W9-AFT-720

ALSO BY NICOLA BEAUMAN

A Very Great Profession:
The Woman's Novel 1914–1939

Cynthia Asquith

E. M. FORSTER

Jess Byford

A wonderful picture

E. M. FORSTER

A Biography

Nicola Beauman

ALFRED A. KNOPF
New York
1994

This Is a Borzoi Book
Published by Alfred A. Knopf, Inc.

Copyright © 1993 by Nicola Beauman

All rights reserved under International and Pan-American Copyright
Conventions. Published in the United States by Alfred A. Knopf, Inc.,
New York, and simultaneously in Canada by Random House of
Canada Limited, Toronto. Distributed by Random House, Inc., New
York. Originally published in Great Britain by Hodder & Stoughton,
Ltd., London, as *Morgan: A Biography of E. M. Forster*, in 1993.

Library of Congress Cataloging-in-Publication Data
Beauman, Nicola,
E. M. Forster : a biography / by Nicola Beauman.—1st American ed.
p. cm.
ISBN 0-394-58381-7
1. Forster, E. M. (Edward Morgan) 1879–1970—Biography.
2. Novelists, English—20th century—Biography. I. Title.
PR6011.058Z62   1994
823'.912—dc20
[B]   92-44378
CIP

Manufactured in the United States of America
First American Edition
Published April 7, 1994
Second Printing, May 1994

The personality of a writer does become important after we have read his book and begin to study it. When the glamour of creation ceases, when the leaves of the divine tree are silent, when the co-partnership [between writer and reader] is over, then a book changes its nature, and we can ask ourselves questions about it such as 'What is the author's name?' 'Where did he live?' 'Was he married?' 'Which was his favourite flower?' Then we are no longer reading the book, we are studying it and making it subserve our desire for information . . . Study is only a serious form of gossip. It teaches us everything about the book except the central thing, and between that and us it raises a circular barrier which only the wings of the spirit can cross.

E. M. Forster 'Anonymity: An Inquiry' 1925[1]

Contents

Contents

Illustrations

———————————

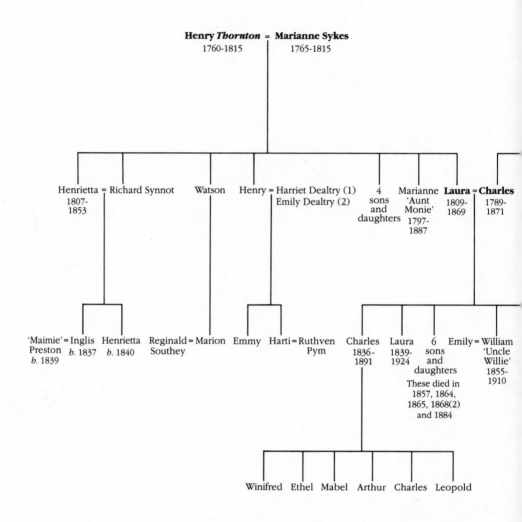

Henry *Thornton* = **Marianne Sykes**
1760-1815   1765-1815

Henrietta = Richard Synnot   Watson   Henry = Harriet Dealtry (1)   4   Marianne   **Laura** = **Charles**
1807-   Emily Dealtry (2)   sons   'Aunt   1809-   1789-
1853   and   Monie'   1869   1871
                                                                     daughters 1797-
                                                                               1887

'Maimie' = Inglis   Henrietta   Reginald = Marion   Emmy   Harti = Ruthven   Charles   Laura   6   Emily = William
Preston   b. 1837   b. 1840   Southey   Pym   1836-   1839-   sons   'Uncle
b. 1839   1891   1924   and   Willie'
                                                                                                 daughters   1855-
                                                                                                 These died in   1910
                                                                                                 1857, 1864,
                                                                                                 1865, 1868(2)
                                                                                                 and 1884

Winifred   Ethel   Mabel   Arthur   Charles   Leopold

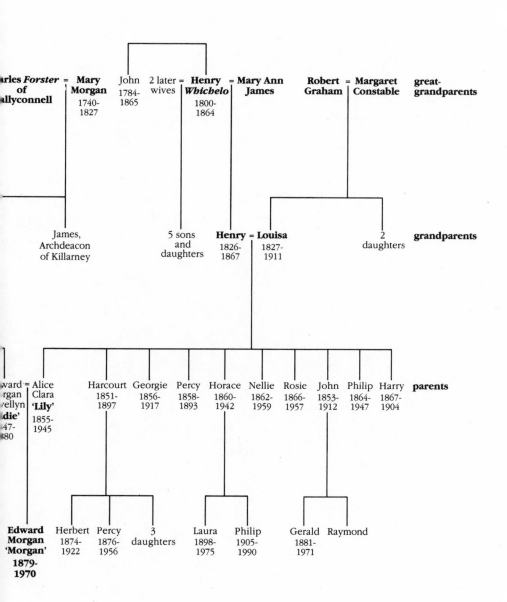

great-grandparents

arles *Forster* = **Mary**
of   **Morgan**
illyconnell 1740-
             1827

John
1784-
1865

2 later = **Henry**
wives   ***Whichelo***
         1800-
         1864

= **Mary Ann**
  James

Robert = **Margaret**
Graham   **Constable**

**great-
grandparents**

James,
Archdeacon
of Killarney

5 sons
and
daughters

Henry = **Louisa**
1826-   1827-
1867   1911

2
daughters

grandparents

ward = Alice
rgan   Clara
ellyn **'Lily'**
die'   1855-
47-   1945
80

Harcourt
1851-
1897

Georgie
1856-
1917

Percy
1858-
1893

Horace
1860-
1942

Nellie
1862-
1959

Rosie
1866-
1957

John
1853-
1912

Philip
1864-
1947

Harry
1867-
1904

parents

**Edward
Morgan
'Morgan'
1879-
1970**

Herbert
1874-
1922

Percy
1876-
1956

3
daughters

Laura
1898-
1975

Philip
1905-
1990

Gerald
1881-
1971

Raymond

E. M. FORSTER

Introduction

_____

This biography tries to answer a question: where did E. M. Forster's novels come from? How was it that a 'provincial of settled habits'[1] wrote five of the greatest novels in our language before he was thirty-five and his sixth before he was forty-five? And why did he then abandon fiction?

Forster wanted his biography to be written, appointing first William Plomer and then, when he seemed to be being rather slow, P. N. Furbank; his excellent two-volume Life was published some fifteen years ago. There is a large Forster industry – conferences, scholarly editions, academic reputations gained through work on the novels, more and more literary criticism.

Yet among the mass of detail in the Life, and among the criticism, I found an unexpected gap. I learnt a good deal about Forster the man, indeed more than I needed to know. And I learnt a good deal about critical method. About Forster the novelist there was a strange reticence.

Take, for example, Forster's childhood. It has been suggested that it was 'a radiantly happy one' because of his 'love-affair'[2] with his mother. But does this kind of smothering closeness, or the resultant loneliness when the child tries to make his own way, augur well for adulthood? On the evidence of the novels, it does not seem that Forster himself looked back nostalgically upon the state of being a child: he claimed to have put a good deal of himself into Rickie in _The Longest Journey_, but wrote of him that 'the only person he came to know at all was himself . . . he would sob for loneliness, for he would see real people – real brothers, real friends – doing in warm life the things he had pretended.'[3]

Was this so of Forster as a child? Or was he in truth radiantly

1

happy? I did not know what to conclude; or indeed whether reaching conclusions by drawing on the novels might not mean, as Forster said, that then 'we are no longer reading the book, we are studying it . . . Study is only a serious form of gossip.'[4]

Throughout this biography I have tried to eschew gossip for its own sake: my aim has been to study the life in order to understand the novels and to study the novels in order to understand the life. Since it was my passion for the novels that spurred me on, the life after the novels would be a coda, a mere rounding-off. And because a biography of a writer should describe the unfolding of his creative development, the meticulous chronicling of day-by-day events would be relevant only in so far as it illuminates the inner life; for the same reason ancestral values and childhood influences are of greater importance than the public plaudits of old age.

My first book tried to evoke Forster's contemporary women novelists who are my first love: in some ways he did everything that they tried to do – and better. My assumption has been that the reader admires as much as I do Forster's feminine emphasis on the domestic and unpolitical, his accessibility and his directness of tone; and I have tried to write in a style that echoes his preoccupations, that is accurate where the facts are ascertainable and intuitive where they are not.

All writing – even biography – is, I believe, a dialogue between writer and reader. I have therefore tried to enter into the spirit of Morgan's remark that 'a book is really talk, glorified talk, and you must read it with the knowledge that the writer is talking to you':[5] I have chosen to have a dialogue with the reader rather than at all times maintaining the strict objectivity that is the biographical norm. I have in general tried to avoid what Lytton Strachey called 'the direct method of scrupulous narration' and chosen instead to be the kind of writer who attempts to

attack his subject in unexpected places; he will fall upon the flank, or the rear; he will shoot a sudden, revealing searchlight into obscure recesses, hitherto undivined. He will row out over that great ocean of material, and lower down into it, here and there, a little bucket, which will bring up to the light of day some characteristic specimen, from those far depths, to be examined with a careful curiosity.[6]

It is for the biographer to decide which recesses to investigate, which specimen is characteristic and which irrelevant; moreover, if one wishes to go beyond the bare fact – Morgan Forster was born in Marylebone – to the insight that may change our understanding of the novels – Morgan Forster's birthplace was later torn down to make way for the railway – then one has to embrace intuition.

Throughout this book I have preferred the intuitive approach to straight *reportage*; I have assumed a familiarity with the novels, directly or through the films; I have opted for the more intimate 'Morgan' rather than the more impersonal 'Forster'; and the comment that has meant most to me is Virginia Woolf's note in her diary that 'Morgan has the artists mind; he says the simple things that clever people don't say; I find him the best of critics for that reason.'[7] It is why I find him the best of novelists.

Preface

One day in January 1895, when Morgan Forster was sixteen and at school in Kent, an item appeared in a local newspaper in London about the proposed extension to the Metropolitan Railway. This grandiose scheme involved joining it up northwards with the Manchester, Sheffield and Liverpool Railway and southwards with the Continent, perhaps by means of a Channel tunnel. In Marylebone 1129 houses were to be demolished and 11,000 people forced to leave their homes – among them the residents of the Forsters' former home at 6 Melcombe Place. The *Marylebone Mercury* commented: 'It seems that this parish with its fine squares and sylvan villas will soon be converted into a smoke begrimed railway centre, with more railways running through the district and having their termini and depots therein than any other parish in London.'[1]

Morgan had no memory of the house where he was born or the beautiful squares – Blandford, Harewood and Dorset – where he was taken out in his perambulator; nor, in his extant writing, is there any reference to the destruction of 6 Melcombe Place. But a constant theme in his work would be disappearing houses, people displaced from their normal surroundings, the importance of an ancestral home: the concept of *genius loci*, the spirit of the place, and the need to cherish it, would be lifelong food for his imagination. And in one of his six novels, *Howards End* (1910), he created what is in effect an elegy to his vanished birthplace.

In that book the house in Wickham Place is a re-invoked Melcombe Place. The one is 'fairly quiet, for a lofty promontory of buildings separated it from the main thoroughfare',[2] the other was protected from the Marylebone Road by a mews at the back and the houses of what was then an east–west section of Gloucester Place; if Melcombe

4

Place had survived, these would eventually have been replaced by the kind of buildings over which the inhabitants of Wickham Place 'lamented greatly when they arose. They were so vulgar and so Babylonian, they robbed so much air and so much sun . . . But one gets used to things – at least the Schlegels did – and they ended by finding the flats rather a comfort: if they shut off the sun they shut off the roar of the traffic also, and one cannot have everything in London.'[3] Alas, the houses in Wickham Place itself 'would be swept away in time, and another promontory would arise upon their site, as humanity piled itself higher and higher on the precious soil of London'.

Throughout *Howards End* the tone is elegiac: in the beautiful description of the threatened street ('The sun had set, and the backwater, in deep shadow, was filling with a gentle haze. To the right the fantastic skyline of the flats towered black against the hues of the evening; to the left the older houses raised a square-cut, irregular parapet against the gray') and in the pained realisation that it would be demolished to make way for flats:

'It is monstrous, Miss Schlegel; it isn't right. I had no idea that this was hanging over you. I do pity you from the bottom of my heart. To be parted from your house, your father's house – it oughtn't to be allowed. It is worse than dying. I would rather die than – oh, poor girls! Can what they call civilization be right, if people mayn't die in the room where they were born?'

The speaker, Mrs Wilcox, has no doubt that to be born and to die in one house and to keep faith with that house is the greatest happiness that life has to offer. When Margaret Schlegel tells her that their house in Wickham Place is only an ordinary London house and can easily be replaced, Mrs Wilcox retorts, '"So you think!"'[4] She foresees that the Schlegel sisters will be punished for the moral failing of not valuing their family home; they will find tranquillity only when, from her, they inherit the mantle of Howards End.

The destruction of Marylebone was soon proved unnecessary and the station was under-used from the day it was built: it was 'the only London terminus where one can hear bird song'.[5] The Forster home need not have been destroyed, for its site on the south side of Melcombe Place remained as waste land. Numbers 1–5 did survive for some twenty years (with exposed fragments of what was number

E. M. Forster

6 perhaps clinging to the propped-up flank of number 5); then they, too, were devoured by a 'promontory', Melcombe Court, which is still there today. The site of numbers 6–10 was undeveloped for many years; later a block named Regis Court was built. Today, on its ground floor, there is a workman's café on the spot where the front door of number 6 once opened on to the outside world.*

During Morgan's years as a novelist the house where he was born was rubble. It was a loss he could never remedy and, throughout his life, the image that was to have the greatest significance for him was that of houses – early Victorian London terraces, eighteenth-century villas set in parkland, mansion blocks. They were real – Battersea Rise, Milton Bryan, Abinger Hall, Rooksnest, West Hackhurst – and they were fictional – Cadover, Windy Corner, Howards End – yet in the end Morgan was to be excluded from all of them. As one of his characters, who is closer to being his *alter ego* than any other, tells his closest friend: "'And then you've got a house – not a metaphorical one, but a house with father and sisters. I haven't, and never shall have. There'll never again be a home for me like Cambridge. I shall only look at the outsides of homes.'"[6]

Morgan, too, was to feel he had in some ways come home at Cambridge; yet the sense of loss never left him. 'I don't feel *of* any where,' he would write in old age. 'I wish I did. It is not that I am déraciné. It is that the soil is being washed away.'[7] Yet his was, as he perceived, with the great writer's ability to universalise individual experience, a shared deprivation, a homelessness understood by millions.

When, fifty years after the first publication of *A Room with a View* (1908), he wrote an anniversary postscript in which he imagined George and Lucy making 'the squalid move from Highgate', he realised that Lucy's 'unsuccessful yet prolific' brother would have been forced to sell the family home to raise capital: 'Windy Corner disappeared, its garden was built over, and the name of Honeychurch resounded in Surrey no more.' Nevertheless, the young, or by-now middle-aged, couple had the same needs as everyone else: even if these were, in the restless and destructive twentieth century, more

* After number 6 was demolished Melcombe Place was re-numbered and number 12 on the north side, which by now stood on its own astride the archway over Upper Boston Place, became number 6. In 1904 a photograph of the new number 6 was taken in connection with the building of the underground railway. Until I realised about the re-numbering I believed that I had found a photograph of Morgan's birthplace. (It is in Marylebone Library.)

6

and more difficult to fulfil. As Morgan said, in disjointed sentences that are sharply expressive of his feelings, George and Lucy wanted a real home – somewhere in the country where they could take root and unobtrusively found a dynasty. But civilization was not moving that way. The characters in my other novels were experiencing similar troubles. *Howards End* is a hunt for a home. India is a Passage for Indians as well as English. No resting-place.[8]

1

Melcombe Place

Mr and Mrs Eddie Forster moved into their house in Marylebone in the August of 1877, six months after their wedding. It was a good address: the previous tenant had been both titled and an admiral. Lily, whose widowed mother had been forced to take in lodgers ('Germans, whom she undercharged'[1]) and who herself had spent the last four years as governess/companion to the better off, could shut the front door on the two maids preparing dinner and, arm in arm with her rather aesthetic-looking husband, take an early-evening stroll across Dorset Square to the boating lake in Regent's Park. Or she and Eddie could take a glass of sherry in the airless drawing-room where the curtains might have been 'pulled to meet, for the carpet was new and deserved protection from the August sun. They were heavy curtains, reaching almost to the ground, and the light that filtered through them was subdued and varied.'[2]

Number 6 Melcombe Place was a house like thousands of others – part of an 1840s terrace with a basement and three storeys, wrought-iron balconies in front of the two drawing-room windows on the first floor and a south-facing garden at the back which was pleasant for afternoon tea. 'Under certain circumstances', Henry James was at that time writing in the opening sentence of *The Portrait of a Lady* (1881), 'there are few hours in life more agreeable than the hour dedicated to the ceremony known as afternoon tea';[3] and Lily Forster agreed with him. The silver teapot (or is it silver plate?) that has ended up in a flat in Hampstead (it is brought out, ceremonially, for admirers), was almost an icon in her household. Ritual surrounded it; for example, it was bad manners for a teatime guest not to stay for a full hour, a rule which on some occasions induced boredom and on others caused offence if broken. Afternoon tea was, indeed, so hedged around with

9

constrictions, and so symbolic of the society that had evolved them, that it is hardly surprising that Lily's son's first attempt at a novel, when he was twenty, would also begin with a description of the ritual: having passed remarks about the new tenants across the road, Mrs Manchett

sat down and talked till tea-time. Beginning with the lady opposite, like all great talkers she gradually reached the universal – the mass of people who were 'not quite'. These fell into three classes: those who had called on her, those who had not, and those whom she did not mean to call on. The third class was the most exhilarating, and on it she declaimed till tea came.[4]

In Melcombe Place, as autumn came, the garden grew dank and the teapot was produced in the drawing-room which, like the one furnished by Mrs Honeychurch in *A Room with a View*, would have had 'the trail of Tottenham Court Road upon it; Cecil [another Forsterian *alter ego*] could almost visualise the motor-vans of Messrs Shoolbred and Messrs Maple arriving at the door and depositing this chair, those varnished book-cases, that writing-table.'[5] Lily was not a rebellious creature: we can assume that her somewhat unadventurous aesthetic perceptions would have been similar to her mother's, and therefore to those of 'Mrs Honeychurch' for whom her mother was in part a model. Apart from tea, meals were taken in the dining-room which, at 'Wickham Place', was 'small and drab, and close to the level of the street . . . Its upper window panes occasionally revealed the figures of draymen or of hansom-cab men.'[6]

Marylebone had the advantage for Eddie and Lily that they themselves could not be observed by their relations. If they had moved to Clapham, where Eddie's aunt and Lily's mother lived and where Eddie's illustrious ancestors, the intellectual, do-gooding Clapham Sect, cast a long shadow of influence, they would have been watched and interfered with to an impossible degree.* As it was Eddie's formidable 'Aunt Monie' had to devise a stratagem in the week they moved in: when Lily, rather childishly, tried to hide from her their exact address, she decided to order a basket of provisions to be sent down to London from her Bedfordshire estate, 'though you don't deserve nothing of the sort because you won't tell me yr. no.

* Yet they were only half a mile away from Eddie's first cousin Harti Pym at 35 Devonshire Place. 'North of Oxford Street' was thought less salubrious than south (with the same slightly unconventional overtones as 'north of the park' nowadays); but the fact that Harti and her husband Ruthven lived there improved matters in the eyes of Eddie's family.

in Melcombe St'. The next day: 'yours just come, a "splendid letter it is" but no mention of yr. number in Melcombe. What can I do with your basket I wonder.'[7]

Marianne Thornton (Aunt Monie) had first met Lily in 1867. The local Clapham doctor thought it would amuse his elderly patient if he brought with him the twelve-year-old girl when he called on her: Lily's father had recently 'got up one morning and opened the window and just died'[8] (the kind of sudden death that was to occur so frequently in his grandson's novels) so the doctor was also trying to be kind to her and to her suddenly impoverished mother. Being spirited and clever, Lily was a success, and was soon spending the day at Marianne's house on Clapham Common and accompanying her on outings; one of these was to Torquay in the autumn of the following year, for there is in the Forster archive at King's College, Cambridge an envelope with a lock of hair inside, on the front of which is written 'EML Forster's hair – Torquay – October 20 '68 inscribed by ACF'. EML was Edward Morgan Llewellyn and ACF was Alice Clara Forster, always known as Lily; even though she used her married initials it seems clear that Eddie, romantically, gave Lily his lock of hair that October.

Although Eddie was then nearly twenty-one, she was only thirteen. But that she was a precocious child, almost a young woman, was confirmed the following year when Marianne took her to Weymouth and from there wrote to her niece Laura, Eddie's sister, that she would not let Lily 'dine late or accept croquet parties by herself, for Emmy says on the Esplanade the young artillery officers were enquiring who she was and whether she was staying on here'. This Jane Austen-ish occasion took place when Lily was a mere fourteen and three-quarters, making it even more plausible that she and Eddie had exchanged locks of hair the year before.

He, an undergraduate at Cambridge, would not have entertained serious thoughts about her, yet Marianne may have had hopes that they would one day marry and perhaps watched over Lily with that in mind: she sent her for a year to a school for young ladies and then found her posts as a governess, one of which was with the family of Eddie's close friend and cousin-by-marriage, Reginald Southey. Feelings that Lily was socially inferior were not entertained by Marianne, for she valued Lily's intelligence and capableness just as highly as Eddie's illustrious ancestors. But Eddie's sister Laura

11

was mortified by his choice of wife; on the day the young couple became engaged it was left to her close friend Effie Farrer, Lily's current employer at the palatial Abinger Hall in Surrey, to try and reassure her:

Dearest Laura, this was my one shadow in seeing so much charming happiness – the disappointment for you. How I hope and trust it may turn out better than you think it. He seems thoroughly to have faced the want on the intellectual side, and I do think there is stuff and character in her – witness her dealings with her own people. I feel sure they'll be very happy, but your question is couldn't he have kept up at [a] higher level.[9]

The bitterness that Lily felt about this kind of condescension was to take a more ironic form in the next generation, but even then it was sometimes nakedly evident. '"I have taken a plunge"' are the words Mr Elliot in *The Longest Journey* (1907) uses to tell his family that he is to marry someone 'not impossible socially'. 'The family, hostile at first, had not a word to say when the woman was introduced to them; and his sister declared that the plunge had been taken from the opposite bank.'[10] Although the aura of disapproval must have been a tremendous intoxicant to the young Forsters (not only did it make their marriage more romantic, it provided a lifetime's challenge for Lily), she would never forgive and nor would her son. There is more than a touch of his mother in Lilia's outburst in *Where Angels Fear to Tread* (1905):

Do you think I'm a fool? Do you think I never felt? Ah! when I came to your house a poor young bride, how you all looked me over – never a kind word – and discussed me, and thought I might just do; and your mother corrected me, and your sister snubbed me, and you said funny things about me to show how clever you were![11]

The marriage took place eight weeks after the engagement, on 2 January 1877. Significantly, they were married not from Marianne's house on Clapham Common, across the road from the church, but from the little house in a side road that Maimie Synnot, the widow of Eddie's cousin Inglis, had recently occupied. Yet Marianne must have kept a controlling grip on the proceedings and her kindness extended even to Lily's family, whom she helped in all ways she could; alas, as she grew older her sympathy overreached itself and she became interfering. Sometimes she was cruel: so annoyed was she by Lily's prudish refusal to tell her the exact date when, in the spring of 1878, she was expecting a baby that she wrote telling her not to be uppity. As a governess Lily had failed to 'strike out some new and superior path' but here she was professing to be 'more "proper and particular" than all the rest of the creation ... I shall look in The Times for the announcement of the Bassinette being wanted.'[12]

But in mid-February Lily miscarried. 'Your safety almost – but not quite – effaced the disappointment' wrote Marianne,[13] who must have been beginning to wonder whether she would live to see the much-anticipated great-nephew or niece. Yet hardly had the spring come and gone before Lily told her that she was pregnant again. The oddity for the biographer, scrabbling crudely about with 1877 and 1878 birth certificates and magnifying glasses to see if the dates on the extant letters have been doctored (it seems not, though there are six months at the beginning of 1877 that are unaccounted for, and the short lapse of time between engagement and wedding is unusual), the oddity is that Lily conceived again so quickly. Enough is known about the strictures laid by Victorian doctors upon their female patients, and enough can be guessed about the rapaciousness of Eddie's sexuality (surely *not* very great to look at him) to make the date of the miscarriage and the date of the next birth (1 January 1879 and not apparently premature) quite mysteriously close together. It seems that Lily, who was to be a strait-laced widow for sixty-five years, had once had a straightforward and eager attitude to sexuality of a kind that would, in different circumstances, have made her a mother ten times over like both her mother and her mother-in-law.

Much Forster censorship and many bonfires have concealed possible explanations, but here and there we find hints: when, in 1910, Lily read about Helen Schlegel's illegitimate baby in *Howards End* she was more disapproving than she had ever been, as far as we know, before or since. September 1910: 'Mother is evidently deeply shocked by *Howards End* ... I do not know how I shall live through the next months ... Yet I have never written anything less erotic.'[14] Indeed, conception was only described as 'she loved him absolutely, perhaps for half an hour'[15] with a result nine months later that most readers were to find emotionally implausible but not shocking. Could it be that Lily remembered the unexpected conception at Melcombe Place during the last days of March 1878, and that her embarrassed, even guilty recollections took the form of indignation?

However, the biggest hint by far was given by Marianne who, in the summer of 1878, with Lily four months pregnant, decided to give the young Forsters a holiday in Paris. They would not, however, travel alone. 'Streatfeild [*sic*],* a friend of my father's, went too,' their son would write in 1956, with no comment. Why on earth did he include this sentence, or the following? Marianne, enclosing £30 (£1300)† for Eddie, told him that £5 of this was being given 'on condition of its being spent on Lily being drawn about in any conveyance she chuses, but by Jengo I won't have her walk. It would be a bad investment having her laid up in a Paris hotel and no Lady companion except Streatfeild who is very nearly one I own, but not quite.'

'No Lady companion except Streatfeild'! What can Marianne have been thinking of? What can Lily have meant by keeping the letter? And by keeping a letter that Marianne wrote to her that hoped 'Eddie wont be too old-maidish to walk you down the Boulevard Italienne at night when Paris is en fête'?[16] It can only mean one thing: that Lily had discovered that the gentle, aesthetic, languid demeanour that she had admired in her husband and that had reminded her of her similarly artistic father had turned out to be something other than she had hoped; and that she had made no secret of it to Marianne. Nor was it a secret that she would keep from her son.

In no Forster novel is there a 'good' father, indeed one might go further and say that in almost all instances the father is either dead or irrelevant to the action and that what we know about him is sexually reprehensible. (The two exceptions are Gino in *Where Angels Fear to Tread* and Mr Emerson in *A Room with a View*, but they are both completely different types from the conventional English middle-class parent, one tender, sensual and almost pagan and the other morally percipient and forward-looking.) Every Forster novel

* The *sic* is Morgan's: because it is Streatfeild not Streatfield.
† When a sum of money is mentioned I have chosen to give an approximation in 1992 terms, using statistics kindly provided by the Central Statistical Office. Despite the vast difference between then and now in terms of relative cost (governesses and houses were cheaper, clothes and food more expensive) a rough estimate is illustrative even if slightly inaccurate.

except *Howards End* has a widow as one of the central characters, and even Mrs Wilcox in that novel is in a sense a widow because her husband has betrayed her.

The most extreme case of a dead and despicable father is Mr Elliot in *The Longest Journey*, the novel whose hero Rickie 'more than any'[17] represented his creator. Mr Elliot was a barrister, one of only three careers that Eddie's father had thought acceptable (the others were the church or 'by a strange concession'[18] architecture); he had 'hollow little cheeks, a broad white band of forehead, and stiff impoverished hair. His voice, which he did not transmit, was very suave, with a fine command of cynical intonation'[19] ('sarcastic' was the adjective that Eddie's son would use about his own father). Mr Elliot marries a beautiful girl, deemed by his family to be beneath them socially; but he leaves her because she chooses a dining-room carpet with clashing colours.

It is the clearest indication, of all the details we are given about Rickie's father, that his sexuality was neither bourgeois nor straight-forward. 'The unhealthiest thing of all,' wrote an Old Tonbridgian in a book about homosexuality, 'was to know anything about decor in the home – a healthy man left that sort of fal-lal to the wife.'[20] By this definition Mr Elliot was certainly not healthy, nor was Eddie; and both of them, believed Morgan, passed on their legacy of unhealthiness to their sons. The attempt by the next generation to reconcile the healthy and the unhealthy within suburban, heterosexual society would be the crux, perhaps the tragedy of their lives.

Mr Elliot was also at fault for *caring* so much about the carpet, because he thereby placed his sterile values above tenderness and love. Could it be that the detail that 'the carpet was new and deserved protection from the August sun' derived from Lily's wounded memory of Eddie's reaction, in the summer of 1877, to a carpet that she had bought for the drawing-room at Melcombe Place? And that she herself had inculcated in her son a sense that Eddie/Mr Elliot had, despite his pretensions,

not one scrap of genius. He gathered the pictures and the books and the flower-supports mechanically, not in any impulse of love. He passed for a cultured man because he knew how to select, and he passed for an unconventional man because he did not select quite like other people. In reality he never did or said or thought one single thing that had the slightest beauty or value.

15

He leaves his wife ('beautiful without and within') because of her lack of approved aesthetic sense; he speaks 'languidly'; he first humiliates his wife and then hits her. When 'at last' he died 'she was much happier, she looked younger.'[21]

The more than oblique hint that the father of this professed *alter ego* was homosexual was to be reiterated a few years later in *Maurice* (published posthumously), another Forster novel with an *alter ego* hero. Again the father has died before the start of the action and is not mourned. He had, however, obeyed the rules by not being found out. '"He never had any unpleasantness"', remarks his widow; he 'had supported society and moved without a crisis from illicit to licit love.' Yet when his son is making a confession to a hypnotist he thinks of him: 'When all was detailed the perfection of the night appeared as a transient grossness, such as his father had indulged in thirty years before.'[22] Since Maurice's night had taken place, according to the real-life time scale of the novel, in August 1909, thirty years earlier would in reality have been just about the time of Eddie and Lily's visit to Paris with Streatfeild. Despite the oddity of Lily's rapid re-conception, the implication is clear: Eddie's son believed him to have been homosexual, and he believed Streatfeild to have been his lover.

Eddie and 'Ted' Streatfeild were distant cousins, both being descended from Marianne's mother. Ted's father had died when he was four and, since he was delicate and the youngest of the family, the child was especially close to his mother. Eddie's father had been a remote figure who took no notice of his children (five of whom died in the years Eddie was growing to manhood), preferring to sit in his study writing religious tracts. The two young men were only six months apart in age but because they went to different schools (Charterhouse and Wellington) it is likely that they became close friends when they were both apprenticed to the London architect Arthur Blomfield. Here they were part of a group that included 'a somewhat depressed managing clerk, two or three assistants and half a dozen cheerful young fellows who were serving their articles as pupils, and most of whom were much more interested in the latest news, sporting or otherwise, than in the latest experiment in Architecture.'[23]

One of Ted's first projects, while he was only twenty-one and Eddie was still in his last year at Cambridge, was supervising the restoration of the church at Fulbourn, on the edge of the Gog Magog hills near

Cambridge. That was in 1869 and it seems that, upon completion of his degree the following year, Eddie joined Ted at Blomfield's office. In the years that followed they both did a lot of travelling in Europe. It is mere conjecture whether they were together. But since Ted's trips with his brother are known to have been in 1870, before Eddie had finished at Cambridge, and then in the autumn of 1877, while the Forsters were settling in to Melcombe Place; and since Eddie's trips were in the years between 1873 and 1876 (it was upon his return from France in the October of this year that he became engaged to Lily) it seems likely that in these years the two did travel together. Certainly a friendship of this nature is one possible explanation why Eddie's rather anonymous sketch-books for these years have been preserved while his diaries, his letters home and any details about his travels have all vanished. It was Lily who jettisoned them.

In 1874 Ted went to live at Great Marlborough Street* where 'he worked and shared expenses with his most attached friend Wm. O. Milne . . . Their friendship was as unbroken to the end as it was sincere and strong.'[24] Along with Lily's mother and Eddie's sister Laura, Ted was witness at the wedding. And the next year he made a third on the trip to Paris. It is possible that Lily left the two of them there and returned home alone; at any rate she spent the August of 1878 in the country, staying with Marianne at Milton Bryan. Then she went back to London and settled down to await the birth of the baby. Eddie was by now overseeing his first commission: his sister had been given the lease of some land on the Farrers' estate at Abinger Hammer in Surrey and he had designed a house for her; he must have been forgiven for his misguided marriage.

Yet, as the weather grew colder, Lily's happiness was slowly eroded by Eddie's state of health: the fever, the irritability and the fatigue of early consumption had already begun. However, on New Year's Day 1879, on a rainy, muggy day that became icy towards nightfall, the baby was born, and he lived. They named him 'Henry' after both Lily's Whichelo father and grandfather and Eddie's Thornton

---

* From 1876–7 Eddie had his office in Duke Street, Manchester Square, half a mile's walk from Melcombe Place, another reason why he and Lily moved there. From 1878 onwards he shared the office at Great Marlborough Street with Ted and his friend William Milne, and it was to here that he walked every day from Melcombe Place. One of the other architects in the building at this time was Basil Champneys, whom Eddie had met the year before when visiting Ted there and who had preceded him at Charterhouse and Trinity. His influence can be seen in the design of Eddie's only building, West Hackhurst, 1877–8.

grandfather, and 'Morgan' after Eddie's Forster grandmother who had been called Mary Morgan. Lily, one imagines, had rather her baby avoided the name of the man to whom her husband was so devoted, even if it was her husband's name as well; but then, on 15 February, the baby was taken for his christening to Holy Trinity on Clapham Common, where Eddie and Lily had been married just over two years before. And Eddie, having written the chosen names on a bit of paper and handed them to his mother-in-law,* who then refused to read them out because she suddenly 'became afraid of the sound of her voice in a sacred edifice', gave the piece of paper to the vicar. He intoned them; but the names he read out were Edward Morgan.

Afterwards there was 'agitated research'[25] as to whether the registered or the christened name took precedence, but finally it was decided that God came before State. Yet when the future novelist Sylvia Townsend Warner tugged her father's beard at her christening in 1892 and he, distracted, named her Cynthia the mistake was 'put right later in the register'.[26] No such dispensation was allowed to the Forsters' baby. In order to spare confusion (and pain to Lily, although this would not have been mentioned) he was to be henceforth called by his second name, Morgan. 'Aunt Monie's reaction was characteristic. She had never liked the name Morgan, it was not a Thornton name, it was a Forster import.'[27] And so Morgan Forster, whose work was to be constantly preoccupied with the idea of muddle, misunderstanding and mistake, began his life with a muddle.

---

* I have been unable to discover who Morgan's godparents were. Marianne's resident niece, Henrietta Synnot, is alleged to have been one. If there were two, the other would certainly have been Ted. It is perhaps because one *was* Ted that Morgan censored this piece of information. Later on he himself was to have extremely ambivalent, almost neglectful feelings towards his godchild John Jermyn Darling; however, he doted on his second godson Robin Buckingham.

2

Clapham

The name may have been arrived at through muddle; what was appropriate was that it happened in Clapham, a few yards from the plaque in honour of the Clapham Sect who 'laboured so abundantly for national righteousness and the conversion of the heathen, and rested not until the curse of slavery was swept away from all parts of the British Dominions'.[1] The baby's great-grandfather, Henry Thornton, was the linchpin of the Sect; and the influence of him and his circle was to make itself felt throughout the baby's long life.

Henry Thornton was not first-generation Clapham. His grandfather had left Yorkshire, where his forebears had for three generations been parsons, and bought a Tudor house on the south side of the Common. Here he pursued the trade with Russia that he had first established in Hull, as well as becoming a banker; his son John continued both careers, but was morally more of a purist and became a first-generation Evangelical. Leslie Stephen, another descendant of the Clapham Sect, wrote about John that, although he was immensely energetic about distributing bibles all over the world or helping impoverished clergymen, he was uninterested in society, and 'his strictness, and some oddities of manner, exposed him to sneers, to which he was absolutely indifferent.'[2]

John's son Henry (1760–1815) was even more devout than his parents, indeed somewhat patronisingly described his father as 'naturally rough, vehement and eager'[3] in his attitude to things religious. He also criticised his mother, perhaps because her charitable endeavours were of a domestic rather than a fervent nature. She preferred, for example, going with her five children to take the air at Harrogate and Tunbridge Wells to accompanying her husband to the seaside retreat where he and his protégé clergymen used to pray.

19

Morgan was to be intrigued by this great-great-grandmother and in the 1950s would transcribe some of her diary into his commonplace book. He was especially touched by the following passage in which she broods upon having reached half her allotted life span. After her death

> ... where am I? Living perhaps in the memory of a few kind relatives who may now and then say thus she did, who may kindly excuse my follies and overrate my Virtues, but in a few years even this imaginary liveing is also over, and perhaps it will never be known but upon old parchment or on a register that Lucy Thornton ever liv'd.[4]

When he gave the name Lucy to the heroine of *A Room with a View* Morgan may have been paying homage to the unusual qualities of this eighteenth-century wife and mother who pottered about Clapham doing good works, looking after her house and keenly gardening; yet who was censoriously described by her son as seeing, during the Tunbridge Wells summers, 'neither present evil nor future danger to her young people from the introduction of them into scenes of vanity and dissipation'.[5]

Henry's resentment stemmed partly from his parents' complete indifference to his intellectual development: 'he started in life, as he said, with "next to no education", and without any political acquaintances.' Nevertheless, he became MP for Southwark; yet although he held many Whig principles he did not join either political party. His dislike of party political conflict, but passionate interest in moral issues, was to be shared by his great-grandson; as was his absolute disinterest in the public gesture: when he considered some aspects of the newly imposed income tax to be unworkable 'he silently raised his own payment to what it would have been upon his own scheme',[6] an attitude to personal financial wealth that was to be inherited by Morgan, who frequently and unspokenly gave smaller sums of money away for reasons of principle.

Henry was one of the most influential members of the Clapham Sect, that 'industry in doing good'[7] that succeeded in abolishing slavery and tried, among other things, to encourage relief for the poor, to abolish cruel sports, to reform prisons. He was an intimate friend of William Wilberforce, who had entered public life – and the Sect – at about the same time and was virtually related to him since Wilberforce's uncle had married Henry's aunt. Before John Thornton's death Wilberforce lodged with the family; then the two

young men set up home together, at a house that was also on Clapham
Common known as Battersea Rise. When Henry married, Wilberforce
married too and moved almost next door on the Common. And when
Henry was known to be dying he was taken to Wilberforce's 'town'
house in Kensington Gore where he spent his last hours; but he was
brought back to Clapham to be buried.

Wilberforce was not alone in living near the Thornton family:
Henry had used his fortune to build houses around the Common
and he then leased them to his friends. The centre of it all was his
own home, Battersea Rise, and most especially the large oval library.
It was the most important room in the house, an almost sacred place,
not merely because of the arguing, praying and do-gooding that went
on here but because it was the heart of Henry's family life. What is
endearing about the changes to society wrought by the Clapham Sect
is that they were achieved in comfortable, domestic surroundings with
the noise of children running about overhead (there were, allegedly,
thirty-four bedrooms), the lawn being mowed and soft white rolls
and drinking chocolate being set out on the sofa table: not in stuffy
committee rooms or in the political arena. It was a direct, unpompous,
domesticated, almost feminine way of doing things that so many
descendants of the Clapham Sect, and the Bloomsbury Group in
particular, were to adopt for themselves.

In the book-lined library Henry wrote two characteristic books.
One was a collection of family prayers ('The Clapham Sect listened,
rose from its knees, ate and then made money – made as much as
ever it could, and then gave as much as it could away. The activity
in either direction was immense'[8]) and the other was a book about
money itself. This was the *Enquiry into the Nature and Effects of
the Paper Credit of Great Britain*, published in 1802 and re-edited in
1939 by the eminent economist F. A. Hayek. The books represent the
two supporting pillars of Clapham Evangelicism: on the one hand the
almost abstract yet ultimately realistic attitude to money, on the other
prayers *at home*. The whole family kneeling at prayer, in the library at
Battersea Rise, was far more sacred to the Thorntons than any church,
and had the added advantage that it obviated the necessity to take part
in the Church rituals to which they so much objected.

Bound up with the Sect's antipathy to religious dogma, to any
kind of godly ostentation, was a persistent dislike of poetry, of
mystery. It was this lack of the mystic element that was to irritate
their Bloomsbury descendants.

Riches, evangelical piety, genuine goodness, narrowness, complacency, integrity, censoriousness, clannishness, and a noble public spirit managed to flourish together in [their] ample bosom without mutual discomfort ... That they had no sense of art goes without saying, nor were they interested in literature unless it was of an intellectual or formative character ... indifference to the unseen seems to me the great defect in my great-grandfather's sect, and the reason why they have not made a bigger name in history ... Poetry, mystery, passion, ecstasy, music, don't count.[9]

Yet this was the atmosphere in which Henry Thornton's great-grandson Morgan Forster grew up for the first eight years of his life. He lived of course with his mother, and he lived away from Clapham; but Aunt Monie, Henry's daughter Marianne, who did not die until she was ninety and her great-nephew eight, exerted a strong influence.

Both Henry Thornton and his wife had died in 1815. Marianne and her siblings were entrusted to the guardianship of the unknown and little-liked Robert Inglis (not to that of the beloved and respected Wilberforce, about whom Mrs Thornton had perhaps had some of the same feelings as Lily was to have about Streatfeild). Robert proved kind, but so pompous and so conventional that the mere memory of his aura was to provoke Morgan to fury. One of the origins of his lifelong anti-establishment, anti-Oxford bias would be his resentment of Robert Inglis:

... an unbending Tory, he dreaded not only revolution but reform, and when he entered Parliament he opposed any measure that promised social betterment or menaced the supremacy of the Church of England. Weightily for twenty-five years did he represent the University of Oxford. Two engravings of him in his robes of a D.C.L. so oppressed my youth that when they came into my possession I took one of them out of its frame, tore it into small pieces, and burnt them in the kitchen range.

The nine Thornton children were able to stay on at Battersea Rise until they married and it would not have been foreseen by anyone that life there would ever have to end. But in 1852 Marianne was turned out. It was the greatest tragedy and the greatest drama of her life, and there is no doubt that it was from her that the infant Morgan first learnt to associate leaving houses with unhappiness; so much so that when he was twice forced to leave his own home without having chosen to do so he elevated these quite normal terminations of the lease into similar disasters. Part of his adult anger was to be fuelled, also, by his childish incomprehension of what had happened to Marianne.

Her brother, Henry Sykes Thornton, had become a widower and left her to bring up his children as if they were her own. Then, after ten years, he proposed marriage to his sister-in-law and 'announced that he intended to marry Emily although she was his deceased wife's sister, that he was going to get the law altered in Parliament, and that until it was altered he and she would live abroad'. One of his chief opponents was his erstwhile guardian Robert Inglis who was 'against the Jews, the Catholics, the Dissenters and now he denounced the Deceased Wife's Sister Bill'. Henry went abroad with Emily, and Marianne, although conscious that 'should the law be altered probably the next generation will wonder at our scruples', left Battersea Rise.

She went to live on the east side of the Common, still within earshot of the Battersea Rise dinner bell, in a house that Morgan remembered as having the unappealing address of Number One,* The Sweep, The Pavement, and as a result was always known as 'East Side'. It was here that Morgan was taken to visit her, and thus grew up knowing, but not quite understanding, that his great-aunt was an exile; later on he would realise that she abandoned her home for reasons of scruple and that 'to the moralist so much discomfort will seem appropriate. To the amoralist it will offer yet another example of the cruelty and stupidity of the English law in matters of sex.'

Marianne never returned to Battersea Rise, and continued to be estranged from Henry and Emily even when they came back to England (they had been married abroad). When Morgan was two, Henry died and Marianne learnt that he had left the house to his wife and her nieces/stepdaughters. It was a painful realisation for, as she wrote, 'I'd set my mind on once more being drawn round the garden before I died.' A week before her death, in 1887, there was a kind of reaching out: Marianne, perhaps thinking of her childhood and the food of children, wrote to her sister-in-law and asked to borrow some milk. 'No biographer could have foretold such a request, no novelist before Proust could have invented it' wrote Morgan, her

---

* It was in fact Number Three.

great-nephew.* After thirty-five years' alienation she asks for some milk.' As Morgan understood, 'Marianne was writing not to a person but to a place. The milk was a sacrament. She knew she was dying and before it happened she wished to be in physical touch with Battersea Rise.'[11] For her, as for her great-nephew, the house was what mattered: the reconciliation she desired was not, after all, with Emily but with her home.

The house proved invulnerable for only another twenty years. While London crept nearer and a once pleasant suburb became less pleasant, the garden for a while retained its overgrown beauty and 'the maids still whitened the white squares and avoided the black squares of the tessellated pavement in the hall'. Indeed:

The whole organism seems to have functioned to the very end – the greenhouses, the special cows, the maps on rollers, the Nankeen Rooms, the gloxinias, the large vase into which they were stuck, the sofa under whose weight two footmen staggered on to the lawn. London knocked and everything vanished – vanished absolutely, and has left no ghost behind, for the Thorntons do not approve of ghosts.[12]

It was in 1907 that the demolition gang arrived, the same year that the marriage bill for which Henry had fought so hard finally became law. Of all the hallowed houses that Morgan was to know or create in his life, Battersea Rise was the most sacred, abandoned because of conventional morality, in the end destroyed. Today, at the junction of Clapham Common West Side and Battersea Rise, where Grandison, Alfriston and Muncaster Roads turn south from the Common, it is impossible to see any trace of the house in which Morgan's Thornton ancestors lived so happily and so serenely. For them the house fulfilled 'that longing for a particular place, a home, which is common amongst our upper and middle classes, and some of them transmitted that longing to their descendants, who have lived on into an age where it cannot be gratified'. For them 'the ritual has ended'.

Morgan's Thornton great-grandmother had had nine children and one or two stillbirths after the age of thirty-two: she had married

* There was some false modesty here. In *Where Angels Fear to Tread* Philip (whose name incorporates the Greek word for love and for friend) 'underwent conversion. He was saved'[10] after the death of the baby. He and Gino then share the baby's milk and the sacrament of the milk completes his salvation. (Morgan was writing ten years before Proust.)

TOP LEFT The Rev. Charles Forster in 1833 TOP RIGHT his wife Laura Forster née
Thornton in 1833 BOTTOM LEFT Marianne Thornton, Morgan's great-aunt in 1873
BOTTOM RIGHT Morgan with ringlets aged about four (p 43). All four drawings are by
George Richmond, although the one of Morgan is thought to have been drawn by
his pupil.

25

late and was to die when her youngest child was only five. Her last daughter, Morgan's grandmother, was born in 1809 and was named Laura. She was only six when her parents died, when responsibility for her upbringing fell to the Inglises. Her grandson was to describe her as 'very tall, tomboyish, shy-ish, animal-lover: probably the least intelligent of the sisterhood', certainly much less intelligent than Marianne. She married a parson twenty years older than herself and within twenty-one years, by which time she was forty-six and her husband, Charles Forster, was nearly seventy, had produced ten children.

Laura had a 'reputation amongst her sisters for unconventionality, but it was unconventionality of the helter-skelter type that flaps about in bonnet strings, puts babies to sleep in the bath, and forgets where they are'. Her husband produced books with titles like *Mohammedanism Unveiled* and *The Three Heavenly Witnesses* while Laura looked after her 'boys with their angelic rather weak faces, the girls with their genuine loveliness' and muddled through. 'The sisters wrote to each other continually over the next thirty years: babies, illnesses, church repairs, illnesses, babies, parcels, when can you all come, when shall I come.' Marianne was often at the rectory and

it was she who worked for the Forsters with her hands and tried to tidy up the confusion into which they were sinking. Sometimes she is ashamed of her 'single blessedness' when she thinks of 'poor dear Laura 20 times iller than I am rushing about after her 10 children and her groaning husband and crying maids and low-sperritted governesses'. At other times she can do nothing but laugh.

Yet Morgan was always to find the memory of his Forster grandparents 'unsympathetic'. Laura he thought silly, perhaps because his mother (who may have met her once or twice at the end of the 1860s) used to say so; Charles he disliked because he 'soon degenerated into a Hebrew Prophet who has nothing to prophesy about. He denounced, he exhorted, he pardoned.' As for his scholarship, 'his method was to accumulate such scraps of erudition as fitted in with his convictions, and to commend them forcefully'.[13]

The Forsters lived at Stisted in Essex. Once Morgan visited the rectory and felt 'pity and admiration', pity because the people who lived there were quite forgotten, admiration because 'it was a real existence – tragical – the Family were loved and have died.' Here was yet another house where his ancestors had lived a teeming, domestic existence that was now ended: 'the beauty that years and memories showed them I have seen in an instant'.[14] Morgan's father, Eddie Forster, the eighth of their children, had been born in November 1847 and was given the Welsh-sounding name of Edward Morgan Llewellyn: Charles Forster's Welsh mother was born a Morgan, the other two names perhaps also deriving from the Welsh side of Charles's family. After Charterhouse, Eddie, as he was always known, went to Trinity College, Cambridge; here he read Classics and won a Greek prize. The year he went up to Trinity, 1866, must have been entirely overshadowed by death, since three of his siblings had recently died; two more, and both his parents, were to die in the next five years. Unless his mother herself died of consumption, which is not known, she surely died of grief.

It was Marianne, at East Side, who now became the focal point of Eddie's life. For some years her 'favourite nephew' had been Inglis Synnot; but he died, too, while Eddie was at Cambridge and from then on *he* undertook the role of favourite nephew, going often to stay at East Side and both enjoying and squirming under the fierce beam of interest that his own son would know in the 1880s. And it was at the end of the 1860s, perhaps while he was visiting Aunt Monie from Cambridge, that he first met Lily Whichelo, his future wife.

Her family had lived in Clapham for a mere twenty years, in a street some distance from the salubrious Common. Her father, Henry Whichelo, came from a family of artists – his own father was a landscape painter and his uncle, John, was 'Marine Painter' to the Prince Regent in Brighton – and had come to Clapham in order to be a drawing-master. In 1850 he married a Louisa Graham whose family originally came from Scotland, 'a lovely lively woman, most amusing and witty, fond of pleasure, generous and improvident'; after the tragedy of her husband's early death she supported her family herself, yet she did *not* regard trials and tribulations as blessings, a kind of challenge sent by God: 'it may have been possible to do this at Battersea Rise,' observed Morgan, 'but she had too many trials and too little room.' It was only one of many contrasts between his Thornton and his Whichelo ancestors, and he was to be aware of them all his life; yet Louisa and the Whichelos were the ones of whom he wrote, 'it is with her – with them – that my heart lies'.

The tug between the two families was something that the eldest

Whichelo daughter, Alice Clara, born in the January of 1855 and always known as Lily, had also to endure. Although she was 'lovely to look at, with a delicate complexion, and full of gaiety and charm', the prettiest of the four Whichelo sisters, she was by nature more conventional than them. In later life, while she remained a kind of crystallised Victorian, her sisters would grow more bohemian. She was an obedient girl, responsible and anxious to please; she was by nature more Thorntonesque. Yet her father, 'a delightful character – unselfish, considerate, sensitive, handsome, cheerful, and alive to scenic and architectural beauty', was, it had to be admitted, an art master, not quite as bad as being an actor or a musician, but bad enough. She was all too aware that, as her son was to write, the Whichelos 'muddled through. They had no enthusiasm for work, they were devoid of public spirit, and they were averse to piety and quick to detect the falsity sometimes accompanying it'[15] – in short, they were the exact opposite of the Thorntons. But Lily was different from her siblings in being drawn to efficiency, to the clear-cut, to social responsibility. Hence the tug between serious-mindedness and high spirits, between Clapham and those outside the select circle, between South Kensington and Bloomsbury. Morgan's lifelong enquiry into contrasts and the possibility of drawing them into one unified whole began with his early awareness of the opposites in his parents' lives and the opposing milieux from which they derived.

Lily was, however, too normal and too practical a person to consider marrying vastly out of her sphere. The Forsters, in the shape of Eddie, were the perfect compromise. She knew them already and had been seeing them continually since she first met Marianne. They were Thorntons and yet not purely Thorntons, the piousness of Clapham having been somewhat tempered by Charles's part-Irishness. They were, like the Whichelos, a family of ten which had lost a parent, or in their case parents. And there was the possibility for Lily of in some way replacing the father she had lost: Eddie not only had a marked talent for drawing but actually looked like Henry Whichelo. As Louisa commented at the time of the engagement: 'He is a man in 10,000. How my dear mother would have liked him! Strange is it not, that you should marry someone so like your own father! I enclose the photo. You will see the likeness for yourself.'[16] But, above all, lock of hair or no lock of hair, it was, on Lily's side at least, a love match. For Eddie seems, from his photograph, to have been a handsome young man, slightly petulant perhaps, slightly what we would nowadays call wet, but good-looking and with a romantically languorous figure.

On Eddie's side there is more doubt as to the strength of his feelings. There was, after all, Ted Streatfeild. But, since he was Aunt Monie's favourite nephew, for this reason as well as for financial motives he must badly have wanted to please her. He was twenty-nine when he became engaged, which is the age when it is generally accepted to be more respectable to be married than not to be. And Lily was pretty, friendly and yet cheerfully domestic. However, there was another obstacle, hinted at by Effie Farrer when she wrote to Laura Forster on the day of the engagement, 7 November 1876: Eddie was 'not wild like Lily but as befitted his seven more years all aglow with happiness and having looked "things" steadily in the face I should say'.

Lily was the daughter of a drawing-master whose wife took in lodgers. The Thorntons and the Farrers would never forget that it was of Lily that Marianne had once written, in her unselfconscious *de haut en bas* tone when commenting on her evident popularity at Weymouth, 'I reckon I have added to it by insisting on shabby dress against [the doctor's] offers of help to any amount to make her "to appear respectable", but strays and waifs are never liked unless they show their lowly estate.' Lily was making an advantageous match. Eddie was not. Hence Effie's remark to Laura Forster, 'your question is couldn't he have kept up at [a] higher level'.[17] The fact that he couldn't meant that Morgan was born. The fact that the question was asked was to determine the direction of every one of his novels.

3

Rooksnest

Poor E. Forster is gone – quietly and as *soon* almost as we hoped. His wife is LF [Laura Forster] says in great desolation, but has her brother with her. What a little tragedy has been acted there under our eyes – and what is to become of that poor helpless child-mother, and that child which looks as if the Forster fate was looking out from its pretty bright face.[1]

These were the feelings of the Farrers at Abinger Hall. But Lily had not hoped Eddie's death would be soon. She had not even imagined it, for 'she was accustomed to young people remaining alive', Morgan would write, 'and although she dutifully carried out instructions, she could not take her husband's illness seriously'.[2] Yet the death certificate stated bleakly 'Typhoid Fever 18 months Pulmonary consumption 18 months', which dated the onset of obvious, recognisable illness to Morgan's first spring. Surrounded as the Forsters were by death, Lily's optimism seems misplaced: the newly-wed Lily must have blithely hoped that her family would be lucky. When it was not, her temperament was rapidly transformed and the sanguine attitude she had once adopted towards days on the beach or winter outings to the park was henceforth quite different. Her subsequent dread of illness shadowed her son throughout their life together and was to have a significant effect on his work: a dislike of action and vigour, which stems initially from the restrictions placed upon those who have continually to be 'careful', often results in literature where both the form and the content is confined and small-scale. At the last minute Lily agreed to do more than visit Marianne's house at Milton Bryan for brief periods of recuperation: she rented a large house in Bournemouth,* healthily by the sea. But it was here, on 30 October 1880, ten days before his thirty-third birthday when his son was twenty-two months, that Eddie Forster died.

Lily now found herself very much alone. Her brother-in-law William at once came down from his job at the Thornton family bank in Mincing Lane, but once the formalities were completed he returned to London. Her mother seemed mysteriously unavailable. Even Ida Farrer, to whom she had once been companion at Abinger and who had become a close friend, had recently married a Darwin and gone off to a new life in Cambridge. And it is most unlikely that Lily would have wanted to see Ted Streatfeild or William Milne, although they were, with her, joint executors of the will and 'Guardians of my infant children'.†

The one close friend she did have was 'Maimie' Synnot. She, too, had been married to a favourite nephew, to Inglis who had also died while still in his thirties. Maimie was a kind-hearted and straight-forward woman, some years older than Lily, and during Eddie's final illness she went down to Bournemouth to be with the Forsters. She stayed on, and then returned with Lily to Melcombe Place. Thus it was that the census for April 1881 described the twenty-six-year-old Lily as 'head of the family, occupation gentlewoman', and said that with her in Melcombe Place were her son ('unmarried, male aged two'), two unmarried female servants called Alice and Eliza, and a visitor, Mary Ann Synnot, a widow of forty-two born in the East Indies.

During the next two years Lily was at home very little. Although she kept on Melcombe Place, she spent the three midwinter months of 1881–2 and 1882–3 in Bournemouth, presumably for the good of 'that child which looks as if the Forster fate was looking out from its pretty bright face'. In the summers she made a round of visits, for example she told Marianne on 1 January 1883 (Morgan's fourth birthday), 'I can hardly believe 82 has gone it seems to have been such an endlessly long year. I did not leave B. mouth until the end of February and was back here on Dec 1st and yet such heap of things happened in between

---

* It was Meriden, 4 Richmond Gardens off Christchurch Road, and had a beautiful garden facing south to the sea half a mile away. The house was demolished in the 1960s and a multi-storey car park was built.
† She did not apparently see either of them again. Ted died of consumption in 1882 leaving £6500 (£300,000) to his widow Katharine whom he had married three months before his death. She was childless, never remarried and lived alone in London until she died aged sixty.

– all my househunting and visits to Clapham Melcombe Pl. Abinger Southborough London Milton Sunbury Bayswater Brightstone.'[3] At about the same time she wrote to Maimie, 'I wish tonight would never turn into day and that I could go on sleeping for ever, it would be so nice.' (In old age Morgan scrawled underneath: 'end of "a very grumbly letter" deeply black-edged one of a series which I shall mainly destroy. Uncle Harry, then an invalid boy [of fifteen], a nuisance, self, a baby, ditto. Friendship with Ida Farrer (Darwin) has already cooled. Only Maimie can have kept her going with love.'[4])

What is unclear is why Lily and Maimie did not simply set up home together. The ostensible reason, given by Morgan, 'was that Maimie (they agreed) was too devoted to the baby and would spoil it'.[5] But there must have been more to it than this: they would have formed such a comfortable ménage and both preferred shared grief to being lonely widows. Possibly Lily wanted to have her child to herself; possibly she felt her chances of re-marrying were better if she lived on her own; or possibly the sixteen-year age gap made her doubtful about spending her life with Maimie; in addition, Maimie did not want to leave her Clapham house, which she had only lived in for five years, and Lily resisted going back to Clapham. Whatever the reason, she decided to live alone with Morgan and to devote herself to him.

The baby was, as she was not allowed to forget, 'the Important One', Marianne's appalling nickname that must have begun as a joke but successfully kept alive in Lily the feeling that her son's welfare was always to be more important than her own. He was, in her eyes, the sole representative of a new generation of Forsters for, although Eddie's elder brother Charles had married in 1866 and had had six children with archetypal Victorian names like Ethel and Mabel, this branch of the family kept only distantly in touch with Marianne and Lily. Apart from these small Forsters, and apart from the children that Lily's elder brother Harcourt had begun to produce, Eddie's son was both fortunate and unfortunate in being the focus of attention.

Her nephew's death had licensed Marianne to renew her grip on Lily, a grip that the fact of her marriage had forced her to loosen. Now she felt it was her duty and her right to oversee the details not only of Lily's life but of the baby as well. Alas, the well-meaning help and sympathy that Marianne had grown used to bestowing on her relations had become interference. It is a fine line, always a difficult one for the older relation to stay the right side of, but during her last years Marianne did not manage it. Her letters to Lily, asking for news of Morgan, asking why she did not spend longer at East Side, demanding anecdotes, must have exasperated the recipient and once, indeed, provoked her to write to an unknown correspondent, 'Well well – I hope in the next world there will be a compartment labelled "Thornton" & that it won't be anywhere near me.'[6]

It was not that Marianne's grip was purely financial. Eddie had left almost £7000 (£325,000), a sum that, together with the gifts and expectations Lily had from Marianne, ensured that she was not poor.* She could afford to continue to rent Melcombe Place, at a cost of £90 (£4000) a year, and to employ two maids. No, Marianne's grip was moral. Just as Battersea Rise had become a symbol of a way of life soon to be destroyed, so Marianne had come to represent the fierce moral standards of the Clapham Sect.

For example, it is a well-known part of Clapham folklore that Hannah More, who was a friend of them all, had two cats called Non-resistance and Passive obedience. The concepts embodied in these cats' names were, in all essentials, learnt by Morgan at his great-aunt's knee; at any rate the time he spent with Marianne ensured that the principles that he upheld throughout his life had been well and truly inculcated in him by the time he was eight: the moral scruples practised and preached by Henry Thornton and by Hannah More were passed on to Morgan. In addition, Marianne must have taught him less quantifiable attributes such as verbal awareness, directness, the ability to see all sides of a question.

Of course in many respects he rebelled. What can it have been like for a novelist to have ancestors who disapproved of novels? Or who invented the devout Victorian Sunday? What can it have been like to go through life loaded with this intellectual baggage of one's forefathers, to follow in the footsteps of people who had such complete confidence in their ability to change the world? It would not be easy for anyone, and, for a child who was the object of such unremitting attention from grown-ups, extremely difficult. Caught between his ancestry, his living relations and his own particular temperament, his rebellion was subtle. He did not hunt or embezzle or become an actor. What he did was disclaim any interest at all in money or in organised religion;

* Assuming that the money was not lost, and that it was invested at a conservative 3 per cent, Lily received an income of about £200 (£10,000) a year; if necessary she could have broken into capital, although it is most unlikely that she would ever have done this.

value the understated, intuitive and small-scale over the declared, the public and the serious; cultivate the mystic sense that he so much condemned the Thorntons for lacking; and veer towards a sexual orientation that was entirely alien to Clapham. (One of the things that must have irritated Morgan was its constant and complacent air of heterosexual rectitude: when the time came for it to be prudent to begin to breed, Wilberforce and Henry Thornton calmly and sensibly got married: but where was passion, where was recklessness?)

The area where all these elements clashed most was, not surprisingly, the financial one. In the last years of her life Marianne spent a lot of time changing her will and fretting about when Morgan should come into his inheritance: 'as to getting at his money when 21 or 25 ... if he *takes* it as they call it at 21 no provision is made for his children. If he waits till 25 he is to leave his money to you and his children. I'm afraid this will put it in to his head to marry . . .'7 The sum she decided upon was £8000 (£400,000), the income from the investments – the money came to Lily already invested in Government securities and such enterprises as the East India Railway Company – being used until Morgan was twenty-five for his maintenance, benefit and education.

The great-grandchild of Clapham, who already had his father's money coming to him one day, was to become inescapably rich. Despite Henry Thornton's fine words when he 'deliberately refrained from leaving more than modest fortunes to his children, and told them that his example of personal frugality and large liberality, inherited from his own father, was better than a large fortune',*8 yet Morgan was to go through life knowing that he need never earn a penny, that he could, if he wanted, live in a style vastly more luxurious than the one in which he and Lily settled for the whole of their lives, that the Clapham Sect were exerting the long hand of influence even from the grave.

What is so much to Morgan's credit is that his money seemed to make so little difference to him – except, that is, as a burden of responsibility, as a moral weight on his shoulders. At first he was too young to understand its implications. When Marianne died he burst into tears but 'They were composite tears. I had not really loved

* But when his son Henry Sykes Thornton died in 1881 he left £60,000 (£2.75 million) to each of his two daughters (one of whom was Harti Pym who lived north of the park in Devonshire Place).

Aunt Monie – she was too old, and the masses of presents she had given me had not found their way to my tiny heart.' Later on, in retrospect, he loved her, and especially so when he came to write his 'domestic biography' of her.

He wrote this not out of guilt, as a way of making amends for his childish neglect, as has been claimed by some; but out of his late flowering of interest in the Clapham Sect, its descendants and their influence on him. When he wrote in the last paragraph of *Marianne Thornton* (1956) that his inheritance was 'the financial salvation of my life' since it allowed him to go to Cambridge and to write, he was being disingenuous and mildly hypocritical. It is true he did not win scholarships, but it was the background of the money that disinclined him to try to do so: his closest friend at school won them and it is surprising that Morgan did not. One can but conclude that something in his temperament, in his perceptions, stopped him from wanting to do so. And when he added that 'after the first world war the value of the £8000 began to diminish, and later on it practically vanished', one cannot but hear the note of relief in his voice that at last, in the 1920s, around the time of the publication of *A Passage to India*, he could know the pride of living off his earnings. Yet his conclusion was that Marianne 'and no one else made my career as a writer possible'.[9] In fact his father's money by itself could have sent him to Cambridge and allowed him to become a writer – many times over. It was not Marianne's money that allowed these things to happen; it was qualities inherited from her, far less definable but far more important qualities, that only became apparent when his life as a writer took hold.

It was to get away from Clapham that Lily decided to move to the country. As long as she stayed in her rented house in Melcombe Place there was pressure for her to move nearer to Aunt Monie and to her mother. But by claiming that the country was healthier for the potentially delicate baby she had a plausible excuse for living on her own. Significantly, she chose a house that was only fifteen miles by carriage to Marianne's country estate near Woburn or two short train journeys (if the timetable allowed for the right connection at Hatfield Junction). Yet apart from the relative closeness to Milton Bryan – could Lily have had fantasies that she might inherit it upon Marianne's death? – there is no obvious reason why she chose to live in Hertfordshire.

The house she found was called Rooksnest and was a part-sixteenth-century farmhouse just to the north of Stevenage.* It is interesting, and typical of his methods as a novelist, that in *Howards End*,† the novel which Morgan was to write about Rooksnest, he never directly described it. The biographer thumbing through the book to find, at this point, a paragraph evoking Rooksnest does not find one. There is only a paragraph that defines its neighbours' voting patterns.

At the church the scenery changed. The chestnut avenue opened into a road, smooth but narrow, which led into the untouched country. She followed it for over a mile. Its little hesitations pleased her. Having no urgent destiny, it strolled downhill or up as it wished, taking no trouble about the gradients, nor about the view, which nevertheless expanded. The great estates that throttle the south of Hertfordshire were less obtrusive here, and the appearance of the land was neither aristocratic nor suburban. To define it was difficult, but Margaret knew what it was not: it was not snobbish . . . 'Left to itself,' was Margaret's opinion, 'this country would vote Liberal.'[10]

Part of the fascination of this passage is that it is paradigmatic Forster: simple landscape description becomes a moral evaluation. More than this, I think, he was making a comment about why Mrs Wilcox (the previous owner of Howards End) and by corollary Lily chose to live in it and to be enchanted by it. It was not just a house, it made a statement about how life should be lived and Lily, despite her melancholy, must have felt a good deal of satisfaction about it. Not only was Rooksnest a pretty house, it was redolent of her social standing, a country estate in miniature where she could forget about impecunious days out at Margate or being a governess. If there had ever been mutters that Eddie had married beneath him, her life at Rooksnest would put an end to them.

So, in late February 1883, Lily and the four-year-old Morgan drove

---

* The house survives unchanged, although it is permanently occupied and can only be looked at from beyond the garden gate. The address is Weston Road, Stevenage. From the A1, take Exit 8 and turn south along the A602. At the first small roundabout turn left, then turn right down North Road. Almost immediately turn left into Rectory Lane and after half a mile turn left by St. Nicholas Church into Weston Road. Rooks Nest House (as it is nowadays called) is half a mile along on the left after a (new) cemetery and a farm: there is a brown plaque on the gatepost with the names of Morgan, and of Elizabeth Poston, the composer.
† Rooksnest was once called 'Howards' after the family that farmed there for three hundred years. Morgan later claimed not to have known this consciously, but since the name changed only the year before he and Lily came there this is hard to believe. Even the modern Ordnance Survey Map says 'Howards' above 'Rooks Nest'.

up the lane and took possession of their new home; their furniture came separately in horse-drawn wagons, and there must have been a good deal of it, accumulated from Stisted, Clapham and Melcombe Place, since it cost the large sum of £33 10s (£1500) to move it. Now began the period of Morgan's life that he would later see as his most formative. More than innocence, more than growth, what he realised the decade at Rooksnest embodied for him for ever was ordinary happiness; the house remained throughout his life an ideal, a paradise. 'If I had been allowed to stop on there,' he would declare when he was in his mid-fifties, 'I should have become a different person, married, and fought in the war.'[11] And, twenty-five years later, 'The impressions received there remained and still glow . . . and have given me a slant upon society and history. It is a middle-class slant, atavistic . . .'[12]

Morgan would, I think, have been atavistic whatever happened to him. Even without Battersea Rise, even without Melcombe Place, he had an intense empathy with the past and the people who were part of it; and Rooksnest was the house where he had his childhood, his own past. It is a fitting tribute that he ascribed his later 'slant' solely to its influence; fitting, too, that one of his earliest pieces of prose, written when he was fifteen and by now living in the house no longer, is about the home of his childhood. In it he begins by claiming to remember that first arrival from the station in 1883, and goes on to describe the Hertfordshire countryside. Then he declares, in that disarmingly direct style that was to become so much his own, 'I don't know what to speak about first but will perhaps tell about the house.' He describes it as 'oblong in shape and built of red brick that had long lost its crudeness of colour' and, despite some detail about the roses, vines and gables, gives little pictorial evocation, in the manner that was becoming so typical of his style.

One of the reasons for the lack of physical, tangible imagery is because already by the time he was fifteen Morgan's writing had become unerringly personalised. Take, for example, the sentences about the hall. This, he tells us, 'was the kitchen when the house was a farm and sad to say once had an open fireplace with a great chimney but before we came the landlord, Colonel Wilkinson, closed it up, put a wretched little grate instead and made the chimney corner into the cupboard.' The reader does not visualise the cupboard; instead one gets an image of a difficult landlord. Again, when Morgan mentions the hall having five doors opening out of it he refers to 'the door to the staircase which was thus quite shut in and could not be found by new people who wondered how ever we got up'. So we at once have an image of 1880s guests for tea climbing down from the fly, squeezing their long skirts in through the porch and being, indeed, rather startled by the absent staircase.

'So much for the house. Now for the neighbours,' wrote Morgan, pleased at being able to turn to what he preferred which was describing the gamekeeper's family and the farmer's family, their idiosyncrasies and the way they spoke (Baby Plum: '"I warnt ter see Maaster Morgin's little gla-a-ass b-a-a-alls"',[13] i.e. marbles). Nor did he flinch from the disadvantages (lack of water, and mice). What he did not do, characteristically, was rhapsodise. Where most fifteen-year-olds writing for themselves might have grieved or despaired or lapsed into lyricism, Morgan sidestepped emotion. The only reasons we know that he cared so deeply are the very fact of his writing this memoir, sitting in his bleak room in Tonbridge with the hated sound of cricket balls on bats, the chapel bell and ladies gossiping in the street below; and that he used the house as virtually the central character in a novel.

In some ways it is not easy to see how a house could have had so much influence on a child. The life Morgan led there was not, after all, so different from thousands of other middle-class 1880s childhoods: wholesome meals, walks along the lane or round the edges of the meadow, pony trap expeditions into Stevenage, tennis on the lawn in front, rabbits, tadpoles, neighbours who called and relations who came to stay in the spare room. The only dramas seem to have been the water drying up and the usually strained relationship with the landlord. Even church was a regular event: so secure was Morgan's life that doubt would not enter it for many years yet.

We were Church of England and she [Lily] read morning prayers to the two maids and me, but she was never intense, and I suspect not very attentive. Her interests lay elsewhere: in helping her neighbours: in running her little house and garden: in district visiting: and in criticising Queen Victoria's Jubilee. The middle-classes kowtowed to Royalty much less than they do now [1959]. They were not under the continuously dripping tap of the BBC which has done so much to sodden rebellion ... We went to church on Sunday, when the mud was not too bad, but I remember no religious instruction there ...[14]

Morgan intimated here that he and Lily led a typical rural existence.

But there was one important difference between them and their neighbours: they kept deliberately apart. Not only was Morgan an only child, he was virtually friendless, and knew little of charades, giggles, messy painting, hideouts at the top of trees or in the stables. There was a 'grown-up' quality to his life which modern parents might deem disastrous. (Could this have contributed to the astonishing maturity of his novels, the first, a perfect work of art, being written when he was a mere twenty-six?)

The isolation separated Morgan, even as a child, from others. For Lily, who had not yet grown into her part of wealthy, respectable gentility, could never let down her guard; if she did the lodgers, the companion at the great house, the sister who was a governess might all be exposed. So she kept herself and her son mostly to themselves, had little to do with the life of the village, with picnics, charity events and intimacy, and ensured that there were only two local families with whom she and Morgan were friends. As her mother wrote to her when the time came to leave Rooksnest, 'it will be delightful to shake yourself free *from all* but Mrs Poston and Mrs Jowitt.'[15] These families, that of the successful stockbroker and the rector respectively, showed to what Lily aspired. When Morgan would one day write of the garden boy that 'my mother in her kindness let Ansell off every Wednesday afternoon so that he could play with me', the bitterness in the word 'kindness' is undisguised. With a little genuine kindness, genuine thoughtfulness for a lonely child, his life would have been quite different. And yet what was more important to him was the ritual, the dailiness, of his years at Rooksnest. It was the very sameness as everyone else, the normality, that Morgan later mourned so passionately. Until he was nearly fifteen he did not feel so very different from other boys. Then, with the move from Rooksnest, he became increasingly set apart. He never recovered.

The 1894 Rooksnest memoir is an oddly polished piece of work given that Morgan was writing purely for his own pleasure with no reader in mind (it remained unpublished until after his death). But at the time of writing he was so homesick for Hertfordshire that it was almost an illness and he saw, perhaps quite detachedly, that the move from the beloved house had destroyed something in him that could never be replaced. Yet what was it about this particular house that gave him such 'a sheltered and happy childhood'? Possibly the most important fact was that he went to live in it at the stage in life when he emerged from babyhood into impressionable and vulnerable childhood. It was his youthful receptivity that made him declare that 'From the time I entered the house at the age of four . . . I took it to my heart and hoped, as Marianne had of Battersea Rise, that I should live and die there.'[16] But there is no doubt that when Lily eventually decided that it was sensible to move to Tonbridge she would have echoed Margaret Schlegel's remark about the house in Wickham Place: 'We are fond of ours, but there is nothing distinctive about it . . . We shall easily find another'; while Morgan, on the other hand, felt like Mrs Wilcox: '"Howards End was nearly pulled down once. It would have killed me."'[17] He loved the house with passion. When I visited it for the first time I felt as if I were meeting the Ideal Woman: Beatrice, Laura or Greta Garbo.

Rooksnest is small: one reason why Morgan loved it.* He, unlike Lily, already felt, and would in the future feel, intimidated by houses like Milton or Abinger, or even beloved Battersea Rise when his eight-year-old self was taken for a glimpse of it through the fence; while Melcombe Place, his birthplace, was only transient. Rooksnest was old enough to be ageless (no one knows whether it was used as a house first in the sixteenth, seventeenth or eighteenth century) and it was unpretentious: it was quite without the pomposity and self-consciousness of so many old houses. It had been home to generations of simple people and had itself remained simple.

Thus it is not too far-fetched to conclude that Morgan's love for the modest charm of Rooksnest was one of the many factors determining his lifelong dislike of the loud-mouthed and the ostentatious and his preference for the quiet and the understated. Rooksnest set in train the directness and simplicity of his attitudes. If you are brought up in an aura of love and happiness, in a place where people have lived in the same way for hundreds of years, you do not feel much drawn either to the convoluted or to the new. When, at Rooksnest or at Laura Lodge (by now called West Hackhurst) in the 1940s, Lily and Morgan continued to eschew mains water and electricity they did so not out of parsimoniousness or eccentricity but out of a deep feeling that what had been good enough for hundreds of years was good enough for them. It was an attitude that Morgan first imbibed at Rooksnest.

* When *Howards End* was filmed in the spring of 1991 a different location had to be found even though Rooksnest remains unchanged; it would have been impossible to fit cameras, lighting, actors into the tiny rooms. And it is not without irony that the house that *was* used was lived in from 1907 to 1911 by Lady Ottoline Morrell, someone far larger, far more extrovert and expansive than the inward-looking Morgan.

Something else that these early years in the country gave to Morgan was a lifelong empathy with rural values. It is a theme that will often recur but at Rooksnest he concluded that life in the country is more 'real', has more integrity, is more in touch with preceding and successive generations. This had, after all, been a key topic for the Victorians from the mid-century onwards. Ruskin's lectures, ostensibly on architecture but also on aspects of social policy, had provoked widespread discussion about the contrast between town and country life, the rich industrialist in control of the impoverished worker, the assumption that the rich man is in his castle and the poor man is at his gate. As Ruskin had told the manufacturers of Bradford:

Your ideal of human life then is, I think, that it should be passed in a pleasant undulating world, with iron and coal everywhere underneath it. On each pleasant bank of this world is to be a beautiful mansion, with two wings ... At the bottom of the bank is to be the mill ... In this mill are to be in constant employment from eight hundred to a thousand workers, who never drink, never strike, always go to church on Sunday, and always express themselves in respectful language.

Is not that, broadly, and in the main features, the kind of thing you propose to yourselves? It is very pretty, seen from above; not at all so pretty, seen from below.[18]

Morgan is likely to have become familiar with these ideas at an early age, perhaps even at Rooksnest when he was thirteen or fourteen; and would have become aware that within a mile lay farms and villages yet within thirty miles lay the slums of industrial north London.*

He realised quickly, because he lived at Rooksnest rather than because of his schooling, that in Britain urban dwellers had increased from one in five to four out of five during the preceding century; he learnt about Ruskin's links with people like William Morris and Edward Carpenter; he could imagine a Britain in which, before long, in the words of a modern critic, 'most of the changes which [Ruskin] advocated – free schools, free libraries, town planning, smokeless zones, green belts – are now taken for granted'.[20] He could empathise with the ideologies promoting country values such as the back-to-the-land ideal, the rural handicraft movement and

---

* One day the working-class Leonard Bast in *Howards End* would rather censoriously think about Ruskin that though 'full of high purpose, full of beauty, full even of sympathy and the love of men' he nevertheless speaks (in *The Stones of Venice*) with 'the voice of one who had never been dirty or hungry, and had not guessed successfully what dirt and hunger are'.[19]

the simple life approach. The very year that Morgan and Lily left Rooksnest, 1893, Robert Blatchford published his best-selling *Merrie England* linking socialism to ruralism:

First of all, I would restrict our mines, furnaces, chemical works and factories to the number actually needed for the supply of our own people. Then I would stop the smoke nuisance by developing water power and electricity. Then I would set men to work to grow wheat and fruit and to rear cattle and poultry for our own use.[21]

Many of these ideas, and the others which are so familiar to us nowadays to do with the destruction of the countryside and the growth of industry, were to reappear in *Howards End*. So when Margaret visits the farm near Howards End she has a vision of pastoral life which was, of course, Morgan's own:

Here had lived an elder race, to which we look back with disquietude. The country, which we visit at week-ends, was really a home to it, and the graver sides of life, the deaths, the partings, the yearnings for love, have their deepest expression in the hearts of the fields. All was not sadness. The sun was shining without. The thrush sang his two syllables on the budding guelder rose. Some children were playing uproariously in heaps of golden straw. It was the presence of sadness at all that surprised Margaret, and ended by giving her a feeling of completeness. In these English farms, if anywhere, one might see life steadily and see it whole, group in one vision its transitoriness and its eternal youth, connect – connect without bitterness until all men are brothers.[22]

While seeing life whole, Morgan yet had the self-knowledge to accept that not all aspects of the countryside were for him. He never pursued the simple life: rearing sheep, making bread and growing vegetables did not attract him. Even when, in his twenties, he took to long Housmanesque tramps through the countryside or when, in his forties and fifties, he lived in rural Surrey, he still felt partly urban. This is why he did not indulge in endless town versus country debates with himself; he knew that it was the philosophical attitude to the pastoral that interested him and that his heart was in both camps, not divided but spread between the two.

During Morgan's Rooksnest years he displayed a certain sensual charm. He was to allege that he kept his ringlets until Marianne died but this is hard to believe as by then he was nearly nine and had lived the life of an outdoor country child for over four years; far more likely that in old age (he was eighty-six when he made this assertion) he liked to pin long-held resentments about familial smothering, confused sexual identity, on to his lingering ringlets. Even without them, however, he had a directness of gaze and full lips which made his adult lack of good looks surprising ('a strange-looking youth, tall, prematurely aged, the big blue eyes faded with anxiety, the hair impoverished and tousled'[23] was to be his vision of himself in the guise of a character in a novel by the time he was thirty).

The directness of gaze is what strikes one. Ever afterwards, that is after the decade at Rooksnest, Morgan would look squinting at the camera, he would turn sideways on or his eyes would stray past the photographer. The extant drawings and photographs of Morgan with ringlets show him looking unabashed at the camera; by the age of eight or nine he looked past it, but he was still an appealing child with strong features that augured well for the future. Then it began to change: the shyly averted gaze of the nine-year-old Morgan started to become wary and almost shifty. There were two reasons: human relations became complicated, mysterious and painful. And he departed from paradise.

4

Kent House

The boy grew up in great loneliness. He worshipped his mother, and she was fond of him. But she was dignified and reticent, and pathos, like tattle, was disgusting to her. She was afraid of intimacy, in case it led to confidences and tears, and so all her life she held her son at a little distance. Her kindness and unselfishness knew no limits, but if he tried to be dramatic and thank her, she told him not to be a little goose. And so the only person he came to know at all was himself.[1]

Morgan was close to Lily, but he did not love her with the almost romantic passion that some boys feel for their mothers. Their relationship was symbiotic in a domestic way, they were openly affectionate (verbally, but physically is less likely) and took the greatest possible interest in each other's daily lives. However, their relationship was not a love affair: the letters Morgan occasionally wrote to her are not redolent of this, nor was his attitude which, while far more filial and concerned than is usual, yet lacked sentiment.

Lily, too, though possessive, seemed to have no feelings that by being together so much they were being anything other than sensible and kindly; she would have been the first to pounce on 'silliness'. The reason that the two were to live together until the end of Lily's long life was to do with mutual devotion, loyalty, concern and a certain degree of laziness. Jealousy and passion were not really emotions that either of the two would have understood in the context of themselves as a family; as regards his own inner life they were feelings that Morgan was to know all too well.

As a child he had few friends of his own age: but his adult friends and relations were always interested in him and in any case there were the children from the farm, and the garden boys. In 1901 he wrote:

44

TOP LEFT and RIGHT Morgan's parents Lily and
Eddie Forster. Morgan owned neither of these
photographs and refused to allow publication of
any photograph of his father. This is the only one
of Lily in which she looks bridal rather than
matriarchal; perhaps like Agnes in *The Longest
Journey* the day Eddie 'asked her to marry him she
went to a shop and had her ears pierced'. Her
earrings, too, look 'copied . . . from something
prehistoric'.[1] ABOVE two of Lily's sisters, Morgan's
Aunt Nellie (left) and Aunt Rosie (right), showing
their lively Spanish ancestry. RIGHT Morgan aged
about eight, still in smocks but minus ringlets.

LEFT Battersea Rise, the Thornton family home, abandoned in 1852 after Henry Thornton's unacceptable marriage. 'Now they were excluded for ever – unless they bent the knee to immorality, which was unthinkable . . . They did not know whether they wished the house to be sold and to vanish off the spiritual face of the earth, or to stand as it was, an empty and dishonoured shell.'[2] It was demolished in 1907.

RIGHT Abinger Hall in Surrey, built by the architect Alfred Waterhouse in 1872, now demolished. Here Lily was companion to the Farrers' daughter before marrying Eddie; her months there gave her aspirations to gentility.

RIGHT Harewood Square, the site of Marylebone Station, a few yards from the house in Melcombe Place where Morgan was born. Here he took the air in his perambulator.

RIGHT on his copy of this photograph of Rooksnest (probably taken in the 1900s) Morgan wrote, 'only record of wych-elm (in Howards End)': one of 'a great number of sacred trees in England, it seems',[3] the tree was felled during the 1960s. The Forsters used the lawn for tennis.

LEFT the Rooksnest drawing-room 1885. 'Still with me in Cambridge 1962,' noted Morgan on the back of this photograph, 'are writing table, mantelpiece with four long dishes etc, fender, carpet.'[4] The mantelpiece went with the Forsters to all their subsequent homes.

BELOW judging by the car, this photograph of Monument Green, Weybridge was taken in the 1920s, just about the time the Forsters moved away in 1925. Harnham is the third house from the right, partially obscured by a tree.

LEFT Rooksnest in 1891: Morgan's Uncle Harcourt with his sons Herbert aged seventeen and Percy aged fifteen. Morgan would never achieve the direct, manly, sporty gaze of his Whichelo cousins. Something of Harcourt and his sons went into Henry Wilcox and his sons Charles and Paul in *Howards End*, with their talk of 'sport and politics'.[5]

RIGHT the bookish and charming Reggie Tiddy at Ascott under Wychwood where, in 1912, he built the Tiddy Hall with a sprung floor for folk dancing; this photograph still hangs in the hall. BELOW boys from School House, Tonbridge in 1890. Their handsome, self-assured expressions, well-cut trousers and waistcoats and general air of empire-building manliness defined the school ethos.

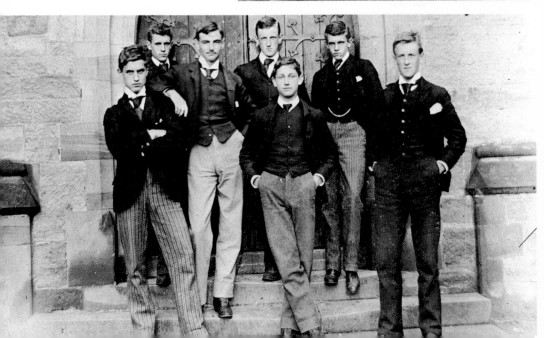

I have forgotten a good deal and probably shall put down things I shouldn't have before, and vice versa. I'm also more discreet. Ansell however will never see this book, and I can speak of him. He was the third/fourth? of our garden boys – Ray, William, Bible,* Ansell, Field, Chalkely were their order, and was the only boy I knew. Wednesday afternoon was given up to me, and there were many extras beside.²

In 1935 Morgan amplified this in his diary. He described Ansell, who was perhaps five years older than him, as 'a pale snubnosed boy, very good tempered. We built a little house between a straw stack and hedge, and often lay in each other's arms, tickling and screaming ... Ansell was my first friend. I told him about the Swiss Family Robinson.'

This was a reference to a book that Morgan loved. His favourite character in it was Ernest: 'I could not bear that Ernest should grow up – he was 13 I think – so the end of the Swiss Family Robinson, which takes place 10 years later, was repellent to me, and I would pretend that Ernest and the others were magicked back into boys.'³ As part of the tradition stretching back to *Alice* and forward to *Peter Pan* and *Le Grand Meaulnes*, Morgan would try to escape from the onset of adulthood. And it is possible that he was prompted to write the 1901 lines about Ansell by the coincidence of Barrie's wife being called Mary Ansell and Morgan's being interested in Barrie because he had read his novel *Tommy and Grizel*, published two years before. In it the writer-hero explains his new book as being about

a little boy who was lost. His parents find him in a wood singing joyfully to himself because he thinks he can now be a boy for ever; and he fears that if they catch him they will compel him to grow into a man, so he runs farther from them into the wood and is running still, singing to himself because he is always to be a boy.⁴

At the end of the earlier paragraph about Ansell, Morgan broke off in the middle of a sentence: 'Sometimes A. and I quarrelled. He used to hide, and leave his billcock as a – '⁵ Since he was by now twenty-two, Morgan could see the double meaning of what he had jotted down and perhaps could not be bothered to rework it.† At the

---

* It was Bible who, in 1894, the year after the Forsters left Rooksnest, was to be the father of an illegitimate baby born to their former maid. In fact Bible was *after* Ansell.

† Fifty-five years later Morgan completed this sentence in *Marianne Thornton* and explained that it was a 'decoy' for the searcher in hide-and-seek.

same time he was made deeply unhappy by remembering their once carefree playing; after the Ansell days at Rooksnest he never found innocence again. And he would fictionalise it in 1902 in 'The Story of a Panic'. In this the fourteen-year-old Eustace, who is the age Morgan was when he last lay with Ansell, 'longed for a friend' but can only keep him by remaining for ever a child and running away into the woods: 'far down the valley towards the sea, there still resounded the shouts and the laughter of the escaping boy'.[6] In 'Ansell' the central character remains a boy by being forced to abandon his intellectual pretensions (his books fall into the river); in compensation he gains the quite unbookish Ansell as a friend.

Ansell has appropriated me, and I have no time to think of the future. I cannot fend him off. I have a bruise on my shoulder from shooting and a cut on the foot from bathing ... Whenever we pass the place Ansell looks over and says 'Them books!' and laughs, and I laugh too as heartily as he ...[7]

The name 'Ansell' would reappear yet again three years later when Morgan began *The Longest Journey*, the novel that he was later to claim as his favourite, and gave the name to the hero's closest and only friend.

The afternoons with Ansell were among the happiest of Morgan's life: uncomplicated, untrammelled by disapproval (apart from that of his part-time tutor who thought the boys 'childish and undignified'), guiltless, and innocent not only of overt sexuality but of politics and class. When, as an adult, Morgan came gradually to accept that it was with working-class men that he felt happiest sexually, he must sometimes have remembered the haystack 'dark inside and very stuffy. "Ow 'ot it is in 'ere! I've got the 'eerd ache already" was the immortal speech of A's.'[8]

Morgan first became conscious of his body and its sensations – one can hardly say of his sexuality because that did not happen until much later – when he was five or six. 'Prepuce being very long I used to play with it ...' he wrote in a portion of his diary headed 'sex' in 1935. 'I knew this was "wrong" and told my mother who must have said "Dirty" for "help me to get rid of the dirty trick" presently figured in my prayer.' Despite Lily's youthful mothering of her siblings, despite her responsibilities as lone parent, she never found the words, or thought it right, to talk to her son about these matters. Even Louisa, who seems to have well recognised the disadvantage of being brought up in a household of women,* could not talk to her grandson about intimate things. Nor were books very informative. 'For years I thought my "dirty" was unique and a punishment', continued the adult Morgan, 'yet looked for the "dirties" of others in Smith's Classical Dict., and was annoyed when they were concealed by drapery in the illustrations to Kingsley's Heroes.'

Morgan, looking back, seems to have had a faint awareness of his future sexual interests at an early age. When he was eleven he and Lily once again went to Bournemouth and, very much as one thinks if so-and-so happens then it's lucky, so 'I remember a queer moment. I stood looking out of the sitting room window at the deserted road and thought "It all depends upon whether a man or a woman first passes." From the right came a gentleman with a brown moustache. I was much relieved . . . This is the first *conscious* preference that I recall.'[10] (It is significant that it was Bournemouth. He may have thought of his father and the few rumours that he had inevitably heard about Ted Streatfeild.)

In the autumn after the holiday at Bournemouth Lily made the decision to send Morgan away to school. 'Mr Hervey, my dubious tutor, left England about then,'[11] Morgan was told, untruthfully; and it was he, 'a fat dark man of about 30', who had suggested to Lily that his pupil should go, having, it seems, been unable himself to mould him into the conventional format. Morgan 'was devoted to Mr Hervey for a time. He could make me wretched by not speaking to me.'[12] It is poignant to imagine what effect for good he might have had if he had been that kind of idealised tutor one reads about in Russian novels: intellectual, knowledgeable, thoughtful, encouraging. But it was not to be, and Morgan went off to a prep school called Kent House, on top of the cliffs near Eastbourne; why there rather than anywhere else is unclear, except that it was by the sea and presumably Lily had heard it well spoken of. It seems to have enjoyed a liberal reputation, for it was this that prompted the future Lord Beveridge's mother to send her son there at the same time.†

---

* For example, when he was about twelve Morgan was apparently encouraged by Louisa to write an anti-feminist poem beginning 'Here come the women! Out they walk In groups of two and three To chatter forth their silly talk O'er filthy cups of tea.'[9]

† Will Beveridge was the future Lord Beveridge, architect of the post-war welfare state and a committed proponent of Economic Planning. By curious coincidence the first four years of his life were spent at Bankipore, the suburb of Patna that was to be the model for 'Chandrapore' in *A Passage to India*.

At first Morgan was perfectly happy. Some of his letters still exist and they are full of normal eleven-year-old detail about stamps, extra blankets, train times, food and colds. They are not the letters of an over-sensitive child wrenched unwillingly from its mother. He even enjoyed the beach, telling Lily that 'when the tide goes out a long way it uncovers rocks, shingle and sand'[13] (an image that was to reappear in *Maurice* twenty years later when he described Maurice being taught about the 'mystery of sex' by Mr Ducie and the tide coming in to cover over the sand-drawn diagrams). By December the tone had changed: he was feeling 'so very nervous somehow. I don't know why it is but perhaps it is excitement, but lately I have always been taking the dark side of things. I have never been like it before, but it is not at all nice. It is very much like despondency.' And he added sadly, 'The worst of school is that you have nothing and nobody to love, if I only had only somebody, I shall be much happier.'[14]

Kent House was turning out to be less liberal than Lily, and Mrs Beveridge, had hoped. The latter wrote about her Will in 1891 that 'he was over-burdened with homework and that she had been forced to intervene to protect him from bullies'.[15] But partly, for Morgan at least, it was the lack not just of someone to love but of someone to confide in. In the spring of 1891, excused football and told to go for a walk on the Downs, he came across a man peeing. It was a mark of his naïvety that he sat down with the man, who then undid his flies and, as Morgan described it in the 'sex' section of his diary, 'told me to take hold of his prick. "Dear little fellow . . . play with it . . . dear little fellow . . . pull it about." I obeyed with neither pleasure or reluctance. Had no emotion at the time but was surprised at the red lolling tip (my own prepuce covering the gland even at erection) and was startled when some thick white drops trickled out. He rapidly lost interest in me, asked where I lived ("Hertfordshire") and offered me a shilling ("no thank you").'

The first thing he did was write to Lily. Not unexpectedly, this letter is missing from the bundle of twenty-five prep-school letters but she told Morgan at once to tell the headmaster. This he did. '"You know your bowels, sir" [the one portion of the intimate anatomy it was, at prep school, proper to mention]. Mr H said he did, and I described how this man's bowels were diseased.'[16] Then Morgan wrote to Lily again: 'I judged both from your letter, and from the way Mr H took up the thing, that you mean to hunt the man up, and make him appear in court, for I should think *it* is an infringement of the laws of England, if so I suppose I should have to appear too; if you are going to do that please tell me, for I shall not be nervous in doing my duty; indeed it would be rather fun.'[17] Lily was brisk: 'darling it won't be "fun", it is such a dreadful thing. I could not talk to Mr H on such a subject unless I was positively obliged to do so. I shall not come to Kent House on Sat. I will write.' They would, she said, have a laugh together 'upon the dreadful subject – & then we will never mention it again & try to forget it has happened.'[18]

What he must learn was to obliterate. A day later Lily wrote again, saying, tenderly and mysteriously, 'I am so glad darling you are feeling all right – you must try & forget about it – except that I think you might remember it as *a lesson*. I will explain if you do not understand when we meet. I need not remind you not to tell any of the boys and of course you will not.'[19] She never did explain. And by dutifully not mentioning his lesson to his contemporaries – there was very little talk of sex among the boys and what there was he did not understand – Morgan never did understand it. When he came home for the Easter holidays Lily asked him if he had cured himself of his '"dirty trick". I said I hadn't and she was so distressed and worried that I decided not to mention it to her again. Thus ended my last chance of a confidant.'[20]

One of the boys who could have been a confidant was Will Beveridge. Occasionally Morgan went to his house on a Sunday and by 1892, the end of Morgan's second year at Kent House, the two boys were friendly both with each other and with other boys. In a group photo marked up by Morgan he is sitting 'between the Profumo brothers – Dick Minor and Dick Major'; either Major or Minor has an affectionate and comradely arm slung round his shoulder.[21] There is no evidence to show that any of them were either teased or unhappy; indeed, although in July Will left to go to Charterhouse,* Morgan stayed on for another two terms, until the spring of 1893 when he was already fourteen. It was unusual to stay on after the age of thirteen and a half, yet Morgan cannot have wanted to leave; and he seemed to enjoy the self-confidence that came with being one of the older boys, for example gaining a reputation as a practical joker. In the last week of term in the summer of 1892 Will wrote to his sister:

Yesterday afternoon when we had come back here, coming into the

---

* His biographer writes that 'this was in many ways a curious choice for Charterhouse in the 1890s was almost entirely devoted to worship of athletics.'[22]

school-room I heard the voice of Crabbe in great excitement and going to his desk what should I see inside but five or six little live crabs who were wandering about while Crabbe* vainly tried to seize them for as soon as he touched one his courage seemed to leave him. Various boys round attempted to screw up his courage for as soon as he felt their legs wriggling round his fingers he retreated . . . On enquiring from the other boys who was the perpetrator of the crime I was informed that it was 'Saint Forster'. I hope that next time you see him you will give him a scolding for his astonishing wickedness.[23]

Morgan liked to pretend that he was downcast, downtrodden and homesick at school, a myth he fostered so successfully that any other details about his more light-hearted side have been obliterated.

He left Kent House in April 1893 and it was arranged that he would spend the summer term at the local boys' school in Stevenage before going on to Uppingham in September. Why there was this interim period is unclear but it can only have been because he was too old for Kent House yet was for some reason unable to enter his public school for the summer term. Nor was the Stevenage school a day school: it shows Lily's insensitivity (by the standards of modern parents at least) that she expected Morgan calmly to fit in with a school for merely three months. At first Morgan 'very quickly got into the ways of the school, I feel I have been there several years',[24] then he was teased, which had not happened to him before, and became hysterical. 'Why have you not come, what are you going to do? . . . If you tell about the boys *do do* take me away or I shall be worse off than I am now . . . I feel utterly wretched, I would like to come away. Every one is against me . . . I have tried to keep from breaking down but I could not help it, and all the boys have noticed it.'[25]

Those few weeks at Stevenage were a turning-point. Morgan was apparently made fun of; he felt wretched; he missed the position of perky authoritativeness that he had enjoyed at Kent House; so much did his spirit crumble that Lily had hastily to make fresh plans for September. Not only was Morgan depressed, almost terrified, by the thought of going to Uppingham with his new schoolfellows; she began to wonder whether he was, in his present state of mind, fit to go to boarding school at all. How different things could have been if he had calmly gone to Charterhouse the previous year with his friend Will, and how Lily must have wished he had. But the damage was

---

* As was to happen so often in the future, Morgan was seizing on the resonance of a name.

done; something in Morgan that had made him robust enough to adjust to, even to be happy at, Kent House now made him nervous and overwrought. Lily removed him from the school and allowed him to spend the rest of the summer, idyllically, at Rooksnest.

What was to be done? She had originally chosen Uppingham because in recent years, under its well-known headmaster Edward Thring, it had greatly expanded, and instituted various educational innovations such as the teaching of French, German, drawing and carpentry. It was also the first English school to have a gym and a swimming pool. Sensibly, Lily thought that Morgan would prefer a school which had the imagination to deviate from the usual regime of Greek, Latin, cold showers and ball games. Now she had to think again: she had to see if there were any respectable public schools that took day boys and if so whether they were in places in which she herself would like to live. In one way she must have been relieved. For the last two and a half years, ever since she had been left alone at Rooksnest during the Kent House terms, she had been thinking about moving. At first she seems to have considered London: Morgan wrote to Lily in October 1890 that he 'was very surprised to hear you are looking at flats. I hope you are looking at them only to live in them till you find a house in the country for I know you would not like London and I should hate it.'[26] Then she must have abandoned this plan but continued to dither. The necessity of moving to a town with a public school would make up her mind for her, and by the spring of 1893, when she still thought that Morgan would be safely settled at Uppingham in September, she had made a definite decision to move. Louisa wrote to her in the March of 1893, referring to a move from Rooksnest, and added, 'I am glad you have not told Morgan, it might have worried him.'[27]

It was a normal enough remark, if somewhat ill-considered. Yet how could Louisa and Lily know that Morgan's worries would have an everlasting effect? No one thought – why should they? – that Morgan might be devastated then and for always. No one thought that a decision of that kind would be better made by at least *pretending* that the Important One had been part of it. When the final decision was made Lily, perhaps not unnaturally, thought that what mattered was finding the right school and allowing the newly morose Morgan to live at home with her; and Morgan could never find it in himself to disillusion her.

The last lines of his Rooksnest memoir, begun in 1894, continued in 1901 and finished after her death, lines that he added when he was going through her papers copying down a few things before destroying them, were as follows: 'Mother to self, 189– You must not mind about the moving because you will be sure to like a new place and I shall always be there (refers to her abortive attempt to leave. She got turned out a few years later, and not unreasonably, I now realize).'[28] The abortive attempt was the flat-hunting when Morgan went away to school. The turning out is less simple. Was she turned out or did she choose to go in order to live at Tonbridge?* We cannot know. But what is clear is that the elderly Morgan, one day in his turn forced to leave his home at Abinger, still felt so bitter about leaving Rooksnest that he *chose*, he needed to feel aggrieved. He was still bitter when, in the 1930s, he referred to '"Howards End", the house out of which the Poyntz Stewarts turned my mother and myself when I was fourteen. They wanted it for a friend of their own, who soon afterwards died.'[30]

Morgan mourned the innocence of his childhood; he regretted, without yet realising it, that Lily had lost her chance to establish a tradition, an ancestral home. But what he missed most of all was the countryside. He noted the following year: 'People who were accustomed to call Herts an ugly county were astonished at [the] view and the surroundings of the house were altogether very pretty, first and foremost the fine view, and to the north a peep of the park with its little woods of firs and oaks.'[31] And Louisa wrote to Lily: 'Never shall we see such a sweet place ... the expanse of *air* and fields, and no chimney pots or railway near enough to be a nuisance.'[32] As a child Morgan of course took it for granted that he lived 'in a district which I still think the loveliest in England'[33] where there were 'hedges full of clematis, primroses, bluebells, dog-roses, may, bryony and nuts'.[34] It was only later on that the same district became symbolic.

What it became symbolic of was an impossible and a liberal dilemma, one that is felt by millions nowadays but that, in the early decades of Morgan's lifetime, was felt by only a few, and those only the most far-sighted. It was a conundrum that Morgan was to make central to *Howards End* when he began writing it in his thirtieth year. In the novel he described an England in which 'month by month the roads smelt more strongly of petrol, and were more difficult to cross, and human beings heard each other speak

---

* It has been claimed that the landlord, the Poyntz Stewart family, 'weary of Mrs Forster's inability to make up her mind whether or not she was leaving, settled it for her by informing her that her tenancy was at an end.'[29]

with greater difficulty, breathed less of the air, and saw less of the sky'.[35] Thirty-five years later he broadcast a polemical talk called 'The Challenge of Our Time'. It described how life had gone on much as it always had round Stevenage until the day when someone was applying for a permit to lay a water pipe and was 'casually informed that it would not be granted since the whole area had been commandeered. Commandeered for what? Had not the war ended?' It had, but for the people of what later became christened 'Forster country' another war was just beginning. A satellite town was to be built ('meteorite town would be a better name. It has fallen out of a blue sky').

'Well,' says the voice of planning and progress, 'why this sentimentality? People must have houses.' They must, and I think of working-class friends in north London who have to bring up four children in two rooms, and many are even worse off than that. But I cannot equate the problem. It is a collision of loyalties. I cannot free myself from the conviction that something irreplaceable has been destroyed, and that a little piece of England has died as surely as if a bomb had hit it. I wonder what compensation there is in the world of the spirit, for the destruction of the life here, the life of tradition.[36]

There was nothing Morgan could do in 1946. There is nothing anyone can do today. People need houses. People need the tradition of the unspoilt countryside. They cannot have both. Nowadays Rooksnest, although surviving in its garden and on the edge of fields (in 1960 it too was threatened, making Morgan reflect gloomily on 'the impending destruction of the countryside, the home, and perhaps of the family'[37]), is yet much changed. On one side there is the throbbing of traffic along the A1 trunk road, on the other the houses of what is by now the outskirts of Stevenage. Although grateful that the house has not been swept away by the demolition men I cannot but mourn the Forster countryside of old. The sense of loss belongs to us all and always will. For Morgan this was first made real in the summer of his fifteenth year.

5

Tonbridge

The school Lily chose for Morgan, hastily when he was fourteen and a half, was Tonbridge. She chose it for one reason and for one reason only: it was a respected public school that had recently made a point of trying to attract day boys and as a result 'many a family moved to the place where living and education were so cheap, where day-boys were not looked down upon, and where the orthodox and the up-to-date were said to be combined.'

Since Morgan had shown himself unsuited to boarding-school life – and he had after all to go to school somewhere – this was the ideal compromise, socially acceptable, intellectually respected and, happily, inexpensive: the fees when Morgan arrived were £18 (£1000) a year for boys living within ten miles of the school and scarcely went up over the next four years. And what could be nicer than having 'Morgie', at home, in the healthy Kent countryside?*

What Lily could not know – how could she? – was that the teaching at Tonbridge was often pedestrian and uninspired and that the sporting ethic was supremely important. What she could not know, also, was that day boys, although an ever increasing group (twenty out of the fifty-seven new boys in the term Morgan arrived lived at home), never quite felt they belonged. At Kent House Morgan had been perfectly happy because in all basic essentials he had felt at one with his peer group; at Tonbridge he did not, and his already incipient sense of being an outsider was made more manifest.

Things did not begin well. July and August were spent in packing

---

* When Eddie went to Charterhouse it was still in cramped Elizabethan buildings in the City; the damp and overcrowded living quarters may have contributed to his breakdown in health.

up* Rooksnest and in Morgan bestowing long farewells on the house and meadow and on Ansell. He then departed for Tonbridge on his own and for the first month lodged with a local family. His letters 'home' were forlorn; and it is hard to reconcile the Lily of this period who sent her son off into the unknown with the Lily of later years who continually fussed about Morgie's breakfast egg or need for vests. It was almost as if at this stage she was herself adhering to the Tonbridge aim of 'producing the average Englishman';[2] or hoping against hope that her son would transmogrify into a 'Trent' in *Nottingham Lace*, his first, unfinished novel, 'brown, athletic and good-looking: a straight sensible fellow who if he had brains would never let them become unduly dominant'.[3] Only when she finally realised that her son would never be thus would she allow mother love to topple over into smothering.

'The school is so huge,' Morgan told Lily, 'in fact after I have begun to make friends with a boy I lose him! and the friendship is closed prematurely.'[4] For, it is clear, one of the most useful lessons Morgan had learnt at Kent House was the importance of having a friend, an ally against adversity. 'In any community', he would write in the 1930s when describing a friend's life at Charterhouse, 'it is necessary to have someone with whom you can consort and who will not turn against you when you are attacked, and it is most necessary in the community of school, where attacks are so capricious, and so relentless when they start.'[5] In his own case he consorted with his mother.

She arrived within a few weeks of the beginning of term, in the early autumn of 1893, and moved with Morgan into their new, rented house (whereas one of the points of pride for the dreadful Manchetts in *Nottingham Lace* is that they 'are almost the only people who have a house of their own here – I am not boasting, I merely say it for what it is worth'). Dryhurst, Dry Hill Park Road,† was an 1860s red-brick villa (so spacious by modern standards that it is nowadays a school). Almost next to one of the boarding houses, it was less than five minutes' walk

---

* They took with them the drawing-room mantelpiece which, Morgan was to write in 1947, 'has followed us to Tonbridge, to Tunbridge Wells, has been stored, followed us to Weybridge and West Hackhurst, and now stands, more effective than ever, in its last home'[1] (Morgan's room at King's College, Cambridge, now the Graduate Common Room, where it looks a little forlorn). It is possible that Eddie designed the mantelpiece for Melcombe Place; or that Lily herself installed it at Rooksnest and regarded it as movable furniture; or that she and Morgan were determined to take some part of Rooksnest with them and removed it.

† Now 38 Dry Hill Park Road.

from the main school itself; from the gabled windows at the top Morgan would have been able to see across neighbouring gardens to the cricket field, to hear the sound of boys shouting heartily to each other and, even on Sundays, the day he was at home with Lily, hear the chapel bell tolling for compulsory Matins at 10.45 and Evensong at 7. The one aspect of Dryhurst that Morgan liked was the view and the garden which, like the Manchetts' garden in *Nottingham Lace*, sloped down to four big pines and a tennis court and 'a black line of hill that stretched across the country from right to left, like a great thick billow that was going to break over the wavelets and wrinkles of the green sea below.'*6

Close as Dryhurst was to the school, for Morgan it came to epitomise domestic life in the suburbs; and it was at this time that he came to accept, half angrily and half contentedly, that 'some people spend their lives in a suburb, and not for any urgent reason. This had been the fate of Rickie. He had opened his eyes to filmy heavens, and taken his first walk on asphalt. He had seen civilization as a row of semi-detached villas, and society as a state in which men do not know the men who live next door.'7 The anger was because he missed Rooksnest. The contentment was because suburban life was undeniably a comfortable one; it was the domestic calm of these years 1893–7, while Morgan was at school but while he was cosily at home with Lily, that were to make him reluctant to escape suburbia in the future: even while he railed against it.

Part of the move to attract day boys was the recent abolition of early school in favour of 'early preparation in the boarding Houses and in the boys' homes'.8 In practice the day boys could come down for breakfast at a reasonable hour, read *The Times* and set off for chapel at 8.30 or lessons at 8.55. Morgan's departure for school was thus little different from an adult male setting off for work, and a routine was established at this time that gave the widow and the introspective, increasingly home-bound boy a closeness, almost a symbiosis, that ensured that neither would ever choose permanently to break the pattern. Since Marianne and Eddie's money would ensure that Morgan did not have to sit in an office, it would make little difference to Lily if he went a short distance to school or sat upstairs in his room 'working'; whatever he was doing she consulted with the maids, set off into town

* Hilden Oaks School still has a large sloping garden with a view to the North Downs spread out on the horizon.

to do some shopping, joined Morgan for lunch, rested, had tea with a friend, joined him again for supper and then sat with him reading, sewing and talking. For fifty years, with infrequent variations, such would be the daily round.

The domesticity of all this, the endless opportunity for motherliness, were what enraged many of the school's teachers (the boys were quite happy, seeing equal advantage and disadvantage in being a boarder or day boy). Tonbridge in the 1890s was neither in the firm grip of an established order nor cheerfully maverick, and for the master obsessed with tradition this was the fault of the day boy.

How can traditions flourish in such soil? Picture the day-boy's life – at home for meals, at home for preparation, at home for sleep, running home with every fancied wrong . . . And then the letters from the parents! 'Why has my boy not been moved this term?' . . . 'Can you let my boy off early to water the garden?' Remember that I have been a day-boy house-master, and tried to infuse some *esprit de corps* into them. It is practically impossible. They come as units, and units they remain.

This is Mr Pembroke in *The Longest Journey*, whose greatest achievement was the organisation of the day boys:

Like the boarders, they were to be in at 7.15 p.m . . . they, too, must work at fixed hours in the evening, and before breakfast next morning from 7 to 8. Games were compulsory. They must not go to parties in term time. They must keep to bounds. Of course the reform was not complete. It was impossible to control the dieting, though, on a printed circular, day-parents were implored to provide simple food. And it is also believed that some mothers disobeyed the rule about preparation, and allowed their sons to do all the work overnight and have a longer sleep in the morning.[9]

At Kent House, 'Saint Forster' may have played some practical jokes but he was, all in all, a compliant child. It was the absurdity of the rules at Tonbridge, the almost manic longing with which some of the masters wanted to impose them but were, of course, unable to do so, that first aroused Morgan's anti-authoritarian instinct. Selfishness was one thing – he always obeyed rules if he otherwise impinged on people's autonomy – but officiousness was another; with this Morgan would have nothing to do and one can imagine the sullen and rebellious pleasure with which he would almost religiously lie in bed before breakfast from 7 to 8. His loathing of all that was implied by the phrase *esprit de corps* was inculcated during these Tonbridge years.

Yet the headmaster of Tonbridge, Dr Wood, was tolerant enough of the individual to make certain concessions, for example Morgan was excused games and instead allowed to go for long bicycle rides into the Kent countryside. Where Dr Wood was less tolerant, indeed unbending, was in regard to teaching methods.* At the time his, and his classics staff's, emphasis upon rote learning and accuracy was taken for granted by Morgan. Later on he would recall not with anger but with mere 'amusement the howls of pain that a false quantity would wring from teachers of verse composition at school'.[11] Nor were classics lessons completely hidebound by accuracy and false quantities. In very old age Morgan, re-reading the *Aeneid*, recalled in his diary how

Mr Floyd, a form-master in faraway & forgotten Tonbridge laid his head on one side when it finished and squeaked, 'marvellous, but you cant see it, wretched boys, cant see it – – – ' We couldn't, and I was puzzled by his enthusiasm, which I realised was genuine, and he helped me by puzzling me and making me realise that I might see more in Virgil and elsewhere, when I was mature. His squeak survives as a fruitful sound, and I remember his fat intelligent screwed up face. Mr Floyd was said to be frightening, but he was never unkind to me, and I pay him this faint far away tribute.[12]

It was only when Morgan arrived at Cambridge that his tutor first explained to him 'that much of my backwardness was due to the time wasted on repetition. He was horrified at the amount learnt, and always thought that Dr Wood was a stupid narrow-minded man with regard to teaching.'[13] And there was to be more than a hint of self-identification when, in old age, Morgan wrote about the 'stupid and wasteful way' his friend Goldie Lowes Dickinson had been taught Latin and Greek and remarked that 'it was only when he got away from them and studied contemporary affairs that he began to discover what they meant. The ancients are modern. That, in brief, was his discovery.'[14]

Yet Tonbridge continued the work of Kent House: both institutions managed to instil in Morgan his passionate and lasting love of the classics. And although neither school could have done this if he had been unhappy, yet for the rest of his life Morgan was to intimate that he *was* unhappy, deeply so, at school. A nameless

* Dr Wood did, unusually, allow boys to specialise in one of the 'Classical, the Modern, the Scientific Sides'.[10]

witness was once produced to give (endlessly re-quoted) evidence of schoolboy bullying ('we took it out of him, I can tell you'[15]), while Morgan's few published statements on the subject of his unhappiness at school, all made when he was well over fifty (and very much part of the 1930s *Zeitgeist* when *everyone* said they were unhappy at school), his statements have also been continually cited to further the myth: 'I did not like mine',[16] 'I was neither very happy nor very unhappy there',[17] 'I certainly didn't like Tonbridge'.[18] Then there is a longer statement, the tone of which is humorous but which has been read, ever since it was first published in the 1930s, as evidence of genuine misery:

If the impossible ever happens and I am asked to help break up a school what I shall say is this: 'Ladies and gentlemen, boys and bies [*sic*]: School was the unhappiest time of my life, and the worst trick it played on me was to pretend that it was the world in miniature. For it hindered me from discovering how lovely and delightful and kind the world can be, and how much of it is intelligible. From this platform of middle age, this throne of experience, this altar of wisdom, this scaffold of character, this beacon of hope, this threshold of decay, my last words to you are: There's a better time coming.' And then that school would break up.[19]

Apart from this there are no letters, no diary entries, no verifiable memories of contemporaries. But there is the myth and there is the novel, *The Longest Journey*, published ten years, only ten years, after Morgan had left Tonbridge. Of course he used the school as a model for 'Sawston', and of course the novel is strongly autobiographical and extremely hostile about the school. But it is a satire and not a polemic: the focus is the ideal of the British Public School; it was not, and was never intended to be, why he, the author, was so miserable at his own public school. He was not entirely miserable. But he spent the rest of his life, or at least his life as a public figure, implying that he was, in perpetuating the myth of his unhappiness at Tonbridge.

There were two principal ways he did this, apart from declaring that his education only began at Cambridge, and these were claiming to have had no contact with the school after he left and claiming to have been friendless. How odd it was, therefore, to discover that a few months after he left Tonbridge, at some point in 1898, he took out a life membership of the Old Tonbridgian Society formed ten years earlier to 'promote mutual intercourse amongst Old Tonbridgians, and good feeling between past and present members of the School'.[20] It was a purely voluntary society, indeed Morgan joined at a time when it was not traditional to do so – only later on did joining become automatic, with the fee being added to the last account. Why should he have wanted this lifelong link with his old school, this annual necessity to read, throw away or in any case take minimal notice of the annual Report and List of Members of the Old Tonbridgian Society? Unless Lily wanted him to (but then later on he could have asked to be taken off the mailing list) it is inexplicable; but the upshot is that every year *for the rest of his life* Morgan received this Report, first at Cambridge, then at Weybridge and then at the Reform Club. It means that while writing *The Longest Journey* he had copies beside him to remind him of Tonbridge/Sawston details. And overall it means that his feelings must have been far less uncompromisingly hostile than he regularly implied ('the best of life began when I left it'[21]) because otherwise he would not have arranged for the Report to follow him about: he would, as is usual in these cases of misery at school, have gone on the Unknown Address List that fellow pupils are annually asked to bring up to date.

Another myth is that Morgan was friendless. What is certainly true is that in later life he did not keep in touch with anyone from Tonbridge, either with the two close friends he made during his time there or with the ex-Tonbridgians such as William Mollison whom he cultivated in his first year at Cambridge in order to have some kind of companionship. But friendless he was not, for there were two, Reggie Tiddy and Edgar Nicolas: the latter appears in Morgan's pocket diary for 1898 almost always called by the abbreviation Nic; the former was mentioned definitively and without hesitation as being Morgan's 'best friend'.

There is a man living at Tonbridge today who came to teach at the school in 1922* and is now in his late nineties; his name is Gilbert Hoole and it was he who told me that Morgan had a close friend called Reginald Tiddy.[22] At first I was sceptical, wondering how this could be remembered over so many years.

---

* He replaced Floyd, who had died suddenly.

Then, as I understood Morgan better, I realised that the very reason it *was* so plausible was because it appeared, as it were, without trace. Throughout Morgan's life story we are submerged with detail about certain areas, certain preoccupations, certain people: but these are the details he wanted us to know about. He told us a volume's worth about Marianne Thornton, yet about Eddie, the person we would like to understand, nothing at all. He told us that he had no friends at Tonbridge. By being supposedly direct and informative about certain things he assumed that we would question no further and take his word for it; he hoped that by transparently revealing certain aspects of himself others would remain submerged. Tiddy was one of the latter category. He did not mention Tiddy, I would surmise, because the friendship resulted in a wound which never healed and which Morgan did not want to think about. He therefore concealed him, he tidied him up in the same way as he was to describe his ancestors doing when he mentioned that 'their letters and the Thornton papers generally have been tidied up by pious editresses. The copies on which I have often to rely may conceal omissions.'[23]

Tiddy became an omission because, I believe, Morgan offered him a passionate romantic friendship of the type later described in *Maurice*, but for some reason this friendship foundered. I make this suggestion for three reasons: the first is the remark of a graphologist who looked at Morgan's handwriting for the mid-1890s and suggested that 'he appears to experience bouts of depression which leave him vulnerable at an impressionable age to influences that might seem to offer the supporting arm of companionable assistance. In our subject's case there are strong suggestions that this was a sexual relationship with another man.'[24] The second is that the friendship must have been a strong, and a famous, one for Gilbert Hoole to have heard about it twenty-five years later and to remember it. And the third is what we know about the character of Tiddy himself.

The first aspect of fascination is the photograph of Tiddy. This gentle, intelligent man appears, in his owl glasses, charmingly intellectual. He *looks* the kind of young man one would imagine Morgan wanting as a friend. Then there is what we know about Tiddy (who was always called Reggie but since he seems in some respects to be the model for Tibby in *Howards End* it is difficult to think of him by anything but his last name*). Tiddy was, like Morgan, a classicist, but was cleverer than Morgan, winning a scholarship to Oxford when he was only seventeen and staying on at school in order to be head boy. From this last detail we gather that he had a greater commitment to conventions and institutions than Morgan, and this impression is confirmed: Tiddy remained at Oxford as a don, first teaching classics and then being one of the earliest lecturers in the newly established School of English Literature. In the vacations he lived in a village near Oxford 'and was one of the leaders in the revival of folk-dancing and folk-song which took place about that time'[25] for 'he had a deep love and comprehension of the country people, who looked upon him as one of themselves – "of the land", as they were'.[26] One of his closest friends was the composer George Butterworth, who set songs from *A Shropshire Lad* to music and was killed on the Somme five days before he was, in August 1916. When Tiddy was killed a writer in the *Oxford Magazine* remarked, in words that in some respects anticipate Fielding in *A Passage to India*:

He was never quite at home, I think, with the well-liking people who are at ease in the world, who win races, and gain prizes, and enjoy themselves. But with those who have suffered any sort of hurt or deprivation he had a magic intimacy. His own mind was so healthy and sane, and his own enjoyment of things so keen, that he was something of the physician in his friendships – wholly devoted, but a little aloof, clear in vision, strong and cheerful, like a good doctor.[27]

Although I cannot rid myself of the image of Tiddy and Morgan walking by the river, lollingly watching cricket, discussing classical texts and English literature, it is an image merely; there is only one mention of Tiddy in any of the extant Forster Papers, which is in the 1898 pocket diary where Morgan mentions him coming to tea one Sunday in July, when Morgan had already had a year at Cambridge and Tiddy was about to go to Oxford.[28] Could it be that there is more than an echo of self-identification in the following lines in *Nottingham Lace*? The ostracised Edgar 'here and there . . . recognized a face and turned scarlet. He passed the school captain

---

* We can also suspect, from the fact that Tiddy's third name was Elliott, that his name and character were in Morgan's mind when he came to choose the name Rickie Elliot for the hero of *The Longest Journey*. The pairing of Rickie Elliot with Stewart Ansell has much the same rhythm and resonance as the pairing of Reggie Elliott with Morgan Forster.

who had befriended him in his brief career. The captain looked the other way. There is no more pity or friendship for those who have put themselves outside the pale.'[29] It is impossible to know: Morgan has so successfully tidied up all references to Tiddy. But it is not difficult to imagine.

It is also the 1898 diary (why, if it comes to that, did Morgan keep it among his papers, all his long life?) which refers to Edgar Nicolas, usually called Nic by Morgan and once Edgar. On 9 January 'Edgar walked over from S'bro', the house at 84 London Road, Southborough where the Nicolas family were then living. (Southborough is one of the places where Lily stayed during her round of visits in 1882. It is unclear whether this is coincidence merely or whether she partly chose Tonbridge and later Tunbridge Wells because of a friendship there, in this pleasant village halfway between the two towns.) Following the 9 January entry there is a tiny drawing of what looks like a sun with six rays and an eye at one end: a hieroglyphic incomprehensible to anyone but Morgan. The next day he 'walked and bussed to S'bro and saw Nic's new house', the following ditto and the two of them walked to the nearby village of Speldhurst. At luncheon 'Mrs N lent me Westcott's religious thought in the West' (Nicolas *père* was a clergyman so the talk must often have been about religious matters). Just before Morgan returned to Cambridge the boys went up to London for the Millais exhibition at the V & A, and played golf. In the Easter holidays it was the same pattern, less so over the summer, presumably because Morgan had by then been at Cambridge for a year and Edgar had just left Tonbridge and had started a job in London. Nevertheless, in September, Morgan 'sent off book on style to Nic'[30] – being a fledgling civil servant he was evidently in need of it.

The impression of the diaries (only two pocket diaries have survived, for the years 1898 and 1899) is of a sociable, cheerful young man given to walks, bicycle rides and tea with friends; not of someone apparently morose and at odds with the world. 'A most delightful Xmas it has been,' Morgan wrote in December 1899, and there is no reason to think he dissembled. Yet, in later life, he did: he exorcised Tonbridge friends, he professed to an unhappiness which was not, at the time, there. It was for this reason that he edited out the Nicolas family, even though he and Lily would have met them very soon after they moved to Tonbridge (they had lived next door but one to Dryhurst*

---

* Their house, Correnden, was separated from Dryhurst by a house called Simla.

and Edgar was a day boy and Morgan's age). It is likely, indeed, that it was the Nicolases' move away from Tonbridge that inspired Lily to move too (although she was not to choose a village but another suburban street, in Tunbridge Wells). It is likely as well that it was the Nicolas family who inspired Morgan to write his first novel, the unfinished fragment called *Nottingham Lace* that he began the year after the move, while he was in his third year at Cambridge.

The hero is, like 'Nic', called Edgar. His surname is Carruthers, a name not unlike that of the Nicolas house Correnden, but having, like Nicolas, three syllables with a hard consonant, two soft consonants and a final 's'. (This is a pointer that will recur in the future: when Morgan identifies a fictional character with a real person he almost always gives the one a name that sounds at least rhythmically like the other, for example Whichelo/Honeychurch, Lily/Lilia and, in *Maurice*, Ernest Merz/Maurice Hall and Max Garnett/Clive Durham.)

It is impossible to know how much Edgar in the novel is like the real Edgar, or, indeed, how much he is simply a self-projection of his creator. But he seems to have had many of Morgan's qualities: he reads Pater, Keats, Swinburne and the *Omar Khayyam*, as presumably did Morgan, for 'poetry was a refuge from the world without'; he knocks things over, clumsily; he feels excluded from 'normal' life and resolves, as perhaps did Morgan, privately upstairs in his bedroom, that 'he would lead two lives. His artistic interests and youthful impulses – all the things he cared for should be on one side, shut up in his room. His everyday behaviour should be on the other.'

Edgar does not fit in at 'Sawstone'* school, for he 'had proved unequal to its vivifying influence and after two terms of misery had ignominiously retired'; he feels disgraced not only because he was destroyed by the bullying but because he had 'proved himself unfit for the battle of life'. If school was a 'world in miniature' and 'if he had capsized in the bay how could he hope to cross the open sea?' Yet if the book was to have a dramatic focus Edgar would eventually have to escape. Since Morgan himself was too unwilling, too unsure whether he wanted to or had the courage, he could not make his hero do something that was beyond his reach and which even his imagination could not encompass. As he wrote about Edgar, 'events to be truly tragic must take place quickly. However important they are they lose

* Sawston was spelt with an 'e' in *Nottingham Lace*.

their impressiveness if they take long.'[31] It was a presentiment of his own future. His escape would not be rapid. It would come, slowly; but not through his novels.

6

To Cambridge

What, as he approached the end of his time at Tonbridge, did Morgan Forster seem like? This, in the words of another old boy, Rupert Croft-Cooke (also a writer and a homosexual who, it must be said, might not have been quite unbiased), this is what Morgan was *not*, a

Tonbridge type, middling, a little smug, quietly successful with a consuming horror of not resembling precisely his neighbours and contemporaries. He has pleasant manners, what used to be called good breeding, he is usually honourable and his only excess is in conventionality. He was a good minor administrator in imperial days; he makes a loyal and sensible but unimaginative officer; he is unobtrusively housed, prosaically dressed, impeccably correct in procedure, appearance and ambition. He is prominent in whatever sport may be fashionable and is pained rather than angry to find that the world holds persons with ideals quite different from his. He is a good chap, staunch, sometimes charming, always reliable – and usually prosperous.[1]

The only respect in which Morgan was like this mythical Tonbridgian was in the quiet unassuming manner; he, too, would not have wanted to be noticed. He by now walked in a slightly hunched way, neither with a self-confident amble nor with a purposeful stride. His clothes never looked quite right on him and never would: not that he ever gave them a great deal of thought, so one cannot assume that he minded.* He was awkward, gauche and clumsy, not so appallingly that it was

---

* The writer Victoria Glendinning once reviewed a book of photographs called *Lady Ottoline's Album* and asked 'And why did E. M. Forster wear his trousers three inches too short?'[2] In photographs his trousers do indeed often expose an unseemly amount of ankle; or they are too long.

humorous but almost irritatingly; his was the kind of hair that looked thin from his earliest years, and which always looked mousey and greasy; his appearance was, alas, diametrically opposite to Duncan Grant's, a friend and contemporary who would always have won the handsomest-man-in-England stakes.

And yet, and yet. There was something attractive about the awkward, pale, seemingly unprepossessing young man that Morgan had become by the time he was eighteen and a half, in the summer of 1897. He was neither brash nor obvious and had a stooping, ill-at-ease diffidence that is so often appealing; it is this type of boy who is gestating: the pleasant, smug boy is unlikely to produce anything more than pleasant smugness. Yet he was also the type who kept his true self hidden, as he described Edgar doing and as he would describe Lucy in *A Room with a View*: on one level she is a nice girl from the suburbs who is 'always quoting servants, or asking how the pudding is made'; on the other she is the girl who 'entered a more solid world when she opened the piano. She was then no longer either deferential or patronizing; no longer either a rebel or a slave.'[3] Like Lucy and Edgar, Morgan 'would lead two lives'.[4] The life that mattered would be revealed, however, not only in music but – and this was a realisation that must have been growing on him very gradually during the Tonbridge years – also in his writing.

At first he had imagined himself a classicist and indeed by some standards he *was* a classicist for the rest of his life: it was only that he did not work in a school or university or a museum. At the end of every year he was at Tonbridge he won form prizes (except in 1896, which was likely to have been the year he had his unhappiness with Tiddy); and in the term he left, the summer term of 1897, he won the Latin verse and the English essay prizes; these had to be partly read out on speech day, and the English essay was printed in the school magazine.

It was this essay, titled 'The Influence of Climate and Physical Conditions upon National Character', that might have made Morgan wonder, privately at least, whether he might be a writer.* The effortlessness and the beauty of the prose strike the reader at once. Nor is it the work of someone hostile or self-deprecating:

* He once told an interviewer 'indulgently': 'Of course, I had a very literary childhood. I was the author of a number of works between the ages of six and ten. There were "Ear-rings through the Keyhole" and "Scuffles in a Wardrobe".'[5]

it is the work of someone confident and subtle. It is also curiously characteristic of Morgan's future writing, in some ways prophetic. 'In the case of emigration,' wrote Morgan, 'a struggle takes place between the man and his new surroundings . . . [but] an Englishman is an Englishman, whether he is on the plains of South Africa or the mountains of Upper India, though his descendants live in these places for hundreds of years they will never in the slightest degree resemble Hottentots or Chitralis.'[6] Nearly thirty years later he was to conclude his greatest work, *A Passage to India*, with the reluctant acceptance that the English and India could never be true friends: 'they didn't want it, they said in their hundred voices, "No, not yet," and the sky said, "No, not there."'[7]

Morgan must have been embarrassed by this eighteen-year-old's essay for the irony is not quite sharp enough: read in a certain light, it could appear both empire-building and self-satisfied. The conclusion to *A Passage to India* was to be reached after an entire novel with evident, palpable reluctance; the author of the essay could be seen to have imbibed the nationalist ideals of his surroundings, more evidence that Morgan did not begin properly to question or to dislike such ideals until after he left Tonbridge. The empire-ruling values that the school inculcated in its pupils had had their effect upon him too. When, in later years, Morgan came to loathe these values there was perhaps just a tinge of shame that he had once, youthfully, failed to reject them enough.

But it was not shame alone that made him turn his back on Tonbridge, indeed that was but a small part of it. The overriding reason was his own temperament. Morgan matured late; as a young adult he was obedient and thoroughly unquestioning, indeed dutiful. Yet this was the 'decadent' 1890s; the Oscar Wilde trials took place in the middle of Morgan's time at Tonbridge; to read literary histories of the period England was full of velvet-jacketed, sexually ambivalent aesthetes drinking champagne for breakfast and publishing their work in little magazines. Not a glimmer of this pierced the calm of Dryhurst – or so it seems.

For Edgar Carruthers 'the life he liked leading and the life his relatives led were incompatible'[8] but he, and Morgan, did not wish or did not dare or could not make a declaration to this effect. Virginia Woolf's remark about Morgan – 'He spends his time in rowing old ladies upon the river'[9] – would have been apt about any period of his life including the period of his schooldays; Lily's friends, Lily's sisters, the maids, the neighbours: uncomplainingly Morgan made them the focus of his life. Even spiritually he was, underneath, less defiant than he might have chosen afterwards to imply. It was not so long since he had been shocked by his contemporaries' spiritual indifference at prep school; at Tonbridge, as he later admitted, the 'spiritual shallows continued – complicated rather than deepened by confirmation'.[10] By the time he left school he was nearly nineteen. The extraordinary almost unbelievable miracle is how far he had to go and how far he got in the three years before he wrote *Nottingham Lace* and the eight years before he published his first full-length novel.

Clearest evidence of this miracle appears in the one full-length diary that survives from this period. In the April of 1895, when Morgan was just sixteen, he and Lily went for two weeks to France. The purpose of this trip was partly to visit his thirty-year-old aunt Rosie Whichelo who was a governess near Le Havre, partly to allow Morgan to see Rouen ('*the* place of north Europe, as Venice is of south Europe',[11] as Ruskin wrote) and the other great sights of northern France. They were kept entranced for five days by Rouen, and in his detailed diary Morgan mingled Ruskinesque description of architecture with personal and domestic detail: 'Shop people, servants, & waiters etc. are much more pleasant than those in England. The sugar for coffee is rather large & thin. Mother says it is made of beetroot. We have to use the same knife & fork through nearly all *dîner*.'

The style of the diary, though evocative, is generally bland ('I have never seen anything so wonderful'); but what it does display is an eye for domestic anecdote ('Madame Poulard & her daughters waited, with the help of a maid with a face like a Dutch doll. When you finished a help of anything they fled at you with more') and, towards the end of the two weeks of diary-keeping, a new mastery of sentence structure:

At length the pitching & rolling began to increase, the passengers scrambled into their berths, the food was cleared away for which we were heartily thankful, the lamps were turned down & we composed ourselves to sleep with many misgivings which increased in proportion to the movement of the ship.[12]

Yet Lily could have had misgivings for another reason. It may not have been chance alone that took her and Morgan abroad in the very month of the Oscar Wilde trials: might it have been her long-repressed feelings about Eddie and Ted that prompted her first holiday in France since Paris in 1878? The hearings against Wilde had begun at the beginning of April. The second and third hearings were on 11 and 18 April. By being away from 10–27 April Lily might have hoped, consciously or subconsciously, to avoid the worst. She could not know that Wilde would be sent for trial and that the first trial would begin on the day they crossed back from St Malo or that 'perhaps never in the Nineties was so much unsavory evidence given so much publicity'.[13] Yet whether or not their departure for France was coincidental, and even if Lily had managed to stop all newspapers at Dryhurst, the atmosphere of sexual repression during Morgan's second summer at Tonbridge must have been appalling. '"So you've never guessed"', says Maurice to the family doctor, 'with a touch of scorn in his terror. "I'm an unspeakable of the Oscar Wilde sort." His eyes closed, and driving clenched fists against them he sat motionless, having appealed to Caesar.'[14]

'The fearless uninfluential Cambridge that sought for reality and cared for truth'[15] first took Morgan to its heart in the autumn of 1897. Almost ever since, or since at least he has been revered as one of England's great novelists, Forsterian imagery has been so inextricably entwined with King's College that one can separate the two as little as Wordsworth from the Lakes or Edith Wharton from Upper East Side New York. Yet he might not have gone there. Eddie, after all, had gone to Trinity and one might have expected his son to go there too. Indeed, one cannot but feel sympathy for the ghost of the pale, effete young man – Eddie – who was rejected so consistently and so cuttingly by his widow and by his son. Nowadays there is much less feeling that a child should follow a parent to the 'old school'; in the nineteenth century it remained a mark of respect and of homage. Yet it was one denied to Eddie.

Ida Darwin née Farrer, Lily's former charge, is likely to have been responsible for the choice of King's. Occasionally, while he was at school, Morgan stayed at Cambridge with a boy from Tonbridge whose father was Dean of Clare College;[16] he would then go to lunch with the Darwins in the house they built themselves in the

Huntingdon Road.* Ida was in some respects a fearsome figure, not because she was bullying but because she was, according to Gwen Raverat (who described her in her classic autobiography *Period Piece*), 'so fine-spun and rare, with her sloping shoulders and shining Victorian perfection'. It seems that, despite her remote aura, Ida had an intuitive grasp of the world. If she proffered advice as to the choice of college, one would be inclined to follow it. And the fact that 'it seemed impossible to live up to her standards' and that she had an 'over-sensitive response to life. She saw the world with very clear eyes'[17] must, in various ways, have made its mark both on her close friend Lily and on Morgan; none the less Ida's perfectionism cannot have been easy for Lily to emulate.

Ida sounds as though she would have understood Morgan; and since she had by now been living in Cambridge for over fifteen years she would have realised that her friend's son would be likely to flourish best in a college which, though 'small, was civilized, and proud of its civilization. It was not sufficient glory to be a Blue there, nor an additional glory to get drunk.'[18] She would have seen that an unsporty, never-drunk boy would do better in the nonconformist, liberal atmosphere of King's than in the larger, more boisterous, more worldly courts of Trinity.

It is possible that King's was a Tonbridge ideal, since the new 1902 chapel was to be modelled on King's College Chapel. Yet overall this seems unlikely: few of Morgan's contemporaries went there and enough was known about the ethics and the atmosphere of King's to make it less than attractive to the Tonbridge masters who advised Morgan about his future. Nor did Morgan know anyone at King's; all in all Ida seems the most likely source of influence. Yet, in a manner she could not have anticipated, its values were to become his values, his values its values, so that the two, the institution and the individual, became quite intertwined. This was despite Morgan's living away from King's for the most creative period of his life; but its aura stayed with him, replenished by visits and by enduring friendships with fellow Kingsmen. If Morgan had gone to a college or a university with a less strongly defined creed, or one which appealed to him less, he might never have found his inner voice and never written his novels. We owe a lot to Ida.

* This house, 'The Orchard' and its garden, was later given by the Darwins as the site for the third Cambridge women's college, New Hall.

What would her Cambridge acquaintances have said about King's? Firstly, and perhaps most famously, they would have pointed to its reputation for the cult of friendship between don and undergraduate, its tradition 'of easy intercourse between old and young. Dons at King's do not live in one box and students in another.'[19] Then they would have defined its anti–public school reputation and the fact that King's values were the reverse of those of muscular Christianity and Tory imperialism (when Morgan arrived at Cambridge he fairly soon shed his lingering religious faith and any vestiges of conservatism). The acquaintances would have known that the existence of God was called very much into doubt at King's (despite the chapel) and that personal relations, philosophic discussion and aesthetic appreciation were what mattered. They would have explained that the authoritarian ethic was despised not revered, that sport was unimportant and that the tripos was valued not shrugged off as something irrelevant: between 1875 and 1906 King's obtained forty-five History Firsts and Trinity (with three times as many historians) a mere thirty.[20] Quite unlike Tonbridge which, in the latter half of the nineteenth century, 'suddenly emitted a quantity of bishops. The bishops, like the stars from a Roman candle, were of all colours, and flew in all directions, some high, some low, some to distant colonies, one into the Church of Rome',[21] King's, since the 1880s, had produced no headmasters – and no bishops. Their place had been taken by liberal intellectuals.

Ida would have understood that Trinity was still a forcing house for bishops, that from the vantage point of the Kingsman it seemed 'stern, arrogant, intolerant, generally rather unamiable', to quote the words of one of Morgan's King's contemporaries, who went on, 'King's has an unconquerable faith in the value and interest of human beings, and finds an interest in the average man – as most people call him . . . what we call "character": I think we care for it more than for intellect.'[22] Faith in others, and faith in moral judgement, were not only innate in Morgan but one of the firmest legacies of the Clapham Sect: despite the radical reputation of his chosen college, despite the vast gulf between its values and those of suburban Tonbridge, yet this is where he felt he belonged. It showed a self-confidence that his otherwise diffident behaviour could not suppress.

When he came to write his two novels with Cambridge scenes in them he placed his heroes at King's but each for different reasons. Rickie in *The Longest Journey* is embraced by the college almost as if he had come home. He realises this, and accepts it, while he is there, and by corollary knows that when he leaves he will be an outcast. Hence the repetition of the metaphor about 'the outsides of homes', which appears again when Rickie's friend Ansell declares that 'To compare the world to Cambridge is like comparing the outsides of houses with the inside of a house', and when Rickie thinks 'Was experience going to be such a splendid thing after all? Was the outside of houses so very beautiful?'

Rickie 'crept' to Cambridge,

cold and friendless and ignorant out of a great public school, preparing for a silent and solitary journey, and praying as a highest favour that he might be left alone. Cambridge had not answered his prayer. She had taken and soothed him, and warmed him, and had laughed at him a little, saying that he must not be so tragic yet awhile, for his boyhood had been but a dusty corridor that led to the spacious halls of youth.[23]

Maurice, by contrast, only chose his college because it was one

patronized by his chief school friend Chapman and by other old Sunningtonians, and during his first year managed to experience little in University life that was unfamiliar . . . they did not care to risk knowing men who had come from other public schools . . . All this suited Maurice. He was constitutionally lazy. Though none of his difficulties had been solved, none were added, which is something.[24]

Morgan, like Maurice, spent his first year in lodgings;* his friends were all from Tonbridge. Lily had stressed the grave importance of being friendly, yet she had evidently emphasised the light-hearted, acquaintance-based aspects rather than the deeper loyalties that were to preoccupy Morgan throughout his life. As yet he was on the side neither of Lily's '"don't rush into everybody's arms, but be very pleasant to all"'[25] nor Helen Schlegel's passionate '"personal relations are the important thing for ever and ever"'.[26] The King's ethic took a while to take effect; convivial breakfasts and rounds of golf with Tonbridge contemporaries were all that Morgan thought important for the moment. Still, he found it all rather an effort: 'I am trying to get some friends,' he told Lily, 'but it is uphill work.' He added, 'all this struggling for friends is very unbecoming, but I suppose all go through it.'

It is piquant to compare this assiduous, eager to please, almost

---

* In Market Square, 'where the Guildhall now stands' he once observed.

compliant Morgan with what he later became – someone who eschewed small talk and disliked sitting around gossiping with acquaintances. In his first year as an undergraduate he could write that a fellow lodger 'does interrupt so – comes in & sits for boring hours'[27] with the implication that he politely tolerated this for the sake of 'getting' friends. In his last years at King's as an old yet still articulate grand old man he often refused to utter even words of courtesy. During a pre-lunch drink with the King's Vice-Provost and a young writer, Morgan one day '*never* spoke, not a word in the hour or so I was there . . . nothing he could have said would have impressed me so much as his silence.'[28] But for a nineteen-year-old conformity was all: whist, expeditions to Ely, concerts, decisions about whether to go up to London for an OT (Old Tonbridgian) dinner: he shirked, 'however several others did not go, so I was not peculiar'.[29] That was what mattered.

What mattered more than anything, still, during Morgan's first year, was not to be peculiar, to play the game. At this time – and it was a period of his life that was to last for a only a little while longer – Morgan did not feel that different from the average undergraduate. When, in thirty years' time, he would write famously that Anglo-Saxon public-school men go forth into the world 'with well-developed bodies, fairly developed minds, and undeveloped hearts'[30] he was, in the last two attributes at least, referring to himself. As someone new to Cambridge, whose umbilical cord to his mother and to Tonbridge was not yet severed, Morgan still wanted to take part in the game that Virginia Woolf was excluded from by virtue of her femaleness but at which all her male relations were adept.

They knew the rules and attached immense importance to them. Father laid enormous stress upon schoolmasters' reports, upon scholarships, triposes and fellowships. The Fishers, the male Fishers, took every prize, honour, degree. What, I asked myself the other day, would Herbert Fisher have been without Winchester, New College and the Cabinet? What would have been his shape had he not been stamped and moulded by the patriarchal machinery? Every one of our male relations was shot into that machine and came out at the other end, at the age of sixty or so, a Headmaster, an Admiral, a Cabinet Minister, a Judge. It is impossible to think of them as natural human beings as it is to think of a plough horse galloping wild and unshod in the street.[31]

Although Morgan cannot have imagined he would be an admiral or a judge, he would not have yet ruled out the possibility: he would not have yet entirely reneged on Tonbridge values. And when he won a College Exhibition a few weeks after his arrival he must have felt nicely part of the machinery. Slowly, however, a change began to take place, a classic change, probably similar to that experienced by Charles Ryder, the hero of Evelyn Waugh's *Brideshead Revisited* (1945). During his first week at Oxford Ryder is called on by his cousin. 'He ate a very heavy meal of honey-buns, anchovy toast and Fuller's walnut cake . . . and . . . laid down the rules of conduct which I should follow . . . "You'll find you spend half your second year shaking off the undesirable friends you made in your first."'[32]

Morgan's relations, while possibly regretting the abrupt breaking of the links with Tonbridge that took place in his second year, could not possibly have objected to his friends. Perhaps, too, they sensed that Morgie was now, in the autumn of his second year at Cambridge, entering upon the happiest years of his life. But they are unlikely to have sensed that, although he was on the threshold of making his most lasting friendships, yet 'the genius of the place – for places have a genius, though the less we talk about it the better' was what was to give him the greatest happiness of all. At the beginning of October 1898 Morgan took possession of his two rooms at W7 Bodley's with its sitting-room looking north to King's Bridge and bedroom at the back overlooking the gardens of Queens'. Like Rickie,

just then he loved his rooms better than any person. They were all he really possessed in the world, the only place he could call his own. Over the door was his name, and through the paint, like a gray ghost, he could still read the name of his predecessor. With a sigh of joy he entered the perishable home that was his for a couple of years. There was a beautiful fire, and the kettle boiled at once . . . He sighed again and again, like one who has escaped from danger. With his head on the fender and all his limbs relaxed, he felt almost as safe as he felt once when his mother killed a ghost in the passage by carrying him through it in her arms. There was no ghost now; he was frightened at reality; he was frightened at the splendours and horrors of the world.[33]

7

King's

'Filthy self righteous place, full of Dorothy Perkins roses,'[1] the thirty-three-year-old Morgan would one day write about Tunbridge Wells, the town to which he and his mother moved in the September of 1898. After much house-hunting they had had to compromise. 'We want low rent, detached house, view, near station, water, drains and in the country';[2] but 10 Earls Road was a semi-detached red-brick villa on the newly laid-out Molyneux Estate without much of a view.* Here Morgan spent his vacations during his remaining three years as an undergraduate, so that at the same time as beginning to form his exalted and exultant images of Cambridge he was also starting to define the appalled view of English suburban life that was to be the theme of all his novels. Tunbridge Wells was where he did much of his concentrated reading and was where literature started to be more important to him than anything else. Like Edgar in *Nottingham Lace* he would, the following year, have 'looked at the spring with the eyes of a reader and lilac and hawthorn filled him with a vague literary pleasure'.[4] For the first time he was observing with a writer's eye, seeing things not just for the sake of it but because they were resonant with books he had read and because they were food for his imagination.

One of the reasons why it all began in Tunbridge Wells lay in his very dislike of it. The contrast between 10 Earls Road in the vacations and King's in term-time served only to intensify Morgan's

---

* It was a pity that Lily chose a house with little character, for parts of Tunbridge Wells are leafy and pleasant (nearly a hundred years on even Earls Road has acquired a certain period charm). Of this part of the town a modern historian was to remember the approach from the west, which was where Earls Road was, as 'unrelievably urban and firmly set in south-east England at its worst'.[3]

hostility to the one and identification with the other: so that it was now, with his termly escape from self-righteous Tunbridge Wells, that he could begin to articulate the values by which his life would in future be measured. The obsession with contrasts and the longing for harmony between opposing forces had begun; as had the fight against his 'old enemy the "undeveloped heart", against which he battled all his life'.[5]

Friends, teachers, intellectual development: of the latter it is now almost impossible to discover detailed information. But we do have Morgan's pocket diary for 1898, and this lists the exams he took in March, after he had been at King's for five months and as a result of which he was awarded a Second (a respectable enough result but disappointing for someone who had just been awarded an Exhibition). On the first day he wrote an essay on the 'Genius of Theocritus', a favourite and influential poet. In the afternoon there was G[reek] & R[oman] History. The following five days went as follows: L[atin] V[erse] comp., G[reek] V[erse] trans., G[reek] Iambics, Grammar paper ('Howling Mess'), L[atin] P[rose] comp. and trans., G[reek] P[rose] comp., L[atin] V[erse] trans., G[reek] P[rose] trans.[6] Perhaps the brevity and clarity of Morgan's prose style came from his classical reading; perhaps his understanding of modern literature came from his understanding of the ancients, and his philosophical insight; but to the non-classicist the level of maturity and technical skill that Morgan was to achieve within five years seems even more remarkable in the light of this vast, intense emphasis on dead languages.

One could conclude, as did a friend of Morgan's, that 'what Forster got from his classical studies is rather intangible', that he suspected 'that the Mediterranean setting and mythological symbolism of one or two of his short stories was suggested less by his classical studies – years later he sighed over an American Ph.D. candidate: "He has come all this way to connect me with Aeschylus" – than by a visit to Greece in 1902'[7] Once Morgan became a writer as well as a classicist, then everything he experienced – Greece, Italy, suburban England, India – became central to his work; his years of classics had their effect but indeed not a very tangible one. It is easier to 'connect' him with one or two authors, for example Sophocles, whose *Antigone* seemed to Morgan as though written in the very recent past rather than 2300 years before. When he declared, in 'What I Believe' (1939), that he would rather betray his country than his friend,[8] he was making direct reference, for those who could see it, to Antigone's putting her loyalty to her brother before her loyalty to the State, and Creon declaring, from his own authoritarian viewpoint, 'No man who is his country's enemy / Shall call himself my friend.'[9] Not only did Sophocles help to determine Morgan's loathing of tyranny and implacability; he also made him even more sensitive than he might have been to Antigone's humanity and courage and to Creon's inhumanity and rigidity.

It was Theocritus who was Morgan's favourite classical poet. He flourished about a hundred years after Sophocles and lived at Alexandria; but Sicily, where he was born, was the setting for his *Idylls*. The word 'idyllic' comes from Theocritus's use of the word and actually means short poem: our present use of the word is because of his poems' pastoral charm. It was not merely the mood of green fields, the simple life and happy shepherds that appealed to Morgan: pastoral poetry as a genre has always, through the use of irony or telling juxtaposition, explored the link between romance and reality: 'Inherent in bucolic poetry is the paradox of a graceful clumsiness.'[10] Shakespeare loved this paradox. So did Morgan.

While Mr Pembroke in *The Longest Journey* is trying to deter Rickie from being friendly to a master (he has the subversive, kindly, lenient qualities of which the school should be intolerant) he says of him that he '"is a classical enthusiast ... He makes the past live."' It is the ultimate condemnation: and why, for Morgan, the public-school method of teaching the classics was so appalling – it made the past die. At Cambridge, slowly, the past, the classical past, revived and the resurrected authors – Sophocles, Virgil, Theocritus – stayed with him for life.

Yet, despite his love of certain classical authors, Morgan himself would, with characteristic emphasis on the living rather than the dead, have attributed his intellectual awakening largely to the dons,

the tutors and resident fellows, who treated with rare dexterity the products that came up yearly from the public schools. They taught the perky boy that he was not everything, and the limp boy that he might be something. They even welcomed those boys who were neither limp nor perky, but odd ... the boys noticed nothing, and received education, often for the first time in their lives.[11]

The three dons who then had the greatest influence at King's were Oscar Browning, Goldsworthy Lowes Dickinson ('Goldie') and Nathaniel Wedd. The first of these was a tremendous 'figure', notorious and larger than life; but he was probably, by this stage (he was now sixty-two), rather a bore, and despite his reputation as a brilliant history teacher is unlikely to have appealed to Morgan. Indeed, when he was supervised by Browning, in his fourth and last year when he changed to History, supervisions were mostly spent with pupil reading out his essay and don asleep behind a handkerchief. It was not for nothing that Browning was described by a contemporary of Morgan's as 'colossally vain, devoid of either reticence or dignity, and incontinently egoistic';[12] his effect on Morgan was not so much influential as negative. Browning made him realise that this was *not* how he wanted to end up. Thirty-five years later Morgan wrote publicly about Browning: 'he shines out with a magnificence which has been withheld from his admirable detractors, he remains as something unique in the history of the university, a deposit of radium, a mass of equivocal fire.'[13] It sounds adulatory but since there is no other evidence that Morgan even half-tolerated 'O.B.' I think this was mere politeness. (Possibly Morgan never forgave him for first suggesting he go to the teacher-training college with which he was involved and then failing to put him forward.)

Goldie was someone with whom Morgan at once felt affinity but their friendship took a while to mature. It deepened after Morgan had left King's and Goldie became a link, and deepened still further after they travelled together in India. When Morgan came to write his biography of Goldie (who was to die in 1932 aged seventy) he was thought by some to have enshrined a haloed image, to have shown only the saintly side of what others thought of as the 'dapper, fussy, sensitive, slightly absurd, but wholly lovable little don, behind whose old-maidish fastidiousness there lurked a rare spiritual integrity'.[14] Because Goldie became such an ideal, Morgan chose to opt for donnish, fussy behaviour and more willingly to eschew any thoughts he may ever have had about himself being 'brown, athletic and good-looking' like the idealised Trent in *Nottingham Lace*.

As an undergraduate Morgan admired the thirty-five-year-old Wedd, a classicist who was then 'cynical, aggressive, Mephistophelian, wore a red tie, blasphemed, and taught Dickinson how to swear too'. In later years Morgan would declare that it was 'to him more than to anyone – that I owe such awakening as has befallen me';[15] and when he was eighty he gave an interview in which he said that

it was Cambridge that first set me off writing. And in this very room where I am now there was at one time my tutor, a man called Wedd, and it was he who suggested to me that I might write. He did it in a very informal way. He said in a sort of drawling voice 'I don't see why you should not write', and I being very diffident was delighted at this remark and thought, after all why shouldn't I write? And I did. It is really owing to Wedd and to that start at Cambridge that I have written. I might have started for some other reason.[16]

But Wedd did far more for Morgan than make this suggestion:* it would, after all, have been obvious to anyone who read his 1897 Tonbridge prize essay or, presumably, his weekly Cambridge essays,† that he might write. 'As a young don Wedd had been an almost farouche radical, the tireless tormentor of smugness lay or clerical':[18] this, to quote a King's historian, was Wedd's effect on Morgan. Wedd impressed upon him again the importance of the liberal ideas and precepts, the humaneness, absorbed at Marianne's knee: and Morgan's spirit re-awoke. Now he began to realise that all his life he had been parched; but with the new understanding given to him by Wedd and the other dons, and by the radicalism of the undergraduates who were becoming his friends, now his spirit could drink it all up.

Ansell, Will Beveridge, Tiddy, Nic, his few 'undesirable' friends from the year before: none of them was to make as much difference to his life as the friends he made at King's during the years 1898–1901. It was they who made a passionately happy Morgan think of Cambridge as 'too good to be real', they who made him see, as Goldie had seen earlier,

that the public school is not infinite and eternal, that there is something more compelling in life than teamwork and more vital than cricket, that firmness, self-complacency and fatuity do not between them compose the whole armour of man, that lessons may have to do with leisure, and grammar with literature – it is difficult for an inexperienced boy to grasp truths so

* In a talk given in the 1920s Morgan declared that Wedd helped him by saying in a lecture that 'we all know more than we think'.[17] But his influence on him has been exaggerated. In 1908 Morgan began a letter (the fourth of the four that survive) by saying that he had been meaning to write to him for several years. He added an exclamation mark to soften the callousness but nevertheless cannot have regarded Wedd as someone to whom he owed a great deal. As so often, it seems, Morgan embroidered in retrospect.
† All, alas, now lost.

revolutionary, or to realize that freedom can sometimes be gained by walking out through an open door.[19]

Because the King's ethos was one of friendship, the atmosphere immediately embraced the new undergraduate, however callow or isolated he had previously been feeling. The mystery is that the decision was *ever* taken that first-year men should live 'out'; they must all have had the same difficulties as Morgan and have tended as a result to stick with their acquaintances from school. But 'during his second year', for Morgan as for Maurice, 'he underwent a change. He had moved into college and it began to digest him.'

People turned out to be alive. Hitherto he had supposed that they *were* what he *pretended* to be – flat pieces of cardboard stamped with a conventional design – but as he strolled about the courts at night and saw through the windows some men singing and others arguing and others at their books, there came by no process of reason a conviction that they were human beings with feelings akin to his own.

Maurice, Morgan then declared, had 'never lived frankly'[20] since he had left his prep school by the sea, thereby confirming the impression that he himself was ever anxious to give that he had withered away during the Tonbridge years but then came to life at Cambridge.

In *The Longest Journey*, more than in *Maurice*, Morgan was subtly to convey the aura of intense happiness that emanated from his hero while he was at Cambridge: the earlier novel begins with an entrancing and famous description of undergraduates discussing whether or not cows exist when no one is looking at them: Rickie's friends are sprawled all round the room and 'the air was heavy with good tobacco-smoke and the pleasant warmth of tea'. Happily he thinks back on his day:

In the morning he had read Theocritus, whom he believed to be the greatest of Greek poets; he had lunched with a merry don and had tasted Zwieback biscuits; then he had walked with people he liked, and had walked just long enough; and now his room was full of other people whom he liked, and when they left he would go and have supper with Ansell, whom he liked as well as anyone.[21]

This, in these years while Morgan was living in King's, was the pattern of his days. He would never be so happy again and, perspicaciously, he realised it at the time. The realisation even marred his happiness. What would his life bring *after* Cambridge?

The biographer is, however, largely reduced to guesswork about this period of Morgan's life. He kept no diary (or destroyed one) and his letters home to Tunbridge Wells are the very model of the dutiful son. It is evident just from the weakness of his prose style that Morgan was concealing his true feelings; thus February 1899, in a letter beginning 'it is a long time since I have written': 'I spent such a nice time last night with Mr Wedd. I went to have a prose looked over and he asked me to stop and we conversed on all kinds of interesting subjects.'[22]

It was the contrast between the demands of his relations, and the conflicting, infinitely more enticing demands of Cambridge, that led to one of Morgan's earliest public pieces: as one might expect, the disharmony between the one and the other made him want to capture something of it in prose. In November 1899 he described a day's visit made by his great-aunt Eliza (Louisa's sister) and her husband. 'On arriving we examined the chapel. Loud were the exclamations of approval. Aunt Eliza repeated "it is so sumptuous, so rich, the glass is so rich – like woven silk, so . . ." and she waved her hands.'[23] This was to become, a few months later, 'A Long Day', a short article that was published in a King's magazine called *Basileon*. 'Of all days a long day is the longest, a day that is when friends or relatives arrive by the first train in the morning and stop till the last train at night'[24] – here, already, was the characteristic immediacy, lack of pomp and domestic humour.

He did not tell his relations much about his fellow undergraduates and even in the spring of 1900, which was towards the end of his third year, was omitting to mention his new friends and still implying that he was loyal to his old ones: 'Nic paid me a visit last Sunday week. We enjoyed ourselves very much in spite of slushy weather.'[25] What is clear is that Morgan felt, quite reasonably, that here was something that, for the first time in his life, could be called his own – and he did not want to share it with Lily, Aunt Laura or all the other female relations with whom he continued so dutifully to correspond. He knew, in any case, that if he had mentioned his new friends he would have been asked a myriad of questions about their relations, their interests; thus they would have become, in some measure, the questioner's. Morgan did what so many people do in this situation: he made a few of his friends public property and allowed all curiosity about them to be satisfied. He censored the rest.

It is the rest who have since become public property in a way that was denied to his relations: there is hardly one who has not been the subject of a biography or at least figured in many footnotes. Lytton Strachey, John Sheppard, Hugh Meredith, Leonard Woolf, Malcolm Darling, George Barger, Edward Dent were among the future academics, writers and scientists with whom Morgan spent his time when he was not alone in his rooms reading or writing essays. They, and all the other undergraduates whom Morgan counted as his friends, were a highly intelligent and original group of young men. Without their influence – if Morgan had gone to Cambridge in a less glorious era, or if he had not gone at all – it is unlikely that he would have become a writer. They contributed enormously to his intellectual development; they also gave him confidence in his own abilities, and they made him happy. It was because of his friends that Morgan felt he had come home:

As Cambridge filled up with friends it acquired a magical quality. Body and spirit, reason and emotion, work and play, architecture and scenery, laughter and seriousness, life and art – these pairs which are elsewhere contrasted were there fused into one. People and books reinforced one another, intelligence joined hands with affection, speculation became a passion, and discussion was made profound by love.[26]

Morgan's sense of coming home was crystallised on 9 February 1901 when he was elected to the Apostles. This was, and is, a secret society, also known as the 'Conversazione Society', to which seven or eight usually King's or Trinity undergraduates belonged at one time; however, those who had resigned to make way for new members could still attend meetings as 'angels'.* Thus it was that the philosopher G. E. Moore, who had resigned the month before, was present at the meeting at which Morgan was elected, and he continued to play an important part in the society during the four years of Morgan's membership. The other six members in February 1901 were Desmond MacCarthy, Austin Smyth, G. H. Hardy, A. R. Ainsworth, Ralph Hawtrey and Hugh Meredith, who were to become, respectively, a literary critic, the librarian at the House of Commons, a mathematician, a philosopher, an economist and an economic historian; more than this, they were all of them to be among the most distinguished in their fields, a characteristic of Apostles before and since.

---

* Ex-Apostles are presumably 'fallen angels' because they have resigned from the society. The title of Morgan's first novel *Where Angels Fear to Tread* was in part an Apostolic joke.

George Moore's influence upon the Apostles was such that the group became almost a mouthpiece for his own philosophy: so that when, as often happens, the claim is made that Morgan was much influenced by Moore's famous book *Principia Ethica* (begun in May 1902 and published in October 1903) the truth is that it was the ideas that influenced him, not the book itself. (Indeed, he was to claim that he had never read it.[27]) Part of Morgan's passion for Cambridge was his passion for Moore's vision, a vision that embraced truth, beauty and personal relations and that eschewed the mechanical and the socially divisive. More than this, it removed the 'scales, cobwebs and curtains', as Leonard Woolf would put it, that turn-of-the-century Cambridge had inherited from its Victorian ancestors, 'substituting for the religious and philosophical nightmares, delusions, hallucinations, in which Jehovah, Christ, and St Paul, Plato, Kant, and Hegel had entangled us, the fresh air and pure light of plain commonsense'. Moore's work allowed Morgan and his contemporaries to reject Clapham Sect values without feeling outcast; it allowed them to question religion, the money-making ethic, conventional morals, without feeling impossibly alienated from the society into which they had been born. This is why Cambridge, and later 'Bloomsbury', mattered so much to Morgan: it became his value system and in this way his family, his background.

'Philosophically', Woolf would continue, 'what, as intelligent young men, we wanted to know was the basis, if any, for our or any scale of values and rules of conduct, what justification there was for our belief that friendship or works of art for instance were good or for the belief that one ought to do some things and not do others.'[28] Here, in abstract form, is the opening scene in *The Longest Journey*, Morgan's novel which, more even than *Howards End*, paid homage to Moore's ideals. And it was in homage to these ideals, rather than out of homage to the man himself, that Morgan came to create Ansell, Rickie's philosopher friend in *The Longest Journey*. As a person Ansell combines characteristics of Moore, Meredith, Ainsworth and Leonard Woolf; as a symbol, almost an icon, he was one of the few ways Morgan could thank Moore for changing his personal philosophy so much for the better. Thus the opening scene of the novel, in which Rickie's intense happiness is evoked, is almost a hymn of praise: in undergraduate, philosophical terms.

It was philosophy. They were discussing the existence of objects. Do they exist only when there is someone to look at them? or have they a real existence of their own? It is all very interesting, but at the same time it is difficult. Hence the cow. She seemed to make things easier. She was so familiar, so solid, that surely the truths that she illustrated would in time become familiar and solid also. Is the cow there or not? This was better than deciding between objectivity and subjectivity.

Rickie does not join in the debate, for which he 'rebuked his own grovelling soul', but he is deeply happy. 'In one year he had made many friends and learnt much, and he might learn even more if he could but concentrate his attention on that cow.'[29]

The questions discussed at this teatime in Rickie's rooms are wryly symbolic of those discussed at the Apostles Saturday evening meetings. One member (in the months before Morgan joined it was often Moore) would read a paper on a subject such as 'Is anything as good as persons?' or 'Should things be real?' and then there would be a vote. The subjects were not always entirely abstract. In May 1899 Moore asked, 'Is self-abuse bad as an end?' Hardy and Robin Mayor agreed with Moore that it was; Smyth, Roger Fry, Bob Trevelyan and Goldie thought it was not. How deeply, unutterably relieved Morgan must have been when he read the minutes, for he was, so he later claimed, a frequent but guilty masturbator. Yet how embarrassed he would have been to vote for the 'No's. It was to be many years before he even began to shed his inhibitions about sex: he, like Rickie, would not have wanted to join in Apostolic debates, happy as he was to listen to them. Things had not changed years later at Bloomsbury gatherings when he would say not a word and then interpose a remark into the silence when everyone had forgotten he was there.

For, even now, and proud as he was to be part of such a group,* Morgan was on the edge of it. The shyness that had built up in him over the last ten years made him hang back, much as he wanted to put himself forward. Thus, when Moore's biographer described the Easter reading parties that Moore organised almost every year from 1898 to 1914, he described them as including 'most of the Apostles who were to become members of Bloomsbury – Woolf himself, Lytton and James Strachey, Keynes, MacCarthy, Harry Norton and even Roger Fry, the single notable omission being E. M. Forster; but

---

* He read his first paper 'Are Crocodiles the Best of Animals?' on 4 May.[30] The text has been lost.

it also included men who were only on the fringes of Bloomsbury like Gerald Shove, Rupert Brooke, J. T. Sheppard, Mayor, Bob Trevelyan, Sanger, the Llewelyn Davies brothers and Ralph Hawtrey.'[31] Morgan, who must have longed to go, was either too diffident for Moore to ask him; or (and it is not clear whether he was asked and refused, or was never asked) he felt he could not leave Lily at Easter. He was the only one of them all who consistently put his duty to his family before his duty to his intellect: that was to be fitted in where it could.

Yet it is in the very nature of a great novelist to be an outsider: the remarkable fact is that Morgan was taken to its heart by Cambridge as much as he was. If he had not remained detached, if he had not, at this time, gained his reputation for being an 'elusive colt of a dark horse',[32] he might well not even have begun to write. Also, he had grown used to being elusive: ever since the beginning of his adolescence he had worn a carapace, and this had advantages and disadvantages. If one thinks of writers like Gerard Manley Hopkins or Alain-Fournier or Denton Welch or Emily Dickinson or Proust, all of whom Morgan resembled in some respects, one realises that he did not 'end up' like any of them. He was never to come near the precipice of insanity. He was never to endure unmanageable depression. He was never even to behave or look like most people's conception of a writer, which is why William Plomer's famous description of him was to be so apt:

In appearance he was the reverse of a dandy. Incurious fellow passengers in a train, seeing him in a cheap cloth cap and a scruffy waterproof, and carrying the sort of little bag that might have been carried in 1890 by the man who came to wind the clocks, might have thought him a dim provincial of settled habits and taken no more notice of him.*

For a *writer* to look like that is unusual. Writers traditionally have hair drooping tastefully over their forehead. Or they scowl. Or they wear velvet jackets. Or they are too sensitive to emerge in daylight. Or they are obsessed with their art. Morgan was none of these things; and this lack of affectation, and his everyday quality, combined with a detachment which was unusual among

* This description originally appeared in an essay published during the Second World War. When Lily saw it she said, according to Morgan and to Plomer, '"There! You see what Mr Plomer says. How often have I told you, Morgan dear, that you really ought to brush your coat?"'[33]

E. M. Foster, a biography
> by Nicola Beauman
. Introduction
52 - 8

King's Parade 1887, painting by Louise Rayner.

his friends but essential to the writer's temperament, was to be characteristic for the rest of his life. Outwardly Morgan's existence was a little dull; inwardly it was of the greatest fascination. Those who could only see the clock-mender found him uninteresting; those who could see the person underneath were for ever enticed.

Reluctant to leave King's, and having obtained another Second in the Classics Tripos Part II, Morgan stayed on from 1900 to 1901 to read History. He had hoped that Goldie would be his tutor, but Browning's force of personality prevailed; he went, however, to Goldie's lectures on 'The Theory of Law and Government' and 'Analytical and Deductive Politics' and he cautiously began to think of him as a friend. There is no doubt that a year of academic history on top of three years of classics provided a good background for Morgan's future career as a writer and, in particular, an essayist; yet if the English School had been founded he would have spent the year reading English. Indeed, if his academic career had been more successful (he also obtained a Second in the History Tripos in 1901) he might have stayed on as a don and helped to inaugurate the English Tripos, as Tiddy was to do at Oxford.*

Morgan's own censorship has efficiently put a stop to our discovering more about this year. The few extant letters are only about people that Lily knew – Ida Darwin and her husband and children, Nic, or anyone connected with the Clapham Sect such as the historian G. M. Trevelyan who was 'a descendant of the Trevelyans the Thorntons knew – Macaulay's great nephew I think. Aunt Laura wanted me to know him so she will be pleased.'³⁵ And although the previous year Morgan had won a Latin verse prize and an English essay prize (his subject was 'The Novelists of the Eighteenth Century and their Influence on those of the Nineteenth') in 1901 he was not so fortunate.

It is possible, however, that he did not go in for a prize because he was busy with other things. Not only had he written half a dozen more short essay pieces for *Basileon*, all of which were published during this year, but it was at this time, in his rooms at 12 King's Parade immediately across the road from the entrance to the college, that he began to write *Nottingham Lace*. He was twenty-one and it was, in many ways, a beginner's piece. Yet reading it nowadays, trying perhaps to come upon it 'fresh' as though one had been shown it over tea and crumpets in the Cambridge of 1901, then assuredly there is nothing amateurish or callow about it. The mark of genius is unmistakable. What is not there is form or content, in other words, as has been noted earlier, Morgan did not know where Edgar was going and accordingly he could not decide on a form. What *was* there was the beauty and the clarity of the prose; the turn of phrase; the wit; and the social observation. When, years later, Morgan said of this handwritten notebook, 'This wasn't writing, though. The apparatus was working, not inaccurately, but feebly, and dreamily, because I wasn't sure it was there',³⁶ he was right about one thing – he wasn't sure it was there. But the apparatus was, perfectly, there.

In the final scene in *Nottingham Lace* Edgar rouses the Manchetts' son Jack to rebellion. It is a distillation of some of the radical ideals that Morgan had, over the previous three years, acquired at King's; and one of the reasons he broke off the novel at this point is that

---

* It has been suggested that Morgan and his future Bloomsbury contemporaries gained relatively undistinguished degrees because of their 'quite extraordinary undergraduate knowledge of English literature'.³⁴

he knew that his, and Edgar's, intellectual rebellion would not be matched by action. Jack tells Edgar, in the last words that Morgan wrote of *Nottingham Lace* before abandoning it, '"You've shown me what to do, because you're strong and . . ."' But Edgar had only been strong in theory when he said to Jack:

You mayn't do this and you must do that, and you get no answer when you ask why, or only that it's always done or it's the thing or what would people say if you did or didn't. And if you disobey you're punished. And then – yes, that's worst, what you don't see but I do – in time you'll think you must do this and mustn't do that on account of what people'll say, and you'll make it your right and wrong and teach your children it, and punish them if they disobey. And we – all the world – will grow up all alike, frightened to think and act for ourselves. It's awful. We're getting frightened already.[37]

The pull between the conformity of Tunbridge Wells and the individuality encouraged at Cambridge was to be the key to Morgan's life. It was all very well to have emerged from King's imbued with the awareness that, as Maynard Keynes was to define it, 'the appropriate subjects of passionate contemplation and communion were a beloved person, beauty and truth, and one's prime objects in life were love, the creation and enjoyment of aesthetic experience and the pursuit of knowledge. Of these love came a long way first.'[38] How to put these ideas into practice at 10 Earls Road, with Lily, Aunt Laura and Maimie Synnot as eager interrogators and demanders of sympathy and time, with as well the unavoidable lack of the necessity to find paid employment? Unless he reneged on conformity he would never be able fully to opt for individuality. Would it be possible to combine them?

8

To Italy

Lily was very much on her own in Tunbridge Wells: Laura still lived in the house designed for her by Eddie, while Maimie lived in Salisbury, to which she had moved when she remarried in the 1880s and where she had remained as a widow. But the three women, always writing, always visiting each other, intensely part of one another's lives, were, apart from Cambridge, the main influence upon Morgan's life.

When, in 1960, Morgan made a list for William Plomer (whom he then thought would be his biographer) of 'Autobiographicalia' he began it with a list of 'Importanti' and the first of these were 'Mother, Maimie, Aunt Laura – 19 cent.'[1] The implication was that their influence was a Victorian one, and also that it had lessened by the beginning of the new century (the first day of which was, by coincidence, the day he came of age). In reality it had not, and the only circumstance that would lessen it would be old age and death. Yet the three lived to the ages of ninety, seventy-eight and eighty-five respectively, a triplicated longevity that no one could have predicted. It was not that Morgan was ever consciously to long for their death; it was that, when he decided in 1901 not to break away for the time being, he could not have imagined that forty-five years would have to pass before his feelings of duty, inertia, fear, love and childish dependence could at last be substituted by something else. By then it would be too late.

What else could he have done if he had not gone on living 'at home'? Most careers were in one way or another ruled out. To go into the civil service he would have either needed the money or been interested in wielding authority; and he was uninterested in law or in stockbroking, the career that was to be chosen by Maurice who, at the age of twenty-three, became a 'promising suburban tyrant' whose

habits became regular. He ate a large breakfast and caught the 8.36 to town. In the train he read the *Daily Telegraph*. He worked till 1.0, lunched lightly, and worked again through the afternoon. Returning home, he had some exercise and a large dinner, and in the evening he read the evening paper, or laid down the law, or played billiards or bridge.[2]

To teach, Morgan would have had to be content to return to the public-school ambiance; to be a don generally required a First, although this was not always true: Browning had secured the right of fellowship candidates to submit a dissertation. 'This would help the shy man who had not made his mark, and the man who might not have been able to show the true quality of his mind in the Tripos exam- inations, hitherto the chief passport.'[3] Morgan, inexplicably, declined to excercise this right. Yet when his friend Edward Dent was, in 1902, elected a Fellow by this means, despite his Third in the Classics Tripos, Morgan opined wistfully, 'it is a very great thing to be a don. I would have given and would give any thing to be one.' It is a mystery why he too did not use the dissertation method to do so. Perhaps it was because he envied Dent for the wrong reasons, since he added, 'I can't think of anybody who is in a better position for making new friends *and* keeping old ones.'[4]

Nor could Morgan do anything hearty like go into the Indian Civil Service: when he later on described Ralph Moore in *A Passage to India* as being not unlike himself ('prematurely aged . . . hair impoverished') he was to add: 'Not a type that is often exported imperially'.[5] And he was right. His contemporaries at Tonbridge and at King's who went into the ICS were of a different temperament and physique: Morgan would not have got through the interview. The one career that would have once been perfectly suited to his temperament was the Church. It was one career that was unthinkable.

In the last year of the nineteenth century, during Morgan's second year at King's, his 'Christianity quietly and quickly disappeared'. Partly he had come to find the personality of Christ unsympathetic, partly he felt antipathetic to 'so much moving away from worldliness towards preaching and threats, so much emphasis on followers, on an élite'. His family were apparently calm about it. Eddie had once lost his faith but 'had recovered it after a short interval . . . My family assumed that I should follow the paternal pattern. They did not worry, and when time went on they got used to my having no faith.'[6]

The real reason why Morgan at this stage became an agnostic was, however, Apostolic. Even before he became a member of that select group Morgan had found himself receptive to its ideals and philosophy. Later on, after the publication of Moore's *Principia Ethica* in 1903, it was often assumed that this book did for late-nineteenth-century idealism what Samuel Butler's *The Way of All Flesh*, published in the same year, was to do for family loyalty: undermine it. But Moore's ideas were imbued with the atmosphere around him, and the philosophy of something like Morgan's famous 1939 essay 'What I Believe', sometimes deemed Moorean, would have differed not at all if Moore's book had never been published.

I do not believe in Belief. But this is an Age of Faith, and there are so many militant creeds that, in self-defence, one has to formulate a creed of one's own ... Tolerance, good temper and sympathy – they are what matter really, and if the human race is not to collapse they must come to the front before long ... My law-givers are Erasmus and Montaigne, not Moses and St Paul. My temple stands not upon Mount Moriah but in that Elysian Field where even the immoral are admitted. My motto is: 'Lord, I disbelieve – help thou my unbelief.'[7]

These archetypal Forster lines were a distillation of all that Morgan absorbed in the years 1899–1901, after he had lost his belief and before he had to leave the moral paradise of Cambridge. Like few other great artists, his ideas remained consistent all his long life.

Thus, if Morgan's attitudes had taken a more conventional, more Christian form, he might very comfortably have become a clergyman like his ancestors; in some ways the radical nature of the ideas he had absorbed left him rudderless. Yet a great writer needs to be detached from received ideas: conventional attitudes are compatible only with conventional literature.

The atmosphere of King's, where friendship between don and undergraduate was considered the norm and friendship between undergraduates the most important aspect of university life, made its impact on Morgan in a somewhat abstract fashion; that is to say, while he was passionately faithful to the idea of close friendship, the remote side of his nature that had come to the fore since the days of

Will Beveridge made it difficult to put into practice. It was not that he was lonely at King's: a glance at the pocket diary for 1899, patchy though the entries are, gives a convivial impression with friends to breakfast, lunch with friends, tea, coffee and so on. What he lacked was an 'ideal friend', a soulmate, a companion, and not only was he to search for one for many years, he was to realise *in retrospect* that his life at Cambridge had been far less exhilarating without one. This is why, in years to come, he would embroider on one of his friendships to make it appear far closer than it was. This was his friendship with Hugh Meredith.

HOM (he was known by his initials) had been on Morgan's staircase in Bodley's, and it was through his gregariousness that Morgan made most of his King's friends; it was he who first introduced Morgan to the idea of agnosticism; and it was he out of all the Kingsmen with whom Morgan kept most closely in touch throughout their lives. An exceptionally intelligent man, HOM was to hold the Chair of Economics at Belfast from 1911 until 1945; a colleague of his there would refer to 'His pink shirts – or as much of them as you could descry beneath the large black beard which, in combination with an arrogant nose and a ramrod carriage remarkable in a man of his age, gave him the appearance of an Assyrian monarch.'[8] His exuberant personality, his gift for friendship with men and women and his wide-ranging intellect were what attracted Morgan; what is sad is that in old age he was to confuse the attraction of these qualities with love. In conversation with the biographer who replaced William Plomer, Nick Furbank, Morgan intimated that his friendship with HOM had been akin to a love affair.[9] That it was an affair in the sexual sense was wishful thinking; that their relationship was a close one cannot be doubted, indeed in the list of 'Importanti' given to Plomer HOM is cited after the '19 cent.' trio as one of only two Cambridge friends. (The other, somewhat mystifyingly, is Florence Barger, who was not to marry Morgan's Cambridge friend George Barger until 1904 and whom Morgan did not get to know well until some years after that, five years or more after he had left Cambridge.)

It is thus not a very resplendent tally, one friend with whom a love affair was later to be intimated but of which there is no evidence, and one friend who was not to become such for a few years: although Morgan had many acquaintances at Cambridge, and felt idyllically happy there, his actual, real friends were few. Later on it would be different, so that by the time he was middle-aged Morgan's close friends were almost too numerous to count. For now, friendship was still an abstraction. Indeed, his attitude to friends was not so different from Edgar's attitude to the spring and his looking at it with 'a vague literary pleasure': Morgan appreciated individuals but from their individuality he extrapolated larger meanings, wider overtones. This is why, in a sense, he did not need constant companionship, a continual social life. He liked to observe and to draw conclusions, he liked the abstract side of relationships. Thus when, in 1910, he wrote in his diary, after having apparently at last and too late been embraced by HOM, 'that I have been attractive excites me most',[10] it was not the embrace or the fleeting sensual pleasure that made him happy: it was that he was part of the universal state of being 'attractive'. The individual affirmation mattered less than the abstract.

So Morgan was little interested in going to London to share lodgings with a friend – which was, after all, what many of his contemporaries were about to do. He himself disliked enforced intimacy and Lily, too, was against it: in 1900, when the idea was put forward by HOM that he and Morgan should share rooms in the following academic year, she had unequivocally pointed out that this would be a mistake. 'You see he has always been considered a *one man* friend,'[11] she wrote, aware that Eddie was twenty-one when he had become one. But Morgan regretted hurting HOM's feelings and one can imagine him in his room at 12 King's Parade during his final year thinking what might have been had he at that moment been ensconced in the same rooms as his friend over the road in college. In years to come his memory of what had happened between them, and his fantasies, became very much intertwined. That there was anything more than one or two friendly embraces seems extremely unlikely; that Morgan imagined, longed for there to have been cannot be in doubt. How he must have wished that he himself had found a Clive figure when he came to write *Maurice* and that he could have had the joy of writing out of personal experience.

Of course Lily was at the root of it all, not just in the obvious sense that men who reject heterosexuality often have dominating mothers but in the domestic sense. She did not want her Morgie to share rooms because she dreaded him becoming too close to one particular person. Nor was she naïve. Homosexuality was something she would rather not think about, yet she must have seen for herself that her son was, like Eddie (about whom she had had her doubts), lacking in some of the characteristics of the active heterosexual: he did not look like someone of whom people would say, 'Oh, he'll marry and leave the nest before you know where you are.' A small part of her longed for him to conform to the norm; the larger part must have been exultant that the son for whom she had 'sacrificed' everything (she used to hint to him that she had rejected a chance to re-marry for his sake[12]) was not about to destroy their comfortable togetherness or to question her dominance. As her brother-in-law Willie wrote to Laura at about this time:

Lily appears to treat Morgan as if still a child, pays his bills and won't even trust him to choose a pair of breeches. He loathes Tunbridge Wells and tea parties, which latter are all reserved for him he says. He is the only man present invariably and if there were any they wd. be quite as bad as the women. My experience of that class is that they spend their time swapping lies and making mischief. He wants country air and pursuits with genial girls. His descriptions of the teas are very nice, being always in the Jane Austen fashion.[13]

When, three years hence, Morgan came to describe himself in the guise of Philip Herriton in *Where Angels Fear to Tread* he was to claim that he used Edward Dent as a model; but there is little evidence of similarities and since Philip is so obviously like Morgan one can but conclude that in most respects he is a self-portrait. This is how the twenty-four-year-old Philip is evoked:

He was a tall, weakly-built young man, whose clothes had to be judiciously padded on the shoulder in order to make him pass muster. His face was plain rather than not, and there was a curious mixture in it of good and bad. He had a fine forehead and a good large nose, and both observation and sympathy were in his eyes. But below the nose and eyes all was confusion, and those people who believe that destiny resides in the mouth and chin shook their heads when they looked at him.

We are told about Philip, when he sets out for Italy in search of his errant sister-in-law, that 'It was the first time he had had anything to do'; and to him Lilia says, when describing her new husband's cousin, he is '"a lawyer just like you are – except that he has lots to do and can never get away". The remark hurt more than he cared to show.' As Morgan himself set out for Italy he was all

95

too aware that, like Philip, he did not have anything to do and that he also could, all too easily, get away; looking in the mirror he might say, '"It is a weak face. I shall never carve a place for myself in the world."' Yet he knew that the world would make a niche for him 'as it did for everyone'. And 'At all events he had got a sense of beauty and a sense of humour, two most desirable gifts.'[14]

Old ladies continued to hold their financial grip, and at this time Morgan was made even richer. Ida Darwin's mother, Lady Farrer, gave him £50 (£2500) to be spent on travel.[15] Since none of the jobs that Aunt Laura had hinted were within her remit (clerkships in the Education Office, the House of Commons or the V & A) had become even possibilities; since there were no other jobs that Morgan considered feasible; and since there was nothing else to do except sit in Tunbridge Wells – he and Lily decided to go abroad.

Greece was on his mind even as far as jobs went; but Aunt Laura 'won't hear a word about the British Museum because someone says it is badly ventilated, – quite inaccurate I believe; but if one is to get on by favour one must put up with such things.'[16] So he promised Effie Farrer that he 'would spend her present in seeing something Greek: if not Athens, and Troy, Sicily and Magna Graecia/South Italy'. He would have liked to join a cruise that was being organised by Kingsmen for Kingsmen but did not like to tell Lily that she would not be welcome: 'you might not care to go since the great feature . . . is a bumpy cruise along the Asia Minor coast in a small boat. And if you didn't it would mean either waiting in Italy or going home alone neither of which would be pleasant.'[17] (When the cruise took place again in 1903 Morgan had the idea of asking one of Lily's Tonbridge friends to come out to Italy to be with her. Here they waited while he went on it, unaccompanied.)

The Forsters, had they so chosen, could have travelled luxuriously, for Effie's present was only a small fraction of their income. Marianne's £8000 and Eddie's £7000 would still have been holding up well and even if most conservatively invested would have brought in £450 (£22,000) a year; this was ten times Morgan's King's Exhibition (which he had managed to retain into his fourth year despite his

Second in Classics) and five times what a Fellow, even a married one, received. With no servants to pay and no rent, and their only large expense being that of paying for the furniture in store, Morgan and Lily could look forward to a thoroughly trouble-free 'Grand Tour'.

They gave up 10 Earls Road at the end of September, ending a three-year lease, and on 3 October crossed the Channel to France. Morgan, perhaps too aware of his weaknesses, was depressed. 'Start as bad as can well be imagined',[18] he wrote at the beginning of a diary that was continued only for the next month. To Dent, the King's friend with whom he was at this time mainly corresponding and who had given some useful advice about travelling in Italy, he wrote that the start was 'devilish . . . comprising wrong tickets, unexpected arrival in Paris, sick headaches, quarrelling, lost luggage'.[19] Yet part of Morgan wanted it to be like this. How much *less* hemmed in, fractious, bathetic would the experience appear if luggage and tempers had not been lost; by anticipating the material upon which his imagination would draw he blocked out that which might skew his angle of vision. The tenor of his own journey, as well as of Philip's, needed to be manipulated in such a way that when he came to write the final line of *Where Angels Fear to Tread* ('They hurried back to the carriage to close the windows lest the smuts should get into Harriet's eyes'[20]) it should be a perfectly modulated conclusion, a seamless whole with what had gone before both in the novel and in Morgan's own experience. His imagination was too much rooted in reality for him to abandon himself entirely to the unexpected.

First the Forsters went to Lake Como, and decided to stay for ten days at Cadenabbia. Morgan described their hotel, the Belle Ile, as being 'crammed with English – mostly Tunbridge Wells old ladies who go on expeditions that are too long for them and come back tired but vociferous'.[21] It was near the Bellevue, later to be described by Gladys Huntingdon in *Madame Solario* (1956):

In the early years of the century, before the first World War, Cadenabbia on the Lake of Como was a fashionable resort for the month of September. Its vogue was easy to explain. There was the almost excessive beauty of the winding lake surrounded by mountains, the shores gemmed with golden-yellow villages and classical villas standing among cypress trees . . . one arrived by the little steamboat that started at Como and shuttled back and forth across the lake, calling at one dreaming place after another in a journey of incredible slowness.[22]

Morgan saw some of this and noted it in his diary; otherwise he took short cuts. 'I see I have given no description of the voyage,' he noted at Cadenabbia, 'but there is a good one in Baedeker.'[23] What he, like so many writers, could not see was the exact truth: he, like them, took his mental baggage around with him. Hence he noticed old ladies, curates, young girls removed from Tunbridge Wells; Gladys Huntingdon, some months later, ignored these and only observed that 'in the year 1906 women wore long skirts that moulded the hips and just escaped the ground; waists were small and tightly belted; busts were full and bodices much trimmed . . . The social atmosphere of that epoch was particularly loaded with femininity.'[24] Can the two novelists have been visiting the same place?

Yet Morgan knew he was seeing life filtered; and since writing was by now an activity he enjoyed (he had packed the manuscript of *Nottingham Lace* and worked on it when he could) he already understood the personal, novelist's quality of his reactions. 10 October: 'The wind was violent, and as usual we were tired, so the voyage was more interesting as a psychological study of myself than anything else.' 11 October: 'It strikes me so forcibly about Italy that I know it already; I have got it up so well that nothing comes as a surprise.' Despite his professed diffidence, some part of him had the self-confidence to go on with his novel; his detached side could observe his creative side and applaud it, believe in it.

They were going to Florence, and the novel which so memorably has it as its setting was clearly on Morgan's mind. When they made an acquaintance, he privately christened her 'Miss Stackpole' after Henrietta Stackpole in *The Portrait of a Lady*; the Jamesian theme of the American encountering Europe was to be adapted by Morgan into the theme that was later to be known as Forsterian – the English man or woman encountering Italy (and, later, India). As Morgan grew into his persona of a novelist he incorporated James's influence into it, in his theme and occasionally in his language. 'You do understand wonderfully',[25] says Caroline Abbott to Philip, and the Master's voice can be heard.

Thus, while Morgan himself encountered the 'real' Italy ('bullocks drew carts: boys of 16 lovingly cuddled babies'), Morgan the would-be novelist was brooding on the English in Italy. If, in his work-in-progress or in another novel, he could make fiction out of his experiences, his depressing weaknesses would be very much obviated. He began to turn into The Writer, spontaneous reactions often crushed by the need to squirrel away anything that might 'come in', that he could 'use'. Publicly to Lily, or privately in his diary, he might rail against the old lady who 'is continually wishing people god speed or welcome or holding their knitting or turning over their music or admiring their clothes'; imaginatively he was turning her into one of the Miss Allens in *A Room with a View*.

After a recuperative time at Lake Como, Morgan and Lily moved on to Milan, where their first day was spent in changing rooms because they smelt[26] ('"our rooms smell," said poor Lucy',[27] in the opening chapter of *A Room with a View*). At the new hotel ('horribly expensive'[28]) 'they got to know two nice prim maidens and one rather nasty old one, and discussed our doings vociferously in the evening';[29] *A Room with a View*, Chapter 1, 'two little old ladies . . . looked back, clearly indicating . . . "we are genteel" . . . Whichever way they looked, kind ladies smiled and shouted at them.'[30]

It was now, perhaps conscious of the fictionalising eye with which he observed his surroundings, that Morgan appeared to condemn his diary as an exercise in futility and gave it up. The tone of the last two entries was downcast: 27 October: 'the English Church was as depressing as ever'; 28 October: 'of course we were too early, and tired ourselves before the start'.[31] With an abandoned diary, and an abandoned novel, a new start could be made. Florence beckoned, and here they arrived at the end of October.

9

Florence

───────────

Lucy could have cried. It was for this that she had given up her home, made endless preparations, crossed the channel in a gale, had endless railway journeys and four customs examinations – that she might sit with a party of English ladies who seemed even duller than ladies in England. This was Florence, but her life would be where she ate and slept.[1]

These, in part, were Morgan's feelings as he arrived in Florence. He had come to see the 'real' Italy, but he could not seem to shed Tunbridge Wells. At times he wondered whether it was worth having come at all: but what else would he have done? If he had stayed in England with Lily, there would have been nothing for him to do except one of the clerkships that Aunt Laura might, in the end, have come up with; if he had after all applied for a fellowship he might have failed, or Lily might have put a stop to it. If, on the other hand, he had tried to travel with a friend he might, terrible thought, have himself been considered 'a *one man* friend'; and a *group* of Kingsmen would have been unwieldy. A girl could escape through marriage. For Morgan there was no such option. By failing to break Lily's grip in the summer of 1901 it was likely that he now never would. Hence the despondency that was to be his familiar companion during the months in Italy.

How had this gluing of mother and son, one to the other, come about? Not all widows with only sons keep them by their side; many only sons have, indeed, been crushed by the weight of their mother's ambition and by their longing for them to succeed in worldly terms. Lily was different because of her social origins. She could not, ever, forget that 'strays and waifs are never liked unless they show their lowly estate'.[2] That she had once been a stray, and that she had been deemed as such by others, was a wound that had not healed. It was as if she had once been Harriet Smith in Jane Austen's *Emma* (1816), to whom Emma said, unforgettably, '"There can be no doubt of your being a gentleman's daughter, and you must support your claims to that station by every thing within your own power, or there will be plenty of people who would take pleasure in degrading you."'[3]

By marrying into the Thorntons, Lily had put an end to people's pleasure in demeaning her and after Eddie died she was determined that not a glimmer of her past lowliness should shine through her almost-aristocratic façade. She did this so successfully that even Morgan, whose novels are imbued with class distinction, snobbery and the pernicious middle-class emphasis upon whether people 'do' or not, even he never commented on Lily being the cause of his preoccupation. It was not just that they lived in a class-obsessed milieu; it was that she herself was obsessed, however much she and Morgan tried, by ironic insight or claims of genteel poverty or by other methods, to deny the fact. Hence Lily's lifelong need for correctness: those who feel they have to hide something, who are playing a part, cannot ever relax in case someone might pierce their armour.

Hence, too, Lily's solitariness and, as a result, Morgan's loneliness. When Marianne told Lily in the summer of 1878 that 'you have almost led the life of a nun as far as gaieties go since you married',[4] she was not to know that she was being prophetic of the rest of Lily's existence. And when Morgan noted in old age that after his father's death 'my mother retired with me into the country',[5] he perhaps unconsciously used the verb in both its senses: Lily took herself away from the distractions of London life but she also relinquished any idea that she might start a new life. Her energies would go into maintaining the armour round the old.

So Lily kept them as a unit. At the same time she tried to manipulate Morgan's choice of friends. And at the same time as well she fended off emotion, which made it even more difficult for the innately introverted Morgan to reach out to people on his own account. Lily, after all, was, like Mrs Elliot in *The Longest Journey*, 'afraid of intimacy'.[6] Friendship, about which Morgan cared so much in abstract, was something that for years he was to be unable to create himself; yet without it he could not dissolve the glue binding him so efficiently to his mother. And the worst of it was that he could see what was happening for himself. And was too weak, and therefore depressed, to do anything.

Lily, if taxed with all this, would have claimed bitterly that she had only done her duty as a young widow. By moving to Rooksnest, for example, she had removed Morgan from the smog and germs of London. As for herself, one can imagine her moaning, what had been in it for her? The house to look after, trouble with maids, the responsibility of a son – when had she ever had any fun? The one time she had had a little flirtation, or at least drives in the pony trap, with (it seems) Morgan's tutor Mr Hervey, he was deemed by Louisa 'the most uninteresting man'[7] and Lily was criticised for being too confiding.*

There was something else as well that kept Morgan trapped in a duo with Lily: he had a rather sweet nature. Despite flashes of bad temper and grumpiness, which increased as he grew older, in general he was a compliant, kindly person who wanted his mother to be happy. He loved her, he could not help loving her, and he could not tolerate a future in which they were not loving companions. Yet he was trapped, and so the theme runs through his work: Edgar was trapped among the Manchetts by his father's lack of interest and his own failure; Rickie Elliot was to be trapped by Agnes and his own inability to withstand her; Adela Quested was to be trapped by her British compatriots even though she arrived determined they should not stand in her way. Lilia, Helen, Leonard, Maurice, they are all ensnared. The one who escapes is Lucy.

She had arrived in Italy as trapped as the rest; but by the end, because her eyes had been opened and because she had married George,† she had got away. Lucy's escape from Tunbridge Wells is wish-fulfilment for Morgan: and although it has been claimed that as a character she is himself *en travesti* I think this emphasis is wrong. It is not so important that Lucy is Morgan sexually, although she could be him in the guise of a girl; what matters is that her *situation* is his. He

---

* It is possible that it was merely Mr Hervey about whom Lily later made hints that she had rejected proposals for Morgan's sake; if this were so, Morgan's feelings about him and his intrusive influence at Rooksnest must have been more complicated than has been thought. There is almost no evidence, so to give a longer-lasting effect to Mr Hervey is conjecture. But the fact that he had 'eyeglasses and moustache'[8] makes it possible that Morgan saw him trying to kiss Lily, and that this was the origin of Cecil's clumsy kiss in *A Room with a View* when 'his gold pince-nez became dislodged and was flattened between them'.[9] Nor are the names Augustus Hervey and Cecil Vyse quite dissimilar, with their 'v' and 's' sounds.
† His name means farmer/husband; also saviour because St George slew a dragon and saved a stranded maiden. While Lucius = Lat. *lux*, light, and St Lucia = patroness of those suffering from diseases of the eye. Lucy had to see the light and cure her damaged sight before she could be enlightened and clear-sighted. Lucy's brother is called Frederick = peace rule.

had become coerced, imprisoned in a way of life which is usually the lot of women; yet, because it was an unusual one, if he had re-created it in a novel it would have seemed implausible. (And he would have been more recognisably autobiographical.) But the world is full of girls who live wretchedly at home until they can escape through marriage; the fact of Lucy's femaleness did not mean that her experiences were so very different from her creator's.

He therefore changed Lucy's sex for plausibility, not because he himself desired George and could not write about it. Morgan's empathy with women was a real one, even those who were married with children: because, later on, he came to accept that he would never feel sexual desire for them, this did not destroy his imaginative understanding. His misogyny was an affectation, one which bound him more deeply to the misogynist brotherhood of which he longed so passionately to be a part. It did not mean he hated women.

In Florence, Morgan followed Lily first to the Albergo Bonciani, 'very comfortable' and with a 'good piano', then to the Pension Simi because, as he wrote to Dent from the Bonciani, 'my mother hankers after an Arno view and a South aspect, so we are not stopping.'[10] Whereas Morgan was perfectly happy at the first pension, Lily, who normally minded a great deal about her comfort and rather less about spiritual and aesthetic matters, was the one who demanded the view.

The importance of views, of looking from an enclosed world out towards a freer, more open one, was a concept that Morgan had already touched on in *Nottingham Lace* in the opening lines – ' "They are Nottingham Lace!" Mrs Manchett turned from the window with a compressed face . . . Edgar looked out: the curtains were opaque and podgy, but only suggested ill-breeding to the initiated' – and in Edgar's realisation that Sawstone in general is blind to the view beyond it.*[11] Lily's paradoxical behaviour surely (but yet we cannot know for certain because now Morgan kept no diary) caused him to brood further about views, and insight, and spiritual blindness even when a view is in sight. The fact that they changed pensions did

* When the Forsters were house-hunting in 1898 Morgan longed for a house with a view. But 10 Earls Road did not have one: unlike Maimie's house at Salisbury which, as if it was in tune with her outward-looking, receptive personality, had a magnificent view.

not just have a logistic effect upon his gestating novel: it provided a theme. For Morgan, the future novelist of ideas, this was as important an impetus as characters, social comedy or drama.

The new pension, where they stayed for six weeks, became the Bertolini in the novel (the name was that of the proprietor of their hotel in Milan). In 1901 the Pensione Simi was on the ground and first floors of 2 Lungarno delle Grazie, with another pension called the Jennings Riccioli above it; in the 1930s the two were to merge and since then the Jennings Riccioli has occupied the entire building. Its current prospectus boasts a photograph of 'l'albergo dove fu scritto "Camera con Vista"' or 'the Hotel where the author of "Room with a View" was inspired', the English version being technically the more correct. There is also a photograph of the view across the Arno south to San Miniato and the city outskirts, and Lucy Honeychurch was indeed to

lean out into sunshine with beautiful hills and trees and marble churches opposite, and, close below, the Arno, gurgling against the embankment of the road.

Over the river men were at work with spades and sieves on the sandy foreshore, and on the river was a boat, also diligently employed for some mysterious end. An electric tram came rushing underneath the window.[12]

It is only in popular imagination, and in the film of the book, that Lucy draws back the shutters and sees the Cathedral and the 'orthodox-Baedeker-bestarred'[13] view of Florence. Morgan himself, and his heroine, saw the less well-known view over the river to the cypress trees and olive groves and San Miniato; both of them considered it more beautiful.

Indeed, Morgan's reactions to Florence were little different to those of Lucy Honeychurch. Yet he could comfort himself with the thought that he was only twenty-two and had the whole of the rest of his life to see the real Italy. Tourist Italy, he told Wedd, 'delights me so much that I can well afford to leave the Italian Italy for another time'.[14] It was Lily who adopted the attitude that this was an unthinkable possibility: Morgan could never travel on his own. 'I never saw anybody so incapable,' she told her mother, having described Morgan 'fidgeting about looking for his pen which is lost regularly every day . . . I never give him more than 3 or 4 francs [£7 or £8] daily' (not because of extravagance but because he would lose them). Even unvoiced criticism was morale-sapping, and

Morgan lacked the detachment to see that it was Lily's fear of being alone that led her subtly to encourage her son to need her help. In a perfectly contemptible letter she told Louisa that Morgan had taken her to call on some friends of friends but had forgotten the address. 'I said nothing,' declared Lily piously, discounting both the lowering effect her tight-lipped expression would have had on her intuitive son, and her carefully-disguised joy that he did mislay things, 'but like the parrot thought a good deal.'[15] One of the reasons Morgan continued to lose things throughout his life (a regular feature of his letters was to be the asking for book, umbrella, vest or watch to be posted back) was that in some subtle, undermining and brilliantly manipulative way Lily *made* him lose them.

Having spent six weeks sightseeing in Florence, the Forsters, after shivering for a while in Cortona, went on to Perugia. Here Morgan's imaginative vision was further extended since, as he wrote to Goldie, 'The pall of tragedy has been affixed to the unfortunate city, and the elderly ladies of the hotel make midnight excursions in the well lighted streets in search of blood and adventure, and come back breathing desolation & woe'; another instance of what was to become typically Forsterian bathos, inherited directly from Jane Austen, where the three words 'well lighted streets' provide the put-down for the ladies' adventure. 'The exalted level', went on Morgan, 'is sustained by an old lady who is understood to be waiting for an inspiration to write a book, and by an old lady who had really written one which was squashed by the landslip at Amalfi':[16] another example of Morgan, limited in some ways as his vision was, making every possible use of the tiniest incident. All in all it was to reappear five times in his work. Firstly in 'Ansell', written at some time during this year or next, the hero's box of books, his life's work and thus his previous identity, falls irrecoverably down a ravine; but it is a release and a freeing ('Them books saved us') and once they have gone 'Ansell has appropriated me, and I have no time to think of the future'.[17] Then, in 1904, falling books appeared in 'The Story of the Siren' and 'The Purple Envelope', and in 1908 in *A Room with a View* when Miss Lavish, who was partly modelled on a real novelist called Miss Spender whom the Forsters met at Perugia, is described as having lost a manuscript at Amalfi after 'the Grotto fell roaring onto the beach'.[18] Finally, in *Howards End*, Leonard Bast was to be killed by falling books.

The efficient use to which Morgan put this one overheard detail is evidence that at this time, the winter of 1901–2, he started seriously squirrelling: it was about now that he began to think of himself as a writer, with a writer's antennae and perceptions. Why now it is impossible to tell, but the most likely reason is the almost predictable effect that Italy had upon his suburban soul: it awoke his imagination, changed his attitudes and transmogrified his aesthetic vision. This happened slowly during the day's Baedeker-following, the evening's veal, salad and an apple, and the late evening's privacy of his own room where he could legitimately be away from Lily. He told Goldie:

I have done no writing – or hardly any – since I have been abroad . . . I'm very discontented with the novel. I've tried to invent realism, if you see what I mean: instead of copying incidents & characters that I have come across, I have tried to imagine others equally commonplace, being under the impression that this was art, and by mixing two methods have produced nothing. I think I shall have a try at imagination pure & simple: though the result will be as unsuccessful it will perhaps be more profitable. I think I have the photo-graphic gift of which you spoke: but till I'm sure I can do no better, I don't mean to use it unreservedly.[19]

In the event, Morgan mostly used imagination pure and simple for his short stories, and for his novels he used realism in the same system of mixing the two methods. And it was now,* in Miss Hayden's pension in Rome, to which he and Lily went for Christmas, that Morgan abandoned *Nottingham Lace*† and tentatively began another novel. It was the first, later abandoned draft of *A Room with a View*, later to be known by Forsterian scholars as 'Old Lucy' (but seemingly known by Morgan as 'The Concert').

'Old Lucy' is about the guests at the Pension Bertolini who decide to have a concert in aid of the English church. Lucy is the accompanist (*not* the soloist) and feels restless and frustrated, although she does not articulate this until she gets to know a young man called, variously, Arthur and Tancred, who asks her why she is 'doing things you don't care for to help people you don't like in objects that don't interest you'. Lucy thinks angrily:

---

* Some time between 18 December 1901, when he arrived in Rome, and 2 February 1902, when he broke his arm. By the end of March he had written about eight pages. We know this because the phrase 'her life would be where she ate and slept' (note 1 of this chapter) appears in a letter to Goldie written on 25 March – 'Our life is where we sleep and eat, and the glimpses of Italy that I get are only accidents.'[20]

† About forty pages had been written before he and Lily left England and another twenty in Italy.

'Why can't I do anything by myself – settle where I'll go, how I'll live! Shall I ever be free? I see now, never. It's only changing one bondage for another.'

She had hit the truth. The night had taught her that bondage was inevitable. There she stopped. The day was not here to reveal that there are degrees of bondage, and that we have the power not only to choose but to change our bonds. And the power to change bonds is not so very far off from what men call Freedom the unattainable.

In the morning Lucy decides to leave her chaperone, Miss Bartlett. Their parting is painful, quite apart from practical details such as who was to have the Rome Baedeker or how to divide a canvas trunk from the Army & Navy bought for their joint belongings. And after a scene set in Rome the fragment ends with Lucy uncertain what to do next.

One of the reasons Morgan was to abandon 'Old Lucy' was that it was far more obviously autobiographical than the eventual novel, and if Lily had ever read it even she would have recognised her son's anger both with her for curtailing his freedom and with himself for failing to escape. It is almost as a defiant fantasy that Morgan allows Lucy (a little implausibly) to travel to Rome on her own; but then, wearily realistic, shows that there is no life for her there either, since there is nothing for her to do.

Although in some ways elated that he was starting a new novel, Morgan was both cold and depressed in Rome ('depression & misgivings had Lucy in their grasp'[21]), bored by the way he had to 'see everything with this horrible foreground of enthusiastic ladies, but it is impossible to get away from it',[22] and all too aware that the spiritual awakening he had anticipated had not yet happened. 'Though I do love Italy,' he told Goldie, 'she has had no such awakening power on me as she has on you.'[23] Nor did he have any hopes of making friends in Italy, of meeting 'affinities'. As Philip Herriton thinks, in a deleted passage of *Where Angels Fear to Tread* that was to be written in four years' time:

O friends, dear friends of mine whom I have made in Italy! cabmen, waiters, sacristans, shop assistants, soldiers . . . we had been friends for years, I think, when we first met . . . You told me everything, and I told you more than I shall ever tell my true and tried acquaintance here. Then we parted with warm hand grasp, wondering why we had been kept apart so long. And thank goodness! oh thank goodness, I shall never see one of you again![24]

Then, a month after Christmas, Morgan first sprained his ankle and a few days later, perhaps as a result of his tottery steps, slipped on the steps of St Peter's and broke his right, his writing, arm. How Lily must have fussed and patronised, how the other ladies in the pension must have proffered advice, how demeaningly dependent he must have been on his mother for washing, dressing, the cutting up of food. Even worse, the double accident was extra ammunition which Lily used to speak out against the still dormant idea that Morgan should join the King's cruise in Greece during April. Reluctantly he agreed with her strictures, and it was decided that together they would see something of Greek culture by going to Sicily. At the end of March they left Rome, and, as the spring came, Morgan slightly cheered up. 'I am getting to like Italy,' he told Goldie. 'I was more horribly Northern than I thought and took some time to thaw. Besides, you are right: winter is not the time . . . Now it is delightful: and Naples is a most delightful place in which to be.'[25] And it was here, in the spring of 1902, that Morgan wrote, for the first time, a complete short story.

10

Ravello

'The English have harmed it less than any other Italian town of any size' was Morgan's conclusion about Naples. 'The Neapolitans are incurably dirty and idle and indecent, and there is something about them which tells that the East has not been far off.'[1] He was being disingenuous: he meant that Naples was the first Italian city he had been to that had no aura of Englishness, that had avoided being judged by the values of suburbia. Only by coming this far south could he find the 'real' Italy: like Philip Herriton he had already absorbed 'into one aesthetic whole olive-trees, blue sky, frescoes, country inns, saints, peasants, mosaics, statues, beggars';[2] now the sensuousness of the East was there, in the heat, noise, squalor, the almost intolerably exotic beauty, the drains and spices: for Morgan, Naples was a turning-point.

Lily was less happy. From Sicily, to which they crossed at the end of March, Morgan wrote to Dent that 'the noise of people expectorating in the street is wafted up and my mother wails. She cannot get used to the sunny South.'[3] He was delighted by the Greek temples at Girgenti, 'imbedded in masses of yellow and purple flowers',[4] and concluded that Taormina was 'the third most beautiful place in the world'.[5] It is unclear which came first and second, nor is it clear whether his rapture was connected with the von Gloeden photographs of nude young men for which the town was at that time notorious.[6] Judging from the sexual overtones of Morgan's one Sicilian story, it is possible that it was.

'Albergo Empedocle'* was later to be ignored by Morgan; although

---

* Empedocles was the most famous citizen of Agrigento (formerly Girgenti), and was known for his belief in reincarnation.

his first story to be published, eighteen months afterwards, he later disclaimed it as his first piece of fiction. This distinction he was to give, after forty-five years, to another story called 'The Story of a Panic'. But why was Morgan to claim that this was his first when 'Albergo Empedocle' had all the hallmarks of being the earliest he wrote? Perhaps it was simply because, as he was to admit, 'I can't myself manage chronology. The River of Time must be left to historians.'[7] Perhaps it was mere inaccuracy, like remembering Marianne's house as Number One instead of Number Three. But the likely explanation is that he *wanted* 'The Story of a Panic' to be first, just as he wanted to forget Ted Streatfeild or to have been unhappy at Tonbridge or to have owed everything to Marianne's money not Eddie's. It was not that he was one of those writers demanding a biography called 'A Hidden Life' or 'The Truth behind the Mask'; but he manipulated the truth if it suited him to do so.

'Albergo Empedocle', about a young man called Harold accompanying his fiancée's family to Sicily, who awakes from a sleep thinking he had lived before as an Ancient Greek, would later displease Morgan for two reasons. One was its sexual overtones: Tommy the narrator declares that his friend Harold is 'the man I love most in the world' and yet finds him, brought back from Sicily, fossilised into insane oblivion. Harold had had a brief, glorious vision of what his life might have been in Ancient Greece; when he realises he is condemned to Edwardian England he prefers catatonia. After the story had been published, at Christmas 1903, Morgan saw that it was a not-much disguised plea for the values, and particularly the sexual values, of Ancient Greece. He was beginning to realise that he had been born out of time; and what if Lily had understood the full implications of Tommy and Harold, a pair of names with such similar resonance to David and Jonathan?

The other reason Morgan rejected his story was that it was not very good. The elements were there, but not enough of them.

Sir Edwin and Lady Peaslake were sitting in the temple of Juno Lacinia and leaning back on a Doric column – which is a form of architecture neither comfortable as a cushion nor adequate as a parasol. They were as cross as it was possible for good-tempered people to be. Their lunch at the dirty hotel had disagreed with them, and the wine that was included with it had made them heavy.

This is perfectly Forsterian, in the Englishness of the perceptions and the irony, but the one is a little obvious and the other not sharp enough: there is something schoolboyish about the column being neither a good cushion nor a good parasol, and the tone of 'their lunch at the dirty hotel had disagreed with them' is petulant. The most successful phrase is 'the wine that was included',[8] which subtly touches on the crucial question of money. 'We are very comfortable', Lily had written to her mother from Florence, 'and pay 15 francs (£24) a day for both, wine (of the country) included. Candles the only extra.'[9] And when Lucy and Miss Bartlett decide to leave Florence and go to Rome they discuss the difficulty of having already paid for a whole week's pension. In Rome, '"Isn't afternoon tea given there for nothing?"' asks Miss Bartlett and Lucy replies, exhausted, '"Yes, but they pay extra for wine."'[10] Morgan knew that English tourists always drink wine that is 'included' but then feel sleepy; and that Italians are less miserly and have a siesta if they want.

This they would do because they are 'dirty and idle and indecent',[11] the three qualities that Tunbridge Wells was forever holding at bay and that at first Harold too reviled: 'What with the smells and the beggars and the mosquitoes we're rather off Naples altogether,' he writes to Tommy.* In Sicily Harold is mysteriously sleepy, even though his fiancée 'endeavoured to recall him to higher pleasures by reading out of her "Baedeker"'. He goes to sleep on a bed of flowers beside a ruined temple 'and the lines faded out of his face as he grasped the greatest gift that the animal life can offer'. Upon awakening he tells Mildred that he had been there before and loved there before. '"Yes, I loved better too," he continued, watching the little drops of blood swell out' from a scratch made by thorns. (It was the first time of the many times in the future that Morgan was to use spurting blood as an image of orgasm: on almost every occasion that two characters, of whatever sex, feel a sexual frisson, blood is shed.) But the new Harold cannot, alas, escape the society in which he was born and it is in an asylum back in England that he begins 'living the life he knew to be greater than the life he lived with us'.[12]

The story was, for Morgan, too transparent a statement of the theme that we are all prisoners of society, and particularly sexual prisoners. So 'Albergo Empedocle', although submitted – and rejected – for

---

* This narrative device shows, like much else about the story, the influence of Edith Wharton, whose second volume of short stories *Crucial Instances* had appeared the previous year. *Howards End* was to show the influence of Wharton's *The Fruit of the Tree* (1907).

inclusion in his first story collection in 1911, was then quietly
forgotten. Forty years later he had convinced himself that he had
never wanted it reprinted at all: and that 'The Story of a Panic' was
his first story.

He and Lily had returned to southern Italy from Sicily, where they
stayed at the Hotel-Pension Palumbo at Ravello 'with a splendid
view'[13] (wrote Morgan somewhat understatedly, for the views are
uniquely beautiful). 'I think it was in the May of 1902 that I took a
walk near Ravello. I sat down in a valley, a few miles above the town,
and suddenly the first chapter of the story rushed into my mind as if
it had waited for me there. I received it as an entity and wrote it out as
soon as I returned to the hotel.'[14] It was the ease that was memorable
for him: perhaps the slow, tentative work on *Nottingham Lace* and
'Old Lucy' would be a thing of the past and now, at last, his writing
and his life would flow. And, as well, he seems to have found his
theme: in all essentials he would never need to search for another.

The idea that came into Morgan's mind was that he 'would bring
some middle-class Britishers to picnic in this remote spot. I would
expose their vulgarity. I would cause them to be terribly frightened
they knew not why and I would make it clear by subsequent events
that they had encountered and offended the Great God Pan.'[15] Here
were all the elements of the future *oeuvre*: the English middle classes
exposed to something other (a foreign country, an expedition away
from their normal territory), who are mocked for their insularity and
obtuseness, who then encounter something so disconcerting that they
are forced to realise, even if subconsciously, that they have confronted
something vaster than themselves; at the end they are either saved
– or not.

Among other elements were the direct, conversational tone, established from the opening sentence: 'Eustace's* career – if career it can
be called – certainly dates from that afternoon in the chestnut woods
above Ravello'; the sardonic but subtly castigating portrait of English
tourists out for a picnic; the layered overtones in the narrative voice
('I always make a point of behaving pleasantly to Italians, however
little they may deserve it'). The most important element was the
story's passionate plea for physical and spiritual freedom, disguised
as fantasy so that Lily and co. would not see it. Eustace's afternoon

---

* Eustace = Lat. *ustus* = inflamed, also Gk. 'fruitful'. St Eustace was a patron saint of
huntsmen.

in the woods ('racing about, like a real boy') makes him long to be free of the stifling conventions that have surrounded him all his life. He manages it, although at the expense of his newly-beloved friend, the waiter Gennaro.*

Lily, whose knowledge of classical literature was limited, as was her reading of the 1890s poetry and fiction in which Pan was a favourite literary symbol, would not have realised that Morgan's first story was virtually an encomium to Pan. This half-man, half-goat figure of classical mythology is a primitive mountain daemon, god of shepherds and flocks, sender of bad dreams, who runs swiftly through the countryside, exudes uninhibited sexual energy and can lead us, if we are receptive, into mystical experiences imbued with ecstasy and fear. If we are not receptive, as is usually the case with 'civilised' human beings, we must die, either spiritually or in fact; only of Eustace are we told that 'far down the valley towards the sea, there still resounded the shouts and the laughter of the escaping boy.'

Eustace had been found by his aunts 'lying motionless on his back' with his hands 'convulsively entwined in the long grass' and 'seemed so natural and undisturbed' as he smiled up at them; there is no blood but, instead, he rolls in a goat's footmarks 'as a dog rolls in dirt'. He also walks 'with difficulty, almost with pain'[16] on the way home, as if deflowered. To most readers, certainly to modern readers, to any readers except Morgan and Lily, he seems to be in a state of post-orgasmic lassitude. But Morgan fiercely denied any such imputations and, he claimed, for years refused to countenance even thinking about them. When he did accept that the pleasuring of Eustace had been his unconscious impulse, he admitted it to close friends but not, of course, to the world at large.

Morgan was to speak about his change of attitude very amusingly in a 1920s paper he read to the Memoir Club, a group with whom he felt completely at home. He described an acquaintance named Charles Sayle discussing his story with Maynard Keynes:

'Oh dear,' he says ... 'Oh dear, oh dear, is this Young King's?' Then he showed Maynard what the Story was about. B—— by a waiter at the Hotel, Eustace commits bestiality with a goat on that valley where I had sat. In the subsequent chapters, he tells the waiter how nice it has been and they try to b—— each other again. While alive to the power of my writing, to its colour, its beauty, its Hellenic grace, Charles Sayle could not believe his

---

* Gennaio = January, the beginning of things. Also Gene, the dim. of Eugene = Gk. 'noble, well-born' (in this case physically downtrodden but spiritually noble).

eyes. He was horrified, he longed to meet me. Of course Maynard flew chirrupping with the news. It seemed to him great fun, to me disgusting. I was horrified and did not want to meet Charles Sayle. In after years I realized that in a stupid and unprofitable way he was right and that this was the cause of my indignation. I knew, as their creator, that Eustace and the footmarks and the waiter had none of the conjunctions he visualized, I had no thought of sex for them, no thought of sex was in my mind. All the same I had been excited as I wrote and the passages where Sayle thought something was up had excited me most.[17]

Here was another reason why Ravello had been so memorable but the writing of 'Albergo Empedocle' in Sicily so unmemorable: he was excited, not, as he was later to claim, just by the act of creation but by erotic identification. It was a sexual watershed.

Southern Italy, and especially the whiff of the East, had revealed to Morgan the potential of sensuality. There were the images, the colours, the flesh bared to the sun; there were statues; there were the photographs at Taormina; there was even a whole new way of looking at life for a boy reared respectably in the provincial towns of England. Morgan had anticipated that Italy would change his vision. It was, after all, something of a triumph that Lily had agreed to go there instead of to the more salubrious and more sober Germany or Holland; for Italy had been renowned, since the Renaissance, as the country where sexual pleasure was not confined to the conventional.

To take one small example, there was a novel called *The Lost Stradivarius* by John Meade Falkner that had come out seven years before and that Morgan was almost certain to have read. An allegory disguised as a ghost story, it describes John Maltravers abandoning his ordered, married existence to travel to Naples. When his sister eventually goes to search him out she is amazed by the 'mirth and careless hilarity' of the people in the packed streets and cannot 'conceive of any truly religious person countenancing such a gathering, which seemed to me rather like the unclean orgies of a heathen deity than an act of faith of Christian people'. At her brother's villa he is sitting 'on a low couch or sofa, propped up against a heap of pillows, with a rug of brilliant colours flung across his feet and legs'; there is a boy seated on a low stool who is singing to him. A *low* chair is always suspicious: Maltravers has been tempted by sensual pleasure of a quite unconventional, quite unmarried kind and that is why he is now 'wasted'[18] and close to death.

Morgan, in his early stories, saved his characters from mere death and found them some other form of allegorical escape; for himself the only way out was abstinence. But despite Morgan's rather pallid, self-effacing appearance, his sexual energy was, he would claim, not insignificant. He would say in old age that 'lust was always lurking inside my head': even as a young man sexual thoughts dominated his mind and although he hoped that as he grew older 'this fever would lessen, even leave me', it did not. 'I was fifty, and then I was sixty, and nothing changed: sexual images continued to spin around my brain like figures on a carousel.'[19]

Yet the torment from which Morgan longed to be released all his life was not just physical longing ('if I could get one solid night it would be some thing'[20] he was to write so poignantly when he was nearing forty and still had not found sexual happiness); what he longed to put an end to was the 'constant search for the perfect love object'.[21] Union, harmony, marriage with the love object was what he so desperately sought: true fulfilment was for him inseparable from spiritual oneness with a beloved. Despite his famous assertion in the future, when referring to a perceived over-emphasis on romance in fiction, that love should in general only take two hours out of the twenty-four – 'surely that is a handsome allowance'[22] – Morgan, privately, would have greatly changed the proportion.

None of these ideas was, in this period of Morgan's life, as yet articulated. It was Italy that began the slow process of his understanding of his sexual nature and it was his novels that completed it; without Italy, and without southern Italy in particular, he would have taken far longer to know himself and he would have been far less precocious a writer. Lust had, up till now, been an important but generally wretched part of his life, associated with being 'dirty', with the half-understood overtones of the back streets of Piccadilly and of Naples. Love, on the other hand, was something that he had spent a lot of his time at Cambridge debating and defining. But how, he was continually asking himself as he sat over luncheon with Lily, would the two ever be reconciled? For 'normal' people they quite mysteriously were; but what would happen to him?

It is difficult, in the years when Morgan did not keep a diary (he was to begin another in 1903) to be sure what he visualised for his emotional and sexual future. He would have liked to have children, to found a dynasty, and would still have yearned for a Rooksnest of his own, a house where sons and daughters played on the lawn, where the kitchen smelt of coffee, oranges and wax polish, where two people created a 'magic in identity of position; it is one of the things that have suggested to us eternal comradeship'.[23] As time passed Morgan was beginning to realise that the Battersea Rise idyll would never, ever be his, since it was, *au fond*, based upon sexual attraction between man and woman.

But Morgan was frightened of women. Those that he met fell into a few, equally terrifying categories: they were either pretty and quintessentially sexual, although he did not meet many of these; or they were like the brash, assertive Girton girls that he and Lily met in hotels; or they were married, they had crossed the sexual divide. The misogyny in which he indulged with his friends, and especially with Dent with whom it was a shared joke, the good-humoured and almost meaningless misogyny was slowly becoming reality. Morgan was never to hate women, or even to wish them ill, and later on some of his closest friends would be female; but the pattern was being set at this time of a man whose first, instantaneous reaction to women was always negative. It was not so much the individual woman, as her symbolic status as curtailer of freedom.

An example of this had presented itself to Morgan at the hotel* in Ravello, where they had also found (or they had gone especially to visit) G. M. Trevelyan's brother Robert, always known as Bob or Trevy. This rumpled, eccentric poet (he had published two volumes of poetry) was older than Morgan but had got to know him in Cambridge, perhaps when he returned for Apostles meetings. Ottoline Morrell, who had been at Ravello the month before, wrote about him then:

He also had not been long married, but marriage and its obligations and ties did not trouble this Pan-like creature. He would spend whole days out on the crags and cliffs alone, writing poetry ... At night we would call him and he would come on to the terrace probably half undressed, and walk up and down, declaiming about Shelley's poetry, on and on, in a loud and half-controlled voice, hesitating yet explicit, very interesting and very full of charm.[24]

Trevy was the first of Morgan's friends, certainly the first person

---

* Two years later there were peculiar happenings at this hotel involving the marriage of the hotel proprietor's daughter to a waiter, a landslip and falling books. The Trevelyans wondered if Morgan, in his stories, was psychic.

with whom he identified, to be married; and he watched him, eternally trapped, never free except for the 'whole days out on the crags and cliffs alone', voluntarily in the kind of situation in which he, Morgan, had involuntarily placed himself with Lily. He imagined Eustace, another 'Pan-like creature' who did not only talk in a loud voice but who managed to escape over the parapet: he 'uttered a strange loud cry, such as I should not have thought the human voice could have produced, and disappeared among the trees below'.[25]

Trevy's wife Bessie, with whom Morgan was much later on to be close friends (it would take eighteen years for him to write 'Dear Bessie – for so I must really call you'[26]), poor Bessie must in part have given Morgan the idea for the appalling Agnes in *The Longest Journey*. Seeing Trevy at Ravello, Morgan could not imagine that his married, procreative future would be anything but restrictive. And perhaps he visualised a novel that began with an idyllic scene in his old rooms in King's (even now, in the May of 1902, some lucky person was sitting on the window seat looking out at King's Bridge) brutally brought to a halt by the intrusion of a tall young woman. '"Wicked, intolerable boy!" She turned on the electric light. The philosophers were revealed with unpleasing suddenness. "My goodness, a tea-party! Oh really, Rickie, you are too bad!"'[27]

To what extent, at this period of his life when he was still in his early twenties, was Morgan aware that he would not marry? My feeling is that as yet he hardly realised it. In the years since Morgan's homosexuality has been revealed there has been a flurry to re-read and re-interpret his novels as though each one was a disguised plea for homosexual freedom. They were, to some extent, but much was unconscious and took the form of a generalised plea for personal autonomy: at this stage Morgan longed for the courage to throw off Tunbridge Wells as much as he longed for the courage to love whom he wanted.

The realisation that he would never marry would come gradually, after years of feeling shy and awkward, of remarking to himself 'I do not resemble other people' (13 December 1907)[28] and, in the years 1907–12, being unrequitedly in love with a man. There is an unforgettable scene in *Maurice* when a family friend named Gladys Olcott responds to Maurice's smile. Everyone is pleased and he is determined to go further.

Something went wrong at once. Maurice paid her compliments, said that her hair etc. was ripping. She tried to stop him, but he was insensitive, and did not know that he had annoyed her . . . having taken her to some scenery that he considered romantic he pressed her little hand between his own.

. . . she knew something was wrong. His touch revolted her. It was a corpse's . . . She arrived home before him with a sensible little story about a headache and dust in her eyes, but his family also knew that something had gone wrong.[29]

This scene has too personal a quality to be made up: it is like those occasions when one wakes sweating in the night because of something one has said. I think it happened to Morgan himself and was an experience of such deep, humiliating embarrassment that he never tried to repeat it.

Gladys, significantly, pleaded dust in her eyes. The women in *Where Angels Fear to Tread* would do the same, in fact dust is always a symbol of sexual unhappiness, either because women are forever washing it out or because they get covered in it as Lilia, on her last walk, was to be by 'choking clouds of moonlit dust . . . There is something very terrible in dust at night-time',[30] and as Adela Quested was to be when she hurtled down the hillside. Lily travelled round Italy complaining about dust in her clothes; then Morgan, with the dexterity of the great artist, turned her trivial moans into a statement of belief: without domestic abandon there can be no sensuality, without tolerance of dust there can be no ecstasy.

When Morgan declared, aged fifty-three, that if he had stayed at Rooksnest he would have married, he did not say this flippantly as meaning he would have been happy, he would have been 'normal'; he also meant that by staying in rural, dusty, sensually rich surroundings he would not have acquired his fear of women's sexuality. One of the aspects of his education of which Lily deprived her son when she took him away from the countryside was every country child's inheritance: familiarity with nature, with the seasons, with birth, with death. This would have been his within virtually months, for Lily took him away at exactly the moment when independence was his, when he could have walked alone with no maid and no tutor, among the animals and the fields. The departure from Rooksnest made Morgan fall back on the cerebral: that is why he castigated himself for being 'insensitive' to Gladys Olcott. His was an intellectual, self-conscious response, not the instinctive one that he might have learnt from nature.

Something else that Rooksnest would have done would have been to educate him sexually. He would not have been able to write that as a schoolboy he thought committing adultery meant a man warming a woman. 'Never connected warming operation with my sexual premonitions. This chance guess, that came so near the truth, never developed and *not till I was 30* did I know exactly how male and female joined.' But by seeing pregnant cows and copulating animals, he would have acquired both knowledge and familiarity about matters sexual. On the other hand, can a great artist be creative without some element in his make-up of naïvety, of innocence? If, for example, Morgan had had more self-knowledge in 1905 about the pleasure he took in seeing 'two most beautiful things: bathers running naked under sun pierced foliage, and a most enormous beech, standing in the village like a god'[31] he might not have wanted to re-invoke this in the bathing scene of *A Room with a View*.

The sensuality of country life would, too, have helped to nullify the clear-cut distinction, so crucial to Morgan's future, between heterosexuality and homosexuality; he would have been more likely to be bisexual. As a contemporary of Morgan's was to write about the second decade of the century, the term 'homosexual' was 'not in general use, as it is now. Then it was still a technical term, the implications of which I was not entirely aware of.' And Morgan's future friend Joe Ackerley was to remember his own surprise when, at the time of the First World War, he was asked, '"Are you homo or hetero?" I had never heard either term before.'[32] When Maurice's classics don says 'in a flat toneless voice' during a translation class, '"Omit: a reference to the unspeakable vice of the Greeks"',[33] he did not mean by vice what is nowadays deemed homosexuality. He meant any kind of sexuality not purely procreative; it was known as inversion. Maurice, and Morgan, were beginning to suspect they were inverts and they already understood that their distance from the uncensorious sexual attitudes of the Ancient Greeks rendered them born out of time. But they would not yet have known what it was to be exclusively homosexual.

It would be some time before any but the most enlightened would endorse Dame Katharine Furse's* view, expressed in 1940, that 'much has been discovered in the last half-century concerning the biological and psychological make-up of the individual, and it has become increasingly clear that clean-cut divisions of individuals into classes,

---

* She was the daughter of the homosexual writer J. A. Symonds.

such as healthy and unhealthy, moral and immoral, homosexual and heterosexual are quite impossible.'[34] Impossible, maybe; but since 1892, when the word 'homosexuality' was for the first time used in English in a translation of Krafft-Ebing's book about sexual deviance, the division had been clean-cut indeed. It is becoming increasingly hard to imagine, and the greatest possible imaginative leap is necessary: but as important as shyness, as lack of privacy (sex, as much as creativity, needs 'a room of one's own'), was fear.

The seventy years after the infamous Labouchère Amendment of 1885 were, for vast numbers of men in Britain, both sexually repressive and frightening because of the following clause:

Any male person who, in public or private, commits, or is a party to the commission of, or procures or attempts to procure the commission by any male person of any act of gross indecency with another male person, shall be guilty of a misdemeanour, and being convicted thereof shall be liable at the discretion of the court to be imprisoned for any term not exceeding two years, with or without hard labour.[35]

Although the death penalty for buggery had been abolished in 1861, it had been replaced by a term of penal servitude and thus it remained until 1967: when Morgan was eighty-eight. No wonder Eddie and Ted had travelled abroad; no wonder Morgan began to look slantingly at photographers. What can it have been like to be sixteen, an acutely vulnerable age, in the year Oscar Wilde was pilloried according to the precepts of the crucial clause of the 1885 Act: when any act of 'indecency' constituted a crime?

So *was* it coincidence merely that Morgan and Lily took their only holiday abroad during the twenty-two years 1879–1901 in the infamous month of April 1895? Or had Lily, by her spiriting away of her son, by her refusal ever to mention an aspect of the human condition of which she was all too aware, had she helped to determine his sexual future by once again keeping silent? Yet even without her insistence that Morgan should 'try and forget about it' (as she wrote after the incident on the Downs when he was twelve), she decided his future in two ways: most notoriously, she was over-possessive. The word 'notorious' is appropriate here because the modern concept of homosexuality largely derives from Freud's attributing it to

the fact that the future inverts, in the earliest years of their childhood, pass through a phase of very intense but short-lived fixation to a woman (usually their mother), and that, after leaving this behind, they identify themselves with a woman and take themselves as their sexual object. That is to say, they proceed from a narcissistic basis, and look for a young man who resembles themselves and whom they may love as their mother loved them.[36]

But poor Lily: wrong she may have been in her dependence and her demandingness and cause she may have been of Morgan's dislike of so many aspects of womanhood; that she or other mothers like her are the entire cause of their sons' sexual orientation seems deeply unlikely. There are a vast number of instances of smothered sons who are happy to live with women and there are far more plausible explanations for men or women preferring their own sex such as genetic disposition, upbringing, or the eclectic sexuality that is so often part of the creative temperament.

Yet in one other respect Lily did determine Morgan's sexual future: she agreed to go to Italy in 1901. She thought, of course, that their trip was in the tradition of the Grand Tour; what she did not fully realise was that writers like Goethe, Matthew Arnold and Samuel Butler had made Italy a symbol of escape: here the traveller could encounter the sensuality repressed by centuries of Protestantism. But to Lily, Italy was respectable enough, in fact not so different from the Paris pleasantly described in du Maurier's best-selling novel *Trilby* (1894). Her attitude was the one defined by the Old Tonbridgian writer Rupert Croft-Cooke: 'Bohemianism was healthy enough but it had to be of the right kind, that was the du Maurier/Trilby variety, wide-brimmed black hats, huge pipes, beefy appetites for food and chorus girls, but nothing aesthetic or precious.'[37]

Lily liked things to be straightforward, to be nice: her worst term of abuse would have been 'decadent'. Italy, although not entirely straightforward, was, after all, in some ways like England. "'It might be London,'" says Lucy Honeychurch about the Florence pension, surveying 'the two rows of English people who were sitting at the table . . . the portraits of the late Queen and the late Poet Laureate that hung behind the English people, heavily framed.'[38] This is what Lily liked about it: the English visitors, the way the more exotic aspects of Italy could be made manageable through the auspices of Ruskin or Baedeker, the way romance was overlaid with a cloak of realism ('A dentist! A dentist at Monteriano. A dentist in fairyland!' thinks Philip when told what Gino's father does[39]); all this made Italy perfectly healthy.

In truth, Italy represented something quite different to those who cared to look: it represented sexual pleasure of a less than licit kind. Morgan did care to look, and although unable to see very much, he sensed an undercurrent, an easy acceptance, a sensual variety that did not occur in Surrey. Nevertheless, what he sensed was so repressed both by Lily and by the atmosphere of the pension that a great deal had to be gleaned from writers like J. A. Symonds: his work echoes throughout *A Room with a View*, and the irony is that his overriding theme was the glorification of homosexual relations. When Morgan paid tribute to him, for example Mr Emerson asks whether anything could 'be more majestic, more pathetic, beautiful, true' than the Santa Croce Giotto, in deliberate homage to Symonds's statement in *The Renaissance in Italy* that 'no painter is more unaffectedly pathetic, more unconsciously majestic',[40] when Morgan did this he was *also* evoking the imagery of homosexual love.

Similarly, when he used blue as a symbol of sexual passion and freedom ('the Ridge had taken a tint of exquisite blue in the afternoon light',[41] Lucy falls into a field of blue flowers) he was drawing on Symonds's *In the Key of Blue*. This was about the poet's passion for a Venetian boy, in the guise of poems written partly on the theme of blue and partly on the theme of his beauty. Morgan even drew on Symonds for the overall focus of his early stories and novels: 'Symonds's description of how, in "May in Umbria", "it is sometimes the traveller's good fortune in some remote place to meet with an inhabitant who incarnates and interprets for him the *genius loci* as he has conceived it" might be a gloss on Forster's early fiction', John Colmer (one of the best Forster critics) has observed.[42] Morgan was so used to hiding himself from Lily that when he began to write it came quite naturally to him to disguise his references through *double entendre*.

Part of Morgan's nature, dutiful and deferential as it appeared, did not want to hurt his mother's susceptibilities which, as regards sensual pleasures, were so pained and negative. Nevertheless, by taking him to Italy, Lily herself had allowed his perceptions to be freed. It was she who had helped to remove him from the constraints of suburbia.

11

To Greece

After nearly nine months even Morgan began to tire of the rigorous round of sightseeing; like the Peaslakes he and Lily had possibly 'done Palermo in even less time than Baedeker had allowed for it, and such audacity must tell on the most robust of tourists'.[1] He enjoyed being in the places that had been the background to his years of Latin and Greek, but told Dent that he had now become 'a little weary of sights & views'.[2] It was at this time, as summer arrived in southern Italy, that he withdrew from Baedeker's vision and began to find his own, his writer's voice. '"Tut, tut! Miss Lucy!"' says Miss Lavish. '"I hope we shall soon emancipate you from Baedeker. He does but touch the surface of things. As to the true Italy – he does not even dream of it. The true Italy is only to be found by patient observation."'[3] By losing her Baedeker, by accepting its loss, Lucy will be free to join the Emersons; Morgan to join his true self.

During the weeks of travel and of pension life he had changed in a few, subtle ways. He had perceived sensuality, and although remaining an observer not participator in Italy's pleasures yet he was awakened to their potential; he had become a little firmer with Lily – evidence of this is his taking notes at about this time on Thomas Hodgkin's *Italy and her Invaders 376–814 AD* (1880–99), a work in *eight* large volumes, the thorough reading of which must have necessitated many evenings peacefully on his own, away from the chattering ladies and the kind of conversations satirised at the beginning of *A Room with a View*; and finally he had discovered that his overriding interest was in human beings and in the workings of the human heart and brain, an interest which he defined as mere psychology but which transcended this. It was from Sicily that he wrote a letter to G. M. Trevelyan which its recipient, alas, threw away but which apparently declared a growing fascination with 'intricate psychology'. Trevelyan replied, in a letter that Morgan was always to keep:

Your intricate psychology will (insensibly, indefinably) become interesting and healthy (not necessarily passionate) if you yourself have *lived*. There are so many sides of *life*, of which however Pension Life is not one ... I believe in your powers, I applaud your zeal for psychology and your desire to do it, but I believe some study or some employment (whether in the ordinary course of your literary work or outside it) will be of great value to you, and will eventually lead you to do psychology in the right way eg. reviewing, or business, or a study of a historical period with a view to a novel, or teaching.[4]

As summer came, Morgan realised that 'the creative element had been freed'. This, his faint weariness with sightseeing, and G. M. Trevelyan's letter with its sensible suggestions as to his future, all combined to make Morgan want to go home. So in June he and Lily turned north, the plan being that they should be back in England by the autumn. They were, however, as industrious as ever, and went to Rome, Siena, San Gimignano, Volterra, Pisa, Lucca, Florence and Verona. They did not go to Venice because of the heat and it was to be another few years before Morgan visited the subject of Ruskin's famous book.

It was 'at Siena or that sort of place' that Morgan found the 'photo-graphic' impetus for what would eventually be his first published novel.

I overheard an English lady talking to another English lady about a third English lady who had married an Italian far beneath her socially and also much younger, and how most unfortunate it was. This sorry bit of twaddle stuck in my mind. I worked at it until it became alive and grew into a novel of contrasts. On the one hand was the English suburbs with the grey inhibited life that I knew only too well, and on the other hand was Monteriano, a romantic hill town which I established in Tuscany on the basis of San Gimignano.[5]

Although Morgan only went for the day to the little hill town (unlike Siena it lacked a pension suitably 'frequented by English travellers') it became, for him, the apotheosis of Italy in its decontamination from middle-class England and in its historical uniqueness; as Baedeker observed, 'perhaps no other town in Tuscany presents so faithful a picture of Dante's time'.[6] Morgan was to reflect his deep sense of connection with San Gimignano's pastness when he wrote *Where Angels Fear to Tread*: Philip, and Caroline Abbott, do not just see present-day Monteriano when they gaze out of their hotel window but also its historical backcloth, for even the back bedroom windows 'are menaced by the tower of the Aldobrandeschi, and before now arrows have stuck quivering over the washstand'.

The reader of *Where Angels Fear to Tread* imagines that San Gimignano is described; the truth is that, as always with Morgan's writing, there is little actual, physical detail. Thus, in the following sentence, more is evoked about Philip than about the town: 'Philip could never read "The view from the Rocca (small gratuity) is finest at sunset" without a catching at the heart'. Similarly, we understand a good deal about the way Lilia and Gino live, even if little about the actual look of their home, from the words 'in half a minute they had scrambled down the mule-track and reached the only practicable entrance'.[7] The effect of landscape on character was what was to matter to Morgan, not the abstract aesthetics of it: form, content, colour, geography of a place would always be less important to him than the feelings of those who lived in it.

So what was his overall aesthetic judgement of Italy after his nine months there? In essence, rather like Lucy Honeychurch's. Morgan may have had the resonance of his classical education to inform his perceptions, but in other respects he meant Lucy to express his own attitudes. This is especially so in the crucial scene in Santa Croce when Lucy first senses her Baedeker-induced values being called into question. '"Of course, it must be a wonderful building"', she thinks ('must' because Ruskin says so, and she has been told so), and then, her real self peeping through, '"but how like a barn! And how very cold!"' Then a few moments later, 'the pernicious charm of Italy worked on her, and, instead of acquiring information, she began to be happy.' When a baby stumbles against 'one of the sepulchral slabs so much admired by Mr Ruskin' she hears Mr Emerson asking irreverently, almost atheistically, '"But what else can you expect from a church?"' Finally she declares, in a spiritual transformation of which she is not yet aware and which will not be complete until the end of the book, '"I like Giotto . . . It is so wonderful what they say about his tactile values. Though I like things like the Della Robbia babies better."'

Anyone who rejects tactile values (that art-historical phrase that is like a password for the initiated) and who prefers chubby *bambini* is close to discovering the real Italy. It is the same discovery that Philip and Caroline were about to make in *Where Angels Fear to Tread*: albeit in a different manner. But for Morgan revelation was more difficult. He carried both the baggage of suburbia and the abstractions of his over-education. And his own inhibitions precluded his throwing them away. Ruefully he felt that he might always be like Cecil,* unable to succumb to Italy's delights, trapped by his deeply imbedded intellectual perceptions. If he had thought about Lucy it would, alas, have been with some of Cecil's detached art-historical appraisal:

Italy worked some marvel in her. It gave her light, and – which he held more precious – it gave her shadow. Soon he detected in her a wonderful reticence. She was like a woman of Leonardo da Vinci's, whom we love not so much for herself as for the things that she will not tell us. The things are assuredly not of this life; no woman of Leonardo's could have anything so vulgar as a 'story'. She did develop most wonderfully day by day.[8]

Yet Morgan knew, as the Emersons knew but Cecil did not, that what matters is to be 'of this life'; that just as babies are better than values, so George's impetuous hug would be a better thing than Cecil's considered embrace. At the same time, ostentation was not admirable: when Ansell admires some statues in the British Museum as being 'monuments of our more reticent beliefs'[9] it was the highest compliment he could pay. These two qualities, directness and discreetness, were to inform Morgan's prose; and would make him forever antagonistic to theoreticians, those who value abstract statements ('tactile values') above the actual, chubby baby.

Slowly, during the second half of 1902, his tone was beginning to emerge; or perhaps one should say rapidly, since few people have found their voice by the time they are twenty-five. It felt slow to Morgan: but then he felt quite ordinarily impatient, ordinarily lackadaisical, ordinarily melancholic. 'Travelling does not conduce to work,' he told Goldie, adding, 'I have written a few sentimental articles on Italy, and have got a plan for a new novel, which may be a little more practicable than the last.'[10] Now his arm had healed, and now the watershed of the two stories had been passed, Morgan had begun to write again, to jot down a few pages of 'Old Lucy'

---

* His name originates from *caecus*, the Latin word for blind.

and to rough out some essays on Italian themes. One was prompted by a visit to the Museo Kircheriano in Rome and by a beautiful toilet case dating from the third century BC. 'Macolnia Shops' scoffs at the historian's reverence for the antique and evokes the owner of the case rather than the artefact itself: '"Praise of Water! Praise of Friendship! . . . I bought the thing because it was pretty, and stood nicely on the chest of drawers."'[11] Morgan managed an extraordinary medley of styles: historical, comic, guidebook and simply evocative.*

In the same bound notebook as he wrote the essays and began 'Old Lucy', Morgan wrote down the name Antinous and then (as if he envisaged a story, novel or play with three scenes or sections) Rome, The Summit of Etna and Egypt. The handsome Antinous was, according to Nettleship and Sandys' dictionary of classical antiquities that had been a standard reference book for Morgan at Cambridge, 'a favourite and travelling companion of the Emperor Hadrian'. He drowned himself in the Nile near Alexandria in AD 130 'probably from melancholy' and was thereafter honoured in various ways. 'Among the features common to the many surviving portraitures of Antinous,' wrote Nettleship and Sandys, 'are the full locks falling low down the forehead, the large melancholy eyes, the full mouth, and the broad, swelling breast.'[†13]

Nothing came of Morgan's noting down of the name, but the three loves of his life – an Indian, an Egyptian and an Englishman – would all resemble the fabled youth. For the moment, lover-less, Morgan could only do what so many people have done before and since: gaze at the statues of Antinous, those in Rome at the Vatican and the Villa Albani and, when he finally got to Delphi a year later, the one there. 'It is one of the ironies that beset the sympathetic person that they never find exactly the right people to live with,' thinks 'Old

---

* The present-day journalist, Bernard Levin, once wrote rapturously about 'Macolnia Shops' that 'although I have forgotten almost all of the Roman history I ever knew, I know that Macolnia and her daughter were real people, and that their equivalent exist today, in no way altered, and buy similar toilet-cases in Harrods'; he also wrote about 'why I like to read "Macolnia Shops" late at night to girls whom I have invited up to see my etchings. (Some of them fall asleep in the middle of it – an irony which Forster would have enjoyed almost as much as I do. More, actually.)'[12]

Macolnia comes to life as one of the small terracotta figures in the Graeco-Roman Museum at Alexandria: Case L in Room 18A. 'They are the loveliest things in the Museum,' Morgan was to write in his guide to Alexandria.

† That Antinous was a universally accepted image of beautiful manhood is clear from the words of a clergyman quoted by J. A. Symonds in 1893: 'I have an inborn admiration for beauty, of form and figure . . . in most football teams I can find one Antinous.'[14]

Lucy' in Rome, adding, in words which are clearly her creator's: 'They only meet their affinities in the street or on a steamer or at a railway junction';[15] or, one might add, marbled in a museum.

As the Forsters moved northwards, Morgan worked steadily on 'Old Lucy'; he was using loose sheets of paper, had not yet decided on a plot and the fragments are sketches of pension life rather than scenes in a novel. He was still very much the novelist searching for a novel, hoping there might be the same flash of illumination there had been at Ravello. In Austria, where they arrived in July, there was one small one. At Cortina there was a fund-raising concert that was such a success 'there is every hope that the place will soon be ruined with an English church'.[16] A concert, in aid of the church decoration fund, became the central event of the first part of 'Old Lucy' and leads to all sorts of activities.

In August, Morgan had five days with Dent at Innsbruck while Lily stayed in Cortina. Their friendship, which was mostly conducted by letter, was based on convenience rather than real empathy; but, for the moment, each needed the other and their time together was pleasant enough. September was spent by the Forsters in Munich, Nuremberg, Heidelberg and Cologne and by the first week of October they were in Belgium. In Brussels they saw something of George Barger, a King's contemporary of Morgan's who was assistant there to the Professor of Botany. 'Mrs Forster unselfishly encouraged the two young men to go about together alone . . . they visited the Brussels Gallery and went to the opera.'[17] Then occurred one of those might-have-beens that biographers love to chew at: Proust was in Bruges at this time and if, as is likely, Morgan and Lily went there on their way to Ostend the two future novelists may have brushed past each other, even sat in the same café.

Morgan had told Dent earlier that 'Money goes so much further travelling than when you are in a house or flat that I expect my mother will be quite disinclined to settle down.'[18] And indeed this was the case. Arriving in London, they went to the Kingsley Temperance Hotel in Bloomsbury, 'a clean, airless establishment much patronized by provincial England'.[19] Their first priority was to visit friends and relations since 'it is bad to be away from all friends for a whole year. In the Pension life I have led I have only met one person whom I shall mind never meeting again . . . Books too, are a minor blessing to which I am looking forward.'[20] Their second task was to find permanent lodgings, 'but they are all occupied, dirty, & expensive'.

What with looking for somewhere to live and seeing people, Morgan had little of the time he had hoped for to ponder his future. Relations at once enmeshed him. 'For the last three weeks,' he wrote at the end of October, 'I have been tearing about from aunt to g.mother from g.mother to aunt, exchanging unprofitable embraces, or else going to lunch & tea with people who cannot well help asking me, because it is so long since they have seen me.' Aunt Laura, Maimie and Lily's Whichelo relations such as her brothers Harcourt and Horace, and indeed her mother, they all placed great importance on Morgan having a job (even if unpaid); so he soon visited Cambridge partly because 'my relatives would, I think, be appeased by an unpaid post in the University Library, and I should like it myself.'[21]

One job proffered itself straight away. Remembering G. M. Trevelyan's question six months before ('would you care to do some teaching at the Working Men's College next October?'[22]) Morgan immediately called in there and was accepted to teach a weekly Latin class. Indeed, the hope that he might find employment at the WMC was perhaps the reason for his and Lily's return to England in early October, and the reason they had chosen to be near it in Bloomsbury; the college also had satisfactory Cambridge connections since Ida Darwin's brother-in-law had for many years been its Secretary. (He was married to the Aunt Etty of *Period Piece* who uttered the immortal sentence, once when her maid was away, 'I am very busy answering my own bell.'[23]) We can imagine Morgan taking the class, which he found unexpectedly rewarding ('I am afraid I enjoy it more than they do'[24]), then returning to a cold supper at the hotel. Yet it was not a very happy autumn; and the future stretched ahead.

Even so, there were compensations: his friends in Cambridge, who were wonderfully welcoming and encouraged him to return whenever he could; books and libraries; the British Museum (just across from the hotel); and the continuing work on 'Old Lucy' which he did not abandon, quite. Above all, there was the pleasure of the teaching which encouraged him, only a month after he had started, to apply for an appointment to the lecturing staff of the Cambridge University Local Lectures Board. This excellent institution, the

129

forerunner of the WEA* and of Local Authority evening classes, was organised with great efficiency by a Rev. Cranage. But kindly as he was, and caring as he was, he seemed to be at first oblivious of the special qualities of the putative lecturer whom he was empowered to employ or reject.

He received Morgan's form on 22 November ('have travelled in Italy. Knowledge of Italian . . . Previous experience: class at WMC Great Ormond Street, Bloomsbury') and, also on the same day, a letter from a King's don named Reddaway (the other referee proffered by Morgan was Wedd):

As teacher and examiner I saw a great deal of his work during the year which he devoted to History. His powers as a writer and thinker are considerable, and there is even a touch of real and rare distinction in some of his literary work . . . Forster is liked by all who know him and would never bring discredit of any kind upon the Extension movement. He is unfortunately not at all robust, and I cannot tell how far his health would endure the strain of a great number of engagements to lecture.[25]

That afternoon Morgan's name was voted on to the supplementary lecture list and he was invited, the following week, to give a trial lecture on his chosen subject, 'The Republic of Florence 1115–1530' ('could he do lantern slides?'). But, unwittingly, Reddaway had created enormous difficulties for Morgan over the next few years. There was one essential requirement for being a local lecturer and that was robustness. The classes were often held in remote towns or villages, in far from comfortable huts or schools, and when they were in the evening they necessitated a night in a cheap hotel or a late train journey home. However considerable a 'writer and thinker' someone was, they were not welcome if their health was in question. Yet Morgan, of course, did not know that this letter was on file and when he asked, almost begged, the Rev. Cranage for more work he was often disappointed. It did not do much for his self-esteem. And where, in any case, had the rumour about ill health come from? Had Ida Darwin spread the news about the Forster relations? Had Lily mentioned Morgie's (quite fictitious) ill health to someone at King's who had repeated her strictures? Or had Morgan's lack of sportiness become translated into feebleness? How surprised Reddaway and Cranage would have been if they could have foreseen that Morgan

* Workers' Educational Association, evening classes for adults in employment.

would rarely be ill and would live to the age of ninety-one. Yet even Morgan, encouraged presumably by Lily, thought of himself as delicate – until she died, and he suddenly realised he was not.

The trial lecture was a success but no work was forthcoming, and soon it was once more proposed that Morgan should join the King's trip to Greece at Easter. Lily had luckily kept up with her friend from Tonbridge, Mrs Mawe, and slowly the plan took shape whereby the three of them would go to the Pension Simi in Florence and the two ladies would wait for Morgan while he travelled alone. It was the best that could be managed, but it still did not seem very bold, very independent, very positive. 'I watch my own inaction with grave disapproval', Morgan had written, 'but am still as far as ever from settling what to do.'26 Slowly though, almost reluctantly, he was edging towards it. When he set out for Greece in the spring of 1903 he felt that he had achieved nothing. Yet in a mere seven years' time he would be on the verge of finishing his fourth novel and would be thought of as one of England's best young writers.

The Greek cruise helped Morgan's writing by making him happy. For twenty-one months he had been marooned in Lily's ambiance, with only brief escapes. Now he was for three weeks with people with whom he felt the greatest possible empathy and shared interests, indeed more than this, with these Cambridge dons and undergraduates he felt spiritual harmony. This renewed taste of Cambridge life nearly two years after he had gone down confirmed for ever for Morgan his passionate devotion to it. Now he had left, but was allowed once more to experience the concentrated effect of its values, he realised fully how much he loved it. His month in Greece in the April of 1903 was what turned Cambridge into his lifelong touchstone of friendship, intellectual awareness and happiness. It was at this period in his life that the loss of King's came to be as important as the loss of Melcombe Place, of Battersea Rise, of Rooksnest; and that the idea for *The Longest Journey*, which mourns this loss, first entered his imagination. How happy he would have been as a don (yet how great the loss to literature).

The pleasures of shipboard life were one reason for Morgan's failure to keep a diary while in Greece: there are in the archive a mere four pages torn out of a notebook. He was to regret this: back in London the following winter he had the idea of a story which began at Mistra, but had nothing written down

131

to revive his memory. It was now that he started keeping a diary again – and would do so sporadically for the rest of his life.

After some days in Athens, the cruise began at Delos on 2 April and went via Santorini, Rhodes, Cnidus, Priène, Smyrna, Troy, Mytilène and Methymna on Lesbos ('most beautiful island in Aegean'), Marathon, Delphi, Olympia, Pylos, Mistra and Mycenae three weeks later. As in Italy, Morgan's assiduous preparation and education ensured that little seemed quite new: 'so well drilled by school books that nothing surprised me.'[27] It would always be thus: October 1912, Egypt, 'nothing was new. It was like sailing through the Royal Academy . . .'[28]

The trip to Greece soothed Morgan's soul. There is a new confidence, and a new gentleness in the piece that most directly resulted some months later: 'Cnidus'. It describes a late afternoon (6 April) when twenty-one passengers from the cruise stepped ashore, umbrellas raised, in order damply to inspect the island. The rain was already characteristically Forsterian, indeed he might not have written the essay if there had not been the opportunity for his ironic, deflationary tone to point the contrast between what the imagination anticipates ('colonnades and sky and sun') and what it finds; between what the imagination conjures up, 'declaring that it heard voices because all was so silent, and saw faces because it was too dark to see',[29] and the reality.

'Cnidus' is not merely descriptive, it has a theme: that of history as an abstract concept versus history as we imagine it; that of the sense of the past versus the visitor's 'sentimental imagination'. It was what Philip and Caroline were to sense when they imagine arrows thudding into the washstand mirror. By describing tourists disembarking to 'see' Cnidus, by evoking what they actually see and what their imagination sees, and by providing a little surreal, ghostly touch (an extra person briefly joins their party, then vanishes back into his past existence) Morgan was writing far more than a mere travel piece; as he already knew, he was not only an ironist, able to point up and make fun: he was a moralist. Morgan the essayist, what will eventually be Morgan the narrative voice in the novel, is *telling us what to think*: albeit in the most oblique way.

Morgan had another reason for finding Cnidus unforgettable. High up on the mountainside was the spot where, in the 1850s, a statue of the goddess Demeter* was found and then shipped to the British Museum; so that while Morgan was looking up at her former resting-place, her sanctuary,

She was there at that moment, warm and comfortable in that little recess of hers between the Ephesian Room and the Archaic Room, with the electric light fizzling above her, and casting blue shadows over her chin. She is dusted twice a week, and there is a railing in front, with 'No Admittance', so that she cannot be touched.[31]

(Nowadays she is far more prosaically in Room 81 and she can, illicitly, be touched.) The Demeter's 'sorrowful eyes' and, as the present-day catalogue puts it, 'the elusive but vividly determined expression of her face'[32] had long been of fascination to Morgan, perhaps since Tonbridge days when he and Edgar Nicolas would come up to the museum for the day, certainly since the previous autumn when one reason for choosing the Kingsley Hotel was that it was but a brief walk along the edge of Bloomsbury Square to the museum's main gate. The reason for his fascination was that 'to her, all over the world, rise prayers of idolatry from suffering men as well as suffering women, for she has transcended sex.'[33]

It would be one of the themes of Morgan's life: the longing for androgyny. It was not that he wanted to be womanly (there were too many aspects of the women surrounding him that were of intense irritation, quite apart from the dislike and fear he recognised in himself of straining bosoms, female smells, bleeding). What he wanted was for none of it to matter: whether someone was male or female, masculine or feminine, sexually attracted to the one sex or to the other sex or to both, if only, he was beginning fumblingly to feel, it could be irrelevant. The Demeter represented that possibility; by transcending sex she suggests that mankind can be quite *unlike* Cecil in *A Room with a View* who 'daren't let a woman decide. He's the type who's kept Europe back for a thousand years. Every moment of his life he's forming you, telling you what a man thinks womanly.'[34] For Morgan the Demeter's androgynous features, her beauty that transcended both sexuality and sex differentiation, was a symbol of such importance that he drew upon it three times in

* 'Her name signifies Mother Earth, the meaning being that she was the goddess of agriculture and the civilization based upon it.'[30] She also represents sorrowing mothers: it was her search for her daughter Persephone that led her to neglect the earth so it became barren. When the latter returns spring arrives and the earth mother rejoices.

The Longest Journey, each time as an image of the love which is perfectly pure, elemental and unselfish.

A week after going to Cnidus Morgan had the same experience he had been hoping to repeat since Ravello: 'the whole of The Road from Colonus hung ready for me in a hollow tree not far from Olympia.'[35] The story is set specifically on 18 April, as though Morgan wanted carefully to link his vision with the finished story. And it is significant that it was the month of April, the month when nature is meant to be bringing forth new life: when Leonard Bast and Mrs Moore die in this month the tragedy is all the greater because of the contrast between blossoming nature and the end of their hopes and illusions.

Like Harold, like Eustace, like Lucy and like Adela Quested was so famously to be, Mr Lucas* in 'The Road from Colonus' is an unreceptive traveller ('Greece was like England'). But he is strangely drawn to a place to which he comes for a picnic with his Tunbridge Wells-ish daughter (there is an ironic echo of Oedipus and Antigone in their relationship and in the title's placing of the story at Colonus, where Oedipus died). After resting peacefully against a vast plane tree, Mr Lucas 'was aroused at last by a shock – the shock of an arrival perhaps, for when he opened his eyes, something unimagined, indefinable, had passed over all things, and made them intelligible and good.'

He would like to stay ('for the first time he saw his daily life aright. What need had he to return to England?') but, like Harold, is almost forcibly removed from 'the dangerous scene'. At home he discovers that the tree had fallen and killed the inhabitants of their picnic spot on the very night he would have been there. But he does not care: his failure to act, to seize his chance of self-realisation and freedom, condemns him to a death-in-life of tetchy fretting about domestic trivia. In addition, by refusing to sacrifice his flawed way of life to the spiritual wholeness of Colonus he caused its destruction: an image of a foreigner in a strange place being a destructive influence unless he gives up his preconceptions.

One of the decisions Morgan seemed to reach at this time was that he personally would not be a destructive force. He might lack courage, he might, like Eustace, be 'pale, his chest contracted, and his

* Lucas = Lat. *lucus*, sacred grove, woods. The word derives, as does the name Lucy, from *lux* = light and *luceo* = to shine, hence it means a clearing in the woods.

muscles undeveloped'[36] but he would not impose himself on others. He would observe, he would try to be sensitive to places and to people, but he himself would not cause trees to crash down. And it is indeed true that at few times in his life could one accuse Morgan of careless instincts. When he fell in love, finally and completely, at the age of fifty-one, he did at first harbour very hostile feelings towards the fiancée, and later wife, of his lover. And as he grew older he increasingly took umbrage about things that most people consider part of life (landlords giving one notice, letters not being answered, friendships not being cherished with the assiduousness they should). Yet never did he destroy or crush. The diffidence that had been increasingly there since the uninhibited days when 'Saint Forster' had played childish pranks was to come increasingly to the fore. The writer had found himself and with this he found his personality.

12

Bloomsbury

After the cruise Morgan and Lily spent May 1903 in Florence* and June and July at the same hotel as the year before in Cortina. But Morgan wanted to get back to England and only a few weeks after Greece was writing home to a King's friend, 'I do very much long for the presence of some male who is neither decrepit, mountain-mad, or clerical.'[1] He had changed since the previous summer, and could now freely admit that what he needed was companionship from intellectual equals.

How much he had changed is evident from a piece he wrote while staying in Cortina. Entitled 'Ralph and Tony' by the Forster archivists, it consists of forty pencilled sheets (now glued into a red-leather notebook). Morgan seems to have seen it in the context of an unfinished novel but in fact it reads perfectly well as an accomplished and revealing short story; yet it was never submitted for publication, and the editor of the 1980 volume in which it was finally printed was probably correct when she surmised that 'the characterizations of Ralph and his mother came too close to home for publication.'

The story is as follows: a young man called Ralph comes with his mother to stay in a hotel in the mountains and there meets a brother and sister called Tony and Margaret. Ralph is deemed 'decadent' by the robust Tony: he worries about his health, pins up postcard reproductions of paintings such as the *Birth of Venus* (which Lucy was to buy in the Piazza Signoria and lose, blood-stained) and longs to be liked. Ralph

did not need health or self-confidence or success or that mystic justice for

* And went to the opera, Luisa Tetrazzini in Donizetti's *Lucia di Lammermoor*: the performance was to be re-invoked in *Where Angels Fear to Tread*.

which he was seeking. He merely needed human love, and then without argument or effort all his doubts and weaknesses and unhappiness would disappear. His mother had devoted her life to him, but she was weak, inefficient and spasmodic, for all her occasional insight. She was led astray by the questions of health and success: she did not realize what he really needed, nor could she have supplied it if she did.

Then the strong, athletic Tony, whom Ralph has vainly implored to be his friend, is smitten with hitherto undetected heart disease while rescuing Ralph from the mountain. Ralph now finds the strength to rebuff his mother's demeaning outbursts ('"I don't understand cleverness or subtleties or higher thought. I am only your poor ignorant useless mother"') and Tony has enough heart to allow him into his and his sister's life. At the end his mother 'retired to send off a picture-postcard to her brother, with guarded generalities as to the behaviour of young people written all round the view'. Margaret 'escaped into the garden' and foresees that she will marry Ralph.

Possibly Morgan could not contemplate Lily reading this and therefore decided not to publish; but it is a wonderful story (and, like *Nottingham Lace* and the other pieces, should have been reprinted for the general public rather than in a volume only accessible to scholars). The writing is of a beauty and technical skill which is extraordinary for someone as young and untried as Morgan was during this summer in Cortina; the plot avoids too many touches of Henry James;* and the themes are full of fascinating resonance. Apart from that of mothers and sons, there is the theme of brothers and sisters and the sister's husband: Morgan's King's friends were sometimes to marry each other's sisters as a way of continuing their friendship in a socially, and sexually, acceptable fashion (for example, Ainsworth would marry Moore's sister in 1908). Then there is the theme of the vastness of the mountains set against the pettiness and constrictions of human preoccupations: when Ralph and Tony are closeted together at the end, having the most important conversation of their lives, Ralph's mother despairs because he 'had left all his things in confusion, and she did not know what books he needed packed and what left out for the journey'[2] – a wonderfully ironic insight into the belief that even if something crucial is about to happen, yet one must not leave one's things in confusion.

---

* The character of Ralph has some similarities to that of Ralph Touchett in *The Portrait of a Lady*.

Morgan's thoughts about convention versus self-fulfilment are also evident from 'Ansell', a story that was written at about this period. The hero, called by Morgan's own rejected name Edward, had gone up to Cambridge six years before, as Morgan had done by 1903. His books fall irrecoverably into the river and the reader might at first conclude that this is a morally unambiguous story about salvation because '"them books saved us"' by disappearing. But the ending is uncertain, with Edward thinking, '"I have not yet realized what has happened"'.[3] It was as if Morgan, during his first winter in London, had himself been unsure whether to opt for books or (could he find one) an Ansell figure; now he knew better that he was going to need both.

It is likely that in Greece he had had some kind of revelation greater than mere shipboard conversations. In his biography of Goldie (with whom Morgan identified so strongly that it is not fanciful to read into it many elements of his own life story) he was to describe Goldie going to Greece in 1899 and experiencing 'Mistra: visionary moment at' (to quote the index entry Morgan used in his 1934 biography) where Morgan, too, went in 1903. 'It was here on this night', Goldie apparently declared, 'that there occurred to me the idea of writing a dialogue on Good . . .' And, Morgan added, 'Mistra might symbolize the synthesis at which Dickinson . . . aimed, and it is appropriate that it should have inspired him to write the first of his dialogues. He often spoke of that moonlit scene.'[4]

He described it to Morgan, who was to some extent affected by Mistra too: he resolved to write something larger – even if not exactly a dialogue on Good – than his tally of four short stories, two half-done novels and a few articles. Hence 'Ralph and Tony' and, as well, a novella called 'The Eternal Moment', which was set in Cortina and which Morgan seems to have planned while he was there and to have written the following summer. Returning a year after the previous visit gave an extra impetus to the story: he imagined what it would have been like if a novelist had published a book based upon Cortina and then returned to view the book's effect upon its real-life setting. He wondered, too, whether and how an incipient romance might have been affected by the novelist's departure, fame and return; and he used as a heroine a Miss Lavish figure whom he had already used in 'Old Lucy' and who was to reappear the following winter of 1903–4 in 'New Lucy'; she would be finally perfected in *A Room with a View*.

Miss Raby in 'The Eternal Moment' has come back to Cortina ('Vorta') after twenty years and tells her companions that an Italian porter had fallen in love with her during a mountain expedition. Of course he had not, and one of the themes of the story is Miss Raby's self-delusion and subsequent self-knowledge. The other theme is the exploitation of Vorta consequent on her book and, by corollary, the artist's responsibility. Miss Raby had not only been the cause of the large pompous hotels and fashionable pursuits and the changes in the village, she had exploited her Italian by putting him in her book. Here was Morgan discussing, in fictional form, in his own equivalent to Goldie's dialogue on Good, the aesthetic impulse and his justification for submitting to it. And as someone who had Goldie's 'photo-graphic' gift, he was exploring the moral dilemma inherent in 'using' the places and people he saw around him; he realised that if he continued as he had begun he was in danger of exploiting them as unscrupulously as Miss Raby.

Having reminded the now-concierge of her declaration two decades before, and after receiving his inexpressibly coarse wink, Miss Raby has a revelation. It is Morgan's first expression of the belief, with which his work was to be through and through imbued, in the vast and enduring power of love. Miss Raby realises that

the incident upon the mountain had been one of the great moments of her life – perhaps the greatest, certainly the most enduring: that she had drawn unacknowledged power and inspiration from it, just as trees draw vigour from a subterranean spring. Never again could she think of it as a half-humorous episode in her development. There was more reality in it than in all the years of success and varied achievement which had followed, and which it had rendered possible. For all her correct behaviour and lady-like display, she had been in love with Feo, and she had never loved so greatly again. A presumptuous boy had taken her to the gates of heaven; and, though she would not enter with him, the eternal remembrance of the vision had made life seem endurable and good.[5]

Miss Raby, as Caroline Abbott in *Where Angels Fear to Tread* was to be, is sexually frustrated yet redeemed through the power of love. Alas, her travelling companion cannot forgive her embarrassing revelation – she has become socially unacceptable. It would be one of the key themes of Morgan's work, in his fiction and his non-fiction, the disparity between people's deeply felt beliefs and feelings and between what they pretended to think and feel; how the whole social structure in which one is so comfortably ensconced would collapse if one suddenly declared, but I love him, or I am too irritated by you to continue with this charade, or underneath it all I am deeply, deeply unhappy. The tragedy, for in some ways it was to be a tragedy, was Morgan's cowardice, his lazy preference for a comfortable way of life, his heartfelt loathing of giving offence. And yet the miracle, for his writing if not for his life, is that he understood himself so well, he had such self-knowledge. He knew, aged twenty-four, that he would never break free: and out of the bonds he would create literature.

Lily was reluctant to go back to the daily tyranny of houses, meals and maids but Morgan, with his growing acceptance of his own needs, was urging a permanent home. The plan was that they would settle temporarily into the Kingsley and meanwhile house-hunt. Without any difficulty he slipped back into the routine of the previous winter: seeing friends and relations, reading, writing, revisiting Cambridge and doing some teaching. In August, upon returning to England, Morgan received a letter from the Local Lectures Board: after half a dozen negative letters the news was at last positive: 'Can you go to Harpenden on alternate Thursdays beginning on October 1 for a 6 lecture course on The Republic of Florence (5°/c)?' The fee would be £12 (£600) plus travelling expenses.

The syllabus was Morgan's immediate task. This was eventually printed and the 1905 edition is still in the University Library in Cambridge; but because the questions for students were too complex the first draft had to be changed. 'One could write a volume in answer to some of them,' wrote Cranage of the Lectures Board. However, even with modifications they enticed only three people, out of the forty or so who attended the lecture, to hand in written papers. Morgan had still not shaken off the rigours of his education, yet as the years went by he would place more and more emphasis on accessibility and would have been embarrassed by charges of complexity. Subtlety, fidelity to the individual voice, spontaneity: these would be the qualities that would interest him in a reader or an audience. He would shrink from displaying his own learning; and he would shrink from undermining others by demanding too much of them. Perhaps Cranage, by pulling him up at the start of his teaching and writing career, made him unafraid of reaching out. He may have had a direct influence on Morgan's uniquely approachable, almost confiding style: a style that would reach its apotheosis during the Second World War

LEFT Morgan with gown and mortarboard, possibly in November 1897 (his first term at King's) when he told Lily he was about to have his photograph taken but 'as I have my cap on I don't think my hair will matter'.[6] BELOW Max Garnett in 1905 looking very much the 'English Gentleman – good-natured, hearty, well-to-do, aristocratic, sporting'[7] (as defined by Ernest Merz in 1906).

King's Third Year May 1900. Morgan back row top left; Mollison, his Tonbridge friend, second from the left second row; George Barger and Hugh Meredith third and fourth from the right, also second row.

LEFT Morgan on Rhodes in April 1903, second from the right in cap, with male companion from the ship. His hands are joined at the tips rather awkwardly, perhaps he is feeling the loss of his Baedeker, or is it bulging in his left pocket? Are the two young men accompanied by a Girton girl (who appears, sensibly, to be carrying a mackintosh)?

RIGHT the two tutors and the two governesses June 1905 (p 171).
BELOW Nassenheide itself in July 1905 showing the flight of steps up to the back verandah (p 175). Morgan was less than complimentary about the 'German garden': in England the grass would at least have been a proper lawn and in Italy there would have been geraniums in pots up the sides of the steps.

RIGHT aerial view of Figsbury Rings near Salisbury, an especially sacred place for Morgan.

BELOW Hotel Jennings Riccioli, formerly Pension Simi, 2 Lungarno alle Grazie, the four-storey building with seven windows on each floor. 'A Room with a View' was on the first floor.

ABOVE RIGHT 'Street scene – San Gimignano' appeared in *Hill Towns of Italy* by Egerton Williams, published in 1904 when Morgan was writing *Where Angels Fear to Tread*. Here is the 'very respectable whitewashed mud wall, with a coping of red crinkled tiles to keep it from dissolution'[10] and, left, what could be Gino's house, with its loggia.
RIGHT The Manor House, Winterbourne Dauntsey near Salisbury, the model for Cadover in *The Longest Journey*.

when, in his broadcasts, Morgan spoke to millions.

The Harpenden teaching proved enjoyable and Morgan was a success with the locals, who even helped him to house-hunt: 'We like him so much and wish we could find for him and his mother a house in this town – He wants one at a rent of £40–£60 [£2000–£3000]. I am going to write to him suggesting that he should try Stevenage or Radlett.'[6] At the same time his career was taking another direction – again, curiously enough, through the influence of G. M. Trevelyan. He, Wedd, Goldie, C. F. G. Masterman and others had decided to start a magazine to be known as the *Independent Review*.

It was founded to combat the aggressive imperialism and the Protection campaign of Joe Chamberlain; and to advocate sanity in foreign affairs and a constructive policy at home. It was not so much a Liberal review as an appeal to Liberalism from the Left to be its better self – one of those appeals which have continued until the extinction of the Liberal Party

wrote Morgan in 1934. Yet it was not an entirely political venture: even those who were not Liberals 'saw avenues opening into literature, philosophy, human relationships'.[7] Morgan was at once asked to contribute in all three areas, in whatever medium he chose. He offered 'Macolnia Shops', and it appeared in the second number of the *Independent* in November. Whether he offered 'Albergo Empedocle' and they rejected it is unknown; but it appeared the following month in another publication called *Temple Bar*. (In *The Longest Journey* Rickie hopes to be published in the *Holborn*.) To have two pieces in print within a month of each other must have been an encouraging experience and, indeed, it was at this period, the winter of 1903–4, that Morgan became more productive.

That autumn he had completed 'Cnidus' and 'The Eternal Moment'. Now, instead of writing another short story, he returned to his Italian novel. He had been working intermittently on 'Old Lucy' all that year, and it seems likely that he wrote the concluding pages upon his return from Cortina: the word 'great' or 'greatest' (as in Rome being 'the greatest thing on the face of the earth'[8]) recurs and was also to appear twice in the key passage from 'The Eternal Moment' ('the incident upon the mountain had been one of the great moments of her life'). It was to be a significant word for Morgan, used only with the most intense meaning, never flippantly: when Caroline has spoken about Gino, Philip realises what had happened 'was even greater than she imagined';[9] when Harold in 'Albergo Empedocle' awakens from his vision he knows 'that I was a lot greater then than I am now. I'm greater now than I was this morning.'[10]

The reason for the greatness is a sexual one, or rather an asexual one. Morgan stopped writing 'Old Lucy' after Lucy had perceived Rome as 'the greatest thing'. From the tone of the passage, from the mention of her sitting in the 'warm sunshine', and from various other clues, it seems clear that Morgan would have liked to write about her sensual life and her sexuality; and, at the same time, about the need for a truly fulfilled person to transcend sex and know the greatness of a pure love. But he could not find the vocabulary – apart, that is, from the one word; hence its reappearance in the same context in other places in his fiction. (A good deal of insight may be gleaned by looking for words that recur in Morgan's work, such as 'muddle' and 'blue' and the wasp in *A Passage to India* and the Demeter in *The Longest Journey*.)

So, in December, Morgan abandoned 'Old Lucy'. Carefully he wrote at the other end of the notebook he had been using: *The New Lucy Novel* Dec. 1903. At the same time, and in the same notebook, he restarted a diary; yet so quickly found this a bad idea that after a mere three pages he confined his (intermittent) entries to the notebook and wrote 'New Lucy' on loose quarto sheets. But even a new novel was not enough for him. Goldie's moonlit scene at Mistra and his own visit there were still feeding his imagination, even though he had failed to describe it at the time. The very first diary entry on 8 December records the 'Idea of a story about Pletone, starting at Mistra': thus 'The Tomb of Pletone' was written at the same time as 'New Lucy' was beginning. 'A short historical story', it is in a genre that Morgan had been brooding about since the time eighteen months earlier when he had thought of writing about Antinous. His former instinct – to abandon the idea – was correct: this story, though competently written, is curiously dull. What it does have is an amoral quality, a vision of civilisation with quite different values, and especially those of violence and brutality.

When, at the end of the following year, Morgan realised that 'The Tomb of Pletone' had 'gone the rounds and failed', i.e. was not accepted for publication, he used some of the material in an essay called 'Gemisthus Pletho'. This did better and came out in the *Independent* for October 1905. Both these pieces, with their preoccupation with classical civilisation, reinforce the impression that Morgan continued to be a frequent visitor to the British Museum. Indeed, he may have sat there to write. Hotels are not usually accommodating to the idea of their guests staying in their rooms in the morning, and Lily would have wanted Morgan to accompany her on errands unless he had somewhere to which to take himself. I imagine him sitting on a stone bench or going across to Museum Street for a cup of coffee and a Bath bun.

It was not a gregarious existence, but it was happy enough: except when the museum gave rise to disquieting thoughts. 13 March 1904,

each time I see those Greek things in the B.M. they are more beautiful and more hopeless. It's simple to say they are gods – down to the bulls going to sacrifice on the Parthenon frieze. But I don't believe gods would make one so unhappy. Up to Demeter & Persephone on the pediment they are human and our perpetual rebuke.

It is so curious, this desire to be simple and beautiful & strong. But our only hope lies through all these complications – not by affecting simplicity. So I'll call the Parthenon not a rebuke but a comment – which makes me feel worse.

Then he reflected on the wonderful quality of light in which a statue 'stands all the afternoon warm in thick yellow sunshine' and decided that 'he couldn't have done it in Greece'.[11] It was a tribute to the British Museum that came unexpectedly from someone who had but recently been in the real yellow sunshine of Greece. His deep affection for the museum was one reason why, in *Maurice*, it is the setting for the scene in which the lovers declare themselves to one another. Indeed the theme of revelation and honesty was what prompted Morgan to write, probably during the previous winter, a fragment known to archivists as 'Simply the Human Form'. It is the beginning of a story about a visitor from another planet or civilisation who cannot understand the attitudes to nudity revealed to him in the British Museum. Its fully clothed visitors have come to admire sculpted nudes whose beauty they do not deny; yet, alas, they will not emulate them, with the result that 'nudity at the present day signifies the highest standard in art and the lowest standard of civilization'.[12]

There was also the paradox, of which Morgan was becoming increasingly aware, that the Greeks admired not only nudes but all the varieties of sexual pleasure that could be given and received by these nudes. Yet two thousand years of Christianity had created a situation where Greek art had to be admired according to the totally false premise, alleged to have derived from Plato and particularly his *Symposium*, that love between those of the same sex was tenable only if 'platonic'. It is no exaggeration to say that by the time Morgan came of age, in 1900, society's fear and loathing of sexual relationships between those of the same sex was at its height. If you were an invert you were anti-God, anti-society, anti-respectability, anti-everything.

What extraordinary ill fate, Morgan must have mused as he walked in the British Museum, placed him on earth during a period when these values were unquestioned by virtually the whole of society? And yet, as he luckily could not foresee, the entire ninety years of his lifetime were to be among the most repressive in modern history. If only he too could, like the fully clad visitors in his story, learn to de-sexualise what he looked at. If only, at second best, he could even enjoy the more intellectual relationship of the *erastes* and the *eromenos*, the lover and the beloved; eventually, maybe, his wayward body would learn to still its longings. Yet why should it? Why should Morgan, as a punishment for being born out of time, have to deny himself all sexual pleasure?

The fact that the British Museum was in Bloomsbury was one of the reasons why Morgan felt so at home there. When, in the spring of 1904, he and Lily took a six-months' lease on a flat at 11 Drayton Court, in a road leading from the Fulham Road to the Old Brompton Road in South Kensington, he felt quite transplanted; 'the gulf which we crossed between Kensington & Bloomsbury was the gulf between respectable mummified humbug & life crude & impertinent perhaps, but living',[13] Virginia Woolf would write one day about her own move from Kensington. Morgan was now marooned on the wrong side of the gulf. But he did not complain to Lily: it was as if, masochistically, he had decided that his external circumstances were irrelevant and that what mattered was inside his head. He was also perfecting his pose of extreme seriousness. He mockingly observed this years later when relating his first meeting with Clive Bell, the future art critic and husband of Vanessa Stephen. Morgan mentioned the poor, Clive said he subscribed to one or two charities and that salved his conscience. 'I was shocked at his levity, for I felt it a duty to be unhappy without reserves whenever the poor entered my mind – as occasionally they did for the purpose of making a point – and I should never have subscribed to anything.'[14]

Yet it was Clive and people like him who were soon to help Morgan to be more light-hearted, not in the jokey sense ('I ragged all the time I was there',[15] Morgan had written somewhat surprisingly about his time in Greece) but in the sense of being able to have the due amount of fun: of not always being serious.

As regards the teaching, he remained a little solemn. Yet attendance was up from an average of thirty-seven at Harpenden to seventy-three at Lowestoft. The Secretary of the Lowestoft Centre, which is where Morgan gave his course in the New Year of 1904, advised Cranage that other centres should 'get him somehow into personal communication with his audience' if his words were not to be smothered by his 'real modesty and unassumingness ... Mr Forster has an even delivery which emphasizes nothing.' Nevertheless he continued to be in demand, always giving the same course on 'The Republic of Florence'. Once Cranage advised him to work up a modern historical subject as 'a great many centres are fighting shy of anything so far back'.[16] But Morgan resisted and stayed with Florence.

Having by now established 'New Lucy', he wrote another short story: he was beginning to think that even if he could not finish a novel he might gather a collection of stories. It is unclear whether he ever intended 'Ansell' for publication or whether it was rejected; in any event he abandoned the idea of publishing it and instead gutted the beginning, reworking it into yet another falling-book opening, that of a new piece which he called 'The Story of the Siren'. Based, perhaps, on a memory of an expedition to Sorrento in May 1902 when a 'mad' boatman distressed Lily because he 'groaned and muttered to himself'[17] in the grottoes, it was a mysterious fantasy on the theme of salvation and showed Morgan in a new light, unafraid of using the methods of mysticism and at the same time political. He appears to be inveighing against both the tyranny of organised Christianity and the tyranny of the State: and he contrasted both to Ancient Greek freedom from repression – of which he was by now so envious. After the Sicilian boatman has related 'the story of the siren' he concludes: '"Silence and loneliness cannot last for ever. It may be a hundred or a thousand years, but the sea lasts longer, and she shall come out of it and sing."'[18]

Some of these thoughts appeared in 'New Lucy', on which Morgan was at this time, the spring and early summer of 1904, working steadily. Yet what remains of it is far less complete than 'Old Lucy' and it seems that in the end the first part was absorbed into the finished novel. The only manuscript sheets Morgan was to keep were rejected 'New Lucy' ones; the others must have been absorbed into *A Room with a View* and the originals destroyed. Thus the sixty extant sheets of 'New Lucy' (eventually found in six different places among his papers) begin at Chapter 12, and are all set in England, after Lucy has returned from Italy. The likelihood is that the Italian chapters of what was to be *A Room with a View* were written at the Kingsley in the new year and early spring of 1904; and that when, in 1907, Morgan came to finish what had by then become *A Room with a View* he only abandoned the second half of 'New Lucy' – what had been written at Drayton Court. It was almost as if he was, superstitiously, abandoning everything he had written in South Kensington.

The loss is not insignificant: there is a memorable scene in the library of the Literary and Philosophic Institute; there is yet another incident when 'the book had fallen out of the tree, blatant and heavy, and all the airy fabric of tact was destroyed'.[19] But in 'New Lucy' Lucy is too shallow and Cecil too unpleasant to be plausible, while George is killed by a falling tree and Lucy resolves that she will never marry. In the finished novel Lucy and Cecil are far more 'rounded' characters, each with good as well as bad qualities; and Morgan, by allowing Lucy and George to marry, would display his passionate belief in love's potential for good and in the importance of sexual passion for happiness. *A Room with a View* is therefore imbued with sexual imagery: Lucy, for example, when she goes on her own into the Piazza Signoria, metaphorically loses her virginity:

The Loggia showed as the triple entrance of a cave . . . the tower of the palace, which rose out of the lower darkness like a pillar of roughened gold . . . seemed . . . some unattainable treasure throbbing in the tranquil sky . . . as she caught sight of him he grew dim; the palace itself grew dim, swayed above her, fell onto her softly, slowly, noiselessly, and the sky fell with it.[20]

Between 1904, when Morgan wrote 'New Lucy', and 1907, when he rewrote it a third time, his sexual awareness, previously suppressed, angry and bewildered, was changing into a far more mature understanding. But it was a lonely development. As he wrote in his diary at about the time he moved to Drayton Court, even the 'minority' has 'sweet waters though I shall never drink them. So I can understand the draughts of the others, though they will not understand my abstinence.'[21] It was not always to be thus.

13

Weybridge

Morgan was now twenty-five and the carefree Cambridge years were three years before. No longer did he sit idyllically over tea discussing whether cows exist when no one is looking at them. No longer did he have the feeling that he was part of a magical world. As he had anticipated, he was an outsider, marooned in South Kensington, shy, diffident and with the growing certainty that love, passion, spiritual harmony, all the things for which he longed so much, would never be his. The Morgan who released crabs in people's desks, who played golf, who 'ragged' in Greece, he had quite, quite gone.

But there was one world where, as he had spent the last two years discovering, he was completely happy: it was the world inside his head. About this time he stopped minding so much what people thought; he stopped making conversation only in order to be pleasant; he stopped always expecting to find happiness from others. He wrote in his diary, 'I'm going to be a minority if not a solitary, and I'd best make copy out of my position':[1] he recognised that an invert is not necessarily a solitary but that he himself would be, and that he had better use this fact not just in the literary sense but in the way he lived his life. He would have to enjoy his solitude, not mourn the joviality that would never be his. His world would be a dream world; he would communicate through writing.

It was a confusing mixture: self-confident in some respects – to the people to whom he lectured in Lowestoft, to Lily (in front of whom he never let his mask fall) – and beset with doubt in others. He seemed not to care about his clothes, about his public persona, about living with his mother or being jobless and identity-less; inside he cared a great deal. There was an example of this during the late spring. A very short story, 'A Day Off'

147

(about two German tourists who come across a bizarre 'brood of seventeen magenta-coloured chickens'[2]), was published in the *Pilot* for May 1904, and 'The Road from Colonus' was published in the *Independent* in June. 'The Story of a Panic' would appear there in August: 'shockingly composed', Morgan told Trevy diffidently, 'and I don't know they ought to have taken it. But I like it more than I ought to.'[3]

Yet on 6 July he received a letter from the *Independent*'s editor about changes made to the stories' punctuation. He was 'absurdly angry and ashamed of so being. Probably shan't sleep.' And, a month later, 'beast Jenks altered punctuation after all'.*[4] Here was an example of Morgan's double-sidedness. On the one hand he professed modesty and healthy indifference; on the other he was deeply possessive of his prose, angry to the point of sleeplessness if it was changed. He had such confidence in his own work that he robustly refused to countenance the whims of others.

So sure of himself was he that during the summer at Drayton Court he began another novel; with *Nottingham Lace*, 'Ralph and Tony' and both Lucy novels unfinished, it was his fourth attempt, the one that was to prove, painlessly and without self-doubt, that he was indeed a novelist. Marooned in a rented flat, with no anticipation of what his future would be, starved of the daily solace of intellectual companionship, he began to write his first, finished novel. The overheard incident at Siena; the memories of San Gimignano two years before; the passionate interest in the theme of the repressed Englishman experiencing Italy; the slowly maturing prose style: it all came together and Morgan's life as a novelist began. As he listened

to the scraps that floated up from the street.

'If you look out of a window in London,' said P. dreamily, 'you hear all the people saying "no" to each other. "Naow – naow – " And here it's all si. Si. Si.'

---

* Edward Jenks, the editor, altered Morgan's punctuation considerably: he was a pedant who preferred little phrases ('As Mrs Forman would have said: "it was all very Greek"') to contain the colon and the quotation marks Morgan left out; and who loved semicolons. Going through the 1904 text and the 1911 one (in which Morgan was finally able to delete Jenks's changes) one can see many instances where Morgan had a comma (understated, subtle) and Jenks imposed a semicolon (pedantic, unsubtle); the changes slow the reader down, remove the poetry, alter the rhythm: 'They had suddenly become unfamiliar, and all that they did seemed strained and coarse' changes in all these ways when the comma becomes a semicolon. 'The Story of a Panic' in August also had the imposed semicolons: 'Poor Rose had brought her camera with her; so I thought this positively rude' is quite different when read with a comma as Morgan meant it.

'Il bel paese la dov'il "si" suona. The beautiful country where they say yes.'
'Where people respond you mean.'
'Yes. [illegible] Where things happen.'[5]

Ostensibly one of the first passages of 'New Lucy', written at Drayton Court at the beginning of 1904, in tone and idiom this is clearly from a draft of *Where Angels Fear to Tread*. It is extraordinarily indicative of Morgan's feelings about himself. His too was a life where people said no and where things did not often happen; yet he accepted that a gregarious life would do little for his writing, that he needed solitude and calm.

And it was now, in the summer of this year, that he made a conscious effort to find both. He started a habit of long, solitary walks – not for him fashionable walking-parties or G. M. Trevelyan's favourite Lake-Hunting, an elaborate game of hide-and-seek conducted on the hills of the Lake District; Morgan was to prefer less strenuous expeditions on his own. On this occasion Lily stayed with Maimie in Salisbury and he went on shortish daytrip-length walks, returning in the evening to the two women who loved him so much and to whom he was so close.

At this period of his life, in the years after his trips to Italy and to Greece, Morgan was developing his passionate love for the English countryside. One of the reasons he did not become an Italophile, or did not return again and again to other countries in the way that would, after all, have been so easy for someone without 'full-time' employment, one of the reasons was his devotion and commitment to England. It was almost as if the countryside was beginning to replace the father, the ancestral home, the children he would never have: the love of landscape was in some ways enough.

Wiltshire was, apart from Hertfordshire, Morgan's earliest love. Since he was small he had enjoyed staying with Maimie in her 'tall sun-drenched house balanced high above Salisbury'[6] on Milford Hill; her straightforwardness, her uncomplicated response to people and to the countryside made her a much-loved figure in Morgan's life, so that the town and the surroundings were, for him, magically imbued with her aura. There are elements of Maimie in Mrs Wilcox and Mrs Moore, but especially in Mrs Elliot,* Rickie's mother, who

---

* Morgan did not use a first name for these three fictional characters in order to make them more symbolic of their roles as wife and mother, of the values of reality and clear-sightedness. Similarly, characters like Mr Emerson and Miss Avery have impersonal names to symbolise wisdom.

149

is praised because she was 'unselfish and yet had such capacities for life':

'Unselfish people, as a rule, are deathly dull. They have no colour. They think of other people because it is easier. They give money because they are too stupid or too idle to spend it properly on themselves. That was the beauty of your mother – she gave away, but she also spent on herself, or tried to.'[7]

Maimie was like this: she had a sense of fun, but was good with it. There is something of her, too, in Lilia in *Where Angels Fear to Tread*. Having, in the face of much Clapham disapproval, married a widower named Aylward, who 'called his home "Olmleigh", and worst of all worsts he was in trade',[8] Maimie was very happy. But she was at first ostracised, as Lilia was, and as Lucy was to be when she marries George.

Marriage, and especially unsuitable marriage, was on Morgan's mind at this time. He was developing his intensely held beliefs in the importance of passion, in the bond between two people mattering more than anything else, and yet was increasingly aware of society's power over this passion. What absorbed him was things going wrong, failing to follow the conventional groove. It was not that he was obviously radical, an aesthete or an anarchist or a bohemian; it was that he wanted to write about the truths underneath the surface, the obverse of the socially acceptable. Yet he was too constrained and his milieu too rigidly enmeshed him for him to choose outspokenness. It would all have to be done by implication; this is why, for nearly ninety years, there has been a proportion of Forster readers who have found him tame, dull, middle-class, without even a tinge of anarchy ('I can never be perfectly certain whether Helen was got with child by Leonard Bast or by his fatal forgotten umbrella',[9] wrote Katherine Mansfield famously in her diary).

As well as frowned-upon marriages, another theme that pre-occupied Morgan was babies: the extraordinary concept, made all the more mysterious for an invert, that one act of lust, one ejaculation of seed, results in human life. And what if the seed was ejaculated in the wrong place, in a womb not approved of by conventional society, where the act had not been blessed by meetings between relations, engraved invitations and lists of wedding presents at the best shops? It was a classic theme, explored in novels like *Adam Bede* and *Tess of the D'Urbervilles*, and was one that would appear in all the novels, in Caroline loving Gino, in Lucy loving George, in Margaret loving Henry Wilcox and in Adela's blood being stirred by Aziz. All these loves, although some (like Lucy's and Margaret's) were made quasi-respectable once 'the astonishing glass shade had fallen that interposes between married couples and the world',[10] all these were interestingly outside the norm. Hence, a month before the visit to Maimie, there was a not unexpected entry in his diary: 'An idea for an entire novel – that of a man who discovers he has an illegitimate brother.'[11] Every unacceptable element could, with propriety, be encapsulated in this theme.

As he walked near Salisbury in the September of 1904 Morgan brooded on marriage, on regeneration, on landscape; as he sat down to eat his lunch he would have thought fondly about Maimie; he may even, if the details were known to him, have imagined his father's life with Ted, wondering half angrily and half enviously about their life together thirty years before. Perhaps he thought of Beachy Head miles away to the east and the grassy place where he helped a man to pleasure himself: the reaction of Sayle, and others, to the sexual overtones of 'The Story of a Panic' when it appeared six weeks before would have made him think anew about his sexuality, and he perhaps wished that his mother had ever been able to give him more of an explanation than mere suppression. If only she had chosen, like 'New Lucy', to see 'the whole world of decency and respectability in flames'[12] rather than consign her son to mystification. And yet it is possible that it was the incomprehension, and the calmness, of Morgan's response that led to his determination to understand it; and to his wanting to explore the hidden aspects of behaviour in his writing. Certainly, he could think resignedly, he had not been traumatised; yet did this in itself signify a disappointing *lack* of neurosis, a thoroughly sensible attitude to life that would not augur well for the intensities of fiction?

With all this myriad of thoughts going through his head Morgan was, on this particular September day (the 9th), in a state of heightened awareness and receptivity. As with Ravello, he would later attribute his 'inspiration', the 'sacred and mysterious . . . process of writing',[13] to the spirit of the place, the *genius loci*. Figsbury Rings, ever afterwards sanctified in Morgan's mind as being the birthplace of *The Longest Journey*, is indeed a magic spot. Two miles north-east of Salisbury, 'a hill fort of the early Iron Age, consisting of a bank and outer ditch enclosing about 15 acres',[14] it is a beautiful, grassy hillock with views all around; when the sun shines and the wind blows gently in the long grass, the Rings still seem mystic and timeless. Here Morgan exchanged a few words with a lame shepherd boy, and would claim that it was he who crystallised his dormant thoughts about half-brothers and landscape. In a curious way, too, for Morgan the novel itself gave birth. 'There was reciprocation . . . I received, I created, I restored, and for many years the Wiltshire landscape remained haunted by my fictional ghosts.' In other words the scenery became an image of Morgan's emotional state; then through the act of writing 'a whole landscape is charged with an emotion, permanent as its origins were transitory.'[15]

This would make a good set piece, yet it was Morgan's own frame of mind that inspired *The Longest Journey*, as much as sacred spots or shepherd boys. He remembered them because of the intensity of the emotions: it was not they themselves that created the emotions.

The Rings were curious rather than impressive. Neither embankment was over twelve feet high, and the grass on them had not the exquisite green of Old Sarum, but was gray and wiry. But Nature (if she arranges anything) had arranged that from them, at all events, there should be a view. The whole system of the country lay spread before Rickie . . . Here is the heart of our island: the Chilterns, the North Downs, the South Downs radiate hence. The fibres of England unite in Wiltshire, and did we condescend to worship her, here we should erect our national shrine.

Morgan's own feelings about Wiltshire were such that he himself did 'condescend to worship her'.[16] Although in the past he had enjoyed his bicycle rides into the countryside round Tonbridge; although he had been passionately in love with Hertfordshire; although he admired the green hills of Northumberland around the home of his (Forster) Uncle Willie; despite all these forewarnings his feelings were now quite unexpected. The day at Figsbury Rings with his sandwiches, his mackintosh and his book was to change his mode of thinking for ever. Everything in his work was in future to be affected by this newly perceived identification with, and passion for, the English countryside.

Yet love for the countryside was not, for someone like Morgan, in itself enough. It cannot be separated from love for others. This is why Rickie's visit to 'Cadbury Rings' is the climax of *The Longest Journey*: here, having surveyed England in all its glory, he learns that Stephen is his brother but, fatally rejects him. And this is why, having told her sister that she intends to marry Mr Wilcox, Margaret Schlegel is at that moment so conscious of the timeless beauty of the English landscape as seen from the Purbeck Hills. 'The water crept over the mud-flats towards the gorse and the blackened heather ... England was alive, throbbing through all her estuaries, crying for joy through the mouths of all her gulls, and the north wind, with contrary motion, blew stronger against her rising seas.'[17] So, when, at Figsbury Rings, Morgan met a shepherd boy with a club foot, he became for him symbolic of the English countryside and of England; his wisdom and simplicity 'assures my opinion that the English *can* be the greatest men in the world: he was miles greater than an Italian ... I suppose I shan't again see one of the most remarkable people I've ever met.'[18]

It was with his thoughts full of Wiltshire that Morgan helped Lily move into the house that they had decided upon: a plain red-brick villa at Weybridge, then a village of some charm near the Thames in Surrey* and only ten miles north of Abinger. Meredith the novelist had once lived there, the Cambridge philosopher McTaggart had been brought up there and Morgan felt, in some kind of wry, ironical mode, that it was just what he deserved. Lily would not allow the country so a return to childhood paradise was out of the question; Morgan's growing reclusiveness and elusiveness refused to countenance central London; with more than a tinge of dismay he must have realised that he was to settle down in exactly the kind of house that so far, in all his thoughts and his writings, he had railed against so consistently.

By now he knew and understood his own potential and his own deficiencies. Rarely would he stray beyond subtle, perceptive, humorous, ironical glances at the English middle class of which he was so much part. Everything he had done in his life so far, everything he had failed to do, confirmed this. And in that case he might as well stick with what he knew – and that involved living at its centre. Weybridge was to be his source material and his inspiration; it would be the base

---

* The Forsters' choice of Surrey not Sussex is in some ways as significant as the Stephens' simultaneous choice of Bloomsbury not Kensington. Surrey is calmer, quieter, nearer to being suburban than the slightly wilder, more defiant Sussex. Charleston is in Sussex: it is hard to imagine it in Surrey.

from where he would comment on this material. Almost as if he were a fortune-teller he half-foresaw that it would be where he would live his novelist's years – and that all six of his novels would be written there. When the last was finished, Aunt Laura would, by a remarkable coincidence of timing, die and leave them her house. Then they would move, and Morgan would write no more novels. For the moment, 'our life is where we sleep and eat'[19] as he had once written from Italy. And this was now Weybridge.

With a population of five thousand, it 'could still claim to be an attractive, country village',[20] combining the rural and urban qualities that both mother and son yearned for. Not quite suburban, like 10 Earls Road, it was more in the Tonbridge mode, while being closer to the centre of village life. Fittingly, for someone who was one day to ask himself 'why do I always find three reasons for everything?'[21] and was always aware of the imagery of the triad, the Forsters' house was in the centre of the village at the apex of a triangle: the High Street with the shops, the hill leading to the station a mile away and Baker Street, then 'a narrow lane with overhanging hedges in some parts'.[22] But the most important aspect of the house, in some ways the most demeaning, was that it was virtually new: it had had only one previous tenant. Morgan would evoke aspects of it in the final version of *A Room with a View* when George comes with his father to live in a newly built house near the smugly old Windy Corner.

The woods had opened to leave space for a sloping triangular meadow. Pretty cottages lined it on two sides, and the upper and third side was occupied by a new stone church, expensively simple, with a charming shingled spire . . . Some great mansions were at hand, but they were hidden in the trees. The scene suggested a Swiss alp rather than the shrine and centre of a leisured world, and was only marred by two ugly little villas . . .

'Cissie' was the name of one of these villas, 'Albert' of the other. These titles were not only picked out in shaded Gothic on the garden gates, but appeared a second time on the porches, where they followed the semicircular curve of the entrance arch in block capitals. Albert was inhabited. His tortured garden was bright with geraniums and lobelias and polished shells. His little windows were chastely swathed in Nottingham lace. Cissie was to let . . .

'The place is ruined!' said the ladies mechanically. 'Summer Street will never be the same again.'[23]

Cissie was in part Glendore and its neighbour Redbrae; they were part of a row of six houses, appearing as three semi-detached pairs but separated one from the other by a couple of feet (Morgan would emphasise the detachment). They had been built in 1901–2, and the Forsters took over the lease from the previous tenant in September 1904, paying £55 (£3000) a year. Immediately they changed the name: '"Glendore" is a little trying. In other ways it's not bad: small and somewhat suburban, but not genteel. Wood and field behind.'*24 The name they chose was Harnham, after the part of Salisbury just south of the cathedral, famous for its thirteenth-century bridge, its ford, its water-meadows and its mill. Harnham Hill and the river at the bottom was the view, beyond the cathedral spire, that Morgan would have often gazed at from Maimie's hilltop house to the east of the city; the Englishness and the almost impossible picturesqueness of the scene would have had a special resonance for him that made the name Harnham, even when given to a suburban house, have a certain magic.†

They settled in comfortably enough but Morgan regretted the lack of garden (there was a small one but compared to Rooksnest and to Dryhurst it barely counted) and found the house small. Although of course spacious by some standards, it had only a drawing-room, dining-room and two large bedrooms over them; while the attics contained bedrooms for the two maids, who were now to become an important and permanent part of Lily and Morgan's lives ('the doings of Ruth and Agnes are far more important to her than mine' he would one day remark25) and a tiny study. The house was further proof that even though the Forsters' income was substantial, yet they chose to live in almost incomprehensibly straitened circumstances. They did not think of keeping a carriage; or shopping anywhere except the Army & Navy; or professing to even the merest glimmer of affluence: they resisted any notion of being thought anything but carefully middle class. Could it be that Morgan thought of his money as a millstone and longed to shrug off his wealth?

For wealth it was. Unless the Forsters' private income had been lost or frittered, and there is no proof that it was, they were the recipients

---

* As the result of a muddle, a plaque in Forster's memory was, until recently, on the wrong house – number 20, called Hailsham. From north-east to south-west along Monument Green the houses were 16 and 17, 18 and 19, 20 and 21: Harnham was 19. In 1925 Harnham, the former Glendore, was renamed Revard, which it still is today.

† Constable painted the real Harnham several times in the 1820s, cf. for example the 22″ × 30″ oil painting 'Harnham Bridge looking towards Salisbury Cathedral' sold in London in 1992; his sketches of 'Harnham Bridge' are in the British Museum and in the V & A.

of about £20,000 a year in modern terms. Yet even this was less than the fortunes enjoyed by Margaret, Helen and Tibby in *Howards End*. Is it merely chance that one of the most powerful scenes in the book is that in which Helen explains to her brother Tibby that she proposes to dispossess herself of part (a part only) of her fortune by making it over to the Basts?

'What is the sum?'
  'Five thousand.'
  'Good God alive!' said Tibby, and went crimson.
  'Now, what is the good of driblets? To go through life having done one thing – to have raised one person from the abyss; not these puny gifts of shillings and blankets – making the gray more gray. No doubt people will think me extraordinary.'
  'I don't care a damn what people think!' cried he, heated to unusual manliness of diction. 'But it's half what you have.'
  'Not nearly half.' She spread out her hands over her soiled skirt. 'I have far too much, and we settled at Chelsea last spring that three hundred a year is necessary to set a man on his feet. What I give will bring in a hundred and fifty between two. It isn't enough.'
  He could not recover . . .[26]

If Helen proposed to give away £5000, and if that would bring in £150 a year, the percentage of income on invested capital was 3 per cent. That meant that if she received £600 a year, her portion of the capital was £20,000 or, in modern terms, nearly a million pounds. Morgan and Lily had originally had £7000 (£300,000) from Eddie and £8000 (£400,000) from Marianne; assuming it stayed much the same and that they too received income at 3 per cent, they would have received £450 (£20,000) a year. We are assuming that they *did not touch capital*, that sacred tenet of the middle classes. Yet sometimes they did: 7 August 1904, 'Sold out £3000 [£150,000] Canada Stock'[27] noted Morgan. What could have happened to it? Perhaps Morgan was behaving like Helen, who had begun 'bungling with her money by this time, and had even sold out her shares in the Nottingham and Derby Railway. For some weeks she did nothing. Then she reinvested, and, owing to the good advice of her stockbrokers became rather richer than she had been before.'[28] Or perhaps he gave it away. Yet, if so, to whom?

Morgan knew enough about the power of the men who built the railways to be ironically accepting of the good sense of investing in them; indeed, he shows Mrs Munt safeguarding her nephew and nieces' future by insisting on the safety of Home Rails. It was because of the railways that Tibby received £800 (£40,000) a year and Helen and Margaret £600 (£30,000)* each, sums large enough for an entire family: Henry Beveridge to his wife, 1894, 'I will allow you £800 [£45,000] a year, or £60 a month and £10 at Christmas. Out of this and your own income you will keep the house, educate the children and with the balance of my income I shall clothe myself etc.'[29] Morgan understood that where money was concerned the family was the prime imperative. When he mentioned selling the Canada Stock he added 'per pare tacere i parenti': roughly translated this means 'in order to keep the relations quiet'. Money was another reason why he could not be responsible for his own freedom, his own autonomy: money was the shackles tying him to his mother.

As autumn came in 1904 Morgan began his new life, sitting in his little study with its view over fields at the back and Monument Green at the front. The small green space onto which the houses fronted was where children played round the monument to the Duchess of York that had once been removed from Covent Garden. This was the perspective that Morgan looked at as he worked; he and Lily were, too, rather less standoffish than they used to be. When he wrote in November that 'the best families are to call presently' he was not being entirely ironic, and when he added that 'I hope to join the new Literary Society, if I am duly invited'[30] he did indeed join and even gave a few papers. Remarking that after his father's death 'my mother retired with me into the country',[31] what Morgan did not add was that in Weybridge Lily was almost sociable. But was there ever the impression that she was acting the part? Did she ever recognise herself in Mrs Honeychurch (alleged by Morgan to have been based on Lily's mother)? She and her late husband had at first been mistaken by their neighbours 'for the remnants of an indigenous aristocracy'.

He was inclined to be frightened, but his wife accepted the situation without either pride or humility. 'I cannot think what people are doing,' she would say, 'but it is extremely fortunate for the children.' She called everywhere;

* In the original version of the manuscript (p 59) the sisters began by having £1200 a year each, £900 was substituted, then £600; Tibby had £1500, then £1000, then £800.

her calls were returned with enthusiasm, and by the time people found out that she was not exactly of their milieu they liked her, and it did not seem to matter. When Mr Honeychurch died, he had the satisfaction – which few honest solicitors despise – of leaving his family rooted in the best society obtainable.[32]

The mental energy that Morgan had felt during this year did not diminish in Weybridge, indeed a settled home and a permanent room of his own spurred him on. He was pondering *The Longest Journey*. He was steadily writing *Where Angels Fear to Tread*. And he was intermittently working on 'New Lucy', although he was soon to abandon this and would not re-start for three years. In addition, he wrote two short stories. One, 'The Other Side of the Hedge', was written in the early autumn and published in the *Independent* that November. It is fantasy, with few pretensions to reality; as Morgan was himself to note in 1944, 'I like the idea of fantasy, of muddling up the actual and the impossible until the reader isn't sure which is which.'[33] The impossible in this story is a young man who finds himself in a dream-like utopia which he cannot understand; it appears to him to be a prison, whereas in fact he had *been* in prison, 'the other side of the hedge'. The actual is the obviously recognisable setting of the two concentric circles at Figsbury Rings, allegorically the outside where one is imprisoned and the inside where one is timeless and free. At the end of the story the narrator sees a man 'returning for the night to the hills, with a scythe over his shoulder' and 'I saw that he was my brother'.[34] It would be the theme of *The Longest Journey*; here, in fantastical form, Morgan was trying it out.

The other story he wrote was a ghost story. Its starting-off point was perhaps a diary entry for the previous December when Morgan mentioned a man who 'breathed his friend's name on a mirror and couldn't rub it out';[35] Figsbury was again an influence in an incident of a pipe-smoking shepherd. Morgan seems to have been encouraged by the editor of *Temple Bar*, which had published nothing of his since 'Albergo Empedocle' a year earlier, to try writing a ghost story, for in *The Longest Journey* Rickie is told by the editor of the *Holborn*, 'Write a really good ghost story and we'd take it at once'.[36] But when Morgan told Trevy in January that 'I somehow think I am too refined to write a ghost story'[37] he was being sensibly self-aware: 'The Purple Envelope', eventually published in 1972, is curiously unsatisfactory.

In a way the failure of this story was beneficial: it helped to show Morgan what he was good at, since mostly he did not feel very good at anything. On New Year's Eve, the day before he was twenty-six, he assessed his life as he saw it (something he was often to do) privately in his diary. It makes rather melancholy reading, yet is tinged with optimism:

My life is now straightening into something – rather sad & dull to be sure, & I want to set it & me down, as I see us now . . . The truth is I'm having a very difficult life: I never come into contact with any one's work, & that makes things difficult. I may sit year after year in my pretty sitting room, watching things grow more unreal, because I'm afraid of being remarked . . . Unimportant as my youth has been, it's been less unimportant than I expected & than other people think. And ardently as I desire beauty & strength & a truer outlook, I don't despise myself, or think life isn't worth while.[38]

14

Where Angels Fear to Tread

And what, so far, of the friends with whom Morgan has come to be so much associated, of Bloomsbury, of Virginia and Lytton and Duncan and Carrington and the rest? It was in the very month that the Forsters moved into Harnham that the children of the late Sir Leslie Stephen* were settling in to 46 Gordon Square in Bloomsbury. 'Instead of Morris wall-papers with their intricate patterns we decorated our walls with washes of plain distemper', Virginia Woolf remembered. 'We were full of experiments and reforms. We were going to do without table napkins ... we were going to paint; to write; to have coffee after dinner instead of tea at nine o'clock.'¹ None of this would have been possible or even desirable at Harnham: life there continued to be robustly bourgeois. As Virginia was to write to Morgan about a visit to Weybridge when he was in India: 'All the family silver was out. The maid ... had a new apron on ... Perhaps though I am wrong about the silver and the apron. That may be your ordinary style.'²

It was. Lily, resolutely, continued the style of life to which she had always adhered and Morgan acquiesced: Harnham would never have painted caryatids round the fireplace or Omega fabric on the sofa or even garlic or foreign cheeses in the kitchen. On both occasions that the Forsters returned from Italy, they did not bring back pottery or tapestry cushions; theirs remained the style of Clapham and of Tonbridge, very English, perfectly comfortable but quite un-painterly, un-arty. The Weybridge house was not, in fact, altogether different from the Sawston house in *The Longest*

* He left £15,700 (£825,000) to his children, the same amount as Lily and Morgan had received from Eddie and Marianne; Morgan and Virginia thus shared the same level of affluence, but were to take the same quiet pride in their earnings.

Journey, with its decent water-colours, its Madonnas of acknowledged merit, its strips of brown holland to save the carpet, its palm. Like this house, 'Shelthorpe', it was sensible and unfussy and, Morgan suggested, if able to speak it would have said 'I contain works of art and a microscope and books. But I do not live for any of these things or suffer them to disarrange me.'[3]

So Morgan's style, his aesthetic response, was not to resemble those of his Bloomsbury contemporaries. That is how he wanted it: the same paradox, as throughout his life, that he railed against Weybridge and yet liked and needed it. Frequently, and kindly, his growing circle of friends would try to draw him physically into their orbit. He would always refuse. 'Tempted' by a suggestion that he should share a cottage in the country, he nevertheless turned it down. 'Weybridge is just nice enough to ask people to,' he wrote, with typical self-deprecation, 'and that means I am very often at home for weekends.'[4] What he did not add, despite the implication of week-day freedom, was that for years the immovable 'given' in his life was the last train back to Weybridge, the 11.50 from Waterloo* getting in at 12.32 and after that the twenty-minute walk from the station and, in a jug in the drawing-room, the cocoa on which a skin had formed and which Morgan would gently fish out with a spoon.

Yet the regime suited him. As the years went by and Morgan's circle of friends broadened he would often stay overnight with people, with Edward Marsh in Gray's Inn or, famously (because Lawrence would offend Morgan with his outspokenness), with the Lawrences at Greatham. Generally, however, he would use Weybridge as an excuse to escape from enforced, and especially late-night, gregariousness. It was only after he and Lily moved to West Hackhurst in 1925 that he acquired a room of his own in Bloomsbury. He was by then nearly fifty and less tolerant of the tyranny both of the last train and of Lily. Gomshall Station in Surrey was much further from where they lived than the one in Weybridge had been; and, most important of all, Morgan was at last, and elatedly, an active homosexual and needed to escape the ambiance of the seventy-year-old Lily.

For the moment he made forays to London and returned at

---

* In fact he used to go from Charing Cross, as being more accessible, catch any train for the two-minute journey to Waterloo East, then walk across the footbridge to catch the Waterloo to Weybridge train.

night. But in the years during which he was at the peak of his creative powers, 1903–13, his circle of friendship was not very wide. Later on, of course, it was to be different, and time-consumingly different. 'Lust, fun, kindness, and fear'[5] were what he would one day describe as his principal distractions, for he was to be an assiduous 'keeper-upper'. Luckily for his fiction, his assiduousness was as yet unnecessary. Or was it the other way round – that when his energies were no longer channelled into his writing then they could be devoted to his friends? It is hard to know – success brings friends and Morgan had always wanted friendship but had been too diffident brashly to cultivate it: one of the myriad of reasons that have been suggested for his 'failure' to continue writing novels may have been his 'success' at friendship. At Weybridge, in the years before the First World War, his success was less conspicuous.

There were friends, and close ones. There was Dent, George Barger, Bob Trevelyan, Meredith, and soon there were to be others. Yet none was as important to Morgan as his inner life at home in his room at Harnham: hardly surprising that he wrote in his diary on New Year's Eve, 'self consciousness will do for me if I'm not careful – drive me into books, or the piano.'[6] For it was at this period of his life that music became increasingly important. He, like Lucy, was perhaps 'no dazzling *exécutante*; her runs were not at all like strings of pearls, and she struck no more right notes than was suitable for one of her age and situation.'[7] But he spent many hours playing peacefully in the drawing-room at Harnham. He went to concerts whenever he could. In later years he listened to the gramophone. And he incorporated music into his novels, to such an extent that he was to be called by his future friend Benjamin Britten 'our most musical novelist':[8] from the opera scene in *Where Angels Fear to Tread* to the description of Beethoven's Fifth Symphony in *Howards End* to the more subtle musical imagery of the trial scene in *A Passage to India*, in all three and in the other novels music, as Morgan himself put it, would be 'deep beneath the arts'[9] and beneath his life.

In the late autumn of 1904, at Harnham, Morgan finally finished his first novel: how appropriate that although he had made beginnings in other houses, other rooms, the house where he was to write all of his six works of fiction was the one where he completed his first.

162

There is no way of knowing whether he polished *Where Angels Fear to Tread* a great deal and copied it out, or whether he wrote it straight off. Yet the few weeks it took him to write, and the fact that at the same time he was writing three short stories and continuing with 'New Lucy', suggests the latter; and it has a certain *élan*, an unforced quality, that perhaps comes from something approaching spontaneity. There were, naturally, some changes (the kind that nowadays, with word processors, can no longer be traced) but they were minor. The overall impression is of a novel written with confidence and ease, as though Morgan knew exactly where he was going and what he was doing. (But do I know where I'm going the biographer asks herself, the moment having come when somehow – but how? – she must convey, not merely précis, the plot, and at the same time try and convey why, to her, this is one of the most perfect novels of the twentieth century, aware that if she uses hyperboles like these her ever-vigilant husband will write 'truly wonderful' in the margin and she will realise that, yes, she has gone over the top. But then what vocabulary will do? Quoting would do. But that great slab of prose centred on the page might repel. Suffice it to say that if she *were* to type out, it would be an extract from Chapter 6: for this is the chapter that makes clear that Morgan, aged twenty-six, had *nothing more to learn* about prose style, narrative, characterisation, insight and all the other qualities that need to be part of a great novel.)

The central character is the Morgan-like figure of Philip Herriton. When his brother's widow marries the son of an Italian dentist hers is not the Dantesque New Life that she had hoped. After she has died giving birth to a son, Philip and his sister Harriet* travel to Italy in order to return the baby to Sawston values; but because of their ineptitude and insensitivity, they are the cause of the baby's death. Philip and Miss Abbott both realise that they too love Gino, although Philip's realisation is obliquely stated and it is possible to believe that it is Caroline he loves.†

'The object of the book', Morgan told Trevy in October, 'is the improvement of Philip'; and he went on to justify the violent overtones of the scene when Philip tells Gino that the baby is dead:

* Harriet = Old German 'house ruler'.
† The plot has some similarities to that of Henry James's *The Ambassadors* published two years earlier: Strether is sent to Paris to bring home Chad, said to be entangled with a less than respectable female.

'P. is a person who has scarcely ever felt the physical forces that are banging about in the world, and he couldn't get good and understand by spiritual suffering alone.' Morgan then described the scene as 'sacramental' (a word he would resurrect in 1956 with reference to Marianne's dying request for some of Battersea Rise's milk) and asked Trevy to tell him whether he was 'unduly facetious'.[10]

Where Angels Fear to Tread is, however, about far more than Philip's growth in self-knowledge: it is about the inhibited values of suburbia versus the warm lack of inhibition of Italy, and yet is subtle enough to show the strengths as well as the flaws of both; it is about the importance of the bodily and the intellectual and the spiritual; above all it is a comedy. And it was only because it *was* a comedy that Morgan felt able to write it, and with such freedom: when Lily recognised herself or Morgan she would think merely that he was poking fun, was laughing conspiratorially at them and their funny ways. She would, or could, ignore the heartfeltness behind Philip's attitude to life and to his mother.

All his life he had been her puppet. She had let him worship Italy, and reform Sawston – just as she had let Harriet be Low Church. She had let him talk as much as he liked. But when she wanted a thing she always got it . . . Her life, he saw, was without meaning. To what purpose was her diplomacy, her insincerity, her continued repression of vigour? Did they make anyone better or happier? . . . But he could not rebel. To the end of his days he would probably go on doing what she wanted . . .

What would Mrs Mawe, Laura, Louisa and Maimie have thought of this if it had not been disguised as a joke? And what would they have thought of Morgie's state of mind if they had read anything of himself into Philip's resigned: 'I seem fated to pass through the world without colliding with it or moving it . . . I don't die – I don't fall in love'?*[11] They would have been deeply disconcerted. But Morgan, like Philip, had found that the way to avoid confrontation with the tragic, unbearable aspects of life was to laugh at them, to be deflationary: he transmuted the self-deprecating quality that had been his carapace throughout life into his art. His first novel was in some ways the first modern novel; and it arrived ten years before the first modern poem, Eliot's 'The Love Song of J. Alfred Prufrock'.

---

* And in the unfinished 'Ralph and Tony' Margaret thinks: '"There is I myself. Have I not watched and studied long enough?"'[12]

There was one Victorian writer whose tone was modern too, although he was never mentioned by Morgan except, once, to observe that Goldie must have studied him: Arthur Hugh Clough. There are so many similarities between Morgan's work and Clough's that it is impossible not to conclude that he had a vast influence, if not directly then by some curious form of osmosis. Clough's forty-page 'Amours de Voyage' (1858) is arguably the most memorable poem of the Victorian era: it has flaws, but these are insignificant compared with its great strength – its unique tone of voice, a tone that was somehow transmuted by Morgan into his first novel. The poem is in the form of letters home written by Claude to his friend Eustace, in which he describes the siege of Rome in 1849 and his friendship with Mary Trevellyn and her family, 'middle-class people these, bankers very likely, not wholly / Pure of the taint of the shop.' Like Lucy Honeychurch, Claude explores Rome – 'Murray, as usual, / Under my arm' (Murray had not at this stage been supplanted by Baedeker) – and sees a man killed. The event is important for him and deters him from whole-hearted pursuit of Mary: the main theme of the poem is the conflict between engagement and disengagement, between the urge to commit oneself and to act and the urge to opt out and to remain a detached onlooker. In so many ways Claude is Philip Herriton fifty years earlier.

> There are two different kinds, I believe, of human attraction:
> One which simply disturbs, unsettles, and makes you uneasy,
> And another that poises, retains, and fixes and holds you.
> I have no doubt, for myself, in giving my voice for the latter.
> I do not wish to be moved, but growing where I was growing,
> There more truly to grow, to live where as yet I had languished.
> I do not like being moved: for the will is excited; and action
> Is a most dangerous thing; I tremble for something factitious,
> Some malpractice of the heart and illegitimate process;
> We are so prone to these things with our terrible notions of duty.[13]

Here is the theme of Morgan's first novel; and the last line in particular summarises both the theme and the tone. Indeed the concept of 'terrible notions of duty' is Morgan's theme *par excellence*.*

His characteristic tone, and his realism, were first displayed in *Where Angels Fear to Tread* and were, in future, to be used only

---

* 'From a Sense of Duty' was to be an alternative, rejected title for *Where Angels Fear to Tread*.

in the novels: he would confine fantasy almost entirely to his stories. Apart from a tinge of melodrama in the death of Lilia and later of her baby, the book could have been written in the first person: Philip Herriton is a great deal like Morgan (despite Morgan's trying to distract the reader from seeing this resemblance by pretending that Philip was based on Dent). The Sawston details and the Monteriano ones in most respects neatly fitted Tunbridge Wells/Weybridge and San Gimignano. Even the chronology was accurate, allowing for the curious and perhaps decoy-like way in which it is deliberately set forward by a year: the story begins in November and ends nearly two years later in August, and Morgan wrote on the manuscript that the years were 1902–4. Yet 'at the time of Lilia's death Philip Herriton was just twenty-four years of age',[14] which for Morgan was the January of 1903; thus the action should run from November 1901 (when he and Lily set out on their trip to Italy) to August 1903 (when they came back the second time). He was, in his first novel, being quite traditionally autobiographical; but to avoid charges of complete self-projection he slightly muddled the chronology, already conscious that readers would scrutinise the author as well as the book.

The change in others' perception of him was to come now, in the spring of 1905. Morgan went, briefly, to Cambridge; here, because of one of the three 1904 stories,

instead of an undergraduate, I was famous: those who had read my story liked it. The change was curious and sudden: and, tho' I like praise & being told that I understand human nature, I think honestly I prefer being treated as nobody by 'nobodies'.[15]

This was genuinely meant: he never looked for fame. At the same time his *amour propre* was delicately balanced, and if wounded could take a long time to heal. What he wanted was not to be patronised, but to be treated friendlily; consorting with the upper ten thousand or the literary élite would have no appeal. He would not, like J. M. Barrie, use his success to cultivate titled ladies or, like Galsworthy, to live in servanted luxury; when he became famous nothing about him would greatly change.

For a modicum of fame was not far away (true fame would wait another twenty years). Morgan had by now sent what he privately thought of as his 'Gino' novel, had considered calling 'Rescue' and had finally planned to call 'Monteriano', to Hugh Meredith. He replied gratifyingly, saying that he had just been reading Turgenev and that George Meredith and Morgan were 'the only living English writers who can stand beside him'. No wonder Morgan was later to embroider a close friendship with HOM into a love affair: the effect of this sentence on him, on anyone, must have been so strong as to be almost erotic. 'You really understand tragedy'[16] was HOM's conclusion; yet Morgan had quite enough self-knowledge to discount this comment and as for the book being a great work, 'I do not think it will ever seem so to me: it is not more than careful and praiseworthy'.[17] A funny novella partly set in English suburbia, concerning some rather unprepossessing people who are obtuse and insensitive: it does not seem the stuff of greatness. Morgan's only preoccupation was whether he could get it accepted for publication.

During these weeks, while he was enjoying the knowledge that he had now finished a novel, Morgan was lecturing weekly at Guildford and, since it was the third course he had given, he applied to be promoted to the ordinary, i.e. permanent, list of lecturers. But he was rejected, on the grounds of inexperience, 'unless there had been some brilliant success to counterbalance the lack of experience'[18] and there had apparently not been. Despite his published stories Morgan still felt, and was made to feel, an outsider. Evidence of this lies in a short story he wrote at this time. 'The Helping Hand' was, as the modern editor was cuttingly to remark when it was eventually published in 1972, 'almost unique within Forster's fiction in hardly even hinting at any values more universal or less worldly-wise than the inadvisability, when plagiarized, of squealing too soon'.[19] Morgan, apparently, was still interested in the kind of stories that Edith Wharton was managing to sell, for his story resembled those in her recent volume *The Descent of Man* and in particular one called 'Expiation'.

Although 'The Helping Hand' had obvious weaknesses, it is significant that it was never destroyed: Morgan liked its focus, the work of an Italian painter named 'Giovanni da Empoli', and its references to the Museo Poldi-Pezzoli which he had visited in Milan. But as well as the Wharton influence there was the impetus of a plagiarising book on Verrocchio that had been published that year by a vicar's wife named Mrs Cruttwell. If Lady Anstey in the story was based on her then he may have had worries about libel, as well as second thoughts about writing in a genre that did not really suit him. Then, just as he had finished the story and was wondering what to do with it, a new author came into his life. He would be one of the three, along with Jane Austen and George Meredith, to whom he would always pay tribute (Proust was only to have influence on *A Passage to India*).

In early February Morgan had finished reading Butler's *The Way of All Flesh*, written in the 1870s but not published until 1903;* it became, for him, a key text. When, years later, Virginia Woolf declared 'that in or about December, 1910, human character changed'[20] and that the first signs of change were recorded in the books of Samuel Butler, and in *The Way of All Flesh* in particular, she might have had Morgan in mind. *Howards End* (1910) was to be the epitome of a change that had first begun, for Morgan, in the early spring five years before.†

Partly Butler mattered because 'he taught me how to look at money when I was young':[22] Morgan meant by this that he taught him how to overturn taboos about money in an era when a child was told, as Morgan was, 'Dear, don't talk about money, it's ugly'.[23] Without Butler, Morgan would not have felt free enough to make the money ethic the central theme of *Howards End*, the novel in which he was to try to resolve his ambivalent feelings about living on inherited wealth; to try to work out who had the greater integrity, the Schlegels for living on 'fortune' but being honest about its origins (and, in Helen's case, trying to give some of it away) or the Wilcoxes for earning it but refusing, honestly, to mention it; and to try to determine whether Leonard Bast would have been 'saved' had he accepted Schlegel money. One of the ironies of the novel is that inwardly Leonard wanted to accept the money. It was his pride and class-consciousness that would not let him; yet, Morgan intimated, he would have been more honest, indeed would have lived, had he had the courage to do so. At the same time Helen displayed her honesty by admitting that once they had made love 'I want never to see him again, though it sounds appalling. I wanted to give him money and feel finished.'[24]

---

* Its editor upon Butler's death was, as Morgan must have realised, Ted Streatfeild's nephew Richard.
† Butler's book at first 'sold very slowly'. It was reprinted, 'widely reviewed and highly praised, but still hung fire. Then, in 1910, the flames caught . . .'[21]

It does sound appalling, and Morgan could only voice it because of Butler; what Butler helped him to voice, also, was a deep hostility to Victorian sanctifying of the family. Morgan loved the idea of continuity, of happy domesticity, and indeed lacked the courage to escape his own familial noose; what he longed for was for others to be able to escape it *if they wanted*. The 'breakdown' of family life in the twentieth century, the loosening of the patriarchal and matriarchal grip, was a Butlerian theme that Morgan took very much as his own. This combined, as well, with a new, questioning attitude to religion, one that made *The Way of All Flesh* the perfect partner for *Principia Ethica*. Butler's hero Ernest Pontifex thinks:

The more he read in this spirit the more the balance seemed to lie in favour of unbelief, till, in the end, all further doubt became impossible, and he saw plainly enough that, whatever else might be true, the story that Christ had died, come to life again, and been carried from earth through clouds into the heavens could not now be accepted by unbiassed people. It was well he had found it out soon. In one way or another it was sure to meet him sooner or later. He would probably have seen it years ago if he had not been hoodwinked by people who were paid for hoodwinking him.[25]

Butler's prose style, also, made its impact. 'The frontal full-dress presentation of an opinion often repels me', Morgan would one day remark, 'but if it be insidiously slipped in sidewise I may receive it, and Butler is a master of the oblique.'[26] Above all he always admired the way Butler 'might indulge in private prejudices, but he never bowed to the prejudices of others, he suspected authority, he took nothing on trust, and he had no use for dogmas'.*[27]

There is a passage halfway through *Where Angels Fear to Tread* when Lilia, by now married for six months, feels especially unhappy; and Morgan, quite without irony, lists the things she misses most in Sawston. It was almost as if he looked into his future in Weybridge and with something approaching happiness, certainly acceptance, visualised the rhythm of the years, undramatic, unintellectual, but friendly and harmonious:

It was September. Sawston would be just filling up after the summer

---

* In 1914 Morgan thought he might write a book about Butler; but he abandoned the idea.

holidays. People would be running in and out of each other's houses all along the road. There were bicycle gymkhanas, and on the 30th Mrs Herriton would be holding the annual bazaar in her garden for the C.M.S. It seemed impossible that such a free, happy life could exist.[28]

This was Morgan's voice. He could see the disadvantages of his life. But he had a largeness of vision, an empathy with the everyday lives led by ordinary people, not to despise the comforts and securities by which he was surrounded. It would be the theme of his life and why, fret as he might, he would ultimately choose not to give them up.

15

Nassenheide

In the spring of 1905 Morgan did, however, give up Weybridge for a while. The previous autumn he had had the idea that there might be amusement and interest in finding a family with whom he could lodge and learn German. Eventually a friend from Cambridge named Sydney Waterlow (whose life was alleged to have been blighted by not having been elected an Apostle[1]) told Morgan about Elizabeth von Arnim, an aunt of his who lived on a large country estate near Stettin in Pomerania in northern Germany. She always had a tutor for her three small daughters and preferred Cambridge men recommended by Sydney. The daughters, and the tutoring, did not tempt Morgan much; Germany, and a definite occupation, did. And then there was the curious fact that his employer was a novelist: she had written the best-selling *Elizabeth and her German Garden* and the daughters were the April, May and June babies described in the book. Morgan agreed to go; it was to be the first time in his life he had travelled abroad without Lily.

When, in the 1950s, his employer's daughter decided to write a biography of her mother, Morgan contributed his reminiscences. He then reworked these by broadcasting a talk called 'Recollections of Nassenheide'. The opening sentences were so characteristic that no listener, switching on the Third Programme unawares, could have failed to realise who was speaking. 'Please open this book on page 128. There you will see a photograph of me. I am a slim youth, for the photograph is over half a century old, and I am standing beside another and more solid young man.'[2] And there, in the issue of *The Listener* that reprinted the talk, which was in fact the issue that bears the date of Morgan's eightieth birthday, is the photograph, the French governess and the German governess wearing white aprons, seated on

171

chairs, and standing behind them the German tutor and the English. The former has his arms nonchalantly crossed and his elegant hand is displayed to full advantage on his sleeve where his cuff is properly shot; the English tutor has, despite his stiff collar and handkerchief peeping out of his breast pocket, an altogether less elegant demeanour. Yet he looks so appealing. I want to be liked, he is saying; but why do I never quite feel that I fit in?

Curiously, Morgan did fit in at Nassenheide, and would look back on his summer there as one of the happiest times of his life. There was the self-respect gleaned from doing a job, even if he did only have to teach the girls Greek history or English composition for an hour a day. There was the friendship with the German tutor, Herr Steinweg, with whom he was to keep in touch despite two world wars. There was the two or three hours a day of academic work on the edition of the *Aeneid* that he had promised Goldie he would do for a series he was editing. Above all there was the glorious countryside all about: 'A clear evening, green wheat against the sun, purple shadows of the birch trees on the sand, deer bobbing away over a ploughed field as big as a county – these things, followed by Rhine Music, have made me happy & useless.'³

And there was Morgan's employer. She had been born in Australia and was a cousin of Katherine Mansfield's. Now aged thirty-nine, she had been married to her titled husband for fifteen years (known to the readers of her novels as 'The Man of Wrath') and, after the success of her first book, published her subsequent ones (there were to be twenty-one) under the name 'Elizabeth'. Morgan, or anyway Lily, would certainly have read *Elizabeth and her German Garden* some time in the seven years since it first appeared and would have been familiar with its idyllic portrait of gardening in wide-brimmed hats among scampering children, a cross between Cranford, Sissinghurst and Peter Pan. In reality 'the German Garden itself, about which Elizabeth had so amusingly written, did not make much impression. Later in the summer some flowers – mainly pansies, tulips, roses, salpiglossis – came into bloom ... But there was nothing of a show and Nassenheide appeared to be surrounded by paddocks and shrubberies.'⁴ Morgan, who was often to ponder about the ethics of using and embroidering upon reality (for example in 'The Eternal Moment') was obviously struck by the gardens being so much less beautiful than they appeared in the novel; nor was he alone in his judgement, for one of his successors as tutor, the future novelist Hugh

Walpole, was to describe the garden two years later as 'beautiful in a wild rather uncouth kind of way, but it is a garden of trees rather than flowers'.[5] (Recently, one of Elizabeth's admirers has remarked defensively that 'Forster must have been too much taken up with proof-reading to pay attention to the garden.'[6])

Elizabeth's book is rather unreadable nowadays and does her some disservice, for she went on to write some excellent novels without a tinge of the archness with which her first one was so annoyingly redolent. Her finest achievement was to be *Vera* (1921) with its devastating picture of the bullying she endured from her second husband, Bertrand Russell's brother Francis. The novel reflects, in some slight respects, the influence of Morgan, but the one that was to pay most obvious homage to his work was *The Enchanted April* (1922). Its starting-off point could have been the passage in *Where Angels Fear to Tread* when Caroline Abbott declares that she hates the respectability and petty unselfishness of Sawston. 'Petty selfishness', Philip corrects her, but

'Petty unselfishness,' she repeated. 'I have got an idea that everyone here spent their lives in making little sacrifices for objects they didn't care for, to please people they didn't love; that they never learned to be sincere – and, what's as bad, never learned how to enjoy themselves . . .'[7]

In Elizabeth's book four women manage to escape to Italy for a month, to leave behind seeing about the dinner and the fish: 'And how astonishing to feel this sheer bliss, for here she was, not doing and not going to do a single unselfish thing, not going to do a thing she didn't want to do.'[8] In a much lighter way than for Philip Herriton or Lucy Honeychurch the experience of Italy sets them free.

The Enchanted April was written many years after Morgan stayed at Nassenheide and may well have been influenced by his Italian novels regardless of his friendship; but Elizabeth realised at the time that her tutor was unusual and was always greatly interested in, though often critical of, his work. June 1923: 'Re-read E. M. Forster's *Howard's End* . . . He has a curious effect of sidling up to one with his whimsies – then suddenly real power.'[9] Her comments when she first read *Where Angels Fear to Tread* had been much less favourable. 'She read ch. 1–3, and said it was very clever, but most unattractive, and she felt as if she wanted a bath,' wrote Morgan to Lily. 'Then she read ch. 4, and said it was really beautiful, and she wanted to retract. Now she has read ch. 6 – you wouldn't remember, but it was the one that you rather liked – and has gone back to her original opinion.'[10] Yet Morgan was privately disconcerted by his impression that 'Gr. [the *Gräfin* or Countess] thinks I write better than she does & is distressed at it . . . I think I do think little of myself, but then I think a good deal about it.'[11]

One reason for his thinking about it was that Blackwood's, to whom he had sent his manuscript in February to see if they might publish it in instalments in their magazine, had now offered to publish it as a book. The terms, which Morgan professed to think unfavourable but none the less accepted, were nothing on the first 300 copies, 10 per cent on the next thousand, 15 per cent up to 2500 and one shilling (£2.50) a copy thereafter.* And having had some regrets about the publishers (Methuen or Heinemann) that would have been his first choice if he had not had an immediate offer from Blackwood's, Morgan acknowledged that 'it is wonderful luck for an unknown to get a 10 chapter book taken at all.'[12] It only remained to choose a title, since Blackwood's disliked 'Monteriano'. Dent suggested 'From a Sense of Duty' and 'Where Angels Fear to Tread'† and the latter was chosen. Lily never liked it, however, and Morgan went on wishing he could have kept Monteriano, even writing it on the title-page when he sent a copy to Leonard Woolf.

The *Gräfin* may have been ambivalent about the young tutor's novel, but having read his new *Independent* article on Cardan, the Renaissance doctor and mathematician, 'she brought it back in a highly chastened mood, saying "You've simply to go on and win, I've no more to say."'[13] This made Morgan even more self-conscious, yet his modesty, his 'dark horse' quality as she put it, made her respect and like him, and although the two novelists were not to keep in touch for long they parted on friendly terms. Something in Morgan's understanding of both eccentricity and creativity made him perfectly tolerant of her changing moods. In this he was unlike Hugh Walpole who was to describe these, puzzled, as '1) Charming, like her books only more so (this does not appear often). 2) Ragging. Now she is unmerciful – attacks you on every side, goes at you until you are reduced to idiocy, and then drops you, limp. 3) Silence. This is most terrible of all.'[14] Yet the *Gräfin*'s moods did once provoke

---

* He was to make £42 (£2000) from two impressions of 1050 and 526 copies each.
† 'For fools rush in where angels fear to tread', Pope's *Essay on Criticism*, line 625, written in 1709 when he was twenty-one.

Morgan into a fierce comment: 'Women are not, I think, sillier than men, but more shameless: as each mood – and most of them are digestive – arrives, they base a view of life on it, and pour out opinions which they must inevitably contradict.'[15]

The months at Nassenheide contributed greatly to Morgan's sense of self-esteem, although what had made him happiest of all was the countryside – and, above all, the house itself. He liked being part of a domestic community, he liked feeling himself at one with ancestral values, he liked observing the busyness that was in many respects no different from that at Battersea Rise less than a century before. He liked living in an ancestral home of the kind that his life had lacked:

The house, with its weathered tile roof, was built of stucco. Its walls were a lovely grey colour, covered over with the green or flaming leaves of Virginia creeper or, in winter, with the delicate tracery of its naked branches. It consisted of two wings, the one facing west being two storeys high, with a gabled roof and a strange little square tower with a flagpole perched on its ridge. The front door, a massive affair, was on this side and led directly into a large vaulted hall . . .[16]

and so on, in the words of Elizabeth's daughter, not of course in Morgan's words since he sent Lily descriptions of the family or amusing incidents or domestic details but few descriptions of the house or countryside however much, privately, these appealed to him.

(The village of Nassenheide is now in Poland and is called Rzedziny. The house has long vanished, destroyed by Russian shells in 1945: all that remains among the undergrowth is the flight of steps that once led up to the back verandah from the garden. Among the silver birch trees there is a low block of flats shared by several Polish families, built with bricks from the old house. The stable block alone has survived; Elizabeth's garden is now only a meadow. The one echo of Morgan that I, privately, could find was that the avenue of chestnut trees, which still exists but is now an avenue leading nowhere, looks very like the avenue of trees leading to the palace in Dewas in India where Morgan stayed in 1921.)

When Morgan left the house in July he knew that he had not only 'coped' with Elizabeth but had turned out 'to be most successful as a teacher, & to have kept wonderful order'.[17] And when the April baby was banished to London to be a paying guest in Earl's Court and go to day school (she had been deemed too fond of a tutor who succeeded

Morgan) it was to him that her sisters wrote in order to beg him to visit her. Then, in 1907, there was a kind of tutors' reunion – except that Mr Gaunt, Mr Forster, Mr Wilson and Mr Stuart had not actually met before because they had not been at Nassenheide together. But they all accompanied Elizabeth and her daughters on a caravan trip round Kent and she later wrote this up in her novel *The Caravaners* (1908).*

The trip took place during the wettest August on record, yet Morgan greatly enjoyed seeing the family again and experiencing the freedom of a horse-drawn wagon: 'Pleasures, all physical, sum up into something else. The happiest felt since Greece.' There was something else as well. Gaunt was about to go out to India and Morgan liked him very much: 'wld. give a lot that India shouldn't swallow him up.'18 Sheltering from the rain in the caravan they would frequently talk about the future facing Gaunt in the East; and when, two years later, Morgan heard that he had died out there of malaria he was extremely upset, as though he had identified with his companion and with his future. Since by then, the summer of 1907, Morgan was growing more and more fond of a young man who was Indian, the imagery of that country began to impress itself on his mind ever more intently.

Morgan did not leave Germany straight away; he had promised Lily that he would visit his Rooksnest tutor Mr Hervey at Kiel and used this piece of filial duty as an excuse to visit other Baltic coast towns. Here he was intrigued by the way genuine beauty blended with bourgeois values: 'The pigs of Rostock become margarine in a fair patrician mansion, pleasingly proportional, delicately carved, and adorned with *vigila et ora*, and other wise remarks,' he wrote in an article called 'Rostock and Wismar' printed in the *Independent* the following summer. Wismar he admired for its beautiful water well ('quite small, and standing as it does in the corner of the market place, might easily be ignored, or mistaken for a newspaper kiosk'†) and for the buildings which, although built from 'the bricks of our Surrey suburbs, look strangely beautiful when set in the midst of

---

* In 1934 the novelist Rachel Ferguson wrote a short, caustic satire on *The Caravaners* in *Celebrated Sequels*.
† This is true today; but what Morgan failed to mention was the startling beauty of the square itself, or that medieval jousting took place there – one reason why the visitor is reminded of Siena. It is a perfect fusion of form and content, architecture and life: which Ruskin would have remarked on appreciatively but to which Morgan seemed virtually oblivious.

bricks that were crude and new some hundreds of years ago.'[19]

As well as observing the burghers of North Germany, Morgan bathed, sunbathed and continued to enjoy the sense of well-being that had been his at Nassenheide. He was aware that when he returned to Weybridge he would know the further joy of being a published author: 'The Eternal Moment' had appeared in the *Independent* in three instalments in June, July and August; advance copies of *Where Angels Fear to Tread* were due any moment.

The reviews, when they came, were gratifying, yet, however modest Morgan professed himself to be, they cannot have been quite unexpected after Meredith's adulatory remarks six months before. The first review appeared on 29 September and it was in *The Times Literary Supplement*; in seventy-five words it found the novel original, well written and sometimes witty. Then came the *Bookman*, at the beginning of October. It must have been one of the few times in Morgan's life as a writer – although he did not comment on it – when he felt that gut-churning excitement and happiness so akin to being in love: it was accepted that he could write.

This is a book which one begins with pleased interest and gradually finds to be astonishing. Its amusing facility becomes amusing cleverness, and then, almost without realising the development, we find that the cleverness is of a larger style than we thought, and the main issues of life are confronting us where we looked for trivialities . . . The story is like the characters, the characters are like the story – at first clever, attractive, and seemingly with no heart, then swept almost into tragedy while scarcely knowing it.

The *Manchester Guardian* disliked the title because it found the book 'not mawkish or sentimental or commonplace' as the title suggested, but approvingly compared Morgan with George Meredith; the *Glasgow Herald* thought it 'the most enjoyable book we have read for many a day'; and so it went on until, just before Christmas, the *Spectator* published a 1000-word, unsigned review of such sensitivity and such perception that Morgan must have been almost surprised that he had been so well understood. When he read that 'the dominant impression left on the mind of the present writer is that under the stress of opportunity primitive instincts reassert themselves in the most carefully educated and studiously repressed natures'[20] a small part of his loneliness and a small part of his introspection must have peeled away; now he would never need to feel that he was speaking into a void.

16

The Longest Journey

He had been away for nearly six months. As the Harwich boat train took him south-west towards London he felt enormously happy to be back in England: a more radical form of escape was something he did not contemplate. The harvest and the early autumn sunshine and the sameness of it all were the things he loved. He was glad to be home. And he wanted to finish the novel he was writing, the one that, more than any of his others, was a hymn of praise to the quintessential Englishness of the English countryside and its beautiful landscape.

Although he had been far from under-occupied at Nassenheide, it seems from the similarity of the ink both on the proofs of *Where Angels Fear to Tread* and on Morgan's letters that his new novel had been begun there. Yet he never once alluded to it in his diary or in his letters, merely telling Lily: 'Should I ever write another book it will be called "The Longest Journey", and the one after that "Windy Corner".'[1] That he had been thinking of writing another novel, another that is apart from the two he was already at work on, is evident from a loose sheet that was found among his papers after his death and is headed 'A "Plot" 17/7/04'. This has as its central theme a young man who 'found happiness at Cambridge' and then made a misguided marriage; his wife 'gradually detached Humphrey from his friends'; he finds he has a brother and wishes to accept him. His wife 'naturally objects, and their dissension begins'. Finally the two men die together; the Epilogue reveals that 'Humphrey's book successful'.[2]

Two months after writing this outline, exactly a year before arriving back in England, Morgan had walked to Figsbury Rings and 'had what may be called a second vision of England'.[3] After that the new novel was never mentioned, except in the offhand way to Lily that implied he was only thinking of writing it. It seems almost impossible, certainly mysterious, that a great novelist can live a domestic, harmonious life with other people, can keep a diary, can have a sense of self-esteem and of the possibility of future success – and yet produce a novel as it were out of nothing. It makes the task of biography almost dispiriting. All one can say is that a novel that *seemed* to have been started in the early summer of 1905 is *known* to have been finished by the winter of 1906: there is nothing more to go on. It is all the more frustrating in that Morgan was to write in 1960, 'I can remember writing it and how excited I was and how absorbed.' Yet he continued, 'it is the only one of my books that has come upon me without my knowledge.'

What he meant was that he was so fond of his novel, in a sense he was so personal about it (it was 'the one I am most glad to have written') that he wrote it as if inspired. But when he added that it was for his other work that 'I have had to look into the lumber-room of my past' he was embroidering on the truth. He may have forgotten his hard work on *The Longest Journey*, it may, in retrospect, have seemed to have emerged almost unconsciously; in fact it was a considered, deliberate re-creation of his own life.

Rickie is a lonely boy with a club-foot whose parents had lived separate lives and had both died when he was fifteen. After an unhappy time at school he is transformed by Cambridge. For various confused, idealistic and self-sacrificing reasons he becomes engaged to Agnes and becomes a schoolmaster at Sawston where she lives with her brother. It is only out of a spirit of duty that he goes to visit his aunt Mrs Failing in Wiltshire at her house called Cadover. She has made a home for an orphaned boy named Stephen but because of Agnes's mischief turns him out. Rickie has, by this time, been told by his aunt that Stephen is his half-brother, his adored mother having fallen in love with a Wiltshire farmer; fatally, Rickie refuses to acknowledge Stephen and in so doing compromises his own integrity for ever. Then, at last, but too late, he rejects Agnes and begins to rediscover the values that Sawston had been gradually eroding. But he dies on the railway trying to save his brother who has wandered, drunk, on to the line.

The novel encapsulates all the themes that Morgan was in the process of making so thoroughly his own: truth and loyalty versus convention and self-interest, the English countryside versus suburbia, the constrictions of bourgeois marriage, the aesthetic impulse versus the worldly, and, as well, the tragic result of ignoring the 'symbolic moment'. Morgan believed that if one fails to take an opportunity suddenly offered, one's life, as a result, may be fatally flawed. 'We accept it, at whatever cost, and we have accepted life. But if we are frightened and reject it, the moment, so to speak, passes; the symbol is never offered again.'[4] Philip and Harriet kill the baby; Rickie rejects Ansell in favour of Agnes: these are their symbolic, or eternal moments. Although Morgan himself was often afraid to seize the moment (*carpe diem*), the implications of his having decided that Rickie should not be saved and must die are painfully resonant. What kind of feelings of self-hatred did he have that he had to evoke such a sad life, and such a brutal end to it, for the character with whom, more than any other, he identified?

In the year he went to Figsbury Rings and began to plan *The Longest Journey*, Morgan made some New Year's resolutions. They are so intimate that it is almost intrusive to read them, even ninety years later with the original sheets neatly glued into the archivist's new, paper-conserving notebook. The first is unremarkable, to get up earlier, and the second is rather sensible, a smoker's charter for writers: 'Smoke in public: it gives a reason for you, & you can observe unchallenged.' The third was to plan out work, at least every week, and it gives the biographer heartache. The plans that have been followed, and *kept*, by lesser writers! The fascination there would be in seeing even one plan, for one week, of the writer's life at Harnham! But then if Morgan had been of the temperament to keep to such a plan, less modest, more conscious of posterity, he would not have been E. M. Forster, he would not have been himself.

Resolution four was the cold shower one: 'more exercise: keep the brutes quiet.' There is something inexpressibly sad about the plural, as though his vision of lust was as ravenous bloodhounds, howling dogs who have to be thrown appeasements from time to time, lonely under the sheets in Weybridge. The fifth is revealing but sensible: 'don't ever shrink from self analysis, but don't keep on at it too long.' Then comes 'get a less superficial idea of women'. But how to do this, with 'Gladys Olcott' realising something was not quite right? Was the novelist speaking? Or did it mean that Morgan had not yet given up hope that, even if he never fell in love, he might woo a Cambridge man's sister? Perhaps the next resolution – not to 'be so afraid of going into strange places or company, & be a fool more frequently' – was a follow-on from number six: it is true that if a man lives with his mother, shuns sociability and remains consistently serious-minded that the Gladys Olcotts are less likely to like him.

Finally, after all this self-knowledge, came the concluding resolution: 'keep accounts'. It was so typical of Morgan that although he knew that the next day, his twenty-fifth birthday, he inherited his eight thousand pounds from Marianne (or what it had now become) he did not mention it: he merely noted that a new financial era necessitated account-keeping. What he did not do, of course, was speculate about how to spend the money. That was not really in question. He would not. And yet, in a small way, the inheriting of the money on the first day of 1904 was the first hint of *Howards End*, Morgan's novel that, more than business, more than the sanctity of houses, more than personal relations, would be about money. Accounts would be a way of making wealth more manageable; of making oneself closer to the middle-class norm. Would they also make it easier if one ever chose to disembarrass oneself of it altogether?

'I've made my two great discoveries,' Morgan had noted on the same occasion as he made these resolutions, 'the religious about 4 years ago, the other in the winter of 1902 – and the reconstruction is practically over.'[5] For a son of late Victorian England these were indeed two deeply important facets of his character: religion, now abandoned in favour of truth and beauty and personal relationships, and the 'other', the nature of his sexuality. It was the specific dating in his diary of the latter that was one of the factors that years later led Morgan to elaborate his relationship with Meredith. Why did I write this? he asked himself in old age when a biography was being mooted; what actually happened that winter? He thought back to the Kingsley Hotel and the Working Men's College (where Meredith too taught a class) and he thought of their occasional suppers together, perhaps in a restaurant in Marchmont Street and, as the winter of 1902 became the spring of 1903, their walks in Coram Fields or round Queen Square; he thought of HOM's exuberant intelligence and of his enthusiasm about *Where Angels Fear to Tread*. Then, sixty years later, he embroidered a harmonious, at times sentimental friendship into 'an affair'. It is the nub of biography: should one believe one's subject? Should one even believe his or her diary? The only way out is to demand two sources; and this, as regards Meredith ever doing more than slinging an affectionate arm round Morgan's shoulders as the Profumo brothers had done in the Kent House photograph, has never been forthcoming. All that *has* is a colleague describing Meredith as 'very much a ladies' man'[6] and the friendship implicit in Morgan's dedicating *A Room with a View* to him in 1908.

So what had happened to Morgan in the winter of 1902? That it was something sexual cannot be in doubt (because what else could it have been?); that it was something specifically sexual is, very much, in doubt. There occurred, I am sure, a sexual awakening, but of a quite theoretical kind. Italy, the British Museum, a new understanding about himself, the way other people reacted to him (he himself may have been insensitive to a Gladys Olcott figure, perhaps 'his touch revolted her'[7]) – it all led him to forge new perceptions about his own sexuality. There may even have been a specific event, never recorded but remembered by Morgan with this oblique reference. For example, he or Lily perhaps came across Ted Streatfield's widow, a not unlikely possibility given that both widows were then living in London and the childless Katharine Streatfeild might have had feelings of obligation to her late husband's ward. She perhaps wrote* to the Forsters in October 1902, the month they returned to England after their year abroad, wanting, exactly twenty years after Ted's death, to have news of them. We cannot know. All that we can be sure of is that the winter of 1902 revealed to Morgan something about himself and his sexuality and prepared the way for the winter of 1906 when he met the person with whom he could soon, for the first time, imagine himself in love.

In the autumn of that year a young man of seventeen named Syed Ross Masood had come to live in Weybridge in order to prepare for his Oxford entrance. He was an Indian, the ward of the newly retired Principal of the prestigious Mohammedan Anglo-Oriental College in Aligarh, Theodore Morison; the college had been founded by Masood's grandfather, Sir Syed Ahmed Khan. Morgan was asked to coach Masood in Latin and, perhaps, to ensure that Oxford the following year would not be too much of a shock. Personal relationships were quickly discussed, for the first time Morgan mentioned the young man in his diary was, fittingly, as follows: 'Masood gives up duties for friends – which is civilization. Though

---

* Since Ted and Eddie had been distantly related she might have found them through Aunt Laura at Abinger.

as he remarks "Hence the confusion in Oriental States". To them personal relations come first.'[8]

These twenty-five words were, in effect, a summary of Morgan's future: the stress on relationships, seeing them as the key to civilised living; the muddle ('crossed wires' as one would say today) that ensues between Indian and English; the giving up of duty (country) for friends and hence Morgan's notorious choice, in 'What I Believe' in 1939, of friends over country, a choice which nevertheless required 'guts';[9] and the delights of intimate exchange that Masood found so easy and the English so difficult. (One of the reasons why Morgan had been attracted to HOM, and made so much of their relationship, was the latter's simple, uncomplicated gift for friendship, almost Indian in its easiness; there was a hint of Masood, and of Aziz, in the way a contemporary described HOM greeting people in the street, affably 'affording the most perfunctory signs of public recognition while on his way to astonishing us all with endless talk in private apartments'.[10])

Yet, as important as Masood's belief in friendship as an ideal, was his personal situation as a ward. Seeing Morison's warmth towards him may have made Morgan think about his own, unknown guardian, to confront his feelings of sadness, long suppressed, about Ted and to begin to mourn his father who, had he lived, would not have needed to appoint his friend guardian. At the same time, the discussions about friendship that he was having with Masood, the latter's presumably uninhibited questions about Morgan's family (one of the salutary shocks for the English when meeting Indians is the unselfconscious directness of their cross-questioning), all would have made Morgan think about Eddie and his friendships – about Ted. The likelihood is that Morgan would grow to love Masood partly because the fact of his being a ward was in itself a liberating quality; almost as if the imagery of ward and guardian was for him 'minorite', that of *eromenos* and *erastes*. It would not be for merely sexual reasons that Morgan's lovers would be younger than himself, the traditional love of the older man for the younger; it would be in some ways a re-creation of, and atonement for, the love between his own father and his own guardian.

In physical appearance Masood must have been like Antinous, tall, handsome, vigorous and with the most beautiful brown, melting eyes. He liked money, practical jokes and extravagant emotions, and had the vast self-confidence that comes from being able to trace one's ancestry back through the Prophet Mohammed at the thirty-seventh generation to Adam at the one hundred and twentieth, and from having as grandfather a man described by Edward Carpenter as 'one of the leading Mahomedans of India, as well as a confidant of the British and of the Government – a man of considerable weight, courage, and knowledge of the world, if a little ultra-Mahomedan in some of his views and in his contempt of the mild Hindu.'[11] Masood was indiscriminately friendly and enraged by any form of stand-offishness: Morgan had never met anyone like him, although he had *seen* the type in Italy, men who grinned, looked one in the eye, laughed uproariously and enjoyed *all* the pleasures of life. 'One might disagree with him but he never left one cold,'[12] Morgan would one day write: Masood was exciting, never enervating, never boring: the side of Morgan that had, since the rare occasions when he released crabs in desks or 'ragged' in Greece, been mostly suppressed, was now given a chance for expression. In a way it was like being in love.

Yet love in the sexual sense it was not. First of all Morgan still hoped, although the hope was more and more receding, that he might become 'normal'; his minorite tendencies were still a private grief and would be for another few years. Secondly, he was timid: it is inconceivable that the diffident Morgan would ever have made the first move. Thirdly, because of the Weybridge connection the friendship with Masood was far too much bound up with Lily and Mrs Morison for it ever to become secret, sensual, sexual behind closed doors. Fourthly, and most important, for Masood it would have been inconceivable. His education had been Western, i.e. classical; and in both Greek and Muslim cultures the lover was always manly and dominant, the beloved feminine and submissive. However attuned Morgan was making Masood to other, Cambridge values, he could never change his attitude to sexuality which was that to *ask* for love, to *ask* for penetration was inherently demeaning. Masood could never have imagined or accepted that someone ten years his senior and already an admired writer would jeopardise his sense of *amour propre* by professing his love. The only culturally acceptable mode for Masood would have been if sexually Morgan was dominant. And this clearly, by his demeanour and his behaviour, he was not: in their physical relationship, in their emotional closeness, in everything except matters of the intellect, Masood was the dominant figure.

* * *

Meanwhile, Morgan was working steadily on *The Longest Journey*. As always he was full of self-doubt: 23 March, 'Doubt whether novel's any good: all ingenious symbols, little flesh & blood. Possibly I'd better finish Lucy first.'[13] But he went on with it and by the autumn, when he and Lily went for a month's holiday to the châteaux of the Loire, he had nearly finished. His imagination was so active at this period that even before he had finished this second novel, and even while he was wondering whether to complete his first, he was planning a fourth. In August, having been to Cambridge to give a lecture at the Local Lectures Summer School on the novelist Samuel Richardson and to stay with a friend named Leonard Greenwood, he made the half-hour journey to Rooksnest. It was, apparently, his first visit since 1893: and it made him think again about the changes to the landscape that he dreaded so much yet, fatalistically, anticipated: Admiral Fellowes at Woodfield House, 'naughty man, has sold a good deal of his property for building – the part that touches the Baldock Road, and made a road into it . . . There is also a whole new street, parallel between the High Street and the railway: that will spoil nothing. Towards us it's all exactly the same.'[14]

Accompanied by the farmer's son Frank, Morgan went over the Rooksnest garden (he did not call at the house because the tenant was ill). There were more flowers than in the Forsters' time and the two cherry trees had gone, as had the apple trees; the paddock was full of laurels and the dell and the pond had become rockeries. To complete the gloomy aura of late Victorian shrubberies 'you can hardly see the house for creepers: huge ivies are growing towards the larder window'.[15] With refreshed memories of how the former, beloved garden had been thirteen years earlier, Morgan went on to Highfield, the house a mile to the south-east of Rooksnest where the Postons lived; they, with the Jowitts, had been the only families whom Lily had consented to know. Elizabeth Poston, who was then a baby of about the same age as Helen's baby at the end of *Howards End*, was later told about Morgan's visit by her mother Clementine: the publication of *Howards End* four years later had made her realise in retrospect what significance it had held. Clementine had been

wearing a sweeping blue gown. It was hay time, and on that dazzling day of sun and scent and flowers, she paused to pick a handful of new mown grass for my rabbits. Looking over into the parkland, she saw a tall gangling young man in ill-fitting tweeds . . . 'My name is Morgan Forster.' My mother welcomed him with her ravishing smile. 'Of course, you're an old friend,' she said. 'Come along in and have lunch.' So he joined the party on the lawn.[16]

It was not, of course, chance that 'she seemed to belong not to the young people and their motor, but to the house, and to the tree that overshadowed it.' The house, Highfield, was the essential backcloth to the domestic scene; without the house there could not have been the family. (Yet without the family could there have been the house?) It was in 1886 that the first Mr and Mrs Poston had moved there and for Morgan's remaining six years at Rooksnest he had been friends with them and with their son and daughter, the former being called Charles like his father and like the Wilcoxes' son in *Howards End*. When Charles Poston senior re-married the ménage went on in equal harmony in the same house: which must have made Morgan ponder the state of being a second wife, especially one who continued life in the same house as her predecessor, almost as if it was the house that was the stability and the harmony not a particular wife. Although it was the first Mrs Poston and the first Mrs Wilcox who seemed at one with their houses, their successors were as well: as if the strength and the spirit of the house transcended individuality. It was this theme, with the Postons transposed to Rooksnest,* that Morgan would explore; so that Clementine Poston and what she stood for was in his mind throughout the book, up until the last chapter when it is August and the hay is being cut and Margaret, the second wife, has in her turn become part of Howards End:

The meadow was being re-cut, the great red poppies were reopening in the garden ... These little events would become part of her, year after year. Every summer she would fear lest the well should give out, every winter lest the pipes should freeze; every westerly gale might blow the wych-elm down and bring the end of all things ... They were building up a new life, obscure, yet gilded with tranquillity.[17]

So Morgan returned from Rooksnest that summer of 1906 with his mind full of these images. At the same time he continued to ponder the mysterious, unknown state of marriage; it was something that he now feared, with vast and inexpressible regret, that he would never understand. Already the fear was beginning to undermine his self-confidence as a novelist, and particularly as a novelist in a

* In 1913 Charles Poston senior died; the following year Clementine and her two young children did move to Rooksnest.

culture where marriage was the unquestioned norm of happiness and the novel therefore a heterosexual art form. 'I can scarcely imagine happiness such as they must have had,' he would one day write about one especially happy couple that he knew, 'my own however intense being scraps, and it's no wonder, since matrimony does offer such prizes, nearly everyone should enter, and ignore the deplorable average.'[18]

In general, he had few regrets. Lily had scarcely hinted at a blissful state of affairs with Eddie; Trevy had appeared trapped; most marriages he knew about seemed to offer far less chance of happiness than was given to the unmarried dons at King's or to the young men he knew who lived in rooms in London. And then, at this time, after the vision of happiness at Highfield, he was presented with another, quite appallingly unharmonious marriage: that of his Uncle Willie in Northumberland. William Forster was Eddie's younger brother and was now fifty-one, and Morgan and Lily, or Morgan on his own, had had several holidays in his large house in Northumberland. In the 1920s Morgan gave a talk about him to the Memoir Club, the group of Bloomsbury friends whom he loved to amuse and gratify and entice, accuracy being a somewhat secondary factor.

Although, when younger, Uncle Willie had been 'handsome, amusing, intelligent, athletic',[19] in later years he was none of these, except that he apparently prided himself on his sexual energy and was 'sedulously masculine';[20] however, 'in the end he was interested in nothing but little girls'.[21] How curious, Morgan must have thought, he who had never had the least interest in little girls; yet Uncle Willie's predilection must have occurred to him when, a few months after his return from a visit, he wrote to Dent about Harnham having 'a little green in front on which little girls roll'.[22] Perhaps it would have been easier, he brooded as he stared out at Monument Green, if he *had* liked small, female children; his uncle, after all, did not feel himself a minorite: his sexual preferences were virtually sanctioned by society. How fortuitous life was: Charles Dodgson, the creator of *Alice*, revered almost as an icon, Oscar Wilde reviled almost as a devil; it might so easily have been the other way round.

The quality that Morgan shared with Willie – apart, apparently, from a certain physical resemblance – was that of being 'acutely resentful of criticism and interference' so that 'sooner or later everyone who went there got into trouble'. Morgan did not last long. The April 1904 visit was the first for five years. He went again in October 1905 and in the summer of 1906. That was the last visit; nor was Morgan mentioned in the will. There was a reason for this: the ménage at Acton, Willie's Northumberland house, 'scarcely considered me as a man'.[23] 'Won't have that pansy in the house' one can imagine Uncle Willie saying, as he encouraged visiting girl cousins to 'be rough to me ... Go with increasing reluctance'[24] added Morgan, with the rather dishonest implication that it was the baiting little girls that kept him away. In fact a summer visit in 1907 would have been made especially unpleasant by a reference to an 'Uncle Willie' in The Longest Journey and by a review in the Nation in April. The reviewer began by quoting the passage in which Agnes asks Rickie whether he couldn't make his stories less obvious. '"I don't see any harm in that. Uncle Willie floundered hopelessly. I had to explain, and then he was delighted."' The review went on: 'In truth it is not easy to explain the subtle quality of Mr Forster's brilliant novel to Uncle Willie and his kinsfolk.'[25] They cannot have liked it; and this is the probable reason why Morgan never went again.

Oddly enough, however, he was able to claim in later years that architecturally Cadover in the novel was based on Acton; an eminent Forster scholar even reproduced a photograph of it in a 1966 book. Yet any visitor to Figsbury Rings sets out from the village of Winterbourne Dauntsey and there is the Manor House, the self-evident model ('"There's Cadover," visitors would say. "How small it looks. We shall be late for lunch"'). Morgan referred to Acton because, I believe, he genuinely forgot about the Manor House; and because his deep-rooted evasiveness, his preference for the secret and the mysterious, had now become innate; and because Acton was a vast house that belonged to his family whereas the Manor House he knew only from the 'outside'.* (Yet it is a disconcerting experience for the biographer: she gets off the bus and begins the walk along the path to Figsbury Rings. There is Cadover, she exclaims, seeing every detail down to the 'triangular area, which the better-class servants knew as a "pendiment", and which had in its middle a small round hole, according to the usage of Palladio',[26] knowing that her sandwiches will be eaten confusedly while she reads Morgan's 1960 declaration that it was Acton that 'provided the architecture and the atmosphere

---

* Its original owners were called Thornton (no relation), later ones Abbott. In September 1904 Morgan visited Figsbury Rings and saw the outside of the Manor House; he was then starting Where Angels Fear to Tread – and found Miss Abbott's name.

for Cadover', knowing that this was not so, wondering whether it matters.)

What does matter is the novel. At the end of his 1960 piece, the same piece, indeed the same paragraph, as the one in which Morgan so oddly declared that Mrs Failing in the novel was derived in part from Uncle Willie, causing more confusion to the biographer who can see no similarities, at the end of this piece Morgan declared that 'the book did not sell, and an uncle of mine, a meddlesome tease of a man, bought a number of remainders at sixpence each and sent them to those of my relations whom they were most likely to upset'.[27] But the book did sell – 1500 copies in the April and May of 1907 and 500 more after the June reprint – with no evidence that any of these 500 were remaindered. In any case, Morgan's relations would have bought copies by then, or been given them by him at the author's third-off discount price of 4 shillings (£10); for it was surely of *The Longest Journey* that his Whichelo grandmother said that if one put one of Morgie's novels down without marking the place one could *never* find it again, evidence at least that they tried to read them; while Morgan's Whichelo cousin Philip was to say that his family did not understand *The Longest Journey*: 'it might have been a foreign language as far as they were concerned.'[28] No, the point of the Uncle Willie anecdote was that Willie was incensed both by Morgan's subversiveness and by his evidently unsedulous masculinity; and Morgan made amusing capital out of it.

More than any of this, however, Morgan disliked Acton because of his uncle's treatment of his wife Emily: 'He was abominably rude to her. I shouldn't think he said anything decent to her during the final fifteen years'[29] (the years when Morgan visited). Not only did it make Morgan think about Willie's brother Eddie, it must have engendered grief and almost bitterness in someone whose ideal in life was lifelong partnership, romantic love, the surrendering of one partner to another in the name of caring, all those facets of contented monogamy that would be kept from him. Yet here was Willie's brutality sanctioned, even approved of. When Morgan returned from Acton in 1906 the theme of marriage was greatly on his mind; and it was perhaps now that he began to conjure up Margaret Schlegel and Henry Wilcox, a couple who know nothing of romantic love or sexual passion or the desire to have children but who achieve a contented, and sanctioned, equilibrium through tolerance and good sense.

So, when asked to give a talk to the Working Men's College in its new home in Camden Town (he still taught a Latin class there), Morgan had his theme. He talked about 'Pessimism in Literature' and, averring that the reader judges a book by the words that are written on the last page, pointed out that marriage, as a happy ending, was no longer the answer to the ending of a book. 'We of today know that it is rather a beginning, and that the lovers enter upon life's real problems when those wedding bells are silent.' Because he is sincere and honest the modern literary critic must 'turn to that despised creature the pessimist, and say "How would you end a book?" And the pessimist replies, quite simply and satisfactorily, "By some scene of separation".

The author looks for what is permanent, even if it is sad; the man looks for what is cheerful, and noble, and gracious, even if it is transitory . . . I uphold optimism in life. I do not at present uphold optimism in literature.'[30]

17

Clun

'"The Longest Journey" published about a month,' wrote Morgan in the June of 1907. 'Critics approve – except the Queen & the World. All say "jerky", "too many deaths".'[1] And that, in his diary, was that. And yet: he was being discussed by critics who did not merely 'approve' but applauded rapturously; and who produced over twenty, mostly lengthy, reviews almost united in their praise. To see, nowadays, the intelligence of the comments, the references to 'genius', the depth of understanding generally displayed is, from the aspect of biography, a rather confusing exercise. How can someone of twenty-eight receive plaudits like this and not be moved? At the same time how could he have had such innate self-confidence that he seems to have accepted the reviews as no more than his due? Is it a necessary, vital characteristic of a novelist that he embraces both modesty and self-approval?

These questions are key to any understanding of Morgan's temperament. And the answer, in part, is that in general it is the introspective, the over-sensitive and the vulnerable who write fiction – for a variety of reasons to do with responsiveness and calm – and that such people are of their nature shy, almost humble. (Rarely does one meet a novelist – not a story-teller – who is the life and soul of the party, sporty, outgoing, gregarious, replete with *amour propre*.) Yet how to explain the self-confidence? Something in Morgan now knew and accepted that he was not merely a writer, but a very good writer indeed. That this affected his inner life in no way at all is part of the conundrum.

Morgan viewed his fiction as something outside himself. When he told Bob Trevelyan, who had written him a long and helpful letter about *Where Angels Fear to Tread*, that 'I know I am not a real artist, and at the same time am fearfully serious over my work and

191

willing to sweat at atmosphere if it helps me to what I want',[2] this was not false modesty: his identity, his sense of self-worth, did not derive from his writing. In some ways he saw it as an occupation, a serious occupation but something merely to fill the days instead of, as it were, working in a library or a museum or in a university. This is partly why he participated so little in the whole panoply of writer's accoutrements: book signings, gossip items in newspapers or the *Bookman*, rituals to do with working methods or a certain number of words each morning, knighthoods (offered and rejected in the late 1940s). It was not mere modesty, mere self-effacingness, it was detachment. So, when asked in the 1950s whether he wrote every day or only when inspired, he answered 'the latter'. He also rejected as improper the idea of consciously putting something in a novel ('I never say "that might be useful"'), adding, 'however I have been inspired on the spot'. And when asked to what extent he was aware of his own technical cleverness in general he replied almost tetchily:

We keep coming back to that. People will not realize how little conscious one is of these things; how one flounders about. They want us to be so much better informed than we are. If critics could only have a course on writers' *not* thinking things out – a course of lectures . . . (*He smiled*)[3]

In other words, as he was to assert throughout his life, writing was a private matter. When he declared that 'I would like books to be anonymous. I believe in inspiration',[4] he was carefully equating inspiration with privacy; the public, publicity-seeking, self-aware writer is, of his nature, uninspired: he is only a journalist.

In 1925 Morgan expanded and expounded this principle in an essay called 'Anonymity'. In it he paid oblique tribute to Lytton Strachey's image of the ideal biographer lowering a little bucket to bring up a characteristic specimen[5] when he said that less than first-class writers (he mentions Charles Lamb and R. L. Stevenson) 'always write with their surface-personalities and never let down buckets into their underworld . . . He and Lamb append their names in full to every sentence they write.' The surface personality, declared Morgan, does things like dining out and answering letters; the other, deeper personality 'is a very queer affair. In many ways it is a perfect fool, but without it there is no literature, because unless a man dips a bucket down into it occasionally he cannot produce first-class work.'[6] Years before, in an article called 'Inspiration' written for the *Author* magazine Morgan had described the ritual of this queer affair.

Experiences vary, but most writers when they compose seem to go through some such process as follows. They start pretty calm, promising their wives they will not let the fire out or be late for lunch. They write a few sentences very slowly and feel constricted and used up. Then a queer catastrophe happens inside them. The mind, as it were, turns turtle, sometimes with rapidity, and a hidden part of it comes to the top and controls the pen. Quicker and quicker the writer works, his head grows hot, he looks far from handsome. He spoils the lunch and lets out the fire. He is not exactly 'rapt'; on the contrary he feels more himself than usual, and lives in a state which he is convinced should be his normal one, though it isn't. On returning to his normal state, he reads over what he has written. It surprises him. He couldn't do it again. He can't explain to the reader how it was done. He can't remember whether plot or character was considered first, whether the work was conceived as a whole or bit by bit . . . The reality has swallowed it up. It is a reality outside his ordinary self.[7]

This, it seems, is how Morgan wrote his novels. When he emerged from his room for luncheon at one o'clock, when Lily asked him how his work had been going and Agnes handed round the cold lamb and new potatoes, when he returned to his work table to look at what he had done, it all seemed something other, something outside himself. He could tell if it was good or not, and could set to work correcting it, but he never quite knew where it had come from. Involvement, pride, possessiveness, intense feelings about reviews belonged, Morgan believed, to lesser writers; the real writer looked at his work aloofly, almost ironically and did not seem to connect the self who dined and answered letters and responded to other people with the self who wrote.

In some ways, of course, this was all a pose. Just before *The Longest Journey* was published, he told Blackwood's that he no longer wanted them to publish his work, and this was simply because of a dispute involving rights in other countries: underneath the professed sense of detachment did lie some sense of self-worth. And he was only partly ironic when he told Dent that he had cut a 'Panic' chapter from *The Longest Journey*, in which a Pan-like Stephen bounds about naked, 'so, probably only students of the Master's Juvenilia will now twig what he's driving at'.*[8]

---

* The 'juvenile' story 'The Story of a Panic' is indeed similar to the jettisoned chapter.

The autobiographical nature of Morgan's second novel was remarked upon by few. Perhaps no one imagined that a writer would voluntarily expose his own weaknesses, or perhaps few believed that a satirical novelist could also be 'a lonely and deformed boy' (*Standard*), 'an anaemic personality' (*Athenaeum*), 'gauche, timid, incurably naïve' (*Revue des Deux Mondes*).[9] What no one could know, although the perceptive might have sensed it, is that Morgan had in fact written a novel of anguish: his anguish at feeling himself an outsider, beyond the pale of what society considered normality. '"Never forget that your greatest thing is over"' Rickie tells Agnes just after they have kissed for the first time. The word 'greatest' again has its sexual connotation: Rickie means, and is obliquely warning Agnes, that the sexual joy she had known with Gerald is over. He continues, repeating the word twice in the unconscious longing that she will rescue them from the tragedy in which they are about to participate, '"What I said to you then is greater than what I say to you now. What he gave you then is greater than anything you will get from me."' Agnes is frightened. 'Again she had the sense of something abnormal.' But she cannot know what it is. Instead, maternally, she 'folded him in her arms' and their tragedy begins.

Morgan put himself into *The Longest Journey*, not only the 'abnormal' Rickie but also his parents' marriage, Tonbridge, Cambridge, Wiltshire, the imagery of the Greeks. There is a good deal of openly expressed bitterness. Rickie's mother thinks: '"Marrying into the Elliot family." It had sounded so splendid, for she was a penniless child with nothing to offer, and the Elliots held their heads high. For what reason? What had they ever done except say sarcastic things, and limp, and be refined?' Morgan could, as well, make fun of himself with charming lack of pomposity. First he described one of Rickie's stories, 'The Bay of Fifteen Islets', in perfectly parodying terms; then Rickie tells Agnes about another story that he would like to write.

For instance, a stupid vulgar man is engaged to a lovely young lady. He wants her to live in the towns, but she only cares for the woods. She shocks him this way and that, but gradually he tames her, and makes her nearly as dull as he is. One day she has a last explosion – over the snobby wedding presents – and flies out of the drawing-room window, shouting, 'Freedom and Truth!' Near the house is a little dell full of fir trees, and she runs into it. He comes there the next moment. But she's gone.

'Awfully exciting. Where?'

'Oh Lord, she's a Dryad!' cried Rickie in great disgust. 'She's turned into a tree.'

It is this story that Rickie's half-brother Stephen settles down on the roof of Cadover to read; he sees on the back 'a neat little resumé in Miss Pembroke's handwriting, intended for such as him. "Allegory. Man = modern civilization (in ˉbad sense). Girl = getting into touch with Nature."'[10] Stephen lights his pipe, gazes out at the village and Cadbury Rings and falls asleep: his uncomplicated sensuality being preferable to pretentious stories about dryads.

In the week before *The Longest Journey* was published, perhaps as a way of staving off thoughts of the reviewers poised to strike, Morgan joined Meredith and his wife Christabel, and George Barger and his wife Florence, for a short walking holiday, in Wales with them and in Shropshire on his own. He must have been somewhat disconcerted, as he lay in his single bed, by the thought of his two King's friends, lying voluntarily under 'the astonishing glass shade'[11] next door; and by knowing that soon, when they returned home and read his novel, they would be confronting his pessimistic view of marriage. Yet, he might have presumed, they would identify him with Ansell not with Rickie: they would imagine that his creed was that defined by the former when he tries to stop his friend marrying:

You are not a person who ought to marry at all. You are unfitted in body: that we once discussed. You are also unfitted in soul: you want and you need to like many people, and a man of that sort ought not to marry. 'You never were attached to that great sect' who can like one person only, and if you try to enter it you will find destruction.

And if HOM and George did see elements of Morgan in Rickie they would have been most sympathetic to his feelings when, on Cadbury Rings, he reads Shelley ('it was natural for him to read when he was happy'); and, having declaimed the passage* from which Ansell had quoted, which concludes that those who *are* attached to that sect 'the dreariest and the longest journey go', yet sees two lovers in the distance and feels them 'to be nearer the truth than Shelley'.[13]

Despite living with those who were undergoing the longest journey, Morgan was able to write in his diary 'Feel very happy'.[14] Since Florence was to be an intimate friend in the future, he perhaps hoped anew that close friendship with a woman was at least a possibility – and might even one day be his within a companionable marriage; or possibly HOM had already read his book and praised it as wholeheartedly as his first; or, as he would claim, it was the effect of the landscape, another *genius loci* experience which became, in retrospect, imbued with even more magical qualities than it had held at the time.

The concept of the spirit of the place, a sacred spot, was inherent in the culture of the Ancient Greeks; and was part of Morgan's anti-mechanistic vision. Like Rickie, he 'was extremely sensitive to the inside of a house, holding it an organism that expressed thoughts, conscious and subconscious, of its inmates. He was equally sensitive to places.' Although, and perhaps because, Morgan never felt '*of* anywhere',[15] houses, places, countryside were increasingly important to him the older he became. He felt so sentimental about Rooksnest or Wiltshire, so unsentimental about Tonbridge, that his feelings were almost religious: in a sense they *were* his religion.

Shropshire, had Morgan visited it more often, might have aroused equally deep feelings, but it was A. E. Housman's poems *A Shropshire Lad* that stirred him more; so that ever afterwards the two emotions, his feeling for the countryside and his feeling for the poems, were intertwined. As Morgan would write about Arnold's Oxford verse, 'though I don't care for the scenery or sentiment of the poems,

---

* I never was attached to that great sect
Whose doctrine is that each one should select
Out of the world a mistress or a friend,
And all the rest, though fair and wise, commend
To cold oblivion – though it is the code
Of modern morals, and the beaten road
Which those poor slaves with weary footsteps tread
Who travel to their home among the dead
By the broad highway of the world – and so
With one sad friend, perhaps a jealous foe,
The dreariest and the longest journey go.[12]

they excite by the sense of give-and-take, of creation from scarcely anything of something, until a whole landscape is charged with an emotion, permanent as its origins were transitory.'[16] Shropshire now became charged with an emotion although the poems came first; just as reading Shelley might have come first for Rickie.

It was not the only time Morgan had read Housman, for he had been introduced to his work by Meredith in the winter of 1898. However, to read the poems where they had been inspired, to experience the *genius loci*, changed his perceptions; he did not of course know that Housman had written six of the poems before visiting the county and then went there 'to gain local colour', or that Housman's Shropshire was an imaginary land, with real place-names being used for romantic colouring not because he himself had a particular feeling for a real place.[17]

What Morgan seems to have sensed, on this occasion, in the April of 1907, was the sexual resonance of *A Shropshire Lad*. Either it was pure empathy with the poetry; or his enquiring side, his literary perceptions, now made him realise that Housman had written his sequence in the year of Oscar Wilde's trial and, as we now know, Wilde's sufferings had been one of his main inspirations. 'Want to write to A. E. Housman'[18] Morgan noted in his diary, and he did. But he had no reply and for years bore a grudge against Housman for not responding to his letter. Eventually he exorcised his hurt feelings. 'He was an unhappy fellow and not a very amiable one', he declared in a 1936 review, concluding (with world-weary regret that the passionate feelings of his younger self had never been appreciated by the great man):

Things might have been much worse: he found an adequate haven at Cambridge, he was fortunate in making a quiet circle of friends who understood him, and outside the college gates an appreciative public cackled, not always unwelcome or unheard. He enjoyed a glass of port. That is something ... Perhaps he had a better time than the outsider supposes. Did he ever drink the stolen waters which he recommends so ardently to others? I hope so.[19]

In Shropshire Morgan felt that Housman was speaking to him, and to him as a minorite: could he have hinted at such in his letter? Yet it is possible that Housman had scores of letters from unhappy young men who had realised that his poems had a 'hidden agenda' and that he made it a policy not to reply. Morgan, with a new self-confidence that he was one writer addressing another, was hurt both on this occasion, and on the others on which he made overtures, that Housman never responded with friendship; while the likelihood is that it was simply *because* of Morgan's empathy that Housman was cool, that indeed he was terrified of their shared knowledge.*

Having parted from the Merediths and the Bargers, and having inspected Shrewsbury ('the more said the better. Unspoilt and alive'[21]), Morgan took the train to Wellington, then walked south over The Wrekin to Much Wenlock. Here he looked down at Housman's 'Hughley steeple' (and perhaps wondered why it was sheltered in a valley and not 'a far-known sign'[22]) before taking the train along Wenlock Edge to Craven Arms and Ludlow. He stayed the night at the famous Angel Hotel and next day walked on north-westwards to Clun. Marriage, houses, the continuity of family life and the discontinuity of minorite life were all on his mind; not merely because of the Welsh holiday, nor because of Housman, but because, just before setting out, he had once again visited the Postons at Highfield and had this time stayed the night: it was almost as if he were allowing himself to re-absorb the attachment to Stevenage that he had given up nearly fifteen years earlier. This new attachment would be the theme of his gestating novel; it would also, now, never be broken: 15 July 1944, 'Strange violence of a dream that the Postons were giving up Rooksnest. It was death and humiliation.'[23]

So it was with his mind full of Rooksnest that Morgan arrived at Clun. 'How lovely to be asked whether Oniton† is anywhere,' he wrote to William Plomer in the 1960s. 'No one but you has ever asked, and those chapters of the book have always given me a particular feeling. It is Clun.'[24] Here he stayed at the Castle Cottage guest house and, in the morning upon leaving, could, like Margaret 'pick out the church and the black-and-white gables of the George.‡ There was the bridge, and the river nibbling its green peninsula. She could even see the bathing-shed . . . She never saw it again.' Morgan only did once more, in the April of 1909, when he returned to Clun: he was writing *Howards End* and perhaps needed to refresh his memory. Here the idea had come to him that his new, his next-but-one novel

* Nevertheless, his love of the poetry never diminished. In the first interview he ever gave, in 1929, he spoke of 'Housman our best poet'.[20]
† The name 'Oniton Grange' in *Howards End* would have derived from the village of Onibury, halfway between Ludlow and Clun.
‡ In reality the Buffalo's Head, a hundred yards away in the square.

(for he was about to spend some months re-starting 'New Lucy' and turning it into *A Room with a View*) could have the tripartite focus of which he was so fond and could be based on three houses – Melcombe Place, Rooksnest and Castle Cottage at Clun.

Why did this house appeal to him so much, when he had no connections with it and stayed for only one night both times he visited? Why did he choose Clun as the setting for 'the wasted day' on which Evie Wilcox was married when 'for a couple of days the little town, dreaming between the ruddy hills, was roused by the clang of our civilization, and drew up by the roadside to let the motors pass'? It was, surely, because of its setting, the hills enfolding the ruins of the twelfth-century castle, the river, the market square and the house itself beside the castle mound. Morgan also responded to the simple beauty of a house like 'Oniton Grange' ('the house was insignificant, but the prospect from it would be an eternal joy',[25] thought Margaret) and the very fact that he had no personal attachment to it made it even more suitable to be Mr Wilcox's house, a rich man's toy abandoned on a whim, without thought for tradition and inherited responsibility, an obvious example of what had recently been dubbed 'conspicuous consumption'.[26] Yet the villagers of Clun were attached to the house and it was attached to them – which made the way Wilcox riches could buy and abandon it even more callous.

The air grew cooler; they had surmounted the last gradient, and Oniton lay below them with its church, its radiating houses, its castle, its river-girt peninsula. Close to the castle was a grey mansion, unintellectual but kindly, stretching with its grounds across the peninsula's neck – the sort of mansion that was built all over England in the beginning of the last century, while architecture was still an expression of the national character.

It is no coincidence that Henry Wilcox's first meeting with Margaret at the beginning of their courtship comes just when she has uttered the significant remark that is, in a sense, the key to the 'panic and emptiness' at the heart of his life: 'I quite expect to end my life caring most for a place.'[27] Here is the central paradox that Morgan wanted to explore, and that Castle Cottage revealed to him anew: human beings must not abandon houses, and they must indeed be sensitive to their spirit. But how, in the twentieth century, to reconcile this necessity with personal relations and with telegrams and anger?

* * *

From Clun Morgan walked west along the drovers' road to Newtown, caught a train and journeyed, via Shrewsbury, back to Weybridge. Apart from the reviews of *The Longest Journey*, he was also faced with the far from positive opinions of some of his friends, such as Bob Trevelyan. Yet these did not seem to disconcert him, and he now began work on 'New Lucy', perhaps spurred on by an offer that had come from the publisher Edward Arnold* and that he had accepted. However, he found that the novel 'distracts me. Clear & bright & well constructed. But so thin. Spent an unhappy day yesterday deciding.'[29] The same day he had told Trevy: 'I have been looking at the "Lucy" novel. I don't know. It's bright and merry and I like the story. Yet I wouldn't and couldn't finish it in the same style, I'm rather depressed. The question is akin to morality.'[30] At this period Morgan turned to Trevy first if he was badly in need of advice about his work.

Perhaps for distraction he now wrote a short story. 'The Celestial Omnibus' is one of his most fantastical stories, being about a small boy's attempt to escape his parents' suburban home by taking an omnibus to heaven. He is submissive and dutiful, yet his mother and father 'though very kind, always laughed at him';[31] they punish him brutally when they decide he is lying, and are implacably convinced of their own rightness. In a sense the story is a homage to *The Way of All Flesh*. It is also a reiteration of *The Longest Journey*'s tribute to Shelley: although the boy has never heard of him, he inherits his mantle. He, like Goldie (as Morgan was to write), knew that

What he wanted was a song which would transport him out of the world in the right direction, wings that would carry him out of the body into a region where good and evil are more clearly opposed than on earth, and where good triumphs everlastingly. Sincere, enthusiastic, and fired with the same social hopes, Shelley provided him with exactly the right pair of wings.[32]

The boy in 'The Celestial Omnibus' goes on a Shelleyan flight, with the omnibus being the prosaic, but effective, equivalent of a skylark. It is one of Morgan's most curious stories, yet one of his most interesting: his own positive feelings towards it would be revealed a few years later when he chose it as the title story for his first collection.

---

* It is not known whether Morgan, having severed his ties with Blackwood's, sought out Arnold himself or whether he indeed 'came to Arnold no doubt as a result of one of the many letters Arnold wrote to new authors and because he proposed terms to Forster which were more generous than those offered by Blackwood.'[28]

In September, possibly because the boy in his story was in part inspired by *The Way of All Flesh*'s Ernest, who 'writhes under the paternal lash, he is stifled by the maternal embrace',[33] Morgan re-read Butler's other great novel, *Erewhon*. He had first read it rather unenthusiastically at Nassenheide, and may have been reminded of it by Elizabeth on their caravan trip the month before; this time he was greatly impressed. 'It's the human race re made', he told Trevy, adding: 'It will help us among the planets when we're dead.'[34] Then, at about the same time, he began work on a short play (though without any thoughts of publication) on a subject that made him 'hot': the Deceased Wife's Sister Bill which had been passed the previous month and at last allowed a man to marry his sister-in-law. There were two reasons for Morgan's fury. One was that opposition to the bill was 'a useful reminder of the poison of organised religion'.[35] The other was that Morgan was well aware that the paradisiacal life at Battersea Rise had been destroyed by one thing only: the refusal by Church and State to allow his great-uncle Henry Thornton calmly to marry his deceased wife's sister. If he had been able to marry his Emily without ructions, Marianne would have gone on living with them, Morgan would have had childhood memories of the house, and indeed Thorntons might have continued to live there until the present day. Instead, as Morgan knew, because he had recently been asked for a contribution to a fund set up to save Battersea Rise from destruction, it was about to be demolished and lines of small red-brick villas would then be built in its place. And the Thorntons were vastly the poorer for the loss of Battersea Rise just as

the Schlegels were certainly the poorer for the loss of Wickham Place. It had helped to balance their lives, and almost to counsel them. Nor is their ground-landlord spiritually the richer. He has built flats on its site, his motor-cars grow swifter, his exposures of socialism more trenchant. But he has spilt the precious distillation of the years, and no chemistry of his can give it back to society again.[36]

It is only the biographer who makes so much of the foregoing, who amplifies a brief mention of friends or Clun or book reviews into a whole segment of a life. For Morgan himself told Dent that 'nothing much has happened this year':[37] nothing much, that is, that he could tell Dent about, to whom he did not confide his inner life. (When he did venture to explain what was in his mind, Dent sometimes responded crudely: 7 October, 'I resented EJD's suggestion on Friday that I should "show up" Pension Life.'[38])

For it was at this period, as Morgan could see, that his outer life was beginning to settle into an unchanging pattern, with no foreseeable reason why it should ever be any different. He and Lily lived domestically in Weybridge, as they had done at Rooksnest, Tonbridge and Tunbridge Wells. Morgan worked, ate his carefully prepared meals, sympathised with Lily and, to an extent, participated in Weybridge life. Occasionally he went to London or Cambridge or to wherever he was at the time giving his Republic of Florence lectures (in the early part of the year it was in Stevenage, hence the night with the Postons). All the time, however, it was as if he were waiting for life to begin: with the clear-eyed realisation that it might never do so. Yet Morgan himself seemed to accept (although he never analysed it as such) that he needed a modicum of routine, of boringness, in order to write. As he was to note in his commonplace book exactly twenty years hence, as if looking back to the year when 'nothing much has happened':

How to get down the first hand experiences of my life – today I heard F.V. was not going to prison, helped to lift garden seats, planted tulips, ate Scotch ham inside bread & butter, read Thomas Mann, fear the elm will be blown down – I might have spent such a day twenty years back, here it is, and what can I do with it? Digested by my literary mind, it will tend to reappear as a young man's day, and all the incidents will be haloed with a spurious novelty and wonder, they will be falsified by "oh this was the first time he . . ." which insensibly perverts and pervades modern literature, and turns the numerous and fascinating noises of life into a mechanical morning song.[39]

It was Morgan's realism, almost cynicism, about the routine of his days, his own particular form of dailiness, that deterred him from keeping a diary. While Virginia Woolf was acutely interested in herself, although not so much in her own ego as in what one might call the 'herselfness' of her perceptions, Morgan was fearful of haloing them with 'a spurious novelty' and so his jottings were sporadic and only incidentally revealing of his own psyche. It was this quality of being loath to put himself even briefly on display that earned him, frequently, the epithet 'elusive'. But Lily, we can be sure, did not think him elusive. She thought she understood her Morgie through and through. And yet what can she have felt about his books? Apart from our knowing that she did not like the title *Where Angels Fear to Tread*, and that she disapproved of Helen's pregnancy in *Howards End*, her reactions are a mystery. We know that Morgan was conscious of her feelings (he chose to forget about 'Albergo Empedocle', he abandoned 'Ralph and Tony'); but we shall never know what she really thought, what insights into her Morgie she gleaned of which she might otherwise have been oblivious.

So the uneventful year continued. In July Effie Farrer's sister, 'Snow' Wedgwood, published a revised edition of her philosophical book *The Moral Ideal*, which had come out first in 1888: Morgan had helped with the revisions and felt a certain quiet pride; in November he read a paper on Dante 'whom I cannot like' at the Working Men's College. Events like these were noted in his diary. But the real event – the completing of *A Room with a View* – was never alluded to at all. In fact the only reason we know that it *was* finished is that, by the Easter of the following year, it had been typed. And (for money occasionally featured in Morgan's diary) an advance of £100 [£5000] had been forthcoming from Edward Arnold. 'Financially, poor,' wrote Morgan, 'but have invested £85 in B.A.G.S. [*sic*] – £25 to follow in March . . . Then also £31 for Epsom lectures [which seem never to have taken place], and in October £100 down for novel. So next year should not be so bad and I ought not to be in arrears with payments to mother. Railway fares the chief cause.'

Was this then the secret of Lily's grip? That although Morgan had once had, or indeed still had, £15,000 (£750,000) worth of capital behind him, he was in debt to his mother? It is almost unbelievable and one cannot imagine it to be serious. Yet there is no hint of irony in the remark; and the other possible explanation – that the capital inherited from Marianne and from Eddie had somehow vanished – is equally unbelievable. Morgan was twenty-eight, a published and successful novelist. But he and Lily counted out his money like coffee spoons. It is impossible not to conclude that behind the remark that followed on from this – 'Mother's rheumatism remains. She will not see a doctor. Should we not leave Weybridge?'[40] – there lies far, far more than this, great areas of unspoken unacknowledged feeling: that what Morgan really meant was should *I* not leave Weybridge?

18

A Room with a View

'"Oh mercy to myself I cried if Lucy don't get wed",'[1] Morgan had written to Trevelyan in the September of 1907: for the second half of *A Room with a View*, the 'Windy Corner' half that joined on to the Italian beginning, was quite different from the previous two drafts in that Lucy did get married. In 'New Lucy' love had 'burst out and shook her with a thousand longings – plain longings of the body, mysterious longings of the inmost soul',[2] but then George is killed; in the finished novel Lucy had 'a feeling that, in gaining the man she loved, she would gain something for the whole world'.[3]

Morgan wanted, in a way, to write a romantic novel: not because he wanted the sales (then, as now, literary novels sold far less well than romantic) but because he would have liked to subvert the convention. He would have liked to take the typical marriage plot and mould it into something new; or he would have liked his characters to live together without being married; or he would have liked them to exchange roles ('I hope that for women, too, "not to work" will soon become as shocking as "not to be married" was a hundred years ago'[4] declares Margaret Wilcox). It was his continuing fascination with the state of marriage, with the 'glass shade', that made him want to write about it; since he could not, through lack of firsthand insight, write a 'straight' novel, he chose to write a romantic comedy. Hence the jocular, slightly self-conscious tone in his letter to Bob, trying to shrug off this 'toshy'[5] little piece of froth, hoping his friend will not notice that, deep down, his feelings were as much engaged as in the first two novels.

The theme of *A Room with a View* is self-deception, using the interwoven leitmotifs of rooms versus views, gloom versus light and lies versus truth. After George has kissed Lucy for the second time she thinks, 'The contest lay not between love and duty. Perhaps there never is such a contest. It lay between the real and the pretended . . .' The passage continues, 'Lucy's first aim was to defeat herself . . . The armour of falsehood is subtly wrought out of darkness, and hides a man not only from others, but from his own soul. In a few moments Lucy was equipped for battle.' At the end, when Lucy has defeated pretence, she has rejected duty: and this is the other theme of the novel (but one that Lily might fail to notice). Mrs Honeychurch is not, by the time of the honeymoon in Italy, at all reconciled to Lucy and George's marriage. Yet this is extremely surprising in a mother who had always indulged her daughter in everything: because Lucy did not choose to 'mess with typewriters and latchkeys' this, one might have assumed, would be something for which her mother would be grateful. But Windy Corner was unforgiving, and although Lucy declares blithely that 'if we act the truth, the people who really love us are sure to come back to us in the long run', George is far less sure. He answers her with 'perhaps' and then speaks 'more gently', implying that the word had been uttered a little harshly as a response to Windy Corner's anger. Mrs Honeychurch, whom Morgan once alleged to be based on his grandmother, turns out to be implacably unforgiving, snobbish and cruel; but the couple have defied her and have thereby found out that 'it was worth while; it was the great joy that they had expected, and countless little joys of which they had never dreamt'.

Through Lucy, Morgan re-created his own situation of unmarried child living at home with mother and proffered two alternatives, life with Cecil (blind to what life has to offer, intellectual, narrow yet with a streak of dignity) and life with George (in touch with reality, sensual, receptive to life and with a streak of coarseness). Lucy tells Cecil, in words that Morgan must have longed and longed to make his own,

you may understand beautiful things, but you don't know how to use them; and you wrap yourself up in art and books and music, and would try to wrap up me. I won't be stifled, not by the most glorious music, for people are more glorious, and you hide them from me.

But Morgan was stifled, not only by Weybridge but also by Cambridge values and even by the 'Bloomsbury' friends he was slowly beginning to make in London. And he was wretchedly beginning to feel, as Lucy tells Cecil in George's words, that he himself was 'the sort who can't know anyone intimately'.

Sexual fulfilment, Morgan was openly declaring in his novel, is the greatest gift life has to offer because with this fulfilment come all the other aspects of life that matter so much: intimacy, unvarnished truth, the rejection of purely intellectual values. What Cecil fails to realise about Lucy is 'that if she was too great for this society she was too great for all society, and had reached the stage where personal intercourse would alone satisfy her';[6] what George realises – and this is made immediately clear in the uninhibited and undeferential way he kisses her, twice – is that she is not too great, i.e. sexual, for this society, but that she can only survive in it within a sexual and loving relationship – 'personal intercourse'. Submerged as he was in the moral code of Weybridge, Morgan nevertheless believed that it was George who held the key to life. 'The Oriental is at his easiest', he was to write in India five years hence, when the sensuality and sensuousness of that country had been beating on his spirit for nearly five months, 'when all – scenery, truth – are subordinated to sex. What a hot adolescence. English women will never stand it – I mean that kind of heat.'[7] In this respect George was happily Oriental and Lucy is able, finally, to stand it.

The image Morgan chose for Lucy's 'greatness' was her music. Between 'Old Lucy', where she was an accompanist, and the finished novel, she has changed into an outstanding pianist able to tackle Beethoven's Opus 111, one of the most difficult pieces in the entire repertoire. It is another clue to the real Lucy, and to the real Morgan, another way of subverting the conventional format without Weybridge noticing: only an accomplished pianist (as Morgan was) or someone with a great deal of knowledge of music would know that Opus 111 is a work that can be tackled by very few. The fact that Lucy plays it is a clue that she will, eventually, be 'wonderful'. Mr Beebe,* the clergyman, understands this when

his composure was disturbed by the opening bars of Opus 111. He was in suspense all through the introduction, for not until the pace quickens does one know what the performer intends. With the roar of the opening theme he knew that things were going extraordinarily; in the chords that herald the conclusion he heard the hammer-strokes of victory

He tells Lucy (who 'at once re-entered daily life') that if she '"ever

* The name was that of one of the boys with whom Morgan had been at Kent House.

takes to live as she plays, it will be very exciting – both for us and for her"'.[8]

In a way *A Room with a View* was the culmination of something Morgan had first encapsulated in his 1904 story 'The Eternal Moment': Miss Raby believed that the long-ago 'incident upon the mountain had been one of the great moments of her life – perhaps the greatest, certainly the most enduring.'[9] It was Morgan's belief too. He did not doubt, not for an instant, that if he had been a heterosexual he would have abandoned himself to love; but being a homosexual, and one for whom female sexuality grew more and more puzzling and offputting and, eventually, alien, this option was not to be his. Had it been, he would have wanted a marriage that was loyal, tender and intelligently loving. This is why, when he wrote the postscript to *A Room with a View*, called, sadly and pointedly, 'A View without a Room',* he envisaged Windy Corner gone, its garden built over, he imagined other horrors, but for George and Lucy 'It was something to have retained a View, and, secure in it and in their love as long as they have one another to love, George and Lucy await World War III – the one that would end war and everything else, too.'[10]

The novel to which Morgan had so spasmodically returned over a period of five years was in the end written very rapidly, between the June of 1907 when he mentioned it to Trevelyan and the end of that year, when he received his new publisher's advance. It seems that there was, in the end, some impetus that hurried him forward. And the impetus was, there can be little doubt, Edward Carpenter. A writer who had abandoned his academic life at Cambridge in order to live the simple life at Millthorpe near Sheffield, his first published work, apart from some early poems, was a lengthy philosophical poem called *Towards Democracy*; this was followed by essays and a book about India. Then, in January 1895, the year of the trials of Oscar Wilde, he circulated a pamphlet called *Homogenic Love*. This was 'one of the first books defending homosexuality to be commercially published in England'.[11] (J. A. Symonds's *A Problem in Greek Ethics* (1883) had explored homosexual passions: it was not a defence.) Morgan would almost certainly not have read it when it first came out; but Goldie (to whom Morgan was not so close while at Cambridge but to whom he grew close in later years) was a friend of Carpenter's and had visited him at Millthorpe. Here, since 1898,

---

* Cf. pp 6–7.

Carpenter had lived in a domestic and loving relationship with a working-class boy named George Merrill who looked after the house and smallholding while Carpenter became, increasingly, a sage preaching love, harmony, the outdoor life and uninhibited, and uncensorious, attitudes to sexuality.

Carpenter's ideas were encapsulated in a pamphlet sequence called *Love's Coming-of-Age* (1896) which was, however, published without the 1895 pamphlet. In 1906 the sequence was re-issued in an enlarged edition including the pamphlet on 'homogenic love' and was retitled *The Intermediate Sex*. Four years earlier Carpenter had also published *Ioläus: an Anthology of Friendship* (nicknamed, among booksellers, *The Bugger's Bible*). It had come out the year Morgan returned from Italy, the year in which he had the freedom, for the first time in his life, to say to Lily that he was going out, on his own, for the day, and thus to begin browsing in bookshops unfettered by the beam of her interest. In 1904, while Morgan was living in Drayton Court, Goldie asked Carpenter to contribute an article to the *Independent*: this appeared in May. In it Carpenter observed that 'so much ... of what is called "living for others" is simply a refined dodge of living on them';[12] he also censored so-called 'unselfish people' and his remarks found a direct echo in Caroline Abbott's remarks about Sawstonian 'petty unselfishness' and in Miss Bartlett's behaviour. The same year the *Independent* had also published a review by Goldie of Carpenter's short book *The Art of Creation* and Carpenter's reply to the review; and Morgan, a few months later, wrote 'The Other Side of the Hedge', his story about a young man escaping a materialistic society for a pastoral community of the kind of which Carpenter was so fond.

The Longest Journey, completed during the year that *The Intermediate Sex* was reissued, was also imbued with Carpenter's ideas. Mrs Failing's late husband had been, like Carpenter, a utopian socialist, believing that houses are smug fortresses, that man must live among nature and that we must love one another. 'The hills and trees are alive,' said Mr Failing, the 'whole of Creation is *alive*',[13] said Carpenter, and so on; while Stephen is the nature-figure who sunbathes, swims in rivers, opens windows to allow the fresh air in and (in the rejected scene) dances naked among the woods and the streams of Wiltshire. For him life had two distinct sides – the drawing-room and the other. In the drawing-room people talked a good deal, laughing as they talked. Being clever, they did not care for animals: one man had never seen a hedgehog. In the other life people talked and laughed separately, or even did neither. On the whole, in spite of the wet and gamekeepers, this life was preferable. He knew where he was.

Where *The Longest Journey* is less Carpenteresque is in its attitude to women. The 1896 pamphlets had been in large part a plea for more equal and more open relationships between the sexes, for at this stage Carpenter was mainly known for his feminism (in the aftermath of the Wilde trials he had been forced to be somewhat muted in his vision of a society that embraced homosexuality and heterosexuality alike). Agnes's remark, '"I wish I was a man . . . They aren't cooped up with servants and tea-parties and twaddle"'[14] was one of Morgan's early responses to Carpenter.

Almost as soon as he had completed work on *The Longest Journey*, given his Stevenage lectures and walked in Shropshire, Morgan re-started 'New Lucy'. It was because of Carpenter. He would use the convention of the romantic novel, he would 'show up' pension life, he would put himself in the position of Lucy, who manages to escape Windy Corner values ('their kindly affluence, their inexplosive religion, their dislike of paper bags, orange-peel and broken bottles'): with all this he would preach the Carpenterian ideal of feminism and of an honest and true relationship between the sexes.

The mouthpiece for Carpenter in *A Room with a View* is Mr Emerson. He is the representative of the natural life, in which emotions are freely expressed; and he is set against the forces of Sawstonian respectability. He is a socialist; and in 'New Lucy' he, like Carpenter, was a mathematician. After Lucy's first meeting with him, when she has been told by Miss Bartlett to be sure to shut the window, she opens her window and 'breathed the clean night air, thinking of the kind old man who had enabled her to see the lights dancing in the Arno'. In Santa Croce Mr Emerson urges Lucy to 'Let yourself go. Pull out from the depths those thoughts that you do not understand . . .' Finally he reveals to Lucy that his son George 'will work in your thoughts till you die . . . love is of the body; not the body, but of the body. Ah! the misery that would be saved if we confessed that! Ah for a little directness to liberate the soul!'

Lucy has achieved everything that Carpenter would have wanted her to achieve. She has shrugged off the society from which she is alienated, opted for truth and love and chosen a man who says, memorably, '"I want you to have your own thoughts even when I hold you in my arms."'[15] All these ideals can be found, virtually spelt out, in some instances direct precursors of Morgan's words, somewhere in Carpenter's work. When Morgan decided to dedicate *A Room with a View* to Meredith, a married, extrovert, urban academic, he chose a superb decoy. No one, least of all Lily, would have suspected that it should have been Carpenter to whom Morgan proffered his book.

However, despite Carpenter's persuasive view of women's lives, of unabashed passion, of the need to be in touch with nature, it was for his views on homosexuality that Morgan admired him most. Morgan had always liked Whitman and had undoubtedly read Havelock Ellis's *Sexual Inversion* (1897) which was, apart from Carpenter's work, the key text for homosexuals. But Carpenter himself appealed to Morgan as a personality: he did not focus on the sexuality of being an invert but took a broader, more philosophical view of life; Symonds, and after his death Ellis, were writers, Carpenter was a cult. It was a cult that Morgan must often have longed to be part of. And it was one that would preoccupy his thoughts during the next few years.

Yet his preoccupation was always silent: the side of him that needed Weybridge was equally as strong as the side that yearned for unconventionality. 'Am anxious not to widen a gulf that must always remain wide' he had written at the end of 1907; 'there is no doubt that I do not resemble other people, and even they notice it.' He wanted someone to love, but would not stray beyond the confines of his world in order to find them. It is significant that Masood, although in some ways on the other side of the gulf because he was an Indian, in other ways was very much part of Weybridge: by living there with the Morisons he accepted its values, so that in some respects his and Morgan's friendship was unremarkable. Even Gaunt, of whom Morgan at this time allowed himself to feel fond (22 December 1907: 'Tiresome but not ignoble to care for people at the same time. In G. poetry latent . . . We plan to walk in July . . .'), was a product of the same background as Morgan himself, indeed the two had met in the rain, in Kent, in a caravan, hardly a meeting imbued with exoticism and strange delights.

Despite his growing closeness to Masood, and the evidently tender thoughts about Gaunt, Morgan was still quite secretly homosexual. He still hoped that somehow he might grow 'normal'. He was horrified, for all the reasons to do with what he had observed among those who were less circumspect, and to do with his terror at giving up his comfortable suburban existence, at the thought of being less diffident about his sexuality. And so he did what so many have done before and since – he read. In his diary for the end of 1907 there is a list of books that looks like a reading-list for post-Victorian homosexuals.[16] It included H. N. Dickinson (whose *Keddy* skirts round the subject but nevertheless makes its point, using Oxford hedonism as a focus), Housman, Symonds, Whitman, Marlowe, Carpenter and Michelangelo. He also noted down Howard Sturgis, author of *Tim* (1891), which is unabashedly about Tim's affection for a slightly older boy and his own untimely death.

One of the books that Morgan had recently re-read, in the June of 1907 just after going to Clun, was Jane Austen's *Mansfield Park*: 'Let other pens dwell on guilt and misery,'[17] she wrote famously in Chapter 48. Morgan, we can imagine, began to wonder whether it was possible to write social comedy which did also dwell, in some measure, on guilt (middle-class) and misery (the poor). His remark at the beginning of *Howards End* was to be a direct echo of the novelist who, more than any, was his mentor. 'We are not concerned with the very poor. They are unthinkable, and only to be approached by the statistician or the poet. This story deals with gentlefolk, or with those who are obliged to pretend that they are gentlefolk.'[18] All during the latter half of 1907, while he was completing *A Room with a View*, Morgan brooded on this: how could he transpose some of his intense anger about the class-bound world he saw around him into a fictional form? He wanted, now, to do more than send up the English middle classes; he wanted, in some way, and without of course upsetting Weybridge, to subvert it. But how could this be done?

One way it could *not* be done was in the Jamesian mode, as he must have reflected in the January of the new year when he was taken by Sydney Waterlow to have tea with Henry James. James (as Morgan years later was to describe in a letter to *The Listener*[19]) mistook him for G. E. Moore, a perfectly plausible mistake; while Morgan, self-consciously, although he did not mention this in the letter, was probably mostly concentrating on his appearance and manners. 'Be as clean and smart and handsome as you can'[20] Lily had instructed him when she heard of the proposed visit while, only two weeks before, he had had a rather bruising experience when he went to tea with the Farrers at Abinger Hall. There he met 'a finished personage who betrayed her inmost soul by starting slightly when I offered her jam at tea. So one does not eat it.'[21] Details like this are more revealing about Edwardian society than any amount of history or economics. How curious that, among 'gentlefolk', jam was placed on the table (presumably in a cut-glass dish and with a special silver jam spoon) but then *not eaten* – indeed, not even offered. It just sat there, was removed, put away in the larder in a coarser pot, and then re-emerged at tea the next day.

Jane Austen avoided writing about misery; so did Henry James. On the other hand, polemic of the Dostoevsky or the Gissing kind did not interest Morgan either: someone who knew that his was the sort of mind that liked to be taken unawares ('The frontal full-dress presentation of an opinion often repels me'[22]) was never going to respond to direct exhortation and would not have wanted to write hard-hitting argument. This is why even Morgan's most deeply-felt and serious essays in some curious way creep up on one from behind: he is subtle, funny and acutely perceptive but at the same time and yet without bludgeoning he writes about the deepest and the most important issues. One of the reasons, I am sure, that so many people fail to recognise his greatness, and value him less than, say, James, Conrad, Lawrence or Virginia Woolf, is because they miss his depths, they cannot fathom them unless they present in a frontal, full-dress form. *Howards End* and *A Passage to India* are among the great novels of the century – but only for those who can see that lightness of touch, humour, domestic observation and psychological perception do not preclude insight into the weightiest, the most crucial aspects of our society.

Morgan was beginning to have a feel for the issues that he wanted to write about next and they would, he hoped, include an even more Carpenteresque plea for the emancipation of women, for the importance of personal relations and for the preservation of the countryside. But there were other themes in his mind at this time, the first half of 1908, and one of these was the relationship between the British and the Germans. His time at Nassenheide and in the Baltic coastal towns, and his caravan holiday with the von Arnims the summer before, had caused him to think more and more about this. He might not have such a vastly negative view as Elizabeth (who would be much chastised by reviewers, when *The Caravaners* came out at the end of 1909, for her almost brutal warning that war between the two nations was inevitable because of the Prussian temperament); yet Morgan himself had ambivalent feelings towards many aspects of the German spirit – its love of order, its emphasis on discipline, its preference for the group mentality.

Then, at some point during the early part of 1908, he read William Le Queux's *The Invasion of 1910* (1906); we can imagine that, once he had sent *A Room with a View* off to be typed, he allowed himself the indulgence of days of reading in the London Library (of which Aunt Laura had made him a life member in 1904 for his twenty-fifth birthday) and that this was one of the books he came across. Le Queux's book is halfway between a novel and popular history and describes, dramatically and convincingly, the day in 1910 (by extraordinary coincidence it is 3 September) when, although 'England was on the most friendly terms with Germany', yet 'the enemy had by his sudden and stealthy blow, secured command of the sea and actually landed.' 'The Government . . . were responsible for it all, was declared on every hand. They should have placed the Army upon a firm footing; they should have encouraged the establishment of rifle clubs to teach every young man how to defend his home; they should have pondered over the thousand and one warnings uttered during the past ten years by eminent men, statesmen, soldiers, and writers . . .'[23]

The military details, of which the book is full, did not interest Morgan; but the links and the differences between the two countries did, and he began to wonder whether he could broaden his new novel out in some way so that it was not only about English people but about the Englishness of the English and whether their difference from other nations could be made irrelevant. He began to think about those of his contemporaries who could *not* trace their ancestry back to Clapham and Yorkshire, to Stisted and Brighton, but whose parents or grandparents had chosen, for a myriad of reasons, to uproot themselves from another country and settle in England; he began to think about displacement and integration and whether the one could ever be forgotten and the other could ever be thoroughly accomplished; he began to envisage the Schlegels.

It was not merely nationalism that Morgan was brooding about but civilisation itself. Some time during this year he wrote his own version of the air-conditioned nightmare. 'The Machine Stops' is one of his best stories, echoing the anti-machine stance of *Erewhon* and responding cynically to the utopian visions of H. G. Wells. It evokes a mechanised world in which a Big Brother figure controls individual destiny, from which one of the characters, Kuno, manages briefly to escape. This story is superb science fiction, one of the early examples of the genre, and demonstrates Morgan's great versatility. It ends pessimistically, with Kuno having had a brief vision of another form of humanity ('I have seen them, spoken to them, loved them. They are hiding in the mist and the ferns until our civilization stops') and of 'the untainted sky'[24] before the crash of an airship causes the 'end of the world'.

The story was also prompted by his reaction to the news, in the January of 1908, that a man had flown an air machine for one and a half minutes.

It's coming quickly, and if I live to be old I shall see the sky as pestilential as the roads. It really *is* a new civilization. I have been born at the end of the age of peace and can't expect to feel anything but despair. Science, instead of freeing man – the Greeks nearly freed him by right feeling – is enslaving him to machines. Nationality will go, but the brotherhood of man will not come. No doubt the men of the past were mistaken in thinking 'dulce et decorum est pro patria mori' but the war of the future will make no pretence of beauty or of being the conflict of ideas. God what a prospect! The little houses that I am used to will be swept away, the fields will stink of petrol, and the air will shatter the stars. Man may get a new & perhaps a greater soul for the new conditions. But such a soul as mine will be crushed out.[25]

This entry was a direct prefiguration of *Howards End*, in its impassioned feeling for the English countryside ('in these English farms, if anywhere, one might see life steadily and see it whole'), in its loathing of 'the kind of scene that may be observed all over London, whatever the locality – bricks and mortar rising and falling with the restlessness of the water in a fountain, as the city receives more and more men upon her soil', and in its vision of a landscape destroyed by the motor car ('month by month the roads smelt more strongly of petrol'). The brotherhood of man, which can flourish only in the country (when Leonard thinks that 'To see life steadily and to see it whole was not for the likes of him' he knows this is because he has been displaced), the brotherhood of man will have to rely on love alone:

London was but a foretaste of this nomadic civilization which is altering human nature so profoundly, and throws upon personal relations a stress greater than they have ever borne before. Under cosmopolitanism, if it comes, we shall receive no help from the earth. Trees and meadows and mountains will only be a spectacle, and the binding force that they once exercised on character must be entrusted to Love alone. May love be equal to the task!

The symbol at the heart of the book would be somebody 'very poor', and the reason that he was thus would be because he had been torn up from his roots. So, perhaps basing Leonard Bast* upon some of the young men that he had met at the Working Men's College, Morgan 'guessed him as the third generation, grandson to the shepherd or ploughboy whom civilization had sucked into the town; as one of the thousands who have lost the life of the body and failed to reach the life of the spirit.'[26] Leonard's pastoral vision, his wanting to get back to the earth, was not the mere wallowing in the pleasant imagery of nature that some have since imagined it; it was a vision, amplified from 'The Machine Stops', of what might happen to anybody who ignores their roots and their traditions – indeed to Morgan himself.

In January of the same year Morgan's story 'The Celestial Omnibus' appeared in the *Albany Review* ('the only thing that I am wanting to publish at present is some short stories'[27] Morgan was to tell Edward Arnold) but by far the most important event of 1908 was the crystallisation of what was to become his fourth novel, *Howards End*. 'Idea for another novel shaping, and may do well to write it down,' remarked Morgan in the small, neat handwriting that he used for his diary (the writing in his letters tended to be larger). He still did not mention its title. But a mere six weeks later, on 9 August, came 'Written some of the new novel, Howards End. A deal too cultured, and from hand to mouth.'[28] This, extraordinarily enough, is how Morgan greeted his new book. And yet one could not imagine him doing it differently.

* Bast = a spiritual bastard, illegitimate in the Clough sense of 'illegitimate process', cf. p 165.

19

Howards End

──────────

'I can't write down "I care about love, beauty, liberty, affection and truth" though I should like to'[1] declared Morgan to a new friend, Malcolm Darling, who had written to praise *A Room with a View* at the end of 1908. He had, of course, written all these things down; except that the detached friend, the onlooker, might have thought him remote, sexually, from the first. But he was not, at all: he yearned for it more than ever.

In September, Gaunt, on holiday from India, had come down to Weybridge, but the visit 'was too tame for him, and perhaps he was bored . . . Nor did I know how much we depended on the background of the caravan.' So Morgan, whose fantasies had recently been divided between the Englishman in India and the Indian in England, began to focus his affection on the latter. But he still linked him only with the life of the emotions and not, yet, with his quite private lust. Noting that Italy (to which he had been for a month in the autumn) and Masood's affectionate friendship had been the only remarkable events of that year, Morgan added: 'He is not that sort – no one whom I like seems to be.'[2]

The hollow was deepening in Morgan's life. It was almost as if, up to now, his homosexuality had been comfortably that of Plato, of A. J. Symonds, of Whitman: romantic more than physical, and that now, as he neared thirty, and as the influence of Carpenter took hold, the bodily became increasingly urgent. One reason for this was the new sense of self he had acquired from being a published, and admired, writer. Another was *tempus fugit* – that the years were going past and his longings were still unfulfilled. And another was that, suddenly, he was becoming distanced from his friends by remaining a bachelor. 'Everyone is getting married,' he wrote at this time. 'Ainsworth, Mollison, Gillett, Doncaster – or writing books – Meredith, Dickinson';[3] Meredith was already married (Christabel was about to give birth to twin sons, conceived soon after the Welsh holiday) and this left only Dickinson – with whom Morgan was increasingly to identify.

Something else that helped to set him apart both from his married friends and from the concept of a purely romantic friendship was the autumn trip to Italy. 'How silly I was not to write it down at the time' he noted remorsefully; but it was evidently a 'splendid' excursion and his King's friend Woolley 'a magnificent companion'. Nevertheless, he 'was too moral & set to take to the natives, and said "the long & short of it is they're unreliable"'.[4] The touchstone for Morgan was whether someone could forget his Cambridge ideals and subsume himself in Italian values. On the other hand, Morgan would not, at this stage of his life, have chosen to live permanently among these values, in a country where people said yes and the sun shone and the ethic of the covered-up piano leg had never held sway; it is evidence of Lily's tight hold, and of the comforts of Weybridge, and of his deep love of the English countryside, that Morgan did not now decide to live in Paris or Florence or Tangiers, in a community where, in some ways, he would have felt very much at home.

But home was Harnham and all that it implied. 'I go down to the river, to row my mother & a friend about,'[5] he told Darling, in echoing anticipation of Virginia Woolf's description ten years hence of him spending his life rowing old ladies upon the river. For, whatever happiness he may have acquired from writing and from friends, his family came first, always. If the housekeeping was disrupted, if Lily was upset (as she was, deeply, in 1911 when her mother died), Morgan could think of little else: it was almost as if he were a wife, trying to escape to a room of her own but conscientiously in thrall to domesticity.

Yet it was at this time that Morgan's mind began slowly to awake to the possibility of an Indian novel. Masood, and Gaunt, had aroused his interest first of all. Then Darling, who had written to Morgan first and who had put out a firm hand of friendship, tried quite openly to pull his imagination in the direction of India. Finally, reading Edward Carpenter's *From Adam's Peak to Elephanta* (1896) made Morgan feel that a whole combination of circumstances were leading him ever more unambiguously to visiting that great continent. The problem, in part, was Lily. On one occasion, he told Masood, she was in Salisbury because her lumbago was better. 'This makes me easy, and able to enjoy my walk, as I know she is with some one whom she likes.' What, however, would she do if Morgan went to India, if only for a few months? 'I know that she will mind me going even if she urges it, and that she will be lonely without me; and yet the problem will be no easier another year, and no one can help me with it. I must muddle it out myself. I long to see India steadily. It's out of the question that she should come with me.'[6]

Masood saw, perceptively, that an Indian novel would be a fulfilment for Morgan, although at first he had seen a novel merely as a kind of deflector for the erotic yearnings that were, in Morgan, to become more and more evident. After they had known each other for about two years Masood left Oxford and moved to London in order to read for the Bar. Masood, whose letters had, to begin with, been typically Indian in their charming demonstrativeness ('you are not to think that the great affection, the real love and the sincerest admiration that I feel for you has in any way diminished') saw that he now had to distance himself. He tried to help Morgan to ignore his burgeoning love – for he was sensitive enough to see it as such – and was to tell him:

You know my great wish is to get you to write a book on India, for I feel convinced from what I know of you that it will be a great book. I do not wish to flatter you in any way but the fact is that you are about the only Englishman in whom I have come across true sentiment and that too real sentiment even from the Oriental point of view. So you know what it is that makes me love you so much; it is the fact that in you I see an Oriental with an Oriental's view of life *on most things*, and, as the Frenchman has said 'Cultivez Cultivez' etc, I say Go on Go on improving your imagination and with it your power of physically feeling the difficulties of another.[7]

The reviews of *A Room with a View* were generally good and Morgan's friends mostly appreciative. If few people seemed to notice its outstanding qualities of insight, humour and extraordinarily beautiful prose, the *Observer* did state that 'Mr Forster's gift for sighting the comedy of ordinary social intercourse amounts to genius' and C. F. G. Masterman in the *Nation* wrote a long and positive review.[8] Masterman's insight into what the novel was trying to achieve impressed Morgan a good deal; he was doubly pleased because he had been reading and admiring Masterman's articles in the *Independent* since 1904. A radical Liberal and East London MP, Masterman shared with Morgan a deep sense of disquiet about industrial England:

Restless, dissatisfied faces haunt [the visitor] along all the city ways; he apprehends something gone astray, the lost key of progress: a people which has lost the object of its being ... the atmosphere is of unsettlement and vague disturbance, as if humanity, fleeing from some threatened destruction, had encamped in any huddled fashion for a night and a day. He sees no evident system, or mutual dependence, or effort towards an organic whole ...

At the same time 'large impersonal forces' lie in wait to ensure any errant citizen does not stray off the allotted path: power, tradition, the cash nexus, habit all conspire together to forestall beneficial change. But what relation 'have these lavatories and these cemeteries, all the busy exercises of Government, its institutions, its inspectors, its smooth and polished mechanisms' to civilised values? Why should we condone 'common humanity condemned to monotonous toil and mirthless pleasure, with no intelligible advance in gentleness and the art of living'?*[9]

Masterman stirred Morgan's social conscience more than any writer since Ruskin. He made him want to write a novel that was not merely amusing, or perceptive, or critical of suburban values, or a plea for individual freedom: he made him want to write about English society at that moment. Morgan had, after all, one quality that was essential for doing this, and that was a rootedness in the here-and-now: his feminine side made him very responsive to his surroundings. As Virginia Woolf was to comment:

The social historian will find his books full of illuminating information ... It is on Tuesday that the housemaid cleans out the drawing-room at Sawston. Old maids blow into their gloves when they take them off. Mr Forster is a novelist, that is to say, who sees his people in close contact with their surroundings. And therefore the colour and constitution of the

---

* The next article in the issue of the *Independent* from which this quotation is taken was by Hugh Seebohm, whose family lived in the 'big house' just north of Rooksnest. His subject was Ebenezer Howard's proposal for a Garden City at Letchworth near Stevenage: it was perhaps Howard's name, as much as that of the previous farmer at Rooksnest, that led to Morgan's choice of name. Masterman's articles were to be published in book form in 1909 under the title *The Condition of England*.

year 1905 affect him far more than any year in the calendar could affect the romantic Meredith or the poetic Hardy.

Of course, she went on, 'he is also the most persistent devotee of the soul' and displays a mixture of gifts that is hard to harmonise: 'satire and sympathy; fantasy and fact; poetry and a prim moral sense'; but above all she saw Morgan as a novelist 'extremely susceptible to the influence of time'.[10] If *Howards End* had been written in 1905 or 1915 it would have been a different novel. This does *not* make it a period piece, dating almost as soon as it has been published; what it does do is present, at the same time as creating a portrait of England in 1910, a novel that rises above the merely timely to explore the nature of what we might call liberal humanism: the sanctity of the individual, respect for nonconformity, the love of rural traditions, of art, of the inner life and personal relations.

The story revolves around two families, the Schlegels and the Wilcoxes. The former consists of two sisters, Margaret and Helen,* and their younger brother Tibby, the latter of a businessman and his wife and their three children. The Schlegels live in Wickham Place and the Wilcoxes at Howards End; the families meet by chance and a friendship develops. The theme of the book is the contrast between their ideals and preoccupations with their two houses, plus the Shropshire house, as the triangular focus of their lives.† Around this basic concept Morgan built a masterpiece: 'my best novel and approaching a good novel' he would remark in the 1950s. 'Very elaborate and all pervading plot that is seldom tiresome or forced, range of characters, social sense, wit, wisdom, colour.' But then he went on, 'Have only just discovered why I don't care for it: not a single character in it for whom I care.'[11]

Yet the reader cares for many of them, and particularly for Margaret, one of her creator's finest achievements. She was, I believe, derived entirely from his imagination: although he would later claim that she and Helen were partly modelled on Goldie's

---

* Margaret means 'pearl' and Helen means 'the bright one': Morgan carefully chose names that were appropriate to the sisters' characters. The name Schlegel has overtones of culture and literature since the brothers August and Friedrich von Schlegel were early-nineteenth-century German men of letters, the former translating Shakespeare into German. In an early draft of *Howards End* Margaret and Helen were distant relations of the von Schlegels.
† The novel was originally divided into three parts, to echo the complex construction focused on the three houses; but six weeks before publication Morgan changed his mind on this.

two sisters, and although others have seen in them similarities to the Stephen sisters, in truth she is entirely herself, with perhaps a touch of Josie Darling and of Florence Barger. It is round Margaret that Morgan wove his themes of whither England, of the life of business and imperialism versus that of the intellect and the imagination, of the intertwining of money and of death because of inherited wealth. It is through her, as well, that he explored the theme, one to which he would return in *Maurice*, of exile, of not belonging, of wanting to put down roots; Margaret could not glibly buy herself homes as the Wilcoxes could do, but yet she was much more rooted in the country in which she was a second-generation immigrant – because she had the right ideals. The Wilcoxes, on the other hand, are so obsessed with themselves, with money and with worldly matters that they are dispossessed.

Day and night the river flows down into England, day after day the sun retreats into the Welsh mountains, and the tower chimes 'See the Conquering Hero'. But the Wilcoxes have no part in the place, nor in any place. It is not their names that recur in the parish register. It is not their ghosts that sigh among the alders at evening. They have swept into the valley and swept out of it, leaving a little dust and a little money behind.

One of the most remarkable aspects of *Howards End* is its modernity. This is not just modernity of tone of voice, as in the Clough-influenced *Where Angels Fear to Tread*, but modernity of theme. It is still, to my mind, *the* great twentieth-century novel about London; and is perfectly contemporary for today in its contrasting of Thatcherism with liberal values. Margaret Thatcher is a direct descendant of Henry Wilcox, preaching the competitive instinct, the pay-your-way mentality, the work ethic; as opposed to liberal kindliness, loyalty to the individual, self-fulfilment. When Mr Wilcox says that 'one sound man of business did more good to the world than a dozen of your social reformers' and when we are told that he cares about 'neatness, obedience and decision'; and when the Schlegel sisters declare, famously, that 'personal relations are the important thing for ever and ever, and not this outer life of telegrams and anger' and when Margaret tries to help Mr Wilcox to achieve 'the building of the rainbow bridge that should connect the prose in us with the passion';[12] then we are reading about capitalist values and the liberal, intellectual classes that are opposed to them. And yet, as D. H. Lawrence failed to do (he absurdly accused Morgan of making 'a nearly deadly mistake glorifying those *business* people'[13]) today's Schlegels do usually understand, with ironic awareness, the importance of the Wilcoxes in our lives. 'More and more do I refuse to draw my income and sneer at those who guarantee it' declares Margaret; and Tibby says about businessmen that they 'give me more pleasure than many who are better equipped, and I think it is because they have worked regularly and honestly'.[14]

It has been suggested that Morgan dislikes the Wilcoxes. This is not quite correct. His attitude is much nearer to Margaret's realism and he was able to explore the flaws of Schlegelism while, personally, preferring it as a way of life; and he could see the strength of Wilcoxism while showing the individual members of the family to be unappealing. Yet, while they were not part of what he would later call the 'aristocracy of the sensitive, the considerate and the plucky'[15] – they were not 'saved' – Morgan nevertheless gives them a good deal of dignity. They do, after all, live at Howards End; they are *all* part of the saintly Mrs Wilcox's family. In fact he dislikes them less, I think, than the Herritons in *Where Angels Fear to Tread*. Morgan's money, too, his comfortable, suburban way of life, was ultimately based on the business mind of the Thorntons. It was his understanding of both sides of the questions that gave his novels their realism, their rootedness in life as it really is.

Howards End, unmentioned in Morgan's letters and diary, gradually neared completion: this was his inner life, part of the one that was never mentioned, the one that took place upstairs in his attic room at Harnham and that was discussed with no one. 'Are you writing another novel, Morgan?' one can imagine people saying; and Morgan replying, diffidently, 'I'm trying to' and deflecting the subject on to books (he was at this time reading *War and Peace*), the theatre or the subject he did like talking about, his short stories. In November 'The Machine Stops' appeared in the *Oxford and Cambridge Review*; despite the eulogies he had received for his novels, and despite the persistent refusal of publishers to publish the stories in a collection, Morgan was still fonder of them than of anything else he had written – except *The Longest Journey*: 3 August 1910, reread all about Stephen with pathetic approval. The LJ is a book to my own heart. I should have thought it impossible for a writer to look back and find his work so warm and beautiful. It fills *me* with a longing for Wiltshire! I have given back to it what once I borrowed. To have written such a book is something. My next heroism will be to stop writing.[16]

These remarks were made in the vulnerable period when Morgan was about to correct the proofs of *Howards End* and was anticipating the reviewers' comments. He had completed three-quarters of the book in March and was given a £130 (£6000) advance from Edward Arnold; in Italy, where he and Lily had gone for six weeks' holiday, he had continued to make good progress, and by July had finished. In August, just before proofs arrived, he was told that another publisher, Sidgwick & Jackson, would publish his short stories (Arnold had refused them); this elated him far more than the universally excellent reviews of his new novel, and made him eager to start writing an Apostles paper on 'The Feminine Note in Literature' which he gave in October. The same paper was read in early December to an informal London gathering at Robin Mayor's house* called the Friday Club, one that included Roger Fry and the Stephen sisters; it marked the beginning of Morgan's involvement with Bloomsbury.†

The title of the paper was in echoing response to a 1904 book by W. L. Courtney called *The Feminine Note in Fiction*, which eschewed all serious analysis except for observing that women like detail and are good at psychological insight. Morgan, naturally, since he had always lived among women and since his vision was androgynous, was also interested in whether men and women wrote differently; and in his paper argued that women are preoccupied with 'personal worthiness' but measure this in relation to another person, whereas men are more abstract, 'have an unembodied ideal': 'In *Villette* we care that Lucy Snowe should learn to love Emanuel. In *The Egoist* we care that Clara Middleton should learn to love the Alps.'[18]

Morgan was also conscious that by now he had developed an almost 'feminine brilliance of perception'.[19] As a reviewer of *Howards End*

---

* Morgan thought the house 'beautifully placed' on Campden Hill Square and found that it gave him a new idea of London: as though, naïvely, he had not realised before that it is possible to live an urban existence, near friends, libraries and the underground railway, and yet be in congenial surroundings. How much happier he would have been if he had, like Mayor, lived in Holland Park.

† Leonard Woolf's return from Ceylon in the summer of 1911 would involve him further. But 'I don't belong automatically,' Morgan would write in 1929. 'And I couldn't go there for any sort of comfort or sympathy.'[17]

£130
17 APR 1910
6/4/10

Howards End
June 30 1910

HARNHAM,
MONUMENT GREEN,
WEYBRIDGE.

Dear Mr Arnold

Thank you for your letter: I need
hardly say how glad I am that you
think well of the book. I shall be
very happy to accept the tern terms you
offer — namely the last agreement with
£130 on account of Royalties instead
of £100. I am writing in a great
hurry, so cannot discuss your criticisms
in both of which I feel great force, o

A letter from Morgan to Edward Arnold in 1910, showing Arnold's noting of the £130 advance paid in June. Morgan was in a hurry because he was just off to Italy; he was not persuaded by Arnold's objection to Helen's pregnancy. *Howards End* was published in October, and this November advertisement was in response to excellent reviews and sales – 2500 copies in October, 5500 in November, 1000 in December and two more reprints the following year.

remarked, 'My impression is that the writer is a woman of a quality of mind comparable to that of the Findlater sisters or to May Sinclair.'[20] While Mrs Dawson Scott, the novelist who was later to found PEN, remarked that she had 'just read *Howards End* by Miss Forster. I like it – the vein of thought, the indeterminate people, the soothing lack of incident, the dreamy way in which it is written . . . [her husband] is *not* pleased with it: "Another of these damned old maids talking about things of which they know nothing." And that's true, too.'*[21]

* The novelist Graham Greene took up this approach forty years later in *The Third Man* (1950). In it there is a novelist named Dexter, modelled on Morgan, who 'has been ranked as a stylist with Henry James, but he has a wider feminine streak than his master – indeed his enemies have sometimes described his subtle, complex, wavering style as old-maidish.'[22]

Yet Morgan's androgynous sympathies helped his circle of friends to grow: people found him easy to confide in, he listened, and he made perceptive and not obtuse remarks in response. He noted in his diary that it was gradually getting to the point, something unaccustomed for him, where people wanted to know him more than he wanted to know them. He was now thirty, his intelligence both sensitive and mature; he knew well that 'a pause in the wrong place, an intonation misunderstood, and a whole conversation went awry'.[23] In the year he wrote *Howards End* this was made tragically clear.

20

Maurice

On 8 July 1909 Morgan had dined with Malcolm Darling, a King's friend of his named Ernest Merz whom he had never met before, and, possibly, although accounts have differed about this, a fourth Kingsman named Jermyn Moorsom. (Merz's mother cited 'Darling and Moorsom'[1] as his dining companions, yet put their names in inverted commas as if to signify hearsay; Morgan, in his diary, mentioned only Merz and Darling.) After dinner Morgan and Merz 'walked a little alone, & he left me, normal, at about 9.40.* Next morning he was found dead, having hanged himself.'[2]

Morgan, quite clearly, never, ever got over this. A normally sensitive person never would; as for an abnormally sensitive person, it does not bear thinking about. And the explanation of what happened was not quite as clear to Morgan as it is, I think, to us. Merz was twenty-seven, three years younger than Morgan, and his first year at Cambridge had been Morgan's last, the one in which he was an Apostle and seemed something of a 'figure' to the younger undergraduates. Merz had been up for four years, reading History and Law, but had gained a Third in both parts and minded deeply about this. He was also in the middle of a classic tug between Wilcoxism and Schlegelism. 'Ernest looking forward to the end of his college life when we hope to have him in business in Newcastle,'[3] wrote his mother, only a month after he had come fourth out of eighty candidates for a prize essay on Byron. It was his great Cambridge achievement; yet Wilcoxism triumphed and he began to train as a solicitor, his sense of identity

---

* Morgan would have known the exact time because he would have allowed five minutes to walk to Charing Cross to catch the 9.46 to Waterloo and the 9.55 to Weybridge. However, at this period he occasionally stayed with Edward Marsh in Gray's Inn, in which case he would have remembered the time fortuitously.

confused and his self-esteem low. Nevertheless, he had many friends who admired him, including Arthur Cole, with whom he had until recently shared a flat, and Malcolm Darling, who had described him as 'a continual bubble of suppressed laughter'; and he remarked that Merz 'has shown me how much true tenderness and sympathy may co-exist with a manly self-reliance and intelligence'.[4]

His father, who was 'in business, but for 25 years has been working at a History of the Thought of the 19th Cent'[5] (to use Goldie's typically Cambridge tone of deploring the business but approving the philosophy) was, however, dominant and exacting. He was famous for reading for three hours *before* going off to his Electric Supply Company; for admiring Goethe and Wordsworth; for his philosophical insight (his History was to be in four volumes); and for being a devout Quaker ('Theo says "I believe E. had a vision & he heard a voice which said "Come to me" & he went'[6] was his reaction to his son's death). All in all he was not easy to live up to;* while his wife Alice was over-fond of her youngest child. Ernest himself was, as analysis of his handwriting has shown, an introvert who had deep feelings of inferiority: 'if you can be satisfied with mediocrity – mediocrity will be very pleased,'[7] he had written to Darling on 5 July about a proposed trip to Cambridge. He longed for the protection that, in childhood, his mother had given him but on the surface was a charming, merry Kingsman who reminded Darling of Morgan. The combination of a weak, conscientious and rather rigid nature, combined with a logical, rational and morally scrupulous outlook, fatally predisposed him to suicide – if the circumstances were right for such a tragedy.[8]

In his case he was, we can be almost sure, miserably homosexual. In early manhood he must have hoped he would 'grow out' of it. 'Dear Father,' he wrote from King's in 1903, 'I wanted to write and ask you what is a good easy book to read upon the subject of Heredity, as I am somewhat interested in it at present.' Later, in London, he had close and happy friendships not only with Darling but with

---

* The Schlegel sisters' father Ernst contains elements of Theo Merz: in Chapter 4 of *Howards End* he is described as a dreamy idealist whose values are those of the philosophers Hegel and Kant. Schlegel was neither the aggressive German described by journalists (such as William Le Queux) nor the domestic German described by satirists (such as Elizabeth von Arnim in *The Caravaners*). After leaving Germany, he began life in England in a provincial university; Theo Merz's father had emigrated to Manchester but chose to send his son back to Germany to be educated at provincial universities there.

Arthur Cole – before his marriage – and with the handsome E. V. Thompson with whom, in the last year, he frequently went away for the weekend. But in the summer of 1909 two Cambridge weddings were imminent, those of Darling and of Cole. Ernest liked the future Josie Darling very much, as Morgan was to do, for she was obviously a kind, sympathetic and intuitive person (and was one day to write a good novel). He wrote home about her, in almost passionate terms that he used rarely, that she was

one of the most remarkable and delightful of women, has a very persuasive way of putting things, and it is not easy to remain critical after hearing her arguments. She is a person of extraordinary vitality and power, more like what I imagine George Eliot to have been than any one else I have met . . . she has a perfect genius for colour, so that her dresses change their hue as naturally and beautifully as the face of the country under the influence of the seasons. But most often they are of a rich autumnal hue.

The letter is full of resonance, of a deeply sad kind: never, Merz seems to be saying, will I myself woo a woman like that. But how much I would like to! How much I would like even to marry the daughter of the senior partner if it would please *famille* Merz and the rest of Edwardian society! He knew that when he went north for the Darling wedding on 21 July, where he was to be a groomsman, he would go in the sad knowledge that he himself might never get married, might never be seen to be 'normal'.

Yet there was someone who imagined herself to be unofficially engaged to Merz. The tragedy is that if he had been made aware of her feelings he might have proposed marriage in the hope that, when it came to it, he might, with some luck and some alcohol and some simple affection, prove to be bisexual enough to have an ordinary married life. But he never knew, seeing her merely as the sister of one of his friends; she, however, never married and kept his photograph by her bed to the end of her days. Her name was Hilda Garnett and she had two elder brothers, Maxwell* and Stuart. Max had gone up to Trinity College, Cambridge the year before Merz, had left the year before him and gone to the Bar; in the early summer of 1909 he had become engaged to be married. Merz was, as so often in these cases, half in love with the whole Garnett family, with the three boys and with the two sisters – and especially with Max.

* His father's mentor at Cambridge had been Professor James Clerk Maxwell, after whom he was named.

The Garnett family are certainly amazing ... in all of them their very stature suggests that they have outreached the confines of the earth and have held conversation with the stars, and have had the clouds for their playmates. Something of sunshine glances in their hair, and their eyes reflect, too, something of the colour of heaven.[9]

Between 1903 and 1909 Hilda and Merz corresponded, for although the letters themselves are lost she kept a list of them in the back of an old school notebook; the rest of the book is extracts from hymns, tracts and sermons and although Merz was never mentioned by name it is possible to see that Hilda truly believed that her putative lover had, after his death, gone to a better place. 'Most beautiful letter,' she wrote beside one for January 1905 (most of the letters were for that year since Merz was travelling abroad) and, again, in February 1907 'beautiful'.[10] Often letters were unnecessary, for example in July 1906, when Ernest had returned from his travels, they were in Grasmere* (both, presumably, reading their favourite Wordsworth) and in October of that year Alice Merz 'had nice visit from Hilda Garnett – much company and coming and going'.[12] The last letter of all was on 4 March 1909. The final page of the notebook has been cut out, jaggedly with nail scissors. It would undoubtedly have referred to Malcolm and to Max's engagements in June; and to the tragedy that so quickly followed.

On the evening of 8 July Merz, I believe, appealed to Morgan. He would not have appealed directly, but his state of mind must by then have been so morose, and yet so clear-eyed in its lack of self-worth, that in some form or another he asked for help. It is even possible that, impetuously and out of desperation, he asked Morgan to be his special friend and that Morgan, almost impatiently as was sometimes his way, rejected him. The other possibility is that Morgan recognised a fellow invert straight away; and that when the two of them strolled along Piccadilly together (Merz had said that he was going to his club, the Devonshire in St James's†) Morgan had made a remark or an allusion that made Merz realise his true inclinations were now unconcealable. If this was the case, it may have been Morgan's intuition that toppled Merz over into suicide. The third possibility is that in Piccadilly,

---

* In *A Passage to India* Ronny thinks about Adela, when the trial is over, that 'she belonged to the callow academic period of his life which he had outgrown – Grasmere, serious talks and walks, that sort of thing.'[11]
† His rooms were in Albany in Piccadilly, the home of Oscar Wilde's 'Ernest' in *The Importance of Being Earnest*.

before going to the Devonshire or to his rooms in Albany, he was accosted by a male prostitute and succumbed; the fourth possibility is that he was blackmailed (the Darlings' explanation).

Unable to live with himself, Merz drank whisky ('had the whisky been drunk neat?' Morgan was rather curiously to ask Darling) and then found a rope. 'My own theory,' Morgan said in the same letter to Darling, 'one must have one – is that he was insulted disgustingly or saw something disgusting. You mustn't be annoyed with me for writing so freely. The man whom I saw has never made a mess of things, I know that.'* The Merz family, whom Darling went to see, attributed Merz's death to a spiritual crisis. Morgan, in his letters, could not accept this, crossed out an allusion to the mechanical, mentioned Whitman and Goethe and told Malcolm that 'it is surely the strangest thing we shall ever meet'.[13] Mysteriously he mentioned E. V. Thompson and said that 'I feel wary about him now',[14] wanting to intimate perhaps, as is possible, that it was the close friendship between the two men that had precipitated Merz's death. Yet – and Morgan could of course never forget this – it was he who had been the last person known to have seen him alive. He also, even more importantly, identified with Merz, not merely because superficially they were alike but because their situation was indeed so similar. Darling would never know this, indeed no one would ever know this, but Morgan was guilt-stricken, miserable and confused. The only remedy, the only form of exorcism, that he knew was a novel. And so *Maurice* was born.

Years later, when he was eighty, Morgan was to write a 'terminal note' to *Maurice* in anticipation of eventual publication. In this he claimed that, on his second or third visit to Edward Carpenter at Millthorpe, his lover George Merrill touched his backside; 'I believe he touched most people's,' added Morgan typically, which is indeed true, as contemporary memoirs by other visitors to the Carpenter household have confirmed. But for Morgan the touch was more than

---

* There were, in addition, two other recent and relevant occurrences. The German book *The Sexual Life of Our Time* by Iwan Bloch, of which Chapter XVIII is a very frank discussion of homosexuality, was published in its English translation in 1908; and in the spring of 1909 a pamphlet was circulated in Sheffield attacking Edward Carpenter. It was vile and vituperative and reading it, or even references to it, would have been deeply upsetting for Merz.

just a sensual caress: 'it was as much psychological as physical . . . I still remember it.'[15] He likened the moment to conception; and noted that he then returned to Harrogate (Lily was taking a cure) and at once began to write *Maurice*.

It was the image of the hanging Merz that, I believe, inspired his fifth novel; but Morgan, for all kinds of reasons to do with self-identification, remorse, anguish, would never acknowledge this, preferring to attribute it to Millthorpe. As so often in Morgan's life there was a convenient way to deflect people's assumptions; why need the painful truth be told if it could be manipulated through bonfires, what passed as memory or even 'accurate' observation? Streatfeild, Tiddy or Merz could all be omitted because it was perfectly easy to turn the attention on to other things. And to some extent this is understandable.

Maurice is a unique novel, one of the few novels about homosexual love to have been written in the years before gay liberation began to ensure that homosexual fiction was as publishable as heterosexual. Indeed, if Morgan himself had been willing to publish at the time, then the repression of homosexuals might have been brought to an end more quickly, we would not have had to wait until the 1967 Act (making legal homosexual relations in private between adults of over twenty-one) and the painfully slow change in attitudes since then; *Maurice* might have been part of the line-up of sexually influential fiction that stretches from *Tess of the D'Urbervilles* through *The Well of Loneliness, Lady Chatterley's Lover, The Group, Couples* and beyond.*

It would emerge directly out of both *The Longest Journey* and *Howards End*. '*Maurice* works out in a particular direction the thesis of the importance of personal relationships generally laid down in *Howards End*'[16] Morgan would one day write, thereby emphasising that his impetus was primarily Maurice's happiness in relation to other people rather than the fact that, as it happened, 'He loved men and always had loved them'. If society was structured in such a way that this did not matter: then Merz would not be dead. Was there any way in which there could be, for Maurice, a happy ending?

The plot of the novel is simple. Maurice, a child of the suburbs, leaves his public school and goes to Cambridge. In his second year he meets Clive Durham, who has understood his own homosexual

---

* It was to be published in 1971, a year after Morgan's death.

inclinations for a long time. Indeed 'His sixteenth year was ceaseless torture. He told no one, and finally broke down and had to be removed from school.' (In Merz's sixteenth year he too was removed from school and spent nine months in Germany.) Clive and Maurice realise they love one another; their love is chaste and very much in the J. A. Symonds mode (when Maurice goes to stay with the Durhams he is put in the 'blue room' as a symbol of the poetic, adoring but unphysical nature of their relationship as described by Symonds in *In the Key of Blue*).

After two years of idyllic friendship Clive goes on holiday on his own to Greece. He determines to be 'normal' and tells Maurice as much; the following year, in the spring, he announces his engagement. Initially Maurice contemplates suicide. Then he tries to change his nature for, after all, 'He wanted a woman to secure him socially and diminish his lust and bear children.' He tries hypnosis; but at the Durhams' house encounters a gamekeeper named Alec. Alec climbs into Maurice's bedroom and they make love: 'By pleasuring the body Maurice had confirmed – that very word was used in the final verdict – he had confirmed his spirit in its perversion, and cut himself off from the congregation of normal man.'[17]

In the final version of the (much reworked) ending to *Maurice*, Clive and Maurice confront one another before the latter vanishes leaving only a pile of evening primrose petals. But in the first version of the manuscript there is an epilogue in which Maurice's sister Kitty meets Maurice and Alec working as woodcutters. She is old before her time and embittered. Her words are cruel: '"What, you're never still in England . . . disgraceful . . . abominable . . ." She spoke not what she felt, but what her training ordained.' Her true feelings are confused. 'But what was the "awful thing"? [in echo of Lily's words to Morgan about the man on the Downs and the dreadful thing]. Why should a sane wealthy unspirited young man drop overboard like a stone into the sea and vanish? – drop without preparation or farewell? The night of the wonderful sunset [had the night of Merz's death been one?] he had not returned . . . It was a man's business, Arthur had implied: women may weep but must not ask to understand, and he warned them against communicating with the Police . . .'[18]

Maurice is here allowed an approximation of a happy ending, although even on the last page of this version he and Alec prepare to leave their hideout in case Kitty betrays them to the police. But she proves unexpectedly understanding and echoes Margaret Schlegel's final plea for tolerance for all varieties of human behaviour: this can be seen as a disguised credo for homosexuality, a hint both that her sister Helen was lesbian ('But I – is it some awful, appalling criminal defect?') and that her own and Henry's marriage was sexless but happy nevertheless ('I do not love children. I am thankful to have none'[19]). In the same way, acceptingly, to Kitty,

> without the slightest shock the truth was revealed . . . 'He must be very fond of his mate, he must have given us up on his account. I should imagine they are practically in love.' It seemed a very odd situation to her, one which she had never heard of and had better not mention, but the varieties of development are endless: it did not seem a disgusting situation, nor one that society should have outlawed.[20]

Significantly Maurice and Alec are living in the woods, in the 'greenwood' as Morgan whimsically calls it. For the novel is not merely a plea for homosexuals to be allowed to have the same happiness in personal relations as heterosexuals; it is also a heartfelt expression of Morgan's belief, which had been with him since Rooksnest days, that country life is pure, unselfish and full of integrity and that town life is the opposite.

By allowing a homosexual couple to find happiness Morgan was not only making amends to Merz; he was not only making a Carpenteresque plea for sexual tolerance at a time which was, alas, too soon for the society which should read it; he was also (by showing Maurice outcast from 'normal' society) exploring the concept of the pastoral; and by corollary values such as love, sensitivity, kindness and spiritual freedom which, in society as most of us know it, come second, Morgan felt, to conventional, suburban behaviour.

In July 1910 Morgan accompanied Lily to Harrogate while she went on a two-week cure. They stayed at Beech Lodge on the Esplanade* and Morgan was free to do as he wanted while Lily drank the waters and took hot baths. On one of these days in early July Morgan could have gone by train to Millthorpe, a two-hour railway journey which could easily have been accomplished without Lily knowing where he

---

* This was at number 2 The Esplanade (overlooking lawns and beeches). It later became the Beech Lodge Hotel and latterly the Alphen Lodge Hotel, but is now (1992) empty and awaiting restoration. The hotel next door at number 1 The Esplanade is now the Beech Hotel.

had gone. And it was now, in 1910 not in 1913 as he was to assert fifty years later, that, I believe, Morgan first got to know Carpenter and Merrill. He and Lily were to go to Harrogate again in 1913, and he was again to visit Carpenter (by the end of 1915 he had been '3 or 4 times'[21]) but Morgan, I am sure, confused the date of his first visit: 1910, on his return to Beech Lodge, was when he began *Maurice*.

There are three corroborations of this date. The first is on the original version of the 1960s 'terminal note' to the novel, among the Plomer Papers in the University of Durham Library. Here the opening sentence reads that *Maurice* 'dates from 1910'; however the '0' has clearly been typed in later and there is a faint pencil mark in the margin. At the end of the third paragraph Morgan wrote that 'it was finished in 1912' – but without any later typing-in or pencil crosses.[22] (In the published terminal note the two dates are 1913 and 1914.) Secondly, in the Darling Papers in the University of Cambridge Centre for South Asian Studies there is a sheet headed '"Maurice" – Begun 1910, finished 1912',[23] followed by notes on what is evidently, from the page references, one of the manuscript versions of the novel; the handwriting is certainly not Morgan's. Thirdly, Florence Barger's son, remembering conflicting accounts as to the existence of a homosexual novel, recorded that 'he did write such a novel, called "Maurice", but way back in 1911.'[24]

These three corroborations, set against Morgan's one version of the terminal note, point to 1910 for the conception of *Maurice*. But why does it matter? It matters because the earlier date, coming only a year after Merz's death, shows this event *as well as* the visit to Millthorpe as being the point of inspiration; and thus changes our reading of the novel. And something further happened in 1910 to confirm this date: Merz's family brought out a privately printed volume of Ernest's letters; and they echo throughout the novel so much that it is clear that Morgan had it beside him as he wrote. There are indeed so many points of similarity between Maurice's and Merz's lives that we can now see *Maurice* as a rewriting of Merz's life – but with a happy ending. 'I was determined that in fiction anyway two men should fall in love and remain in it for the ever and ever that fiction allows,' wrote Morgan in 1960; and this is indeed what he did: in the novel the point at which Maurice contemplates suicide comes at exactly the point in Merz's life when he contemplated it and carried it out.

Looking back, I cannot now remember when or specifically why I one day realised that the novel was Merz's life story rewritten. The name alerted me early on, since Morgan so often used significant names: in this case the clue was that the name is German and I realised that if one wanted to anglicise Merz one would end up with Maurice (Merz/Moritz/Maurice). Then I read Merz's letters and thought about what I had been told of Hilda Garnett's love; and one day I realised that the similarities between the Garnett family and the two families in the book, the Halls and the Durhams, were too numerous to be mere coincidence. Max Garnett was the 'slight academic acquaintance' from whom Morgan derived some initial hints for Clive: 'The calm, the superiority of outlook, the clarity and the intelligence, the assured moral standards, the blondness and delicacy that did not mean frailty, the blend of lawyer and squire, all lay in the direction of that acquaintance';[25] the Garnett sisters, Hilda and Dolly, were given to Maurice and became Ada and Kitty.*

With all this in mind I re-read the novel and could see that *Maurice* was more than a work of the imagination: it provides almost documentary detail of the life of one particular segment of Edwardian society, more evidence of Morgan being, in Virginia Woolf's words, 'extremely susceptible to the influence of time'.[26] To read *Maurice* is to be allowed imaginative empathy with the misery of being a homosexual at the time it was written. (And yet, alas, things had not entirely changed sixty years later when it was published.) Morgan decided on a form for his novel which, although similar to *The Longest Journey*, approaches the biographical. So he turned Ernest Merz into Maurice Hall and Max Garnett into Clive Durham[†] not merely through the resonance of their names (they have the same number of syllables and the same feel, yet are different enough not to be too obvious) but also through the similarities of their lives. And he took as his fixed points the dates of birth – 1880 for Garnett and Durham and 1881 for Merz and Hall – and the 'crisis' in July 1909 when Merz dies but Hall rejects suicide and when Garnett is newly engaged and Durham newly married.

Within this framework the outlines of the lives tally in every respect, except that in the novel Morgan compressed everything a little ('Clive had turned towards women soon after he reached the

---

* Ada and Hilda sound alike, as do Dolly and Kitty; these last names have the link, and the resonance, of both being in *Anna Karenina*, a novel that does end in suicide.
† Durham is only ten miles south of Newcastle, where the Merzes lived and where the Garnetts had lived for nearly fifteen years. One of Darling's closest friends at Cambridge, Robin Quirk, won the Chancellor's Medal for English Verse for a poem on 'Durham'.

age of twenty-four') and in reality the Garnett figure (for there is no evidence at all, apart from Morgan's novelist's vision, that he was ever anything but heterosexual) became engaged when he was twenty-nine.* Thus in the novel Hall and Durham travel for only a few months, during the winter of what is on the time-scale 1903–4, whereas Merz travelled for two years, from 1904 to 1906. And Maurice and Clive started work in, supposedly, January 1905 but Merz not until January 1907.

Max Garnett went up to Cambridge the year before Merz in 1899, just as Clive Durham went up the year before Maurice Hall; Max was married on 1 June, as was Clive; Max's and Clive's birthdays were both in October; Maurice's birthday was in August but Merz's in November (yet to make *all* the details synchronistic might have been too obvious, if not libellous). During these Edwardian years, the lives of the four men, two real and two fictional, overlapped in too many respects for it to be mere coincidence: Morgan did it deliberately.

The one moment where his timing seems implausible is at the end, in 1909, when Clive and Anne become engaged in April and marry on 1 June. It is unclear whether there is an echo here of Eddie and Lily's short engagement – once someone homosexual has determined to get married he might want to get it over with as soon as possible – or whether Morgan did not realise that couples generally had far longer engagements (Max was married on 1 June 1910 and had become engaged just before Merz's death in the early summer of 1909). At the same time as Clive in the novel becomes engaged, Maurice's sister Ada becomes engaged to Arthur Chapman, the son of the other half of Chapman & Hall:† just as Arthur Cole had become engaged to Margaret. The effect was to make Maurice, and Merz, feel that everyone they knew was getting married.

The overlap in the lives of these four men is not just a question of matching dates, but of the even more important creation of character. 'The "Hampstead" family, particularly the daughters, are a mirror image of the Garnett family'27 was the comment of one of Max's daughters when she read *Maurice*; yet in other respects what Morgan did was pick out characteristics and distribute them here

---

* He was to be happily married for fifty years and to found a dynasty: all his children were successful and influential; one of his granddaughters entered the Cabinet in 1992.

† When he realised that he had used the name of a real firm, Morgan changed it to Hill and Hall. Maurice was originally Maurice Hill – until, in the 1950s, Morgan met a Cambridge don called this and changed the manuscript so that it became Maurice Hall.

ABOVE Charles and Clementine Poston with their children Elizabeth and Ralph at Highfield near Rooksnest. Mrs Poston's maternal calm, observed by Morgan on his visit in 1906 (p 185), may have contributed to the character of Mrs Wilcox in *Howards End*.

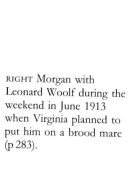

RIGHT Morgan with Leonard Woolf during the weekend in June 1913 when Virginia planned to put him on a brood mare (p 283).

ABOVE Virginia painted by her sister Vanessa Bell in 1912.

ABOVE Morgan in Mahratta turban in India. RIGHT Vishwanath Singh Bahadur, Maharajah of Chhatarpur, 'the ugliest little man you can imagine'[12] (p 267) but 'a most unusual character – mystical, and sensual, silly and shrewd',[13] perhaps the original of Godbole in *A Passage to India*: 'polite and enigmatic . . . his complexion was as fair as a European's. He wore a turban that looked like pale purple macaroni . . .'[14] BELOW the guest house at Dewas where Morgan stayed for Christmas 1912 and then lived for six months in 1921. The European woman on the first floor balcony might be Josie Darling.

ABOVE statue of Antinous, Hadrian's favourite, drowned at Alexandria (p 127). J. A. Symonds wrote in 1879: in sculpture he is 'eighteen or nineteen years ... The whole body combines Greek beauty of structure with something of Oriental voluptuousness . . . The lips, half parted, seem to pout; and [give] a look of sulkiness or voluptuousness [which] Shelley has well conveyed ... [in the] phrases, "eager and impassioned tenderness" and "effeminate sullenness".'[15] RIGHT Morgan in relaxed Alexandrian mood 1917. BELOW bathers at Alexandria in 1917, perhaps off Montazah where Morgan frequently bathed, and probably parted with respectability for the first time (p 299).

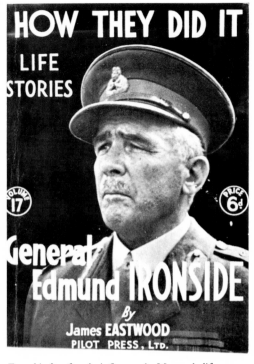

Four kinds of male influence in Morgan's life:
LEFT Edward Carpenter ABOVE Edmund Ironside
BELOW LEFT Constantine Cavafy BELOW
Goldsworthy Lowes Dickinson (painted by
Roger Fry in 1925).

and there. To take a small example: Merz described Hilda Garnett being distracted one day from moving the drawing-room piano by a heated discussion about socialism; but it is the Halls' Kitty who has a socialist friend to stay, while the piano-moving appears in a scene at the Durhams' house at Penge. As always, Morgan was not presenting a mirror-image; he was using pertinent qualities. Having decided to base his central character on Merz, he needed a different family setting, and yet not too different. The little glimpses of the Garnetts gleaned from Merz's letters were perfect for his purposes. In any case they had one, crucial characteristic: they had a security, a rootedness, a feeling of continuity that the suburban Maurice and the immigrant Merz so regretfully lacked. 'When I remember the German blood in my veins,' wrote Merz, 'I remember also that I can never be an English gentleman.'[28]

It was, Morgan realised, a sense of identity that, more than anything, Merz had needed. So he decided to write *Maurice* not merely to describe being homosexual; he wanted to explore this sense of being something other: by using the handsome, sporty, self-confident Garnetts with their leader-of-men qualities and their achievement ethic he could evoke the contrast with the outsider who had none of these things. But to try to connect the one type with the other by simply setting Max against Merz would not only have been too like the pattern of contrasts in *Howards End*; it would also have been too obvious.

After Ernest's death Mrs Merz and the Garnetts kept in touch: 17 December 1909, 'Hilda Garnett showed us the letters Ernest wrote her – chiefly on serious subjects. She and he were great friends.' In 1910 the two mothers watched Edward VII's funeral together, and in July, on the anniversary of the death, there were flowers from the Garnetts among the others on the grave. When, three months later, *Howards End* was published Hilda was given a copy: 'H. Garnett from E.V.T.' reads the inscription. Then, in 1912, just before he himself became engaged, E. V. Thompson visited Mrs Merz; in the autumn of the following year 'Mr and Mrs M Darling came for one night – most interesting and delightful.'[29] Cambridge did not forget. But Morgan never found it in himself to make the visit. And it is possible that one of the reasons he refused ever to contemplate publishing his novel was because of the susceptibilities of the Merz family.

21

The Celestial Omnibus

The initial impetus for Morgan's fifth novel emerged out of his unhappiness at Merz's death, an unhappiness that he shared with no one. The two men had been acquainted for barely two hours; but a fellow human being had reached out to him and Morgan had failed to respond. What should he have done? How could things have been different? All the winter of 1909–10 the thought must have obsessed him. Yet his discipline as a writer was so profound that the questions remained in a quite different part of his mind from that which was slowly and calmly producing *Howards End*. It was as if he told himself that, once he had finished, *then* he would allow himself to think.

There was, at this time, another, in some ways symbolic, change in his life. He had written about Merz's death on 13 July but failed to make another entry in his diary until 30 August: this recorded the death of Gaunt in India from malaria. 'Worlds into which the literary imagination cannot penetrate. I feel that I cannot feel,' Morgan wrote, fretting at the paradox that even the sensitive can remain untouched by death. 'It is only when they have thrilled our blood that the sense of loss is sharpened.'[1] Because neither Merz nor Gaunt had thrilled his blood, his deepest emotions were not affected; but the rest of him was. And almost as though he wanted to make a statement that he *was* touched, Morgan now, after six years, stopped using the notebook in which he had begun 'Old Lucy' and which was, as yet, far from used up, and two weeks later began a new diary, one which had a lock. The book had belonged to Inglis Synnot. It may of course have been pure coincidence that Morgan decided, at this point, to use this notebook. But it is hard not to link the new beginning with the endings in death; and with the diary having belonged to Inglis, Marianne's favourite before Eddie, who would have remained her favourite and her heir if he had not died young; whose death therefore cast a long shadow on Morgan's circumstances.

Lockable as the notebook was, Morgan continued to be circumspect. He did not suddenly move from partial self-concealment to complete revelation and was always aware that what he wrote might one day be of interest to others. 'A glance through in Jan. 1963 disappoints' he would write, quaveringly, at King's in his eighties. 'The personal entries are uncontrolled and niggling, and I should like them used sparingly in any personal account.' The habit of secrecy, the feeling (one that had been with him since Kent House) that some thoughts were too hidden to mention, was never now to be dissipated. 'We begin to understand people', he noted in 1911, 'when we realise they don't say what they mean';[2] of no one was this more true than himself.

Outwardly Morgan's life had continued on an even course and seemed satisfactorily filled with writing, friends, a peaceful existence at Weybridge, and lecturing. This still continued every year: the eleventh lecture course, as always on the Republic of Florence, would be at Harrow in the October of 1911, again for the University of London.[3] The audience, which included 'woolsorter, organ builder, clicker, engineer, compositor, carpenter, lithographer, shipwright, boilermaker, railway porter, painter, baker, blacksmith, carrier, brushmaker',*[4] would by now have been listening to a highly polished series. It was the last he would give until 1922; perhaps he was no longer willing to compromise himself for the sake of his audience. When he described Goldie giving Extension Lectures in the 1880s he concluded: 'Things do not alter much. I remember, thirty years later [i.e. 1914] a lecturer upon Euripides at Weybridge having to defend himself against the charge of condoning the conduct of the Bacchae.'[5]

But the satisfactory life – the writing, lecturing, being the dutiful son – was only on the surface. In the autumn of 1910 a period of depression began and was not to lift for more than a year. In part it was to do with Merz's death and the turmoil Morgan experienced when he visited Carpenter and began *Maurice*. He himself, having written in his diary that 'the last 4 or 5 days have been so unhappy

---

* This was the audience for the Portsmouth class, where Morgan did not lecture, but nevertheless provides a good idea of their make-up.

that I cannot keep an outward cheerfulness', attributed his gloom to a misunderstanding with the Waterlows (whose marriage was collapsing), to Lily's reaction to Helen's pregnancy in *Howards End* ('I do not know how I shall live through the next months'[6]) and, incredibly enough, some domestic worry of Lily's Tonbridge friend Mrs Mawe. The most probable reason he did not want to acknowledge, and did not yet perceive: he would soon be the same age as Eddie had been when he died.

The biographer must, of course, beware of too much psycho-analytical interpretation because it is inevitably so speculative. But the psychiatrist Anthony Storr has made a special study, in several of his books, of the creative personality and has made various observations that apply to Morgan. The loss of a father would have left a void in Morgan's life which he tried to fill by over-attachment to Lily; he was then over-dependent on her approval for his own self-esteem; and would adopt a placatory attitude in order to avoid incurring disapproval. 'Because the price of approval is compliance, which must involve some degree of dissimulation, this type of individual needs to get away from people in order to be himself unimpeded by the need to please.' (Morgan's diary, 5 March 1912, about a remark of Lily's: 'The speech more unbearable than the thing. No armour against it but cheerfulness, and that hardens one. Not to feel is part of courage ... Mother freezes any depth in me. Alone, I can cling to beauty ...')

The same psychiatrist shows, with detailed examples, that 'the gifts which enable a person to become a writer can be set in motion by loss and isolation' and quotes Simenon's remark that 'writing is not a profession but a vocation of unhappiness.' He shows too that early bereavement 'seems often to predispose the sufferer to react to any later losses with particular severity'; but that the creatively gifted who are bereaved 'are often able to use their talents in what can be described as a process of repair or re-creation.' And he points 'to the tendency of those who have been bereaved in early life to look for the lost parent in those to whom they become attached'.[7]

Now, much of this could be overturned with example: there are many creative writers who have lost a parent yet are not depressed and do not seem to need a parent substitute; in some respects Morgan did not display a classic psychoanalytical pattern. But there are too many matching details for Storr's observations not to be intriguing; and nowhere is this more so than in relation to the winter of 1910–11, and the year that followed, when Morgan was, as is shown in his diary, profoundly gloomy. Some have attributed this to the enormous success of *Howards End*, with reviewers almost unanimously recognising it as a great novel. It has been thought that Morgan could not 'cope' with fame, could not 'come to terms' with being a well-known writer. This is not true. Self-deprecating and modest as he may have been on the surface, and hostile to becoming part of a literary élite, he nevertheless welcomed being taken seriously and being appreciated. No, his real cause of depression was his personal situation and his thoughts about his father; yet these were unacknowledged except on the one or two occasions when he noted Lily making a comment of the you-are-just-as-clumsy-as-him variety, and when he refused a 1960s critic permission to reproduce Eddie's photograph.

The realisation that he was now the same age as Eddie had been when he died in October 1880 filled his mind in the months preceding this gloomy anniversary; indeed, in the winter of 1910–11 he visited Stisted. He had turned thirty and was looking just ahead towards the mid-life and thirty-five: it seems likely that he had a 'mid-life crisis' early. He had, after all, achieved so much so soon and yet now, for all kinds of reasons, something in him, he thought, seemed to have reached a stopping point. Lily knew little of this, nor would Masood have known that he was in agonies. Yet they both cherished Morgan as well as they could; and were deeply perturbed when it momentarily seemed that he might have his father's disease – tuberculosis.*

In addition, at the beginning of 1911 Lily's mother died. 'A happy & dignified career,' noted Morgan. 'She knew how to live, and to the end took it out of those who did not, like Mother.'[8] Louisa, it seems, had a gregarious, life-giving nature of which Lily tended to be censorious and Morgan envious: because, years before, in the late 1860s and early 1870s, Lily had so often taken charge of her siblings, she had lost her own sense of fun and begun to incubate her over-careful side. Louisa (who, we may suspect from Morgan's hint, enjoyed a merry widowhood) was never too serious-minded. When Morgan was to declare of her and the other Whichelo relations that 'it is with her – with them – that my heart lies'[9] we may take it he meant that he *wished* his heart had lain with her. So that when Louisa

---

* This was, in those days, a frequent label for depression. In 1913 Cynthia Asquith spent three months in a sanatorium as a tuberculosis-suspect; when in fact she was overwrought after the birth of her son.

died, by misfortune at a time in Morgan's life when he was already feeling morose and rudderless, the age-old tug between the puritan values of the Thorntons and the hedonism of the Whichelos again filled his mind; again, as so often before in his life, he wondered how to reconcile his two sides. And especially with Lily in tow.

Harnham was, at this time, an unhappy household. 'Here we are both without occupation for the coming year,' wrote Morgan in his locked diary, echoing his 1905 phrase about Mrs Herriton, 'Her life, he saw, was without meaning'.[10] He went on, 'I at the flood of fame, but with no further prospects. I will love, though.'[11] The love he spoke of was a far broader one than infatuation with one person; it was love as a creed, as a way of life, the emotion and the impetus that clergymen speak of in church on Sundays. The longing to love, the need to love, was something that Morgan had himself preached in his novels; how unutterably sad that he himself had found no one on whom to lavish this love. His longing to be tender, to subsume himself in someone else, to give, was one reason why, as Morgan himself later suspected, he *could* have been married if chance had ever brought him together with the 'right' woman. Another cause for misery in 1911, after Louisa had died and he and Lily were bound together even more tightly, was that he now began to realise that this way of life would never end. He began to imagine that it was he who would die in Lily's arms and not the other way round.

Sometimes, though, he must have wondered if another form of escape might be possible. Maimie had, after all, managed to escape into an unconventional marriage, something for which Morgan much admired her. Nor had Morgan's Whichelo aunts, Georgie, Nellie and Rosie, led lives of model conformity. His aunts – that portmanteau term for female rituals, afternoon tea, umbrellas and good works – were not, however, typical. Now, in 1911, they were fifty-five, forty-nine and forty-five (Lily was fifty-six), and Georgie and Nellie were almost bohemian in their unconventionality. Georgie 'was a character larger than life, to whom everything was either hysterically funny or devastatingly tragic, middle courses did not exist for her, and a feeling of carnival seemed to develop when she was around' (in the words of her nephew Philip, Morgan's first cousin); she was always enthusiastic, whether about embroidering, playing the piano or playing croquet. So, too, was Nellie, although her enthusiasm sometimes led her into domestic 'scrapes' from which Lily and Morgan had to rescue her. 'She was a very talented designer, and became head designer of the Royal School of Needlework and worked on the embroideries of the coronation robes of Edward VII, George V and George VI, as well as teaching Queen Mary to do tapestry.' (Her photograph features in a book about women in the Arts and Crafts movement.) She was shrewd, intuitive and highly artistic.

Then there was Rosie who, in 1884, had gone to France to be a governess and, in 1895, was one of the reasons behind Morgan and Lily's trip to Normandy. In 1904 she returned 'more French than English' and taught French before marrying an elderly widower named Robert Alford. 'She was Morgan's favourite aunt', partly because of her tremendous spirit and intelligence (as can be seen in her photograph), partly because she was only thirteen years older than Morgan and in some ways like a sister. It was with her much more than with any of the other Whichelos that Morgan's heart lay.

The male Whichelos did not appeal: the Spanish liveliness (it was discovered after Morgan's death that Whichelos had come from Spain to England in the seventeenth century to escape the Inquisition) was inherited more by the women than the men. Among Lily's brothers were Horace (Philip's father) who worked at Coutts Bank 'and was given the job of outside representative on account of being so well dressed';* Harry, who had been Lily's responsibility in the 1860s and who emigrated to South Africa where he died young; John, who 'had the fatal good looks of his brothers' and went on the stage until his looks faded and he took to drink; and Percy, who had the strangest life of any of them. When he was sixteen he met a retired general in a railway carriage and was 'practically adopted' by him, inheriting his entire fortune, including a palace in Venice. Percy, however, spent all the money and was forced to marry a rich widow who promised to pay off his debts. 'On their honeymoon at Dinard he died in mysterious circumstances which have never been cleared up,' wrote Philip. Percy's widow kept in touch with the family and sounds, apart from her financial circumstances, very much like Jackie Bast in *Howards End* (blowsy and dyed red hair). Her second husband also died suddenly – more evidence that the sudden deaths

---

* According to Philip, Mr Wilcox in *Howards End* was based on his father. He also suggested to me that Lilia's daughter Irma in *Where Angels Fear to Tread* was based on his sister Laura. She was seven in 1905, the year Morgan was writing the novel, which was the same age as Irma at the beginning. Laura stayed with the Forsters in 1905 while her brother was born.

of which Morgan's novels are full are not, in the light of his own experience, so out of the ordinary.

All these details were provided by Philip Whichelo, twenty-five years younger than Morgan and also an actor like his Uncle John. He had Adonis good looks yet was curiously like Morgan: to see him was to look at the reverse of a mirror and see how Morgan might have appeared given a little luck, and different colouring. Both men had beautiful, pianist's hands; Philip, too, was homosexual, of a more flamboyant kind than Morgan, and was a close friend of Quentin Crisp: the two were known as 'P and Q' and 'flaunted around London together in arty clothes'. He had the fun in his life that Morgan, so often confined to Weybridge, did not: although, in the following anecdote, we learn that 'once or twice' Morgan did join in the fun.

In 1895 [that year again] Georgie and Nellie rented a cottage at Whitstable in Kent as a seaside holiday retreat and [Percy's widow] and her second husband took the adjoining cottage. The convivial weekends they had with the Whichelo brothers and friends became legendary, the local residents were shocked by their unconventional and rowdy behaviour. I think Morgan stayed there once or twice, but Aunt Lily never did, she did not approve of Whitstable or the goings-on . . .[12]

The important event of 1911 was, for Morgan, the publication of *The Celestial Omnibus*, an umbrella title for six of his short stories.* The reviews must have seemed curious to him, for they were along the lines that he wrote them for himself rather than for his readers, and this was true; he inhabited the world of his stories, and to some extent of *The Longest Journey*, imaginatively, whereas the world of the other novels was observed by him with more irony and detachment. Yet only a few weeks before these reviews appeared Arnold Bennett had published an article in which he said that if Morgan continued to write a book a year, refraining from certain themes and being discreet, he would become the most fashionable novelist in England in ten years' time. 'If, on the other hand, he writes solely to please himself, forgetting utterly the existence of the *élite*, he may produce some first-class literature. The responsibilities

* The stories were 'The Story of a Panic', 'The Other Side of the Hedge', 'The Celestial Omnibus', 'The Other Kingdom', 'The Curate's Friend', 'The Road from Colonus'.

lying upon him at this crisis of his career are terrific. And he so young too!'[13]

Was *Maurice*, were the two 1911 short stories 'Mr Andrews' and 'The Point of It', self-indulgence? Or could and should Morgan go on writing fashionable books like *Howards End*? It was an absurd distinction, but one that Morgan himself believed: the brutal way his lack of self-worth mingled with his innate confidence in his own prose left him bewildered. He could *not* escape from what people thought, in all aspects of his life, literary as well as sexual; 21 July 1910, 'How ever gross my desires, I find that I shall never satisfy them for the fear of annoying others. I am glad to come across this much good in me. It serves instead of purity.' Sexuality could be repressed, or confined to beneath the sheets in the back bedroom at Harnham ('I must try to be less lustful, not because I don't like doing it, but because the habit induces unhappiness' he would write two years later). But literature could not be hidden under the sheets, and Morgan refused to try.

Yet there was his remark, made just before the publication of *Howards End* when he was at his most vulnerable: 'My next heroism will be to stop writing.' The writing and the sexual loneliness were closely connected, and Morgan knew it. 'Weariness of the only subject that I both can and may treat – the love of men for women & vice versa. Passion & money are the two main springs of action (not of existence) and I can only write of the first, & of that imperfectly.'[14] It is unclear whether Morgan felt that he personally as a novelist could not write about money or whether it was merely that it was indelicate, 'ugly', to do so. What aspect of money did he mean? Perhaps the money-making motive so alien to him, acquisitiveness, the miserly instinct described by the French novelists; or perhaps he meant the gradations of male wealth that are the crux of 'marriage' novels and that Jane Austen wrote about so expertly.

Passion, on the other hand, he felt he did know about, for by now he had convinced himself that such was his feeling for Masood. Since they had first met at the end of 1906 their friendship had deepened considerably, so that by 1911 Morgan considered him to be the great love of his life. At the end of 1908 he had remarked mournfully in his diary, 'He is not that sort – no one whom I like seems to be.'[15] Then, after a short holiday in Paris together a year later, he wrote, in a passage he then, or later on, deleted, 'Is the enigma him or his nationality?'; and concluded a few sad lines about their relationship with 'I love you, Syed Ross Masood: love.'[16]

They were so at ease with one another by now that at this time Morgan ended a letter 'from Forster, member of the Ruling Race to Masood, a nigger. And let the latter buck up and write';[17] it was a prefiguration of the charming intimacy that he was to evoke at the start of the relationship between Aziz and Fielding in *A Passage to India*. But Morgan imagined himself in love; and wondered whether, if he changed himself in some way, Masood might respond to his longings. In the summer of 1910 he resolved, once he had finished *Howards End*, 'to devote August to athletics and personal appearance'. This rather odd remark is surely because he thought that if he became more athletic, more hearty in the Garnett family sense, rowing, swimming, playing hockey on the beach, not always having his nose in a book, then Masood might like him better, might respond physically. But it was not to be. Masood, with infinite tact, confided in Morgan about his merry time with girls: a subtle way of fending him off without having to say, definitively, no.

Yet he was not entirely tactful. With true Oriental uninhibitedness he told Morgan how fond he was of him; 5 September 1910,

extract from a letter this morning received. 'I have got to love you as if you were a woman or rather as if you were part of my own body. Pray pardon the singularity of the remark, but I hope it will help you to understand what I mean to convey by it. One of the dearest things I shall leave behind – '*

This can only be Masood (the charming 'pray pardon the singularity of the remark' could not have been written by any of Morgan's English friends) and the letter must have thrown him into an even greater sense of turmoil. Yet, at this time, he experienced 'a decreasing tendency to lustful thoughts': but it was only temporary, or perhaps wishful thinking. By the summer of 1911, when he and Masood went to Tesserete near Lugano for a holiday, his physical longing for Masood had re-asserted itself and he said as much: 'Near the beginning, I spoke, seeing that after all he did not realise. He was

---

* The letter itself has not survived. Masood's declaration was to reappear at the end of Chapter 9 of the 1914 version of *Maurice* with Clive telling Maurice 'I love you as if you were a woman'. In 1915 Lytton Strachey wrote Morgan a long letter about *Maurice*: one of the things he objected to was this phrase, saying it was a lie. As a result Morgan changed it to 'I love you'.

surprised & sorry, & put it away at once.' Indeed he had the courtesy to continue as friendly as ever ('it was clear he liked me better than any man in the world, so I did not mind'[18]) but to run boyishly after any available girl. Years later Morgan remembered that 'we were at the stage – so familiar to me – where the other person has ceased to be interested'; he remembered too 'Masood having an ugliesh waitress, or visitor; for I think he had her, but thought me too much of a muff to be told.'*

Morgan could write acceptingly, at the end of the year, after Masood had returned to India, that 'I bear his going better now, for we shall never be nearer & do seem firm at last.'[20] (And they were to stay firm until Masood's death in 1937, even though Morgan would eventually tell Darling: 'I drifted away from Masood in recent years – he became too reticent and too pompous.'[21]) Yet 1911 had been for Morgan a 'terrible year on the whole' and eventually he was to discover one of the reasons for his gloom, although he never explored it. At the beginning of November:

Last night, alone, I had a Satanic fit of rage against mother for her grumbling and fault finding, and figured a scene in which I swept the mantelpiece with my arm and then rushed out of doors or cut my throat. I was all red & trembling after. I write it down partly in the hope that I shall see its absurdity & so refuse it admittance again.

He did, usually, refuse it admittance. But then, the following year, he made a note on the opposite page to this entry: 'Discover, some months later, that Oct 31 is the anniversary of my father's death.'[22]† One part of his mind acknowledged his grief, his anger, his bereftness; the other ignored it.

But at some point during this gloomy autumn, and partly inspired by the holiday in Switzerland, the idea of another novel began to evolve. The 50,000 words of this other new work would, however, never be published and would remain, like *Nottingham Lace*, an unpublished fragment which had, nevertheless, the distinction of not being destroyed. In the novel, which he called *Arctic Summer*, Morgan would portray a young man who, he imagined, was what he himself might have become if he had married. Martin Whitby (the

---

* In 1960 Morgan tore up the letters he had written home from Tesserete to Lily and to Laura. 'They convey nothing at all. Tesserete, like most of everyone's past, is lost . . . why, having already published 3 [*sic*] novels, did I write such wet letters?'[19]

† It is hard to believe, but if this is true he was thirty-three before he found out.

name has the same resonance, and the same rather English solidity as Morgan Forster) is a civil servant and a (non-resident) fellow of a Cambridge college. His childhood has been prosaic and, although his aesthetic impulse is unaroused, he is not averse to it: 'His mind had been prepared for beauty, and as soon as books and pictures and music touched it, it flowered.' He is married to the daughter of the master of a Cambridge college; her name is Venetia, and Morgan perhaps based her in part on Florence Barger and wondered about the romantic nature of her name: were girls who were named after cities, like Florence and Venetia, perhaps conceived there? But what paradoxes are summoned up by these gruff, intellectual English women being conceived in, of all places, Italy? Yet Martin has married the wrong woman. Her sister Dorothea is altogether gentler and spends her time collecting folk songs: like Tiddy, of whom Morgan was possibly to be reminded, while writing *Arctic Summer*, when he saw his appointment to the Oxford English Literature School announced in *The Times*.

Venetia, Morgan imagined, was the kind of wife he, too, might have married had he followed a more conventional pattern, and was indeed the kind of wife whom so many of his contemporaries were at this time choosing for themselves.

Passion passed in time. For the Whitbys, as for all married people, the sea began to ebb after a few months, and they had to face whatever it uncovered. Now came the critical moment of their career. With what joy did they see the comradeship of the past re-emerging, but softened by a tenderness that had not been in the past. They had produced a wedded love. They had solved one modern problem, and if they became a little intolerant to those who had not solved it, if they sometimes forgot that money and outside interests, and a healthy child, had helped them, nevertheless they were receiving the reward of merit; the lustful and the insincere will never be rewarded.

On their holiday in Italy the Whitbys, who are accompanied by Venetia's mother, meet a young man called Clesant March.* As Morgan said years later about his unpublished novel, 'I had got my antithesis all right, the antithesis between the civilized man,

---

* Elements of his character were drawn from Rupert Brooke, with whom Morgan had recently begun a tentative friendship, occasionally staying with him at Grantchester. They were not close, but Morgan was intrigued by him, admiring his intelligence, charm and unaffected friendliness.

The name Clesant would reappear in a 1927 story 'Dr Woolacott', about a convalescent soldier facing death; T. E. Lawrence was extravagant in his praise of it.

who hopes for an Arctic Summer, and the heroic man who rides into the sea. But I had not settled what was going to happen, and that is why the novel remains a fragment. The novelist should I think always settle when he starts what is going to happen, what his major event is to be.'

The other reason Morgan was to stop writing *Arctic Summer* was, perhaps, that he felt it to be repetitious: once more it set the stuffy English (again always worrying about dust) against the unfettered Italians; it explored the themes of marriage versus comradeship; it was, further on, set in Cambridge. It even showed Clesant to be more 'real' than the Whitbys because he has come to Italy to explore his ancestral roots, whereas Venetia deplores sentimentality about one's family; and it showed Martin being drawn to Clesant and thinking (when he stops him slipping over at the station) that 'a fellow creature had saved him'.[23] But the novel is not, as it stands, on a par with the others. The sadness is that Morgan did not ever work on it, for the potential is, in all essentials, there.

The next year was, however, to be different. Somehow the passage to India that had been so long mooted was to become reality. Darling urged it, as did Masood, who had by now returned home. Morgan's reading and interests also pulled him towards it; even money could not be seen as an obstacle since *Howards End* had made enough for him to feel that he was paying his own way. Then there were two pieces of luck. Goldie was awarded a travelling fellowship; and Bob Trevelyan decided that he wanted to see India, but without Bessie because she needed to stay in Surrey with the children. So it was that during the early part of 1912 the idea came into focus that the three of them should go together. It seems that Morgan, who had despairingly written at the end of 1911 that he now could not respect his mother and was 'only happy away from home',[24] was at last to have the chance to be away, and for a long time. He wrote and told Masood:

I come to be with you . . . I can't describe how much I long to see you again. You have made me half an Oriental, and my soul is in the East long before my body reaches it. I don't *understand* the East or expect to understand it, but I've learnt to love it for several years now . . .[25]

The summer of 1912 went by in a haze of lists, inoculations, guidebooks and clothes for the tropics. Perhaps Masood would, in the exotic East, be as responsive as Morgan hoped. Or 'perhaps when I come out she will find a wife for me'[26] Morgan wrote to Malcolm of Josie, referring to a King's friend's engagement that had recently taken place in India. If only he could marry someone like the real Florence or the fictional Venetia. But he feared, as he looked forward to a new life in India, that it would never be. His hidden self, his socially unacceptable self, longed for Masood's embrace. His inner self longed for another novel. All of him longed to escape Weybridge. But it would never let him go.

22

India 1912

The two-week voyage gave more time for thought and anticipation than is allowed to the modern traveller. Morgan had looked forward, as the sea miles slipped past and Europe receded north-westwards, to acquiring an Eastern outlook, to shedding the Weybridge aura that had accompanied him as far as Naples. 'Too much gab today,' he noted sharply on day two. 'Hardly a quiet minute to think that I am going to India.'[1] The leisure to think, to adjust his frame of reference was, for Morgan, as important a part of the preparations as the reading and the tropical kit. As he said fifty years later, 'it was a long sea voyage that prepared you for a strange world . . . even in our seagoing days, when we theoretically had time to readjust, some of the English went to pieces . . . there was a cultural shock, a mystery forever unplumbed . . . not even a long sea voyage could prepare you for that.'[2]

For much of the time he sat contemplatively in the deck-chair which, in August, he had asked Bob to have delivered to the ship at Liverpool. This had been bought from the Army & Navy Stores and cost either 4 shillings (£10) plain or 11 shillings (£26) reclining; it travelled round India and then returned to Weybridge 'comfortable but rickety'.[3] It is curious, and yet symbolic, that Morgan chose to take such a blatant reminder of the Army & Navy with him: he needed it at the same time as he longed to escape it. The shop had, after all, been the setting for Agnes's spiritual nadir in *The Longest Journey*; and she anticipated the English women in *A Passage to India* both in her egoism, her insensitivity – and in her reliance on the Army & Navy. Here she and Rickie have tea before buying the linoleum for the school cubicles, seated 'amid ladies in every stage of fatigue – haggard ladies, scarlet ladies, ladies with parcels that twisted from every finger like joints of meat. Gentlemen were scarcer, but all were of the sub-fashionable type, to which Rickie himself now belonged.' Climactically Agnes insults Ansell's sister Maud: as a result 'she moves as one from whom the inner life has been withdrawn.'[4]

Alas, the women on board ship appeared little better ('pretty rotten'[5] was Morgan's epithet) and they would eventually commingle with Agnes, Gladys Olcott and the others to form the appalled picture of Anglo-Indian* women that would be central to his novel. Morgan's vision was not, however, quite objective: there was almost no social exchange between them and the three Cambridge men on board (nicknamed variously 'the Salon' and 'the Professors' by the other passengers). Instead Morgan spent the time enjoying the weather, the flying fish, the dolphins and sharks, the sunsets and, especially, the sea ('watched water again, which sends *back* foam from the prow's point, seeming to bounce on the blue'[6]). The voyage itself was rather stately since the ship could do only twelve knots an hour owing to '1000 & 1000 of sacks of potatoes',[7] the chaotic loading of which, and shedding of the surplus on to a barge, had delayed departure from Naples by a day.

When writing his life of Goldie (who joined the ship at Port Said 'looking dishevelled and tired') Morgan was to describe the journey as 'fascinating' but claimed that 'we hated the boat'.[8] The drawbacks, apart from 'poor food, cabins small and full', were twofold: the women and the 'rather military'[9] passengers, the latter being an aspect of British life with which Morgan had unregretfully had little contact since Tonbridge. The four men played chess ('on Sundays', somewhat oddly, of which there were two), 'compared Dostoyevsky with Tolstoy publicly, argued over the shape of the earth at the breakfast-table, balanced on bollards instead of playing deck games'.[10] The Bloomsburyesque aura must have seemed noticeably set apart to the other passengers, pursuing as they did a more conventionally jolly shipboard existence, and it was on only rare occasions that the two strata met: once the famously un-gamesy Morgan consented to join in a shovel-board tournament 'to please the "Pariahs" as Bob calls them – two commercial gents who are not quite and one of whom is rather offensive'. As always, the joining was far less interesting than the not-quiteness.

The friction between the two groups was, of course, partly

---

* The year before this term had officially replaced 'Eurasian' to describe people of 'mixed descent' but Morgan still used it to mean the British living in India.

sexual. The gulf, the unconnectedness, between homosexual and heterosexual runs deep in British society, as does that between Tory and socialist, patriarchal and feminist, aristocrat and working class. It was something Morgan had been observing, sadly and resignedly, throughout his writing life. Now his most important expression of the gulf was to come in *A Passage to India*.

His constant awareness of the sexual divide was explicit in his mention of the 'greatest trial on board . . . a little showing off girl, much noticed by the men: I look at her stonily when she approaches me.'[11] It did not come naturally to Morgan to look stony: sideways and hoping not to be noticed, yes; hostile, no. But the adverb is a measure of the gap between him and the flirtatious, husband-hunting girl sailing on the 'fishing fleet' for the start of the Indian Season; just as his mentioning the gap to Lily is an example of their near-complicity about things sexual. She was one widow who could be absolutely confident that she need not dread a shipboard romance. So instead, during a concert, Morgan 'sat reading by the sea, thinking now and then of the (apparent) happiness of sea-creatures'.

Yet there was someone else who 'reads apart' in a solitary deck-chair. This was the handsome, Byronic-looking Kenneth Searight, an officer returning to the North-West Frontier. 'I like him,' noted Morgan on 14 October, adding, 'he is good to the little Indian.' It took only a day for him to discover why he was so good: 15 October, 'The minorite story of S's. Amazing conversation. His diary.'[12] Searight clearly recognised a fellow invert straight away; although Morgan was different from him in never being interested in young boys, the tone of their shipboard conversation would have been disconcerting in the extreme to anyone who overheard it.

If it had not been for the chance discovery of a manuscript notebook in a shop in the Charing Cross Road, Searight might have been merely remembered as someone who 'pursued romance and poetry'[13] – to quote Morgan's words about him in his book about Goldie. And his diary might have been imagined, from Morgan's mention of it, to have been only vaguely salacious. But Searight is unique in being the author of a paederastic manuscript that has survived. Until the recent reprinting of gay erotica by publishing houses like the Gay Men's Press even homoerotic works of erotica were unusual, almost the only example being the notorious *Teleny* (1893) (thought by some, on little evidence, to have been written by Oscar Wilde).

Searight's manuscript was found in the 1960s and is now 'in a private collection'. Even the article describing it, which was printed in academic-looking format in the now defunct *International Journal of Greek Love*, is vague on particulars, and the author 'Toby Hammond' has remained elusive, at least to the present author. It seems, though, that Searight's 'blank ruled notebook, small quarto, bound . . . in semi-stiff dark green roan boards . . . lettered only on the front cover, PAIDIKION' is the 'story' and diary Morgan saw because this six-hundred-page book consists of erotic stories but also a kind of diary: pages 560–6 list the 129 boys to whom Searight made love between 1897 and 1917. By 1912 there had been nearly forty.

A recent writer, on sex and empire, has evidently been able to see *Paidikion*, although he is circumspect and gives no source for his extract from Searight's autobiographical poem 'The Furnace'. He concludes that this alone is what Morgan was shown, since Goldie, in his reminiscences, remembered that Searight showed them parts of his autobiography, 'in a style which also seemed to belong to Byron – not good, I suppose, but curiously moving'. But if Morgan had *only* seen this would he not have referred to it as an autobiography in verse rather than a diary? The likelihood is that he *was* shown the listing of forty boys and the poem and the stories. He can never have seen anything like them before.*

It was a measure of Searight's instant complicity that he trusted Morgan and Goldie enough to show them the book at all: nowhere in the notebook is there a mention of the author's identity, for obvious reasons to do with criminal law, and 'Toby Hammond' had to discover it from working out that he was at Charterhouse, with a boy called Stanley, and that his name was 'Ken' ('"Why, Ken, old boy . . . you are so beastly slack I thought you were not coming!" But he took / My trembling body to his breast') and that he was in the same house as Stanley. 'The author's identity was clinched by my discovery of a copy of his only commercially published work, *Sona*, at the London Library. This copy bears a presentation inscription in Searight's hand, dated November 1943, which exactly matches the calligraphy in *Paidikion*.'

Hammond further deduced that the original owner of the notebook was the semanticist C. K. Ogden, once believed to have been the owner of 'Baron Corvo's' 'Venice Letters' on the same subject as that

---

* Goldie referred to Searight being 'perpetually in love with some boy or other'.[14] *Could* he already have been 'in love' with three boys a year for fifteen years, an average that was to go up to eighteen a year from 1912 to 1917? Hardly. Goldie, it seems, found the sex more acceptable if graced with love.

which interested Searight. How the notebook 'got onto a remainder stall is anyone's guess'. (My guess is that whoever cleared out Ogden's papers did not actually want to throw it away but gave it innocuously with some other books to a second-hand book-dealer.) Morgan was naturally involved in none of this and in any case never lusted after young boys: he wanted someone who was in some ways an equal, an ideal companion, and although he liked being avuncular to his lovers (in a guardian-and-ward relationship) he did not want to dominate, humiliate, hurt or exploit. Where he did resemble Searight was in his longing to return to the childhood paradise where he had had a friend like Ansell; in the same way Searight's writings portray someone who 'loves another boy at school, then wanders through many countries trying to recapture the magic of that initial experience'.[15]

So, although one would not know it from the diaries or letters, the voyage was a revelation to Morgan. Whatever conversations he had had with Carpenter or Merz or Goldie, he had never before met someone who openly and kindly accepted him as a minorite, who showed him his collection of von Gloeden photographs from Taormina (which Morgan was likely to have seen in 1902 but would not have dared buy because of Lily) and his diary listing the forty boys he had pleasured himself with over the last fifteen years, with symbols referring to a scale of activity, frequency and intensity that must have seemed, to Morgan, quite extraordinary, and unforgettable. He never forgot Searight; virtually his last short story* was the most erotic he ever wrote (of the ones that were not destroyed) and was inspired by Searight and the little Indian. Almost salaciously, fifty years later, Morgan evoked their pleasure on the bunk bed on board ship. The twist of the story derived from the door being found not to be locked; Morgan had never forgotten how he used to pace up and down on deck, even walk past the door and think, what if it were *not* locked and I looked in? And, infinite catastrophe, if the fishing fleet looked in? How poignant, how typical of life as we know it, that the life of the Tunbridge Wells fishing fleet is divided only by a door from the life of Kenneth and the 'little Indian'.

When they docked at Port Said it was, as always, the people that interested Morgan most:

* 'The Other Boat'.

A barge full of coal was towed up, on it black figures squatting and lying. They awoke like an operatic chorus, more and more excited, till they rushed on deck, each with a basketful. Quickest coaling station in the world. But they had time to sing, fight and fondle. Some were women. At night one stood with a beautiful lamp by the plank-way, and the East appeared as something happy and terrible.

And the first time he awoke on an Indian train he noted 'people walking beautifully, and it is these motions that strike me even more than their colours or clothes'.[16] Entries like these raise the perennial question: do writers like Morgan or Virginia Woolf or Marcel Proust know, when they are scribbling down their hauntingly lovely turns of phrase, that they are creating art in the process? Each day, when Morgan wrote in his small, leather-bound, lined notebook in black ink now faded to grey (writing equipment was such an important item of luggage that the final and summarising paragraph of Morgan's first Indian letter to Lily began 'My pen, and indeed everything goes well',[17] clearly implying that 'the important one' was the tool for writing), did he think, self-awarely, 'that's rather well put' or 'that might make a story'? It is unanswerable.

Yet Morgan went to India knowing that 'it will probably be the time of my life'[18] and had for some time been planning an 'oriental novel'; he hoped that India would change his perceptions and therefore needed to record this process. Although the 'I', Morgan's ego, appears quite rarely in the letters and diaries (as for that matter does his health and the weather, a preoccupying topic for most diarists) he was constantly reacting and perceiving in an entirely personalised, in a literary way; the degree to which his prose was consciously finely wrought is, however, unfathomable.

After twelve days at sea it was so warm that Morgan had his bed moved on deck. Now he was beginning to feel the pervading 'sense of joy never conveyed by the air, nor by the dashing waters of the north. Coleridge knew of it.' As land came closer, butterflies fluttered among the baggage, then 'false India – a cloud bank – turned into true, a queer red series of hills a little disquieting, as though Italy had been touched into the sinister.' Soon there were palm trees, rather than cypresses, and the clustered buildings of Bombay, the most prominent of which was the Taj Hotel, 'our destination, but a rumour of cholera came. The last horrid meal on the horrid ship'[19] and they went ashore.

They went to the Pyrke's Apollo instead of to the famous Taj. Uninterested in architecture as he was, Morgan would not have regretted the high Victorian Gothic of the Taj with its curious mixture of the Natural History Museum and St Pancras Station; it would in any case have reminded him of British institutions he disliked – schools, law courts and so on. His first preoccupation was with the need to buy a new hat from the Bombay branch of the Army & Navy; the pith helmet Bob had taken on board ('quite light and will be in a cardboard box'[20]) had 'not been the success we hoped; everyone roars with laughter'[21] Lily was told, 'and Searight refuses to ask me to Peshawar unless I buy a new one.'

(Bombay did not impress Morgan and it was, I think, overactive empathy that led me to imagine him walking round to the Taj, making his way up the famously large and ornate wrought-iron staircase to the Sea Lounge with its windows wide open to the sea, palms in brass pots, painted wicker chairs with shiny chintz cushions and fans, huge fans flapping their wings like birds, a faint breeze coming in from the boulevard along the front. Nevertheless I sat there pinkly among the plasterwork and faded elegance and visualised the four pale Englishmen in tropical suits having tea and scrambled eggs as they might in Cheltenham or Weybridge or the Army & Navy. All that has changed is the noise; nowadays it is scooters and Ambassador cars and crowds round the Gateway of India, which was built in 1927, a mere twenty years before the British departed through it for the last time. Nor can I tell, from Morgan's rather impressionistic notes, whether he discovered the Asiatic Library, a quasi–British Museum in its façade, inside wrought-iron shelves, wooden floors and readers asleep in armchairs that would have reminded him of the London Library.)

After only a day in Bombay there began 'the most expensive, most comfortable, most enjoyable journey of my life'.[22] A year later Morgan was to write an article about this experience for a short-lived London magazine called *Golden Hynde*. It is written in the direct, unaffected, almost domestic style that Morgan had by now made perfectly his own.

When the European enters his first Indian railway carriage, he feels himself in a moving palace, so many are the luxuries that surround him. There are sofa beds, racks, hooks, washing apparatus, electric lights, a white lincrusta ceiling from which electric fans depend, and there are windows of which no Westerner has ever dreamed – shutters to keep out the glare, wire screens to keep out the flies, blue-grey glass to keep out everything. Meals are served on the train, or else the train stops while they can be eaten, gay little timetables and maps of India hang framed in the embossed wallpaper. Housed in such comfort, might one not travel for ever?

This enthusiasm, Morgan admits, can wear off: there are the large amounts of unruly luggage, the tap sending 'an empty sigh' instead of water into the basin and, above all, the unpunctuality.

Yet what he never ceased to admire was Indian affection for the railway; and, as well, he perceived an image in the three classes that prefigures the tripartite imagery in *A Passage to India*. Mosque/Caves/Temple, Cold Weather/Hot Weather/Rains, as well as all the other symbols of a triad, were first mooted in Morgan's compassionate vision of the train as a symbol of India herself. 'The first class – white skinned and aloof – the second and intermediate where the two races mingle – the third class many-coloured, brightly clothed, and innumerable as the sand – the train has brought them together after so many centuries and is dragging them towards one goal. Palace and boxroom and truck have this in common: they do move.'[23]

Masood met Morgan at Aligarh station and took him to his mother's house. (Alas, she would not see him because she was in purdah; although Morgan had told Masood in August that he was 'particularly anxious to see you when you are with your mother'.[24]) It was six years almost to the day since the two had first met in Weybridge, and Morgan's first glimpse of Masood on his own territory must have been a moment of great significance; more than Malcolm's invitation or Goldie's fellowship or the longing to have a real enough excuse to get away from Lily, it was Masood who had brought Morgan to India.

Their week together was spent largely at the Anglo-Oriental College founded by Masood's grandfather which was, during this period, divided between Muslim traditionalists and modernists – although the greater gulf was between Indian and English. In 1892, in a book that Morgan had read, Edward Carpenter had described Aligarh as 'the only place in India which I have visited where I have noticed anything like a cordial feeling existing between the two sections'. He concluded that this was due to the college being 'run by Englishmen whose instincts and convictions lie a little outside the Anglo-Indian groove'.[25] Twenty years later this was no longer so. Morgan noted: 'The English staff complained that they were not trusted to give the help they had hoped to give, but would be turned adrift as soon as the Mahommedans could stand without them.'

It was the Indians among the faculty that Morgan enjoyed meeting most; 'I was complimented by our host for "fitting in so easily with us"' was his diary comment after a dinner, and again, 'Much enjoyed myself and was never conscious whether it was an Indian or an Englishman I was talking to'.[26] One day there was an expedition into the countryside 'in a sort of starved omnibus'; they saw the 'India which baffles description because there is nothing to describe – the cultivated earth extending for ever'.[27] Yet Morgan managed all the same to evoke the day memorably for Maimie: throughout his trip he was a devoted correspondent, with the usual letter-writer's dilemma. 'It sounds conceited,' he told Aunt Laura, 'but I should be so glad to see my own letters again when I come back! my diary gets behind, and what I write to you and mother will be the freshest chronicle of my doings.'[28]

On 30 October the two men travelled to Delhi* and stayed with a doctor friend of Masood's. Here originated the scene in Chapter 9 of A Passage to India when Aziz is ill: 'Meanwhile Masood lay sick – not very sick – of the plague-inoculation, and all his friends came to see him, and we sat on his bed and on my bed – we shared a room – and on the luggage, and on one another's laps, and more food came in and the cockatoo screamed for grapes.'[29] Despite Searight's revelations, and despite his state of mind in the months before his India trip, Morgan seemed to be nearly resigned both to Masood's heterosexuality and to his own celibacy; his lusts remained private. It was an infrequent occurrence for him to share a room, as he was now doing, indeed to sleep in a different place from Lily, yet he seemed to have subdued his sexual longings for the moment: there is only the faintest hint in his diary that he had been hopeful that visiting Masood in India might change their relationship; two weeks after leaving him in Delhi he 'woke up in the middle of the night very unhappy – thought of him who might be slipping away.'

The Delhi 'sights' such as the Red Fort proved disappointing but Morgan liked the countryside outside the city 'which is like a glorified Appian Way': Italy was still the touchstone, Gwalior, for example, glimpsed from the train, being 'like a finer Orvieto'. On his last evening he was taken to a Nautch (songs and dancing) where he was unexpectedly beguiled by the dancers.

---

* The year before it had replaced Calcutta as the capital.

The ladies had already arrived and salaamed us – one with a weak but very charming face and very charming manners: I was never tired of looking at her. The other was younger and fat with a ring through her nose indicating virginity. This made her arrogant, they said, and she didn't attract me. Both were short. One could easily 'lapse' into an oriental; I found myself discussing their points dispassionately.[30]

'I was never tired of looking at her' – this rather surprising phrase reminds one how rarely Morgan revealed his true self even in his diary and, by corollary, how often he slightly fudged the truth because, surely, he knew that one day it might be read by others. In the early days there were Lily and the maids who might have pried; later on there was fame and thoughts of a biography; yet an elliptical prose style ensured that even when posthumous publication seemed not unlikely (though this has not happened yet) the elderly Morgan felt no need to consign his diary to the flames. Indeed, seeing how little he had to excise when he did eventually publish extracts in *The Hill of Devi* in 1953, it seems likely that all the time he thought he might one day publish it.

What he had not yet thought about was the thematic focus for the novel that he hoped, that Masood had first spurred him into hoping, would result from his passage to India. He knew about the genre of novels by writers like Maud Diver, 'Sydney C. Grier' and Alice Perrin (whom he had read in 1911), formula Indian romances in which English soldiers stationed on the North-West Frontier try not to let affairs of the heart interfere with their military duties; and he would certainly have skimmed through the best-selling *The Way of an Eagle* by Ethel M. Dell, which had been published in the January before he left for India and was to supply most people's image of English life in India for the next twelve years – until the publication of *A Passage to India*.

Yet there were so few English novels set in India, and those so stereotypical, that Morgan could not envisage how he could break the mould: unless he could gain enough understanding of Indians to write about them and not, as was usual, about Anglo-Indians. For he knew that he was one of the few who had had the rare privilege 'of dropping straight into native life'[31] and that the only reason he claimed to have 'enjoyed myself in India ever since I landed'[32] was that he had lived with Indians for a full week before setting out for 'Lahore and Anglo-India' to meet up with Bob and Goldie and to stay with the Darlings. But here, alas, 'Indians to breakfast but no sense of intimacy

... don't like Lahore ... all is unfinished and dreary, dissevered from home life and native. The distances are immense and one rattles about in ill-informed tongas'[33] ('O tonga-wallah, Club, Club. Why doesn't the fool go?' screech the Turtons and Burtons in an early scene).

This was Morgan's first encounter with real Anglo-India, with the world of the cantonment, the club and the kind of Englishman whose 'self-complacency, his censoriousness, his lack of subtlety, all grew vivid beneath a tropic sky', the dinner whose menu was:

Julienne soup full of bullety bottled peas, pseudo-cottage bread, fish full of branching bones, pretending to be plaice, more bottled peas with the cutlets, trifle, sardines on toast: the menu of Anglo-India. A dish might be added or subtracted as one rose or fell in the official scale, the peas might rattle less or more, the sardines and the vermouth be imported by a different firm, but the tradition remained: the food of exiles, cooked by servants who did not understand it.[34]

It was not merely that here was the world of Weybridge and Tunbridge Wells that Morgan so longed to escape; it was the falsity that he deplored. Within a matter of days of arriving in India he had decided for himself (although his liberal leanings and milieu had already predisposed him to his point of view) that the English position was untenable.* He realised straight away that, like Fielding, 'he had no racial feeling – not because he was superior to his brother civilians, but because he had matured in a different atmosphere, where the herd-instinct does not flourish';[36] and soon his hostility to the herd-instinct made him increasingly antipathetic to the Anglo-Indian creed. In some ways he was confronted again with the Tonbridge values that he had managed to avoid for the last fifteen years (it is no coincidence that of the fifty-seven boys who arrived at Tonbridge with Morgan in the September of 1893 ten were in India).

---

* His visit to India took place three years after the Morley–Minto reforms that tried to lessen the autocracy of the Raj; and a year after the Great Durbar that, with vast pomp and circumstance, celebrated the accession of George V. There were four strands of political activity in India at this period: moderates who wanted self-government through constitutional means; minority Muslims who wanted the British to safeguard their interests; a small terrorist movement that tried to rid India of the British through sabotage; and radicals who wanted independence through non-violent agitation.

About two-fifths of India was run by Indian maharajahs, each assisted by a British Resident. Seventy-five years earlier the historian Macaulay had described Moghul India as a place where 'a succession of nominal sovereigns, sunk in indolence and debauchery, sauntered away life in secluded palaces chewing bang, fondling concubines and listening to buffoons.'[35] This, alas, was still Anglo-India's attitude to much of princely India when Morgan was there.

Another effect that Anglo-Indian Lahore had on Morgan was to tug his thoughts about women into the insistent foreground. When he wrote about the woman at the Nautch that 'she didn't attract me' he did not add, even unspokenly by intonation, the words 'of course'; it seems that somehow, and for some reason, his thoughts were now, potentially, much more bisexual than they had been during the years of writing *Maurice*. As he was to note in 1927, 'The occasional feeling that e.g. one's sexual outlook was not inevitable brings a gloomy reality into the cell.'[37] It might have been Searight who awoke in Morgan, temporarily at least, the idea that to be lustful only towards adult males was somewhat restrictive; it might have been staying with Malcolm and Josie that made him receptive to the idea that marriage can bring enormous joy even to someone of Malcolm's type; it might have been the unusual and sweet nature of Josie, whom Merz too had greatly admired; indeed the yearning for bisexuality, for so it seems briefly to have been, might have in part resulted from talking to Josie about Merz and feeling that a compromise marriage – were such a thing achievable – would be far, far better than Merz's fate. Whatever the reason, Morgan's thoughts at this time turned often to women.

The myth grew up, in the years after the publication of *A Passage to India*, that in his novel Morgan was hostile to Anglo-Indian women. It is indeed true that by and large they are unpleasant and do little to give the lie to Fielding's discovery that 'it is possible to keep in with Indians and Englishmen, but that he who would also keep in with Englishwomen must drop the Indians'.[38] They seem to exemplify the belief, often expressed by writers about India, that Indian and English were quite harmonious, until the latter started to bring their wives to live with them; then dissension began. But Morgan knew that Josie was not unique; he might have read Maud Diver's 1909 *The Englishwoman in India* in which she tries to account for 'the restlessness and irritability, in certain temperaments, and, in others, that curious slackness – mental and moral – of which the Anglo-Indian woman stands accused';[39] above all he had enough insight and enough empathy to realise that his own situation was little different from that of most English women in India – and of Adela Quested.

When, in the summer of 1913, a few months after his return from India, he started to write the novel in which she was the heroine, Morgan, as always in the past, poured a good deal of himself into the character of his central protagonist: Philip, Rickie, Lucy, the

Schlegel sisters, Maurice – they all had elements of their creator, and so would Adela. She had been, in the first draft, at Cambridge and had there learnt 'that one ought to show when one's bored'. We assume that, because she is a woman, she had then found no purpose in life other than her biological one. In another passage in the first draft she imagines herself as 'a bird, an unimportant one, shut up in a cage with two perches labelled "marriage" and "not-marriage" and that she hopped from perch to perch in order not to notice the cage'; and later, climbing up to the caves, she thinks that:

If the ideal lover had come her way, she would have thrown Ronny aside, but he never would come. For Miss Quested had no illusions about her personal attractiveness: always, from a little girl, she had been meagre, so she dare not expect a perfect mate.[40]

Thinking about Anglo-Indian women, and seeing them from his own perspective, Morgan imagined what his life would have been if his mother had released him from Weybridge – as indeed Lily had – and he had come out as part of the fishing fleet to find a husband; he knew that his job-less, wife-less situation was so unusual that in all essential respects his situation was entirely feminine. The one aspect that was different was that he was able to travel on his own 'seeing Indians' (which is what Fielding was to advise Adela to do if she wanted to see the 'real India'[41]). So many aspects of his trip were similar to a fishing fleet visit. It was for this reason that the people he identified with were, above all, the English women.

23

India 1913

A week after they had arrived in Lahore, the three Englishmen set out for Peshawar on the North-West Frontier to visit Searight. At the Khyber Pass* they sat (as Morgan was to write about Goldie) 'by the edge of the track, watching the caravans pour past . . . out of central Asia, and registering this new proof of the restlessness of the world'.[2] That evening occurred an incident which, in transmuted form, appeared in *A Passage to India*. Morgan lost his collar stud, was late for dinner and found the whole Mess waiting; he was mortified, although everyone else was kind. Aziz's giving of his stud to Fielding is the opposite of a loss, it is a gift, but the English, who observe his studless state, are blind to this and imagine him humiliated. Their attitude contrasts with Fielding's kindly directness, something of which derived from the Peshawar soldiers, 'so charming, and without the least side, and their hospitality passes anything I could have imagined'.[3]

Watching the after-dinner dancing ('White pillared veranda and scarlet coats bounding; jolly outpost to Empire, which one realizes on its edges as nowhere'[4]) Morgan appreciated Goldie anew: 'This is the time', he would write, 'when I began to use him as a touchstone, and to condemn those who fail to appreciate him.'[5] So unexpected was it to see *soldiers* loving Goldie that Morgan could condemn those who did not see the 'point' of him rather than be embarrassed by Goldie's eccentricities. The realisation that both of them could 'get on' with people whom previously they would have imagined quite

---

* The pass, on the border between India and Afghanistan, was guarded twice a week to allow people to pass in both directions: 'at 2.30 the Pass was cleared, and left to barbarism until the next caravan day.'[1]

alien not only made Goldie a touchstone but gave Morgan himself new standards, and new confidence in his capacity to make friends. It was almost as if his intellectual belief in personal relationships as a transcender of all barriers was becoming reality. He had hoped to get to know Indians; he did not anticipate getting to know English men whom, as a breed, he had previously disliked ('Aziz liked soldiers – they either accepted you or swore at you, which was preferable to the civilian's hauteur'[6]).*

Back once more at Lahore, Morgan met a missionary called George Turner, 'the only Englishman I have met who seems to care for the people' (a phrase that might have been used of Fielding). He was comfortably off, having married an American heiress. She was soon to weary of her life in India, go off to France to nurse throughout the First World War and, as Mary Borden, become one of the best-known novelists of her generation. Her book *The Forbidden Zone*[†] (1929) is unique among war novels for its almost clinical description of life in military hospitals, in which Morgan too was to work for three years.

An already well-known novelist (albeit a very middlebrow one) was to be his next hostess: Mrs Everard Cotes, otherwise Sara Duncan,[‡] was 'clever and odd – nice to talk to alone, but at times the Social Manner descended like a pall'. She was a friend of the Morisons and was living with her husband at Simla, that personification of Anglo-India in an alpine setting with Malvern overtones. Here Morgan 'forgot I was in India: there is nothing there but government and scenery';[7] being in this atmosphere must have crystallised his feelings about the governing class and it is no coincidence that the Lieutenant-Governor

---

* Both Goldie and Morgan tried to keep in touch with the Byronic but military Searight by letter. And although neither of them could forget him or his sexual proclivities (when Morgan began his first affair he immediately wrote to Goldie telling him that it was more like an affair of Searight's than anything else, cf. p 304) they never seem to have met again after Peshawar. In his diary for July 1920 Morgan recorded the ending of the friendship but gave no reason: the likelihood is that he longed to meet Searight again and was hurt when he evaded a meeting. However, Morgan kept Searight's letters at least until the late 1930s, when he copied a sentence into his commonplace book to the effect that with only one life to be lived we must not be timid.

† Cf. the present author's *A Very Great Profession: The Woman's Novel 1914–39* (Virago 1983, reprinted 1989), pp 32–5, for a description of this novel.

‡ She was Canadian and had been a successful reporter in the 1880s. Once her husband had proposed (at the Taj Mahal) she turned to novel-writing: some were set in India and one is an 1890s 'new woman' novel. *On the Other Side of the Latch* (1901) was set in Simla and *The Imperialist* (1904) became a classic of Canadian life.

of the Province in *A Passage to India* ('exempted by a long career in the Secretariat from personal contact with the peoples of India, he was able to speak of them urbanely, and to deplore racial prejudice') returns 'to his Himalayan altitudes well satisfied'[8] – it can only have been Simla or Darjeeling that he lived in and more likely the former.

It was at Simla that Morgan attended 'a Mohammedan wedding on rationalist lines . . . It was depressing, almost heartrending, and the problem of India's future opened to me. For at one end of the garden burst a gramophone – "I'd rather be busy with my little Lizzy" and at the other, on a terrace before the house, about twenty orthodox Muslims had gathered for the evening prayer.'*[9] The gloom was not, however, relayed to Lily. She was told merely, in the jolly, cheering-up tone that 'Poppy'† often adopted, that 'very queer it was'.[10] In the same way, when he walked up into the Himalayas and was unhappy in the night at the 'thought of him who might be slipping away' and 'in the morning the mountains were less wonderful' (Morgan was beginning to realise that he and Masood would never be so close again), Lily read merely that 'then I did long for dear mummy again: the road was smooth and not steep, and she would have come in a rickshaw.'[11]

Lily was thousands of miles away but Morgan still could not escape her aura. The depression with which he had continually to battle, the lack of self-worth that had been his all his life, even in India he could not get rid of them. Some years later he would write a revealing entry in his commonplace book:

Idea of Mother and son. She dominates him in youth. Manhood brings him emancipation – perhaps through friendship or a happy marriage. But the mother is waiting. Her vitality depends on character, and asserts itself as the sap drains out of him. She gets her way and reestablishes his childhood, with the difference that his subjection is conscious now and causes him humiliation and pain. Is her tyranny conscious? I think not. Could the same relationship occur between father and daughter? No.

'A ruthless and unpleasant writer', added Morgan, 'might make something of this. But two people pulling each other into salvation is the only theme I find worthwhile.'[12] The tragedy of his life would

---

* When Morgan reworked this diary entry as 'Advance, India!' for the *New Weekly*, 11 April 1914 (later reprinted in *Abinger Harvest*), he asked the question 'How could this jumble end?' after this reflection.

† It is not known why this nickname was sometimes used between themselves by Lily and Morgan; it was perhaps a variation on poppet or popsie.

be that he could only pull himself into salvation by escaping Lily's tyranny. And yet, even in India, reachable only by letter, the sap continued insidiously to drain out of him: 'the mother is waiting'.

'The only idyllic place I have seen yet'[13] was Morgan's next destination. It was Chhatarpur, and for two weeks he lived in the palace guest house just above the city, looking down through mist at the spires of the Jain temples and the monkeys playing on the hillside. Their host, the Maharajah of Chhatarpur, 'was a tiny and fantastic figure, incompetent, *rusé*, exasperating, endearing. He lived for philosophy and love, and he hoped that the two were one.'[14] He had been tutored by Morison and, although supposed to be 'absurd ... he *will* talk about Herbert Spencer and Marie Corelli* till one nearly screams', Morgan found him 'so sensible and shrewd, and so full of fun, that listening and talking to him are both delightful'.[16] He very soon came to love his mélange of Western rationalism and Hindu dogma, his openly expressed affection and concern: it was typical of Morgan's insight that he could easily see beyond the Maharajah's ugly, Pekinese-ish face and his little hobbling body.† And he could recognise a fellow homosexual searching for an ideal friend; hence the procession of Private Secretaries – of whom Joe Ackerley was to be one in 1924 – and, later on, tutors for his son. When not talking philosophy in the palace the three men went on expeditions, once to a favourite local picnic spot at Mau; this was to reappear in the final section of *A Passage to India* when Aziz has journeyed 'some hundreds of miles westward of the Marabar Hills' to escape the British aura. He goes to Mau, which represents the peace and cut-off quality that Morgan found at Chhatarpur and is described in very similar terms to the real Mau in Morgan's diary; for example the real and the fictional both have a ruined stucco palace by a lake

* These were popular late Victorian writers hardly likely to appeal to Morgan and his friends. When Marie Corelli died in 1924 during Joe Ackerley's stay at Chhatarpur, the Maharajah was 'broken-hearted. He wants me, with my own hands, to lay a wreath on her grave for him. I said I'd sooner read another of her books.'[15]

† Some Forster critics, for example Robin Jared Lewis, have claimed the Maharajah as the original Godbole in *A Passage to India*, pointing to their similar dress, their mixture of East and West, their deep belief in the importance of religion and philosophy. The Maharajah was endearingly immortalised in the highly successful *Hindoo Holiday* by Ackerley published in 1932. Others were not so fond. Beatrice Webb told Morgan in 1934 that she stayed with the Maharajah in 1911 and 'thought him the last word of Hindu decadence and especially repulsive when he asked my husband to help him to save his soul'.[17]

where birds 'flapped across the gloaming' (*A Passage to India*),[18] or 'beat the surface with their wings' (diary).

Mau was memorably beautiful and contrasted sharply with the nearby cantonment: 'polo; officers' wives with hideous voices and faces of that even pink. Though not more attracted by Indians than I was, I am irritated by my countrymen more. They made dogs beg.'*[19] Especially painful was the English chaplain who made remarks like ' "Come Maharajah, why don't you eat beef? Do you good." ' Yet while the sensitive trio 'winced with horror' the Maharajah could see him for what he was, a bumbling but well-meaning oaf; while the Private Secretary commended him for having 'no interest whatever in religion, and that is suitable for a clergyman'.[21] This was not said ironically but made the quite accurate assumption that an English man of religion would, compared with an Indian, have very little interest in the subject, whereas Indians thought about little else. Morgan had been unusual in his declaration, six months before setting out, that 'what I want is to see natives, scenery, and if possible religion'.[22] Hence the long conversations with the Maharajah, and even with the Private Secretary: one day 'P.S. burst out to me about the hatred between Hindus and Mohammedans, which might be laid if the one would give up Hindi, the other Cow killing'.[23]

While recognising that religion was the dominant force in Indian life, Morgan was not yet as personally responsive to it as he was, in later years, to become. When, for example, he went to the temples at Khajuraho (in remote countryside twenty miles east of Chhatarpur, entailing a night in tents) he described them to Lily as 'very wonderful but nightmares'.[24] His muted response may have been because he did not want to describe the erotic sculptures to Lily; in any case they are heavily heterosexual, the main impression being of bosoms, pouts and curving thighs with rather fewer penises and muscle. Then, in a broadcast talk years later about an exhibition of photographs of Hindu temples, Morgan declared about those at Khajuraho that 'I have never understood what they were about':

---

* This last observation anticipates *Hindoo Holiday* and perhaps indicates that Ackerley had read Forster's diary when he wrote it. On his second day at 'Chhokrapur' Ackerley had breakfast with the other guests. During a conversation between the two women which Ackerley found 'so remarkable that I began to note it down on the backs of envelopes under cover of the table'[20] the two dogs wandered round the table begging. Ackerley, with his passionate devotion to dogs, always hated their being made to beg; even Morgan thought it a poor trick.

They were just a group of impressive buildings, very ornate outside, and rather poky inside. I grasped nothing further. Now I learn that the Hindu temple symbolises the world-mountain, on whose sides gods, men and animals are sculptured in all their complexity ... The inside is a very different story. The inside of the Hindu temple is a promenade leading to a dark central cell, the sanctuary, where the individual worshipper makes contact with the divine principle. The Hindu temple is not for community-worship. It is for the individual.

When Morgan made this broadcast it was the middle of the Blitz and some form of personal, spiritual inspiration was much needed. What he had found, in the photographs of Khajuraho, was a timely emphasis on the individual, at the expense of community spirit; he went on to say, in a style of peroration that was almost Churchillian and yet perfectly his own:

Besides our war against totalitarianism, we have also an inner war, a struggle for truer values, a struggle of the individual towards the dark, secret place where he may find reality. I came away thinking, 'Yes, the people who built these temples, the people who planned Khajuraho and Orissa and Madura – knew about that. They belonged to another civilisation, but they knew, they knew that the community cannot satisfy the human spirit.'[25]

On another occasion Morgan went on an expedition from Chhatarpur by elephant; it was his second, but this elephant walked more quickly and easily than the other one had done (at Gwalior). Again the experience would be brought to triumphant fruition in an article but this time Morgan's acutely sensitive ear for dialogue was exploited in the subtle cadences of Indian English:

'Ought we not to start? The elephants must be waiting.'
    'There is no necessity. Elephants sometimes wait four hours.'
    'But the Temple is far.'
    'Oh no, there are thirty of them.'
    'Thirty temples! Are they far?'
    'No, no, no, not at all – fifteen really, but much jungle; fifteen to come and fifteen to go.'
    'Fifteen of what?'
    'Fifteen all.'[26]

Here, during the years in which *A Passage to India* was in his mind, Morgan is seen refining his understanding of India and the English in India: there is the English emphasis on time, alien to Indians;

there is the misunderstanding; there is the kindly Indian wish to say what the English questioner wants to hear, not (Western concept) what is accurate; and there is the humour at the end. Suddenly an image flashes into one's mind of a tennis court in a jungle, perhaps of elephants wielding rackets, of the pith-helmeted English playing against – what? It is a muddle, a joke, it amuses one but it also makes one pause – without, ever, being pompous or heavy-handed. The dialogue anticipates the 'bridge party' scene in Chapter 5 of *A Passage to India* where, with the same humour, the reader is aware of the vast linguistic gulf between Adela and Mrs Bhattacharya: with great subtlety Morgan makes one aware that English is, to the Indian, an alien tongue with different idioms and different assumptions.

By the time he left Chhatarpur Morgan's perceptions had been transformed not only by its beauty but also by its separateness: it came to seem representative of India as a whole. And this was so for all three of them, Bob, Morgan and Goldie. When the latter left India he felt (to quote Morgan twenty years later) 'that the main cleavage in civilisation lies not between East and West but between India and the rest of the world'. And he concluded, with almost mystic resignation, in a letter to Hugh Meredith written just after leaving Chhatarpur: 'There is no solution of the problem of governing India. Our presence is a curse both to them and to us. Our going will be worse.' However, his declaration that 'the Indians *bore* the English. *That* is the simple adamantine fact' met with Morgan's disagreement: 'Perhaps he was overtired, perhaps temperamentally averse, but he never found in Indian society either the happiness or the peacefulness which have made my own visits to the country so wonderful.'[27]

When the moment for departure came it turned out that it was not auspicious. 'Journeys begun on Monday always end disastrously,'[28] the Maharajah declared, before agreeing that Tuesday was just about lucky enough for the eastward-bound. Poor Morgan was going west but accepted without demur that his host 'could scarcely hesitate where the safety of Mr Dickinson was concerned'.[29] 'He likes me least,' he noted in the matter-of-fact way so typical of someone whose self-deprecating streak was an ironic carapace rather than a destructive reality. The Maharajah *did* like Goldie best: he had been more willing to talk philosophy and was so wise ('Ah Mr Dickinson, if only you were in power what a different world it would be'[30]).

It was a thirty-mile journey to the nearest railway station and from here another short train journey to the junction at Jhansi. Here Goldie and Bob duly turned east to Benares (it was because their destination was the holiest Hindu city in India that the Maharajah had deemed the astrological predictions of especial significance) and Morgan turned west to Bhopal. On the way he stopped at Sanchi but this was disastrous for Baldeo, the servant who had been with him since Bombay and of whom he had become fond ('he continues a great comfort to me') as they journeyed across India. At Sanchi, Hindu food was unobtainable so Baldeo 'had little to eat all day. He sits on the luggage at the station, holy and cross . . . They certainly act up to their religion', Morgan commented, 'though it is hard to make head or tail of it.'[31]

At Bhopal – 'built on the shore of a long blue lake, but the country is barren and ugly' – there was 'Oriental hospitality plus Oriental confusion': letters of introduction to the Begum from Masood had not had the desired effect. 'I didn't enjoy myself much', Morgan told Lily, 'and shouldn't have been happy but for all your sweet letters.'[32] So he went on to Ujjain, where he found it difficult to persuade his driver to take him to the ruins of the ancient city rather than to the water palace, and then on to the famous marble palaces and lakes of Udaipur, 'the Venice of the East'. Turning south, he paused at Indore, a small town on the east–west route from Bombay to Agra with a large Anglo-Indian community, and stayed with the Private Secretary to the Maharajah of Indore.

Morgan felt at home here because he preferred to read rather than to talk. In these unlikely surroundings 'I read *Wuthering Heights* and very seldom stop thinking about it',[33] he told Josie. Apart from reading, there was the English Club, little described by Morgan at the time but which was to reappear as of central importance in *A Passage to India*:

The third act of *Cousin Kate* was well advanced by the time Mrs Moore re-entered the Club. Windows were barred, lest the servants should see their memsahibs acting, and the heat was consequently immense. One electric fan revolved like a wounded bird, another was out of order. Disinclined to return to the audience she went into the billiard-room, where she was greeted by 'I want to see the *real* India' and her appropriate life came back with a rush.

This short passage is full of Forsterian overtones. The English have chosen to imprison themselves thus and will see nothing more of the 'real India'; the women are imprisoned even more than the men, forced to act in a comedy in which the heroine, a successful novelist, wants only a husband and children; the two fans are the transmuted image of Adela hopping from one perch, labelled 'marriage' yet wounded, to the other, labelled 'not-marriage' but out of order; finally there is the vast gulf created by the English refusal to allow Indians to glimpse them acting – but this for them is 'appropriate life'. It was the Club that came to represent all that Morgan loathed about Anglo-India and it was here that he would set perhaps the greatest scene in the novel when, in order to receive news of Adela, 'people drove into the Club with studious calm – the jog-trot of country gentlefolk between green hedgerows, for the natives must not suspect that they were agitated.'[34] It is no coincidence that Fielding's stand against his fellow countrymen was to be marked by his resignation from the Club.

But at Dewas, some twenty miles from Indore, Morgan found a party of English with whom he felt very much at home. Ever since Malcolm had ceased to be the Maharajah of Dewas's tutor he had kept in close touch with him and, since his marriage, a tradition had grown up that he and Josie travelled, often hundreds of miles, to spend Christmas at Dewas, inviting any English friends that His Highness ('HH') and they would like. For one week out of the fifty-two Malcolm and Josie knew that they would have around them people with whom they could re-create the conversations that they so desperately missed during the rest of the year. Christmas, for the Darlings, had become an annual re-creation of King's values, with much discussion of books, friendship, personal liberty, votes for women, aesthetics: all overlaid with the unforgettable atmosphere of an Indian palace. Morgan felt in his element and confided in Josie: 'his mother took him twice to Italy, and as he talked of it, I seemed to see the two going through the vistas of pictures and statues and sunlit cypresses, the shy quiet widow and the shy sensitive talented little boy, who must have been, even then, the centre of her universe and her husband only a faraway tender memory.' At a wedding there was dancing and 'Morgan, in wine coloured satin, leaped and bounded and whirled in the centre'.[35]

Dewas, Morgan told Bob, is 'a charming place – tents on the edge of a lake; scenery nothing striking, except for an acropolis, an holy hill, which stands over the town'.[36] But he thought HH's New Palace, begun in 1907 and semi-completed the year before, a hideous building, 'shoddy, ignoble, colourless – a yellow-white impression prevails'.[37]

(Nowadays, distanced as it is from the sprawl of Dewas by a drive and a rough garden, it has a faded glamour and is not colourless – it is pleasantly pale yellow.) It was this building that was to provide the setting for *The Hill of Devi*, and where Morgan was to work for six months in 1921 as HH's Secretary, living in the nearby guest house; even now leaving was like 'parting from old friends'.

There was a good deal of muddle over tickets and luggage; but eventually, after two nights' travelling, a tired Morgan arrived at Allahabad where, on a hired bicycle, he was shown round by a friend of Masood's, 'the first Mohammedan I have met with any feeling for Art'.[38] In the evening he endured dinner at the house of the Collector, who tended to remarks like 'I despise the native at the bottom of my heart';[39] the next day he tried, and failed, to find the meeting place of two sacred rivers with the Ganges ('so abased, so monotonous is everything that meets the eye, that when the Ganges comes down it might be expected to wash the excrescence back into the soil'[40]) and travelled on to Benares to stay with the English headmaster of a school there. He proved 'touchy as well as dictatorial' and 'would not let me look at what I liked'.[41] Yet the Ghats, the steps up from the Ganges covered in temples, impressed Morgan more than he anticipated; and he enjoyed talking to a fakir, to whom he had been given an introduction by William Rothenstein, about literature and inspiration. At the station, as he left, he saw the words 'God *si* love' engraved on marble; he jotted them down and they would appear memorably in *A Passage to India*.

Now, in the second week of January 1913, Morgan travelled to Patna* to see Masood again or, more specifically, to its suburb, Bankipore, described by Emily Eden seventy-five years earlier as 'a sort of Battersea to Patna', an epithet which would certainly have appealed to Morgan had he come across it. Like Emily Eden, who was led to conclude that India had 'the most picturesque population, with the ugliest scenery, that ever was put together',[42] Morgan found Bankipore 'horrible beyond words';[43] he was to write in *A Passage to India* about 'Chandrapore'† that 'the streets are mean, the temples ineffective' and, of the 'sensibly planned' Civil Station, 'it has nothing hideous in it, and only the view is beautiful'.[44] None

---

* Here he visited a circular building called the Golghar with a spectacular echo: this may have given him the idea of using an echo in the novel as a symbol.

† This means 'moon city' giving overtones of dreams and of the alien, the other, as well as of the female.

the less, unattractive as Bankipore proved, it was here that Morgan's greatest novel began to germinate. Accepting, at last, that his lingering feelings for Masood were to remain unfulfilled, Morgan saw that the alternative to a *grande passion* was indeed the 'great book' on India that had first been suggested by Masood two years before.

Morgan's empathy with Indians, even the calm state of his digestion (in contrast to Goldie's), made him rather proud, made him feel in small part the self-respect which is most people's inheritance. Once he arrived at Bankipore to stay with Masood he became a less assiduous diary-keeper – January 20: 'Can write nothing outside letters' – and one reason must have been that he was depressed by Masood's uninvolved, if friendly, treatment of him. The one time there was a chance to talk properly, after a pleasant dinner at an Indian friend's, Morgan noted tersely 'oratio minima after it'.*45 But he remained the devoted letter-writer, reminding Lily to go on keeping his letters because 'I find it so very difficult to write an account of anything in my diary when I have once written it elsewhere. Aunt Laura says that it is impossible to write both, and that diaries rob relations of their "dues" – which is very true, I find.'46 (The implications of the word 'dues' are intensely sad. Rarely was it used by Morgan, because so deep was his anger about the boa-like constrictions of his relations that it was as if he dare not let it surface. Yet posterity must wish that Weybridge and Abinger had been less demanding of their dues. The Indian letters are humorous, descriptive, memorably phrased; yet in some ways they are ciphers, concealing so much more than they reveal. As Morgan was to write in the preface to *The Hill of Devi*, apologising for any possible shortcomings of the reprinted letters: 'I was writing to people of whom I was fond and whom I wanted to amuse, with the result that I became too humorous and conciliatory, and too prone to turn remote and rare matters into suburban jokes.')

Since he was used to self-concealment, we can never know his true, his absolute state of mind. But at Bankipore, it is clear, he was deeply unhappy. He had his final chance to woo Masood, and it eluded him. On the last night they had a talk and Morgan seems to have made some form of declaration; in his room alone he was as wretched as he had ever been: 'Aie – aie – aie – growing after tears' he wrote tersely in his diary. 'Mosquito net, fizzling lamp, high step between rooms.

* Bearing in mind that *os/oris* is the Latin for mouth, this phrase may have referred to some form of minimal sexual contact; or merely to a discussion of it.

Then return and comfort a little.'⁴⁷ The comfort took an elegiac, a companionable rather than a sexual form; Morgan now accepted that he and Masood would never be lovers. Possibly Masood told him that he had definitely decided to find a wife, as indeed in the summer he was to do; and this dark night of the soul was for Morgan a miserable finale to the previous six years of his love for Masood.

It was in this state, wretched, weary, having had no sleep but having spent the night staring into the shadows cast by the fizzing lamp, hungry (breakfast was a mere dab of omelette at 6.00 a.m.), that Morgan left Bankipore to go, by train and elephant, to the Barabar Caves; and his misery was compounded by the humiliation of Masood, presumably exhausted by the night's emotions, failing to get up to say goodbye. When he entered the caves, tired and lonely, their effect was overwhelming. Typically, however, nothing of his great depth of feeling and reaction was recorded in either his diary or letters. It had to wait until the following winter, when he wrote the first draft of what was to be the caves scene in *A Passage to India*; and then wait another eleven years until he completed it.*

In the caves, as he told Lily, there was not much to see except highly polished granite walls and not much to do except to try to wake the echo. But the emotion of the night before and the effect of the caves themselves – 'motion more than sound, not a warning as much as the expression of upset,'⁴⁸ wrote a visitor in 1988 – all made 28 January 1913 an unforgettable day. The one clue to this in Morgan's diary lies in the jerky, unmellifluous style, harsh vowel sounds and short consonants unconsciously conveying mental dislocation; and in what was to be his last novel. For it is likely that it was now, as Morgan recovered his equilibrium during a late lunch, that he tentatively began to envisage its rough structure; and that to begin with it was far more closely based on his own experience. An early outline shows that the setting was 'Moradpore', the real name of the part of Bankipore where Masood lived, and that the heroine, variously called Janet and Edith (and much more like Morgan himself) is attracted to a Muslim (who was much more like Masood than Aziz was eventually to be).

Morgan's Murray's Handbook described the third-century-BC caves as 'among the oldest Buddhist monuments in existence'.⁴⁹ In themselves they are not spectacular, which is why they were

* Chapters 1–7 and some of 8, 10, 12 and 14 were written in 1913–14; the novel was finished in 1922–4.

only visited by tourists with an especial interest in the region,* but as symbols, as an image they are redolent of a vast spectrum of spiritual significance; as Norman Douglas was to observe, in his travel-writing classic *Old Calabria* (published in 1915 when Morgan had begun and abandoned *A Passage to India*), 'cave-worship is older than any god or devil. It is the cult of feminine principle – a relic of that aboriginal obsession of mankind to shelter in some Cloven Rock of Ages, in the sacred womb of Mother Earth who gives us food and receives us after death';[50] here was the Demeter in another guise. The cave did not have anything special about it, it was just a cave ('nothing, nothing attaches to them'[51]). For Morgan, when he went in, sexuality was the key; only later did he turn Adela's experience into something more spiritual. This is why in the final, considered version nothing tangible happens to her but in the earlier, 1913, drafts 'Aziz & Janet drift into one another's arms – then apart' and, in yet another draft,

She struck out and he got hold of her other hand and forced her against the wall, he got both her hands in one of his, and then felt at her breasts. 'Mrs Moore' she yelled. 'Ronny – don't let him, save me.' The strap of her Field Glasses, tugged suddenly, was drawn across her throat. She understood – it was to be passed once round her neck, she was to be throttled as far as necessary and then . . . Silent, though the echo still raged up and down, she waited and when the breath was on her wrenched a hand free, got hold of the glasses and pushed them into her assailant's mouth. She could not push hard, but it was enough to hurt him. He let go, and then with both hands on her weapon she smashed at him again. She was strong and had horrible joy in revenge. 'Not this time' she cried, and he answered – or the cave did. She gained the entrance of the tunnel, screamed like a maniac lest he pulled her in when she stooped, and then [sic] the open air, her topi smashed, her fingers bleeding.[52]

Why was Morgan to abandon this version of the caves scene in favour of Adela herself explaining what happened ('He never actually touched me once'[53])? Why, when in the original version Aziz does feel 'Janet's' breasts, was Morgan to prefer vagueness, so that ever afterwards readers never quite knew 'what happened' in the caves? That he would be for a long while unsure what to do is clear from surviving drafts. Of one hundred rejected but preserved sheets of manuscript, fifty-five are drafts of the caves episode, showing that

* The film of *A Passage to India* used far more spectacular caves in southern India.

it was this part of the novel more than any other that would cause Morgan to rewrite. But in the end he chose to be non-specific, to be symbolic. He would tell Plomer in 1934: 'I tried to show that India is an unexplainable muddle by introducing an unexplained muddle – Miss Quested's experience in the cave. When asked what happened there, *I don't know*.'[54] If Aziz really had touched Adela, India would, as Morgan saw it, have been less of a mystery, it would have been more obviously divided between good and evil. After many false starts his final decision would be to make the truth of the caves episode unknowable.

Morgan made only three more brief entries in his diary before abandoning it for an entire month: just as, after Merz's death in the July of 1909, he had soon stopped writing his journal and only re-started in a locked book. In both instances the strength of his mental turmoil kept him away from his diary, yet as a result his psyche was able to direct all its energy into a gestating, putative novel. It was at this time that he told the writer Forrest Reid in Ireland, in answer to an enquiry about his work, 'I am dried up. Not in my emotions, but in their expression. I cannot write at all . . . Please do not mention this, as few people know. It often makes me very unhappy. I see beauty going by and have nothing to catch it in.'[55]

In the last weeks of his trip he began to grow weary. 'Feel rather sleepy and "undescriptive",' he apologised to Lily on revisiting the Taj. It was as if his brain was refusing to absorb and his body needed to take control: staying at Allahabad it was the riding in borrowed jodhpurs that he enjoyed most and at Lahore,* staying with the Darlings, turning somersaults for the delight of John Jermyn. Yet there was one other tremendous pleasure at Lahore which was observing the

---

* In early March, Morgan lectured here on 'The Enjoyment of English Literature' at Government College where the Darlings' friend Gerald Wathen was Professor of English and History. Twenty years later Wathen gave John Jermyn Darling a job at the school in Hampstead of which he was headmaster; the intensely political John Jermyn quarrelled with Wathen over his teaching methods, which he saw as authoritarian and abusive. The quarrel resulted in a court case initiated by John Jermyn, the conviction of Wathen followed by acquittal on appeal, the dismissal of John Jermyn, and the severing of all relations between him, his father and his 'godfather' Morgan who, in November 1910, had refused to be actual Godfather but had written out an atheist's catechism for the new baby, 'Liking Being Alive'. John Jermyn's crime, in the eyes of Morgan, Malcolm and their circle, was that he chose to betray a family friend.

atmosphere in the Darlings' house. On his first visit he had not fully realised how unusual it was, but now he could see that Malcolm and Josie 'are the only officials I have met who care to see anything of the educated Indian socially; others see him, but at formal garden parties and banquets' ('bridge parties'). He told Josie:

I am so depressed by this hatred between the educated native (barrister type) and the I.C.S. I have always told the former that they were touchy and suspicious, but it is now borne in on me that they see no more than there is to see – much of the rudeness is studied and all of it springs from conscious superiority. Granting the type is unreliable and egoistic, and granting that a type with these defects can possess no virtues, it yet seems so unwise to snub it continually, and so (to use a word I never use) ungentlemanly . . . How is it going to end?[56]

Josie herself represented all that was opposite to the kind of woman described by Goldie when, as part of a diatribe against Anglo-Indian society, he told Hugh Meredith: 'It's the women more than the men that are at fault. There they are, without their children, with no duties, no charities, with empty minds and hearts, trying to fill them by playing tennis and despising the natives . . .'[57] (Josie had at once noticed Goldie's 'unconsciously donnish' attitude to women: 'one doesn't feel that one is [a factor] in the conversation; but that one is a woman, who will presently leave the room'.[58])

On leaving Lahore, Morgan visited Jaipur* and Jodhpur, 'after Agra – the finest place I have been to yet'. But more than 'the city tossing purple and golden with the desert beyond' he was impressed by his hosts, friends of Malcolm's named Goyder and Spartali. 'It sounds like a Bond Street firm, but the first is financial adviser to the Jodhpur State, and the second an engineer making a new railway.' Of the former, Morgan noted in his diary, 'Here at last is the perfect Anglo-Indian, seeing the faults of the Indian but not brooding over them till he stifles enthusiasm and love'; while the latter 'spoke of the immense freedom: he loves to be away from the conventions, being unable to neglect them; only the sophisticated can do that and he is simple, and prudish before women.'[59] Like Fielding was to do, Goyder ('one of the best people I've come across yet'[60]) and Spartali both tried to understand India rather than merely to dominate it.

---

* On the way he stayed briefly with another novelist of Indian life, Edmund Candler, a teacher at the Government College in Patiala, whose intellectual isolation Morgan found rather depressing; his major theme was the British as misfits in India.

The now re-started diary records that Morgan returned to Bombay in order to get the train to Hyderabad and visit Maimie's friend May Wyld who was headmistress of a school; her direct, approachable manner ('May entered shops and squatted to bargain. Very nice with people') perhaps contributed something to the character of Mrs Moore. Having stayed with her, Morgan set out north for Aurangabad to stay for a week with a friend of Masood's named Saeed Mirza. He was assiduous in his duties as host but once, as they were out riding, 'burst out against English. "It may be fifty or five hundred years but we shall turn you out." He hates us far more than his brother. Horse curvetting all the time in the sunset.' Although lightly described at the time, it was this scene that was to be the ambiguously pessimistic finale to *A Passage to India*; while Saeed's house, with 'a lovely wooden hall: two rows of triple arches which, like the internal pavilions, were painted blue . . . Square tank of green water'[61] was to be the model for Fielding's house with its 'very beautiful room, opening into the garden through three high arches of wood'[62] and blue-painted pillars inside.

In the last week of his visit Morgan went on an expedition to the famous caves at Ellora, 'more amazing than anything in a land where much amazes',[63] and was so impressed that he went back for a second look. 'The caves are cruel, obscene things,' he told Masood, 'the work of devils, but very wonderful.'[64] Yet he noted, when filling in his diary on board ship, that 'their impression is already fading, I think because there is no beauty and I do not believe in the devil whose palace they are.' Then there was a hurried and confused return to Bombay: the boat left earlier than anticipated so there was 'no time to buy photographs or eat mangoes or repack comfortably or go to the Elephanta caves, nor even to buy cakes for kind Saeed and his friends at the smart confectioner's which I particularly wanted to do'. Morgan noted sadly in the last diary entry of his trip: 'It's as if I am to do nothing for him, however slight. "The accounts of friends are written in the heart" is his explanation. I have ended with a visit typically Oriental.'[65]

24

Weybridge Again

When Morgan arrived at Harnham he gave Lily, and the maids, lengths and lengths of Indian material: like all travellers to India he had been unable to resist their beauty and their cheapness. Lily admired them, exclaimed over them, and put them reverentially away in drawers and trunks. After she died 'they were still in the drawer – never had been opened – and where the folds were they had just rotted away.'[1] Lily would not have *used* the material, as tablecloth or wall hanging or evening skirt, although she expected some tribute from the returning traveller; but it had to be on her own terms, and the idea of thanking Morgan properly by finding a use for his present would not have occurred to her.

So their relationship, the mother in her mid-fifties and the son in his mid-thirties, resumed its former tentacle-like quality, neither being able or willing to start afresh. In later years Morgan would imagine that things had worsened between them after Louisa's death in 1911. In fact it was a combination of circumstances. Lily *was* very unhappy when her mother died; but Morgan was depressed too at the time. Then he went to India and Lily was lonely; when he came back he was preoccupied; then he went away for three years during the war. The approximate harmony that had existed between them during the years that Morgan was writing his first four novels could never return; but it was not just Louisa's death that destroyed it.

One important factor was Lily's ambivalence about Morgan's success. Widows with only children can create a much closer, more enclosing relationship if their child has little life outside the domestic circle. Usually daughters are thus ensnared. When, in Radclyffe Hall's *The Unlit Lamp* (1924), the mother accuses her daughters of wanting 'to hide me away in a tenement house, while you two lead the life that amuses you. This home is to be broken up and I am to go to London – my health doesn't matter', we can hear Lily's voice. And, when Edward Carpenter was to write in 1916 about unmarried women having 'nothing to do except dabble in paints and music ... and wander aimlessly from room to room to see if by chance "anything was going on"',[2] we can imagine how Morgan must have empathised with this. As he told Florence Barger in 1915, 'I am leading the life of a little girl so long as I am tied to home.'[3]

He could, of course, have escaped. There was no financial tie holding him to Lily: quite apart from his private income he could, after *Howards End*, have begun to live on his earnings alone;* the choice was his. Deep down, complain as he might, as he frequently did in his diary, Morgan did not want to break away. Was he forced, a year after he returned from India, to write to Lily while she was staying with friends, 'I am very anxious about you. I not only love Mummy more than any one else, but feel she is *worth* so much more'?[4] He was not. His temperament and his upbringing induced him to, and he knew it.

What was disquieting about the Forster ménage, and this is what made the writing of the novels even more extraordinary, is that Lily resented her son's achievements. She liked him writing; it was, after all, necessary to tell people that he was doing *something*, but she was never able, or never wanted, to rise above the kind of cheery, applauding, jollying-along tone into which mothers of small children often relapse. After Morgan's second collection of short stories was published in 1920 she told him that she had re-read them 'with much pleasure, darling. "The Road from Colonus" is one of my favourites, although it always makes me very sad because it is so true to life – written some time ago – but my darling was always observant.' Since, after this sentence, she added depressingly, 'still pouring and church bells ringing', Morgan's gloom upon receiving these words must have been total. Lily never pretended to be an intellectual. But better for a mother, in that situation, to gush or be awestruck than to revert to the language of the nursery: 'my darling was always observant'[5] was addressed to a man of over forty. No wonder Morgan would say of Lily that 'she is always wanting me to be 5 years old again'.[6]

---

* In 1910 *Howards End* sold 7662 copies, by 1913 it had sold 9959. It cost 6 shillings [£15]. With a royalty of 10 per cent Morgan would have made £150 on top of his £130 advance, a total of £280 [£13,000] over three years. (By 1946 it had sold 250,000 copies in Penguin.)

In another respect, too, Lily could not give up on the vocabulary of nursery life. She thought it her duty to see that Morgan did not become stuck-up, uppity or above himself, to use the language of nannies, and often said as much. 'I hope so much praise won't make you uppish'[7] she would remark after the publication of *A Passage to India*. Alas, would that it had.

It seems so sad to us, Morgan's admirers, that he was not cherished. Yet in some ways this is what he needed. If he had been surrounded by an atmosphere of intellectual complicity of the kind Cecil Vyse lived in he might never have written, he might have ended up only 'for society and cultivated talk'.[8] If Lily, too, had joined the London Library or if she had tried, in the evenings, to discuss his 'work in progress' intelligently, he might have been stifled for ever. In some curious way it suited Morgan to be cramped in Weybridge. When he remarked, in the August of 1913, that 'India has obliterated & makes me careless of this suburban life',[9] he was recording only part of the truth: he was not as careless as he thought he should be. And this ambivalence, this continual wavering between the claims of suburbia and the claims of Bloomsbury, set him apart from both in a rather suitable manner. As Leonard Woolf would write:

He was strange, elusive, evasive. You could be talking to him easily and intimately one moment, and suddenly he would seem to withdraw into himself; though he still was physically there, you had faded out of his mental vision, and so with a pang you found that he had faded out of yours ... Lytton [Strachey] nicknamed him the Taupe, partly because of his faint physical resemblance to a mole, but principally because he seemed intellectually and emotionally to travel unseen underground and every now and again pop up unexpectedly with some subtle observation or delicate quip which somehow or other he had found in the depths of the earth or of his own soul.

Weybridge was the hole into which the taupe withdrew; Bloomsbury was where he sometimes popped up.

Initially, however, Morgan's friends were not always tolerant of his set-apartness. When Leonard Woolf wrote the above passage in 1960 he prefaced it with the remark 'he was a fascinating character and what I knew of him I liked immensely'.[10] Things had in fact been different in 1904. '"The taupe" ... just as querulous & apologetic as usual,' he told Lytton; and, three months later, 'the taupe has asked if he could come & see me, so he lunched here today, & has absolutely depressed me.' Before Morgan became famous few of his contemporaries took him seriously; for example, Leonard, writing from Ceylon in 1905, quite failed to see *Where Angels Fear to Tread* as anything more than simply clever. 'I can imagine the taupes in their half-lit burrows making jokes at one another in it or old ladies in musty close smelling suburban rooms revelling in it if they ever had any humour at all.'[11] How this must have depressed Morgan, he who so longed to be liked; nor was the situation much better in 1913, with Leonard and Virginia newly married. The Morgan who wrote in his diary: 'Growing sense of my own futility doesn't sadden me, though I shall grow queer & unpopular if I go on as I am now'[12] remarked that Virginia and Lytton were rude to him two weeks later. Which they evidently were. 'You will find Forster here,' wrote Virginia from Sussex to a friend, 'but he is going to be put on the brood mare, who had become very fresh, so we shan't see much of him.'[13] There is a photograph of Morgan taken during this weekend: he looks as though he has just got off it.

But it was only a few weeks after this weekend that a happier period of Morgan's life was about to begin, because it was the time when he re-started and nearly finished the novel that had been gestating in his mind since the summer of 1910, *Maurice*. He was also, it appears, writing the first seven chapters of what was to be *A Passage to India*; but since the *only* evidence we have for this is that the colour ink he was using at this period, green, corresponds with that used to write letters at the time, the evidence is not substantial. What is clear, since the green ink is the one clue for the archivist to work on, is that, as always, the writing of the novel was a secret, almost secretive process that Morgan mentioned to no one.

Maurice was, however, mentioned in his diary. He and Lily were again at Harrogate and again (or allegedly for the first time) on 13 September Morgan visited Millthorpe. It was this visit that he remembered and that he then claimed was the beginning of his novel, the occasion when Merrill caressed his bottom. The additional impulses, apart from Merz, were Searight's unabashed sexuality and some erotic short stories which, apparently, he had in the last two years begun to write. One of these was shown to Goldie, who expressed 'disgust'; his reaction, just before Christmas

1913, brought to a halt the 'three-months spurt'* that had lasted since the September visit to Millthorpe. 'So here I am with 3 unfinished novels on my hands', wrote Morgan in his diary (the third was *Arctic Summer*). 'Even mother must notice I'm played out soon.'

Nor was a second visit to Millthorpe that year, although 'it preserved joy', as exultant as the September one. Nevertheless, after his usual New Year's Eve summing up, Morgan wrote, sprawlingly across the page, 'Edward Carpenter! Edward Carpenter! Edward Carpenter!' It was a measure of the freeing effect that the two visits had had on him: not only did he feel able to re-start *Maurice*, he felt freed as a person. Carpenter made him feel that the platonic, Symondsish, Maurice-and-Clive type of homosexuality *must* now be part of the past; and that a Carpenterish, physical, Maurice-and-Alec type of relationship was due to him. He had suffered enough. Yet how to change things? Searight, India and Carpenter had induced a resurgence of lustful visions in Morgan and a new self-knowledge, but also a new disillusion. Once, in December, he saw 'my ideal man'. Ten years earlier 'I shouldn't have done anything for thinking of him. Now it's all nothing': only the depression that lust left behind.

By the spring of 1914, a year after his return from India, Morgan planned 'to finish Maurice in a fortnight?'[15] *A Passage to India* was still not mentioned in his diary, or anywhere else, but that he had been thinking a good deal about the country of its setting is clear from his remarks to Masood that he was 'feeling awfully cut off from India which chiefly owing to your damned self has become part of my life. I meet no one who is interested in it'; and, some weeks later, 'no doubt it is ridiculous to have fallen in love with a continent of 60,000,000 people, but apparently this is what I've done.'[16] With curious symbolism *Maurice* seems to have been finished by August: not only did it encapsulate something of the pre-war era, it also would have been written differently, I am sure, if begun post-war; by an accident of timing the novel was finished and war broke out during the same summer. This was, for Morgan, a lucky chance. The depression he endured from knowing that he had finished an unpublishable novel could be subsumed into his feelings about the

---

* 'Lady writers can be very unfortunate' Morgan would write in 1926. 'I remember a passage in *Elizabeth of the German Garden* where the heroine cries gaily "I mean to call you Roger. Tell me – do you like it and have you ever been Rogered before?" '[14] But sometimes Morgan could be just as unfortunate, although it is a little different in a diary. (There is no such remark in *Elizabeth and her German Garden*.)

war. No wonder he wrote, with frank egoism, 'Irritated not with war but with my relation to it'. But how we sympathise with him when he writes, on 1 August and two days later, 'Mother is nice to me – I had to tell her my work is all wrong . . . Mother happier since I confided I feel done up, & couldn't work, but respects me less.'[17]

Morgan's response to the 1914–18 war was muted. He was against it, and in all essential respects aligned himself with Bloomsbury's pacifism. But he seems not to have opposed it passionately. He never inveighed against it in print. He never marched or signed petitions or expostulated. He even, when his Whichelo cousin Gerald was imprisoned for being a conscientious objector, remained detached; yet here was a first cousin, the nearest he would ever have to the brother for which he had always longed so fervently, prepared to be ostracised for his ideals.

Morgan, still, could not contemplate being ostracised: his moral courage would emerge only later, after *A Passage to India* had made him famous and his ideas respected, after he had had a sexually fulfilling relationship. For the moment he was simply not brave enough to risk offending Weybridge, even though he felt that he thereby alienated Bloomsbury: 'from 1916 the gulf was bound to widen',[18] he would write when brooding on what he felt was his exclusion. In Morgan's eyes the war was rather like school, something he disliked, avoided if he could, but would not stand out against in any conspicuous way. Just as he did not run away from Tonbridge, did not declare at the time that he loathed everything it stood for, so, now, he resisted any open anti-war declarations.

By the standards of the Darlings he was, however, virtually white feather material: they were so passionately in favour of the war that Morgan wondered whether his friendship with them could survive. Josie wrote to her mother:

Where is the Whiteheads' *salon*, and all the Chelsea Liberals? H . . . lets others die to save *him*. It is something very like being a coward, is it not? As for Morgan, the poor dear fellow is not nearly strong enough to enlist; and his work could be done by no-one else, as he has a good deal of genius in him, and he is the only child of a widowed mother. But he too seems hopelessly out of touch with reality. Does he not realise that our little army, the flower of our manhood, must be wiped out if we don't send more and more troops to help?[19]

285

Much of this sentiment was expressed to Morgan too; and the reason the friendship did survive is that with some of it he was in agreement.* He loathed the whole concept of war ideologically. Yet had he not written, in *Howards End* only four years before, that a certain remark was 'of the kind which, if stated often enough, may become true; just as the remark "England and Germany are bound to fight" renders war a little more likely each time that it is made'?[21] And even to Malcolm he said that 'I am sure we could not have kept out of this war.'[22]

Yet for Chelsea liberals, Bloomsbury intellectuals, and all the others of his contemporaries who were fiercely anti-war, Morgan vacillated too much. This was made especially apparent when, for the first time in his life, and immediately upon the outbreak of war, he found a job. In his eyes it was coincidental. The Director of the National Gallery lived in Weybridge and offered him a part-time cataloguing post at a salary of £100 (£5000) a year; here at last was an interesting, suitable way of escaping from three unfinished novels and three meals a day with Lily. But because of the timing it seemed to other people that Morgan had only taken on the position in order to appear employed in a time of war.

What did Morgan feel as he travelled by train from Weybridge to Charing Cross (conveniently, the gallery was a mere step across Trafalgar Square from the station)? How did he react as his contemporaries began to be killed (out of fifty-seven young men who arrived at Tonbridge in the same term as he did, seventeen fought in the war and six were killed, Tiddy among them)? None of this is recorded: even though the war and his job must have been much the most preoccupying part of Morgan's life at this time. Friendships were recorded, though: *they*, not wars, are the true stuff of diaries; they can also be charted in other people's letters. So we know that at the end of 1914 Goldie wrote a letter praising *Maurice* (perhaps he had been allowed to read it because of the shared link with Searight): 'I think he's much the best thing you have achieved'[23] he wrote extravagantly; we know that the twenty-five-year-old Masood was married and that Morgan was mournful but not unduly sad; we know too that at this period Morgan and D. H. Lawrence tentatively began a friendship.

The two novelists had met at Ottoline Morrell's and were naturally

---

* But he broke off relations with Mrs Beveridge and her son because the former wrote criticising Morgan for not joining up; and he was never again so close to Josie. Lady Morison, too, was cool, although by 1920 was 'nice to me again ... My war record is either forgotten or forgiven, apparently.'[20]

curious about each other; when Lawrence invited Morgan to stay with himself and Frieda in Sussex (they were living in a cottage at Greatham belonging to the Meynell family) Morgan accepted.* But the relationship, though intense, was too volatile to last: Morgan was hurt by Lawrence's criticisms yet was too polite to say what *he* thought. He was also made angry by Lawrence's imputations against his sexuality, and the implication that Morgan needed someone like Frieda to loosen himself up. Uncharacteristically he wrote a sharp thank-you letter, saying that although he liked Frieda, and the Lawrence who was restful and wrote *The White Peacock*, he did not like the 'deaf impercipient fanatic who has nosed over his own little sexual round until he believes that there is no other path for others to take, he sometimes interests & sometimes frightens & angers me, but in the end he will bore him merely, I know.'[25] Lawrence respected the frankness of this approach. In any case, the day Morgan wrote his letter Lawrence had been writing one of his own to Bertrand Russell, describing Morgan sucking his dummy long after his age and being 'bound hand and foot bodily. Why? *Because he does not believe that any beauty or any divine utterance is any good any more* . . . Will all the poetry in the world satisfy the manhood of Forster, when Forster knows that his implicit manhood is to be satisfied by nothing but immediate physical action.'[26] Morgan was intuitive enough to suspect Lawrence of penning letters like these, but he did not seem to resent it and the two men were to keep, slightly, in touch; in years to come Morgan was to describe Lawrence as 'most alarming and explosive but I like him'[27] and to declare him to be the greatest novelist of the twentieth century; he began, although never finished, editing an edition of his letters.

Apart from new friends such as Lawrence there were old ones. There was HOM, of whom Morgan had some months before noted rather unexpectedly, 'He remains the ground work of my life, but more unconsciously' but who was growing steadily more distant: 'He will always like me & be very good in ways he will select, but

---

* This occasion was the one time the subject of my first biography, Lady Cynthia Asquith, and Morgan *nearly* met. Morgan stayed at Greatham from 10 to 12 February, Cynthia stayed from 16 to 17 February. She did not write in the Meynell visitors' book. Morgan did: he copied out (or remembered?) the beautiful passage from the end of Chapter 19 of *Howards End* about Poole harbour and England 'lying as a jewel in a silver sea', partly quoted above p 153. Since the first Zeppelin bombs had been dropped the month before – the first such attack in England's history – Morgan chose, in his own words, to re-affirm that England was alive and eternal.[24]

I must not hope for any general interest.' (Indeed his lack of interest in *Maurice* caused Morgan to consider abandoning it unfinished.) There was Goldie. There was Leonard Greenwood, now a Cambridge don, to whom Morgan had shown *Maurice* and who, it seems, went through the manuscript making amendments either of his own or of Morgan's choosing. (He then kept it until he died in 1967 when it was returned to Morgan; the published version is based on this manuscript.) For one brief period the two men seem to have been very close, for at the end of December 1914 Morgan wrote 'LHGG. I am to blame. I ought not to have.'[28] What he did is unclear; but that the two were momentarily friendly is evident from Greenwood having been entrusted with the *Maurice* alterations. (And was there a pun on his name, given that Morgan was always so insistent that Maurice and Alec went off together not just into the woods but into the greenwood?)

Then there were Dent, Waterlow, Lytton Strachey, Roger Fry, the writer Forrest Reid whom Morgan visited in Belfast (where he also saw HOM), Florence Barger, who was becoming more and more of a confidante: he was not friendless. There was even the unusual situation, as he told Masood, that 'a young lady has fallen in love with me – at least so I judge from her letters'.[29] This was Florence's sister Elsie Thomas, and Florence was the go-between when, finally, Morgan managed to rebuff her. He told Florence, 'I have heard from her. She understood and couldn't be nicer, and is happier I think, but I'm not, for she says she now loves me more than ever, and having now known both I can tell you that it is more terrible not to requite love than to love unrequited.'[30] This situation was not mentioned in his diary so we cannot know whether he ever, briefly, considered marriage; but Florence's daughter-in-law (who wields Lily's silver teapot in Hampstead*) did say to me, 'Wasn't Forster briefly engaged?'[31]

'What's to occupy me for the rest of my life, I can't conceive'[32] Morgan had written to Goldie at the end of 1914, replying to his friend's adulatory letter about *Maurice*. And during the whole of 1915, despite the tensions generated by the war, despite the National Gallery job, despite the many and varied friendships, he felt quite

---

* Cf. p 9.

Four portraits of Morgan: TOP LEFT a painting by Roger Fry 1912 TOP RIGHT a drawing by Duncan Grant 1919 BOTTOM LEFT a drawing by William Rothenstein 1923 BOTTOM RIGHT a painting by Vanessa Bell 1940s.

rudderless. Then, in the autumn of that year, a name was mooted that seemed to Morgan to be the most enormously lucky chance, a name that had been, for him, full of resonance almost all his life. It was the name of the city of the beautiful Antinous, of Cleopatra, of Theocritus, and of the meeting between Southern Europe and the Orient: it was Alexandria.

25

Alexandria

Morgan's first idea had been to go to Italy with an ambulance unit organised by G. M. Trevelyan: but Lily had strenuously objected to the dirt and danger. Then came the suggestion of Malta or Egypt with the Red Cross to do 'Enquiry work . . . Malta would be pleasant in the winter' Morgan told Lily, 'and absolutely safe which is a comfort, as I should know Mummy wouldn't worry – or at least have no excuse for doing so . . .'[1] Three weeks later, however, on 27 October 1915, 'have enjoyed all the excitement of quarrelling with Miss Bell'[2] about Egypt. He was never again to see the redoubtable Gertrude Bell, the much-travelled Middle East expert, but liked his encounter with her; in later years he remembered her as

not sympathetic, she was hard and severe as became the daughter of an Iron Magnate and of course extremely busy . . . she had no time for trimmings . . . I remember asking her what the inhabitants of Alexandria would be like. She replied I should have no opportunity to find out. I should only see them in the streets as I went to and fro on my work.

Morgan was a Searcher, helping to trace missing soldiers; it was 'a quiet enough quest' and yet 'a thrill of Foreign Service came in it for the reason that a Turkish invasion of Egypt was at that date expected.'[3] This was true. With Turkey now at war with Britain, Egypt (which in 1914 had become a British protectorate) had become a vast staging-post; but it might easily have become a battlefield. Although he tried to disguise the fact from Lily, at the time Morgan set out Alexandria could have become the important theatre of war that it was to be during the Second World War (the battle of El Alamein was to take place only seventy miles away).

He did not take his diary with him when he left in the November of 1915 and we therefore know nothing about 'the voyage out' (the phrase, the title of Virginia Woolf's first novel, would have been in his mind because he had reviewed it in April; it was only the second novel he had ever reviewed but Virginia never despised him again), only that he reached Port Said on 20 November. He went straight to Alexandria and settled into a hotel; he expected only to stay for three months.

Now, as the Mediterranean winter turned into a warm spring, as the crisp air that came off the sea turned into muggy afternoons with a sense of the desert not far away, in the Greek cafés and the quasi-European apartments, on the trams and in the horse-drawn carriages, Morgan discovered a city to which he had been brought by chance yet with which he found a true affinity. In Alexandria, away from everything he had known for nearly forty years, he acquired equilibrium. It had not happened in India because there he was a tourist, the traveller who had his ticket home in his pocket; here his life acquited an infinite quality. As the days passed, the pale sunshine and the orderliness and the green of England seemed ever more remote. And Morgan came to life. When Bertrand Russell was the recipient of the following letter in 1917 he must have wondered how perceptive Lawrence had once been in his own remarks about Morgan:

Here I have been for nearly two years, harmless & unharmed ... It has been a comfortable life – how unreal I shan't know till I compare it with the lives others have been leading in the period. I don't write, but feel I think & think I feel. Sometimes I make notes on human nature under war conditions ... I love people & want to understand them & help them more than I did, but this is oddly accompanied by a growth of contempt. *Be* like them? God no.[4]

This was the Morgan of the future. He did not want to be like other people because he had found the self-love to want to be himself; but he loved people, he loved humanity.

It is hard to know exactly why this happened, whether it was a personal growth or the impact of the soldiers with whom Morgan came into daily contact or the influence of Alexandria's lively population. But all Morgan's belief in the idea of individuality, in the idea of the sanctity of personal relationships became real: almost as if, before, he had read about the ideological concept in books but was at last experiencing it himself; so that now his loathing of institutions and of power became much more strong. He wrote to Goldie in 1917,

An observer from another planet who watched not only the earth's wars but its public institutions would never infer what sweetness and nobility there can be in intercourse between individuals. Gulf between 'private' and 'public' has in the last three years grown dizzying, and thanks to scientific organisation more and more of man's energy is diverted to the public side.[5]

Did Morgan see that his pleas in *Howards End* for the public not to be allowed to overwhelm the private were already prophetic? Or that when he said that all he cared for in civilisation had gone for ever that he had already foreseen this happening? It is unlikely that he thought about it. As, from the vantage-point of Egypt, he saw his past, his tradition being destroyed, he did not look back at the work he had done in his own past – he looked forward.

Alexandria helped him to do this even more than the people he met. For, unlike other cities, in some odd way Alexandria is itself despite the people who inhabit it, not because of them. When I was researching this book I was very doubtful whether I needed to go there. 'What is there to *see*?' I asked the present-day editor of Morgan's *Alexandria* and himself the author of the best modern guide to Egypt. 'Nothing,' he answered, 'but that isn't the point.' And I couldn't see what the point was. Until I got there; when I understood that Alexandria is a city where the sense of its own past is by far the most important fact about it. As my lunch companion has written, 'Alexandria is all intimation: *here* (some spot) is where Alexander lay entombed; *here* Cleopatra committed suicide; *here* the Library, the Serapeum, etc . . . and there is nothing physically there.'[6] In a sense the past is all Alexandria has; the historical artefact, the monument, the readily identifiable left-overs of history have all, or nearly all, gone. There *is* nothing to see – except what there was, once, for Alexandria is, in some ways, merely an idea, 'the spurious East'[7] as Morgan called it. He would remark one day, 'it symbolises for me a mixture, a bastardy, an idea which I find congenial and opposed to that sterile idea of 100% in something or other which has impressed the modern world and forms the backbone of its blustering nationalism.'[8]

In more obvious terms, Alexandria has been destroyed and has been destroying itself for centuries. For all the years that it has been a city it has regularly built, been destroyed and built again. This is not a case of the wicked twentieth century destroying; Alexandria's inhabitants have always destroyed. This is why it can be such a depressing city for the tourist. There is nothing to look at and nothing to do. Yet of what does it consist?

It is, as Morgan wrote to Lily, a 'clean cosmopolitan town by some blue water',[9] a Mediterranean town, Egypt's elegant summer capital, with roads along the seashore where people strolled, once, but which is today dominated by traffic. Nowadays there is a hotel called the Cecil which was full of palm trees in pots and men in linen suits and women in crêpe-de-Chine dresses; today its charm is too faded to be charming. There are Greek cafés where, once, the Greek community drank Turkish coffee and retsina and ate baklava; the Greeks have almost all gone. In Morgan's day the Cecil had not been built and there were many more Greeks. But what did exist was an identical sense of sadness. Alexandria lives upon its past and always has.

Its historical past was Greek and Roman, its recent one cosmopolitan: it was the home of the foreign community in Egypt. In 1917 Alexandria had a population of 450,000 of which one-sixth was non-Egyptian, Greeks and Italians predominating over English, French, Armenians and Syrians. Life in Alexandria was as smartly Parisian as the foreigners could make it: 'eternally well-dressed people driving infinitely in either direction – that is its ideal' as Morgan put it. But his own ideal was re-creative, re-constructive, being not to drive up and down the Rue Rosette but to look into the past and imagine it as the Canopic Road: 'it was not genteel or smart but presented throughout its length scenes of extraordinary splendour ... The street was lined with marble colonnades from end to end, as was the Rue Nebi Daniel, and the point of their intersection (where one now stands in hopeless expectation of a tram) was one of the most glorious crossways of the ancient world.'*[10]

In some ways Alexandria was the themes of *Howards End* made real. When Margaret asked, about Wickham Place, 'Why had it to be swept away?' and, later on, said how much she hated 'this continual flux of London. It is an epitome of us at our worst – eternal formlessness; all the qualities, good, bad and indifferent, streaming away – streaming, streaming for ever'[11] she might have been speaking about Alexandria. Because of its position, on the Mediterranean yet in Africa, Westernised yet Oriental, it has been in flux for all the years of its existence; more than any other city Alexandria has *always* been streaming.

*   *   *

* Now that Alexandria has become a totally Egyptian city, the Rue Nebi Daniel has changed, again, into Sharia Nebi Danyal.

Having gone to Egypt for, as he thought, three months, Morgan now found himself staying as long as the war lasted. His task was to 'go round the Hospitals and question the wounded soldiers for news of their missing comrades . . . though technically a civilian, I wear officer's uniform.'[12] It was a job Morgan did well. In 1917 one of his reports, giving news of a missing flight sub-lieutenant, was published in Lord Northcliffe's *At the War*. After the concluding letter, printed anonymously but evidently by Morgan, which congratulated the family in England on their son's survival, the book commented: 'This, then, is a labour of love, belonging in its essence to Red Cross work as that work has come to be understood throughout our land. It is a labour which eases the sorest wounds of warfare and which indirectly brings great comfort to the fighting men themselves, many of whom are haunted by the fear of being numbered among the lost and so becoming a source of suffering to their friends.'[13]

Morgan liked feeling useful. What he liked less and less was the war. Without the restraining influence of suburbia and of respectability, without the almost unthinking pacifism of his friends, he saw it in a new light. And he saw, almost for the first time, its vast potential for destruction. This was not merely in the bodily sense (he only referred to wounded, maimed soldiers briefly on one page of jotted notes made his first winter in Alexandria[14]) but in the sense of the values inherent in the world as he knew it; so that his first letter to Masood, written in the December of 1915, declared bleakly that 'All that I cared for in civilisation has gone forever, and I am trying to live without either hopes or fears.'[15] He wrote to Goldie, soon after arriving, that he was so oppressed by the war in its viler aspects that he now felt that 'the suffering and disease I see ought to be stopped at the cost of *any* humiliation'; and, a few weeks later, ' "we must fight again as soon as we are strong enough" is all I expect the war to teach Europe.' He added, 'I consort only with Tommies and others who have no interest in, or illusions about, bloodshed.' By October 1916 his view was that 'war also entails an inward death. It has taken the place of all the old healthy growths – love, joy, thought, despair – deluding men by its semblance of vitality.'[16]

Yet a few months before leaving England he had given a talk to the Working Men's College on the function of literature in wartime and had stressed the importance of avoiding the sensational, the fleetingly exciting, and of turning to books that portray 'a world of greatness, the world of the spirit, that helps us to endure danger and ingratitude and answer a lie with the truth.' Great literature, he argued, makes one detached and therefore braver, less purely egocentric, it 'helps us to abstain from fear, from hatred, from tribal religion'.[17] Now Morgan made these precepts part of his everyday life. Instead of succumbing to fear or angrily railing against the war or retreating into depression he turned to literature and to the ideals embodied within it.

He also turned to the city of Alexandria itself, establishing a fulfilling and soothing routine of working during the day and spending the evening seeing friends, writing letters home, playing the piano and, after some months, writing articles for the two English-language newspapers. His work was mostly on the edge of the city, at the hospital at Montazah where, in Morgan's words, 'the road leads by roses, oleanders and pepper trees' to the ex-Khedive's summer palace; behind it is 'the Selamlik (men's quarters), built by the Khedive in a style that was likely to please his Austrian mistress ... From the terrace, *View* of the circular bay with its fantastic promontories and breakwaters ...' The hospital was in the palace; Morgan stayed for a while at the Selamlik* while convalescing from jaundice and was entranced by the sensuality of his surroundings, where the convalescing soldiers 'go about bare chested and bare legged, the blue of their linen shorts and the pale mauve of their shirts accenting the brown splendour of their bodies; and down by the sea many of them spend half their days naked and unrebuked and unashamed'[19] (the last two words were deleted).

Although Morgan did not feel as much at home with the Egyptians as he had with the Indians, he made friends both among the Greek community and among the English; Alexandria soon began to cast its spell. For it certainly has one, despite its lack of 'sights' ('nothing to divert one into the tourist for an hour except Pompey's Pillar'[20]) and its intangible melancholy. For one thing there is the wonderful climate. Despite the occasional cold wind and rain, it is a place of Mediterranean breeze and sun perfectly combined. There is the bustle and cosmopolitanism of a large city on the edge of the desert. And there is a plangency, a historical resonance, a sad happiness of a kind that does not often appeal but that some have tried to recapture (most memorably the novelist Lawrence Durrell). Few people come

---

* Michael Haag has accurately observed that 'The Selamlik is now a hotel, one of the most pleasant places to stay in Alexandria, though the view is impaired by the new Palestine Hotel, the most vulgar in Egypt.'[18]

to love Alexandria but those that do love her passionately. This does not mean they want to return – but they have her lodged in their imagination.

Morgan did too, but it was Alexandria the poets' city that impressed him most. Euripides in Weybridge had been a droll paradox; now he was in the city of Theocritus, of Callimachus* – and of the celebrated Greek poet Constantine Cavafy, linked, it has been observed, to his poet ancestor through being 'the first Greek poet since Euripides we read with that kind of demonic self-recognition'.[22] The influence of Cavafy freed Morgan as much as Cambridge had done twenty years before. But it did not turn him into a poet; it helped to free his mind and his attitudes. Nevertheless, Cavafy was the kind of poet Morgan would have been if he had been a poet.

The two men met in March 1916, a few weeks after Morgan arrived in Alexandria. It was an intellectual friendship, although their homosexuality gave them a shared understanding. Morgan would one day describe the meeting when 'the first English translation of Cavafy was made by Cavafy': †

The occasion is over thirty years ago now, in his flat, 10 Rue Lepsius, Alexandria; his dusky family-furnished flat. He is back from his work in a government office; the Third Circle of the Irrigation employs him as it might have employed many of his heroes. I am back from my work, costumed in khaki; the British Red Cross employs me. We have been introduced by an English friend, our meetings are rather dim, and Cavafy is now saying with his usual gentleness, 'You could never understand my poetry, my dear Forster, never.' A poem is produced – 'The God abandons Antony' – and I detect some coincidences between its Greek and public school Greek. Cavafy is amazed. 'Oh, but this is good, my dear Forster, this is very good indeed' and he raises his hand, takes over, and leads me through.[23]

Cavafy had spent the 1870s, the years when he was a young man, in England; English literature was a strong influence on his poetry and was one reason why he and Morgan had a shared sensibility.

---

* Callimachus was a 3rd century BC Greek poet who wrote witty epigrams on homosexual themes. Theocritus had been a favourite of Morgan's since Tonbridge days, for he loved his mixing of the pastoral mode with everyday life and wrote of his work: 'History is too much an affair of armies and kings ... Theocritus, wielding the double spell of realism and of poetry, has evoked an entire city from the dead and filled its streets with men.'[21]

† Morgan was to expend much time and energy in the future seeing that Cavafy's poems were eventually translated into English and published.

They were alike, too, in their loathing of rhetoric, in their use of spoken rhythms, in their historical sense, as well as in their cynical attitude to power and politics. Cavafy's poem 'The Afternoon Sun' was written in the autumn of 1918; although we can only read it here in translation, it is clear why the subject matter and the tone appealed to Morgan so much.

> This room, how well I know it.
> Now they're renting it, and the one next to it,
> as offices. The whole house has become
> an office building for agents, businessmen, companies.
>
> This room, how familiar it is.
>
> Here, near the door, was the couch,
> a Turkish carpet in front of it.
> Close by, the shelf with two yellow vases.
> On the right – no, opposite – a wardrobe with a mirror.
> In the middle the table where he wrote,
> and the three big wicker chairs.
> Beside the window the bed
> where we made love so many times.
>
> They must still be around somewhere, those old things.
>
> Beside the window the bed;
> the afternoon sun used to touch half of it.
>
> . . . One afternoon at four o'clock we separated
> for a week only . . . And then –
> that week became forever.[24]

Cavafy's own rooms in the Rue Lepsius are now at 4 Sharia Sharm el Sheikh (there is a plaque outside; the papers and furniture are in a small museum in the Greek Consulate). In atmosphere the street has changed very little. I went to the 'dusky' flat 'in the evening' (the title of a 1916 poem, dusk being for Cavafy, and for Alexandria, the most resonant time of day) and, looking down from the balcony into the narrow street with overhanging washing and echoing voices and the noise of distant traffic and over towards the Greek Hospital where Cavafy eventually died, it was as if I too might see Morgan making his diffident way down the street to share bread and cheese by the light of candles with the Greek whose 'talk would sway over the Mediterranean world and over much of the world within'.[25] The room with the balcony, the room where Morgan and Cavafy sat has a faded and wonderful wallpaper, a kind of murky grey with the outline of something that looked like surreal giraffes; it reminded me of the grey-patterned wallpaper of the dining-room in Vanessa Bell's house in Sussex – Charleston, which Morgan would visit for the first time just after his return from Alexandria.

Cavafy talked to Morgan a little less indirectly than he was used to, or rather less indirectly than anything he had encountered since Searight four years before. Cavafy had been an active homosexual since he was twenty, thirty years earlier. Was his relationship with Morgan such that he could have said to him, 'What, you have never had a lover?' Or was it merely that the open way in which he spoke about his own preferences, and perhaps the way he made the assumption that Morgan shared these preferences, was another element in the freeing of Morgan's body and spirit? For it was in October 1916, only a few months after Morgan had first met Cavafy that, as he told Florence Barger, at this time his chief confidante, 'Yesterday for the first time in my life I parted w. respectability' (the words 'in my life' were crossed out, as if to indicate some hesitation). He added, 'I have felt the step would be taken for many months. I have tried to take it before. It has left me curiously sad.'

The man may have been one of the soldiers on the beach at Montazah. Seeing them made Morgan 'happy yet very sad', although it was a different kind of sadness from that he felt after he had parted with respectability. The earlier sadness was because the beautiful young men were soon to return to the 'unspeakable'; the later one was a purely physical reaction because Morgan realised that he was now tethered by habit 'to the life of the spirit': had he taken the step when young he would not have had that feeling.

Morgan was nearly thirty-eight. It was the following year that he managed to part with respectability entirely. On the tram going to and from Montazah he had got to know the conductor: he was eighteen, his name was Mohammed el Adl and soon Morgan was going for walks with him and returning with him to his room. By the summer of 1917, he told Florence, they had only parted with respectability to some extent: Morgan wanted to but Mohammed would choose to talk about tenderness and affection. In September, although Morgan felt that 'all is far greater than I have yet realised', respectability still held firm. (Semi-respectability seems to have meant mutual masturbation and loss of respectability fellatio. Buggery never seems to have taken place between them: in a note about their affair made in 1922 Morgan recalled that the year before he had resolved, too late, to ask for it.) Finally, on 3 October,

R. has been parted with, and in the simplest most inevitable way, just as you hoped. I am so happy – not for the actual pleasure but because the last barrier has fallen; and no doubt it has much to do with my sudden placidness . . . I wish I was writing the latter half of Maurice now. I now know so much more. It is awful to think of the thousands who go through youth without ever knowing. I have known in a way before, but never like this. My luck has been amazing.[26]

How can it be to have one's first full sexual experience in one's fortieth year? And why did it take so long? The latter is fairly clear: the freeing of Lily's grip, the freeing effect of Alexandria,* the freeing of entrenched morality and of inhibition by Carpenter, Searight and Cavafy; indeed, Morgan rather understated the case when he told Goldie in 1916 that 'In some ways I have never been so free'.[27] As to the former, the first orgasm that was not self-induced, Morgan left no account. But we do know that he was avid for it. 'Dear Edward,' he wrote to Carpenter his first April in Alexandria, his senses aroused by the sun and the remoteness of Weybridge and the bared flesh of the soldiers,

You continue the greatest comfort. I don't want to grouse, as so much is all right with me, but this physical loneliness has gone on for too many months, and with it springs and grows a wretched fastidiousness so that even if the opportunity for which I yearn was offered I fear I might refuse it . . . I am sure that some of the decent people I see daily would be willing to save me if they knew, but they don't know, can't know . . . If I could get one solid night it would be something . . .[28]

We know, too, that when sex finally came into Morgan's life there was not very much of it. During the summer of 1917 Morgan and Mohammed could only meet on alternate fortnights. No sooner had respectability been parted with (how significant that right until the last Morgan saw the sexual act as something social, something sanctioned or not sanctioned; he could not think of it as the act itself, amoral,

* The Australian writer Patrick White, a homosexual, would also respond to Alexandria's lack of constraints: in 1941, aged twenty-nine, he began an affair with a Greek named Manoly Lascaris that was to last for the rest of his life.

BELOW West Hackhurst
(designed by Eddie in
1877), from the garden in
the late 1920s, probably
taken on the same occasion
as the photograph below.

ABOVE Morgan and T.S.
Eliot, at Monk's House,
the Woolfs' house at
Rodmell in Sussex 1920s.

RIGHT Morgan with Lily by
the door to the garden at
West Hackhurst late 1920s
(p 361). His pianist's hands
are clearly displayed. Of
Lily, Siegfried Sassoon
wrote at this time, 'she has
the same face as EMF but
a more condensed nose
and chin.'[16]

BELOW RIGHT Morgan speaking at the International Congress of Writers in Paris in 1935, Charles Mauron beside him. LEFT Bob and Morgan. BELOW Morgan and Benjamin Britten with Billy Burrell, an Aldeburgh fisherman, and an Aldeburgh boy during the writing of *Billy Budd*. These two photographs were taken within a few weeks of each other in 1949 – which is rather surprising given the youthfulness of the pose on the left.

ABOVE RIGHT the official portrait: a Cecil Beaton photograph mid-1950s.

ABOVE Morgan with Bob's grandson Clive 1958 at Turnham Green.

RIGHT Bob and Morgan in the 1960s. The once skinny Morgan has become charmingly tubby and has a definite look of Lily in her last years.

socially irrelevant), then, only a week later, Mohammed went away to take up an army job that Morgan had found for him. He did not return for seven months; then he was preoccupied with the deaths of his father and his brother and, very soon, consequent upon his inheriting the family house, his approaching marriage. For, of the three loves of Morgan's life, two were married when his affair with them was at its height, and the third, Masood, was married only a few months after Morgan's devotion had begun to fade.

Not only was Morgan not jealous of his lovers' wives; it almost seems as if, pandar-like, he encouraged them. This may have been because his kindly nature wanted his lover to be as happy as possible; it may have been coincidence; it may have been, indeed, that he was sexually excited by the thought of his lover also making love to a woman. Yet the fact that this did not disgust him is further proof that Morgan himself was not repelled by women. Indeed, his 'dear honest competent kind Greek landlady',[29] his friendship with her opera-singer employer, the bohemian Aïda Borchgrevink, his correspondence with Florence, were all making him feel better about women than he ever had before; especially now that he was removed from the misogynist jokes of people like Dent and Goldie. As he wrote to Carpenter about Aïda, 'When women *do* understand, they are even better than men, but as a rule it doesn't so much as occur to them to start understanding'.[30]

Apart from 3 October 1917, and apart from some weekends in the July of the following year, and in the autumn, Morgan and Mohammed's sexual encounters were infrequent, and restricted by the precautions that Morgan felt were necessary. Although he told Florence that 'the whole ending of *Maurice* and its handling of the Social question now seems such timorous half hearted stuff. The question never occurs to me and to A. very rarely',[31] nevertheless they both made every effort not to be seen together in public. Sexually, therefore, their opportunities were limited. Yet Morgan, to Florence and later on to other friends, embroidered their relationship into a great love affair: understandably, he so much wanted to have a lover, to be a lover, that, as often in his life, the boundary between fantasy and truth became blurred. It was not until four years later that he admitted in his diary: 'Determined my life should contain one success I have concealed from myself and others M's frequent coldness towards me. And his occasional warmth may be due to politeness, gratitude, or pity. The prospect of his death gives me no

301

pain.'[32] Although the death of his lover, when it came, *did* give him pain, nevertheless the important aspect was that he had *been* loved: the experience of sex in 'nearly a slum'[33] was what he had longed for.

Nor was the slum irrelevant. Middle-class gays often search out working-class lovers for the reason that someone who takes a lover of the same sex then has to *create* otherness, the other: class, and an unordered relationship, are the obvious means. This is not mere 'nostalgie de la boue', it is the search for difference. When Edward Carpenter wrote that his 'ideal of love is a powerful, strongly built man, of my own age or rather younger – preferably of the working class'[34] the latter aspect was quite as important for him as everything else. And when Morgan, in direct echo of this sentence, wrote 'I want to love a strong young man of the lower classes and be loved by him and even hurt by him. That is my ticket . . .'* he too would have stressed the class more than the strength, the youth, the love and the hurt.

There are other reasons, of course, for someone like Morgan having a preference for the garden boy, the tram conductor or the policeman (quite apart from the classic fascination with uniform, something which Morgan did not happen to share). A gay couple (living, with extraordinary appropriateness, opposite the British Museum) talked to me about guilt: that sleeping with someone of a different class, in a master/servant relationship, diminished the guilt factor. They also said that since living in a marriage used to be, for most gay couples, an impossibility because of social pressure, then gay men were free to look outside their class in a way that marrying heterosexuals were not. And they made the point, often reiterated by others, that the inhibited, repressed middle class needs the working class to free it from its inhibitions; thus gamekeepers, soldiers and policemen become symbols of virility. As Morgan wrote in his diary in 1920, '[Edward Carpenter] has explained why I like the Lower Classes. They are not self conscious. I am and therefore need them.'[35] At the same time Morgan wanted a definite symbol of his escape from respectability. When he told Florence, about his weekend in the near-slum, 'never before did I so bless my adaptability. Where would I be if I had gone in for "requiring" things like Plugs and

* Morgan added: 'The "hurt by him", by the way ought to be written in fainter ink. Although it is on my ticket, it is not as vivid as "perfect union", and it is not underlined by the desire to be trodden on or shat on which characterises extreme cases.'

Plates', the adaptability was all important. Sex in the clean calm of the Albany, with food brought in from Fortnum's instead of by 'a semi-slave from outside, who squatted in the passage while we ate',[36] would not have been what he sought.

Something else that Morgan needed before finding sexual fulfilment (because of course he *could* have had sex before had he wanted to, it was only now in Alexandria that he found it on his own terms), what Morgan needed as well was a confidante. How odd, I thought, on first reading the letters, that he told Florence all these details. Then I realised that the details would not have existed but for someone to tell them to. Morgan was not exactly boasting, he did not flaunt, but he needed to define in some other way than in a private diary: the act was negated unless described to someone else. But the dating of the letters to Florence, especially the two letters for 8 *and* 11 October 1917 describing the red-letter 3 October, must have made her feel almost voyeuristic as she looked after her children, followed the war news, ordered meals – in Englefield Green, Surrey, a mere five miles from Weybridge.

Yet Florence was part of the act, almost as if her tolerant acceptance of whatever Morgan told her cancelled out the guilt. During his first year in Alexandria he wrote to her a mere half a dozen times; but between May and December 1917, once the affair had begun, he wrote over twenty times, and it was the same the following year. Wonderful ironies ensued. In November 1917 Morgan began a letter, 'Your visit to mother gives such pleasure . . . I am anxious about the Raids for her – she is going to the dentist as you know' and then continued with a lingering description of the October weekend when 'We ate off the same plate and he pushed the tenderer morsels against my fork or spoon'.[37] Some might say, but I am not sure I would go as far as this, that for Morgan Florence *was* Lily, her interest and concern making the sex acceptable for the guilt-ridden little boy without having to go so far as telling his mother about it.

In many ways the two women were very alike. And it cannot have been coincidence that once Morgan was in England, and back in the same routine of seeming to involve Lily in his life while secretly barring her from it, then Florence as a confidante became redundant. 'Florence here,' he wrote in 1922, 'bores me, so long winded and self-satisfied. Mother far shrewder than most of my friends . . . [Her] comments always to the point.'[38] Lily had reasserted her control. But it was a control she had partly relinquished to Florence while Morgan was in Egypt, although she retained what she could. Florence sent over Morgan's more 'public' letters.* And he continued to send Lily letters that began, for example, 'my dearest and my darling'; to tell her (when she was balking at going to Harrogate for a cure) 'do *do* give insidey a good washout. It is sure to need it and now is the time, when the summer rush of flies and fish is over and you have some leisure'; and, when arguing against buying Harnham for £850 (£17,500) instead of an annual rent of £60 (£1250), '*What* a worry! How you could fill your letter with other things and postpone it to the end I don't know ... There is so much to think about, it makes one feel very trembly.'†39

With Goldie Morgan had no need to be placatory. A few weeks after meeting el Adl he was telling him that 'It is more like an affair of Searight's than anything else I can indicate! This will convey to you age, race, rank, though not precisely relationship.' Although the references to race and rank are distasteful, they are less distasteful than a comment to Florence: 'I can scarcely believe him the son of Egypt, for there is no Nile mud either in his body or mind.' Mud had always been a resonant image for Morgan, and was to recur in *A Passage to India*: it evoked sluggishness and unreceptivity to the new. As Morgan wrote to Masood on first arriving, 'It is only at sunset that Egypt surpasses India – at all other hours it is flat, unromantic, unmysterious, and godless – the soil is mud, the inhabitants are of mud moving, and exasperating in the extreme: I feel as instinctively not at home among them as I feel instinctively at home among Indians.'40

So the last year in Alexandria was, for Morgan, the year of Mohammed. Albeit that the hours they spent together were few, everything else that happened was as nothing. As the war drew to its close, Morgan continued his routine of searching, seeing friends, playing the piano, writing articles (twenty-four in the three years he was there‡) and getting to know the city that was his temporary

* Lily herself wrote continuously: thus, not untypically she wrote on 8, 9, 15, 17 and 21 September 1918.
† 'I was always against buying' wrote Morgan revealingly. 'More than ever at a time like this when securities have fallen: you do not mention that when you call £850 "cheap".'
‡ These were on historical aspects of Egypt such as 'Lunch at the Bishop's (A.D. 310)' or 'Handel in Egypt', or contemporary aspects such as the Alexandria Cotton Bourse or 'Army English'. Fourteen were later reprinted in *Pharos and Pharillon* (1923) by Leonard and Virginia Woolf's Hogarth Press.

home. The articles gave him the confidence that three unfinished novels had jarred: towards the end of his time in Alexandria he began to think of writing a guidebook. Firstly his academic instincts to collate and classify were aroused ('what a funny task to set yourself – though I always remember the thrill you got out of that National Gallery Catalogue'[41] Lawrence would write when it was finished, patronisingly but not unperceptively). Secondly it had long been at the back of his mind to write an antidote to Baedeker and Murray.

The latter, which Morgan is likely to have taken with him, does little to evoke the city and is written in a negative tone, stressing that Ptolemaic Alexandria has disappeared and that the only relics of interest, Cleopatra's Needles, have been taken to England and to America; the only thing to see is Pompey's Pillar and the Catacombs. In a sense this was perfectly true, in 1916 as today; but, somehow, indefinably, there is so much more. Could one, Morgan began to think, subvert the Baedeker ethic and write a guidebook about a city where there is so little to see and yet so much, basing it upon the premise that 'the "sights" of Alexandria are in themselves not interesting, but they fascinate when we approach them through the past'? It would be the ultimate illusion, the ultimate elusiveness, a guidebook about things that are not there, continually reminding the visitor that 'the situation of Alexandria is most curious. To understand it we must go back many thousand years' or that 'he should not visit the [museum] collection until he has learned or imagined something about the ancient city.'[42] Most tourists, the kind whose 'noses were as red as their Baedekers'[43] lived only in the present, ignoring both the past and the reality of the country they were, temporarily, exploring. Morgan would tell them that the best way to see the bazaar and mosques of the old Turkish town 'is to wander aimlessly about'; Baedeker, with its planned walks and itineraries, would never, ever do this. For fifteen years he had been fascinated by the guidebook culture; now he would write an anti-guide.

In the January of 1919 Morgan left Alexandria. He had recently defined it, on the first page of his guidebook, as 'a maritime gateway to India and the remoter east';[44] for him personally this is what it would prove, a fictional gateway that would bring him nearer to the completion of his Indian novel, one that linked East and West within his own imagination.* He would one day publish a short story in the rather grandiose guise of 'Entrance to an Unwritten Novel;'[46] it was Alexandria that was the entrance to *A Passage to India*.

* Later writers about Alexandria were also to stress its bridging quality between East and West, for example Lawrence Durrell, D. J. Enright and Robert Liddell. And cf. V. S. Naipaul's *An Area of Darkness* (1964): 'It was clear that here, and not in Greece, the East began: in this chaos of uneconomical movement, the self-stimulated din, the sudden feeling of insecurity, the conviction that all men were not brothers and that luggage was in danger.'[45] (The last phrase, with its deliberate bathos, its humorous acceptance of the petty preoccupations that must beset every traveller, is a direct echo of Forster.)

26

India Again

The war was over at last but Morgan, who had narrowly escaped a threat of conscription in the summer of 1916, had not quite lost the 'slightly heroic mood'[1] in which he had arrived in Egypt at the end of 1915. He had done his job with admirable tenacity and tact (even, in the end, being appointed 'Head Searcher', much to the chagrin of the formidable and eccentric Miss Grant-Duff under whom he had been working); and he had made a life for himself in a place that was not only remote from England but remote from almost everything with which he had hitherto been familiar. It was not going to be easy, placidly to return to England and to 'a joyless, straggling place, full of people who pretended' (as he had once described 'Sawston'); or to go back to the old, purposeless life when for three years in Alexandria, like Philip Herriton, 'it was the first time he had had anything to do'.[2]

He professed to find things unchanged: 'isn't it awful', he wrote to Siegfried Sassoon, with whom he was beginning a correspondence and who was to become a close friend during the 1920s, 'how all the outward nonsense of England has been absolutely untouched by the war – still this unbroken front of dress-shirts and golf.'[3] In the same way Vera Brittain was to find that the dons at Oxford greeted her after her four-year absence with nothing more personal or enquiring than 'How do you do, Miss Brittain?'. 'Once again, as in 1915, Oxford from Carfax to Summertown was warm and sweet with lilac and wallflowers and may; it seemed unbearable that everything should be exactly the same when all my life was so much changed.'[4] But for Morgan far less had changed: none of his relations and few of his friends had been killed and Lily's life had been unaffected except that getting up to London to go to the dentist had been rather complicated.

Immediately, after an extended visit to the Bargers in their new house in Edinburgh, he returned to the old routine.

It need not have been thus: a few weeks after his return he was offered a job in Germany, 'something secretarial in the Inter Allied Commission ... at a salary of £600 [£15,000] a year; plus billeting allowance.' He refused, because of Lily. The opportunity, which the three-year stint in Egypt had made less surprising, was rejected 'after three wretched weeks of indecision'[5] because he did not want to leave her again. Implicitly they both accepted that, apart from extended 'visits', he would never live without her; the chance to escape, for which Alexandria had set a precedent, would not be utilised; 'this unbroken front' closed around him.

Part of Morgan was pleased that it had. When he went down to Dorset to stay with Goldie he remembered that 'The world seemed settling down into its lost armchair for a moment's rest' just as they had: 'the impression is happiness, hopefulness, clouds lifting.' Yet much of their conversation was about the war and its aftermath. 'It is possible that Dickinson invented the phrase "League of Nations"; it is certain that he was the first person in this country to formulate the idea',[6] Morgan would write in Goldie's biography, when introducing the subject of his commitment and assiduousness in that direction. In true Apostolic fashion it was the concept of the League, not the day-to-day running of it, that interested both men; Morgan did not bother to mention, although Vera Brittain did, that 'the League of Nations came into existence at the end of April by the adoption of the revised Covenant at the Fifth Plenary Session of the Peace Conference.'[7] Symbolically, in a way, Max Garnett, the doer, the extrovert, the athletic paterfamilias, was the first Secretary of the League of Nations Union.

But, unsurprisingly, Morgan was now more aware politically than he had ever been before. 'What *is* it? What *is* it?' he had asked Sassoon the previous spring after having been in more contact than usual with British officers. 'I believe it's the possession of power. Give a man power over the other men, and he deteriorates at once. The "troops" are decent and charming, I believe, not because they suffer but because they are powerless – And the devil who rules this planet has contrived that those who are powerless shall suffer.'[8] Morgan did not want power for himself, indeed he never had wanted it and never would; but he was growing increasingly aware of its destructive influence. Over the next twenty years he would explore this influence in his last published novel and in his essays and reviews; so that by 1939 he would be seen as the embodiment of the democratic outlook, someone for whom power in all its manifestations had truly become a dirty word.

In 1919 his ideas were not yet so clearly defined – he had not found his secondary, his essayist's voice. But all during that year, and the one following, he was on his way to finding it. During these years he wrote nearly one hundred articles (whereas in 1914 he had only written four, about India*) and fewer than a dozen book reviews. Why was he suddenly so prolific? It was, I think, because of his time away from Lily. People like Cavafy, like Aïda Borchgrevink, like the other people at the Red Cross and in the hospital, had all treated him with respect; even the people with whom he exchanged letters in England like Bertrand Russell or Leonard Woolf attributed an intellectual and emotional maturity to him which Lily, during his twenties and thirties, had done her best, consciously or unconsciously, to suppress. Some might say it was the beneficial effect of holding down a job, and a useful job, in a time of international crisis; others that it was the effect of sexual fulfilment; but more than either of these it was freedom, it was a new vision that he found in Alexandria. Here Morgan found that he was truly a writer. He did not articulate this; he did not behave differently; but it was only from his Alexandrian period onwards that he behaved as one.

This new willingness, and eagerness, to write articles was in part helped by his ever-widening circle of friends. In November 1919 he went with Sydney Waterlow to spend the night with John Middleton Murry in Hampstead;† around the spring of that year Murry had taken over the editorship of the *Athenaeum* and Morgan had been writing for it – reviews, articles about Egypt (including one about Cavafy's poetry) and so forth. In fact by the time of his visit he had

---

* Reprinted in *Abinger Harvest* in 1936.
† Katherine Mansfield was spending the winter in the South of France; in June she had given supper to Morgan and told Virginia Woolf, 'I *don't* care for him. Partly perhaps because he dreadfully dislikes me – But I could forgive that. What I can't get over is a certain *silliness*. Is that unfair?'[9] Despite these strictures she said to Murry six weeks before her death, about the Gurdjieff Institute where she was staying, that Lawrence 'and E. M. Forster are two men who *could* understand this place if they would'.[10] Morgan told Murry, rather mystified, that he 'did not know that I should have understood anything of her state. What you say has given me a curious feeling. I had never for an instant thought that she might be thinking of me.'[11]

written nearly twenty pieces for Murry and was delivering to him a three-part article about the lighthouse at Alexandria* that was to appear in three issues of the *Athenaeum* just before Christmas. As he was also writing for the *Daily News* and the *Daily Herald*, of which he was, for two months, temporary literary editor while Sassoon was in America, it was with some justification that he wrote in his diary, to which he had returned after being without it for three and a half years, 'I am happiest when busy. How fatuous! I see my middle age as clearly as middle age can be seen. Always working never creating. Pleasant to all trusting no one. A mixture of cowardice and sympathy. Blaming civilisation for my failures.'[12]

As for fiction, as for creativity, he continued mostly to stagnate. The exception was an 'Unfinished Short Story' apparently written during the winter of 1919–20 and labelled 'not bad' by Morgan. It is about an Englishman who, spending two days in the 'sensuous and venal' atmosphere of Alexandria, is disorientated enough to visit a prostitute: 'He felt no repentance now, only a relief that he had imitated the rest of the world. Everyone deceives his wife now and then.' Next day he is further disorientated by his first aeroplane trip. 'This was Alexandria. Here was the lake and the twin harbours, and between them, not expecting to be examined from above, many houses. At this altitude they resembled decaying teeth.' The description was based on Morgan's first flight the year before, after which he too 'had come to rest on the surface of the aerodrome feeling very hot and a little sick and trembly'.[13]

Morgan was still, apparently, trying to carry on with his Indian novel, although the only evidence for this is a flippant remark to Sassoon: 'While trying to write my novel, I wanted to scream aloud like a maniac, and it is not in such a mood that one's noblest work is penned.'[14] But he did not *feel* like a writer. Although Arnold were about to reprint *A Room with a View* and *Howards End*, the print run was far too small to make him feel like a leading novelist, nor did the two thousand copies of *Where Angels Fear to Tread* that Knopf were about to publish in America. The joy of the latter, only the second of his novels to be published across the Atlantic (*Howards End* had appeared in 1911) and the first with Knopf, was somewhat diminished by Hugh Walpole, whom Morgan considered

* One of the Seven Wonders of the World.

lowbrow,* having been asked to write an introduction to it before Morgan himself had been consulted: he vetoed the suggestion. But it must have made him wonder where – exactly – was his level? And had the reading public, either lowbrow or highbrow, ever heard of him? It was doubtful.

In 1916 Morgan had received a letter from the Maharajah of Dewas asking him to take up the post, then vacant, of Secretary. Morgan told Lily, having detailed the reasons why he should and should not go, that 'another attraction is that I have begun a novel on India, and would finish it – it is stuck now because all the details of India are vague in my mind not for any other reason.'[15] (Since seventy pages had been written by the time Morgan went to Egypt, it throws curious light on his and Lily's daily lives together that all during the years 1913–14 he had not, apparently, mentioned his Indian novel to her *once*.) In 1920 the post of Secretary again became free, and although Morgan was feeling 'awfully East-sick' and could not 'remain severed from the East and from [Masood] indefinitely in this cruel fashion',[16] he felt he could not leave Lily. Then, in 1921, the post became temporarily vacant. Partly because he was able to tell Lily the appointment was for a limited period, Morgan decided to go.

A second passage to India (the title for the novel did not occur to him until he had nearly finished writing) was evidence not just that he longed to return to that country, and was deeply interested in the changing political situation; it was clear that his identity, the way he saw himself, was still that of a working novelist. *Maurice*, he believed, could never be published (to try to publish it as a polemic, as a way of changing laws and attitudes, was not of his nature); *Arctic Summer* he did not want to finish: somehow his thirty thousand words about the Whitbys and Clesant March did not inspire him. The only hope was the Indian novel, and a return to the country of its setting might be the fulfilment of that hope. The 1913–14 manuscript, together with two or three pages of the 1919–20 re-start (the one he had mentioned to Sassoon) was the key item of his luggage (miraculously it was never lost or stolen . . .)

---

* One of the reasons Morgan was to refuse a knighthood in 1949 was that Hugh Walpole had had one.

He left England in early March 1921 and arrived at Port Said on the 16th; in the same month Tonbridge's most illustrious old boy (even nowadays the only one who is honoured with plaques, portraits and so on) Sir Edmund Ironside* arrived there as well, for the Middle East Conference in Cairo. Winston Churchill, as Colonial Secretary, had convened it in order to settle the outstanding issues of the region and, advised by T. E. Lawrence† and Gertrude Bell, made a number of critical decisions designed both to safeguard British interests and to satisfy the demands of the Arabs; Churchill also authorised the final leg – from Cairo to Karachi – of a regular air passage to India. The conference was at once the apogee of British imperial influence and the beginning of a withdrawal. Ironside was sent to be Commander-in-Chief of British troops in the region just when their numbers were to be greatly reduced: British influence now depended increasingly on British character. Would Ironside be any different from Ronny? 'Wherever he entered, mosque, cave or temple, he retained the spiritual outlook of the Fifth Form, and condemned as "weakening" any attempt to understand them . . . One touch of regret . . . would have made him a different man, and the British Empire a different institution.'[20]

* His mother had, like Lily, moved to Tonbridge to be one of the 'great concourse of retired officers, civil servants, widows, and fathers of large families who "squatted" within the radius and got a cheap education for their children.'[17] Her son, known as 'Tiny' because he was so large, arrived in the same term as Morgan, became a soldier and, when his life was written up in the 'How They Did It' series in 1939, was described rousingly as 'a giant among men and a born leader of them. His life is one long epic of self-sacrifice, bravery and adventure . . . Standing six feet four, lean and powerful, with bull-dog jaw, masterful brows and eyes as piercing as those of the eagle that haunts his native Highlands.'[18] Ironside's daring escapades as a secret agent during the Boer War (1899–1902, while Morgan was at Cambridge and in Italy) are alleged to have suggested the character of Richard Hannay in John Buchan's *The Thirty-Nine Steps* (1915).

Morgan must have had an aspect of Ironside in mind in a 1939 unpublished story called 'The Obelisk': two sailors called Tiny like Ironside ('merely because he's so large. Another joke') and Stanhope separately seduce a couple called Ernest and Hilda (*could* they have been based on what Morgan thought Ernest Merz and Hilda Garnett might have become?). Each lies to the other by pretending to have seen an obelisk 'erected – to some local worthy'. Only Hilda discovers that it had fallen down the previous week; and why, therefore, her husband 'looked handsomer than usual, and happier, and his lips were parted in a natural smile'[19] – it was Tiny's attentions.

† Morgan and Lawrence had been briefly introduced in London two weeks before and were to establish a literary friendship in 1924, exchanging long letters about literature and showing each other their work in progress. Morgan was setting out to stay with Lawrence at his house at Clouds Hill on the day in 1935 that he heard about his death.

Ironside and Morgan would have had little to say to each other had they met at Port Said. The former had fulfilled all Tonbridge's ideals; the latter had not. But Morgan, the observer, the chronicler, would have appreciated the irony of the contrast that at Port Said he did, however, have a visitor: el Adl. During their evening together 'I found him more charming affectionate and intelligent than ever', Morgan told Florence, adding, 'and since the time was so short we decided only to speak of happy things.'[21] The consumption that would, in little more than a year, be the cause of el Adl's death had evidently, as with Eddie Forster in 1880, not yet manifested itself. Morgan had no idea, when he later wrote a 'letter' to his dead lover, that 'it was the last time you had full vigour. I hadn't seen you for two years and took joy in touching your stiffened flesh again. You said "foolish": I: "All have their foolishness and this is mine."'[22]

So Morgan continued the voyage 'in great peace of mind'[23] and it ended happily in '"feverish gaiety, concerts, juggling with prizes, quarrels between elderly men over a game of deck quoits, special meeting of Sports Committee to adjudicate same" in fact in all the things I was about to escape' – and had managed to avoid in 1912. At Bombay there were again the muddled arrangements of eight years before but eventually he boarded the night train to Indore ('the Indian trains have gone downhill in the last ten years') where he was met by car and 'I sped along the chaussée for 23 miles – a dull drive and a dull evening: the road was straight and rough and edged with small dreary trees and we passed a dead cow round which vultures were gathering.' (Another terrifying drive, I wrote in 1990. Dusty straight road, scrubby trees, people living along edges, lots of scraggy cows wandering about. One sees the Hill of Devi from a distance – it is brown, bare and table-shaped. Dewas is quite a large town with industry, 'suitings' and such. I am not surprised Morgan described Dewas so little. There is little to describe. Figsbury Rings is far more beautiful. Yet the two are not dissimilar.)

Morgan, without fully realising it, was entering the chaotic world which, as he had observed in 1912, 'can have no parallel, except in a Gilbert and Sullivan opera'. His employer, HH the Maharajah of Dewas, Senior Branch (the extraordinary division of Dewas into two meant that there was a 'Junior Branch' as well, complete with its own palace, court, army, flag and so on) was a man of great character and complexity, a charming creature, gay, witty, affectionate, generous and with a strong religious element in him. I am tempted to call him a saint, but saints are supposed to be reliable, anyhow by the British, and the Maharajah certainly wasn't that. He loved intrigue, he could lie if he wasn't trusted, and since besides being deceitful he was unpractical, he made a tragic mess of his life in the end.

The New Palace, where Morgan had stayed for the Christmas of 1912–13 with the Darlings, was 'still building, and the parts of it that were built ten years ago are already falling down. You would weep at the destruction, expense, and hideousness, and I do almost,' he told Lily, always careful to note down the domestic details for her and the maids in Weybridge.

We live amongst rubble and mortar, and excavations whence six men carry a basket of earth, no larger than a cat's, twenty yards once in five minutes ... This is the scene under my window, but for acres around the soil is pitted with similar efforts, slabs of marble lie about, roads lead nowhere, costly fruit trees die for want of water ... I look into a room – dozens of warped towel-horses are stabled there, or a new suite of drawing-room chairs with their insides gushing out. I open a cupboard near the bath and find it full of teapots, I ask for a bookcase and it bows when it sees me and lies rattling on the floor. And so on and so forth. I don't know what to do about it all, and scarcely what to feel. It's no good trying to make something different out of it, for it is as profoundly Indian as an Indian temple.

These were not the circumstances for writing a novel; although Morgan had 'expected that the congenial surroundings would inspire me to go on. Exactly the reverse happened.' He concentrated instead on his duties, only vaguely defined as those of Secretary, by trying to put to rights some of the intrigues, rescuing some of the palace contents from further decay, trying to stop money being frittered away. Yet, as Morgan told Malcolm, 'to check the idleness, incompetence and extravagance is quite beyond me. I knew I should find them, but they are far worse than I imagined.' The main reason, apart from lack of calm, why Morgan could not even think of working on his novel was lack of privacy. In April he reported to Lily, 'I cannot get over the constant publicity. Even when the doors are made to shut they do not, owing to warping; and servants not thinking it polite to knock, you may any time find yourself amid creeping forms. Plenty of sentries, but they generally sleep face downward. We lie as open to the countryside as to one another. It is indescribable and unimaginable – really a wonderful experience, for it is the fag end of a vanished civilization.'

Sexually, the constant publicity was a great problem. Morgan had resolved, on arrival, to repress all thoughts of sex: in 1912 he had once heard HH censure homosexuality and he did not want to give trouble. But the heat 'provoked me sexually' (he was to write the following year in a private memoir called 'Kanaya') 'and masturbation brought no relief'. He decided to seduce an eighteen-year-old Hindu coolie but no sooner had he made an assignation on the road near the guest house ('for the least I could do for HH was to avoid any carryings on in the Palace') than the news was whispered round the palace and, miserably, Morgan thought HH had found him out. He shunned the coolie, considered resigning from his post, then spoke. But HH had heard nothing and responded sympathetically when Morgan told him that he had no feelings for women, declaring 'you are not to blame'. Eventually HH himself organised a young barber called Kanaya and 'for a time all went well. I couldn't get from Kanaya the emotional response of an Egyptian, because he had the body and soul of a slave, but he was always merry and he improved my health.' Then rumours spread, Morgan felt that HH's authority was undermined, and eventually there was 'the incredible silliness of Kanaya' trying to 'establish himself as Catamite to the Crown'.*24 Morgan boxed his ears, was unable to dismiss him 'since it would "look suspicious"' and went on having angry intercourse with him that 'was now mixed with the desire to inflict pain'.

I've never had that desire with anyone else, before or after, and I wasn't trying to punish him – I knew his silly little soul was incurable. I just felt he was a slave, without rights, and I a despot whom no one could call to account ...

* A recent book about novels by English novelists with Indian settings finds the sequence of events, as related by Morgan in 'Kanaya', quite improbable, believing that HH must have always known Morgan to be homosexual and 'that from his first arrival at Dewas the Maharajah orchestrated an elaborate series of manoeuvres designed to tempt Forster into active homosexual behaviour ... throughout the six months that Forster spent at Dewas he was the victim of a very unpleasant game devised by an accomplished sadist.'25 According to this interpretation Morgan, while a little suspicious about HH's true attitude, could not contemplate disillusion about him; yet his vague unease destroyed his sense of truth and reality just as the echo Mrs Moore heard threatened 'in some indescribable way to undermine her hold on life'.26

The same writer makes the interesting point that Ruth Prawer Jhabvala's *Heat and Dust* (1975) draws its inspiration both from Ackerley's *Hindoo Holiday* and from *The Hill of Devi* and that Harry, the Nawab's secretary in her book, is in part based on Morgan.

When I look over that year, my verdict is unfavourable on the whole. I caused so much trouble all round, and my intimacy with HH, the only gain, would have been achieved anyway I think. I see myself disintegrated and inert, like the dead cow among vultures at the edge of the road. I thought 'This is how it will end,' and thus it ended. I asked HH once whether I could dominate lust as he seemed to – for he visits his wife but rarely and her alone. He replied: 'Oh one can't teach those things. When you are dissatisfied with your present state of existence you will enter another – that's all.'[27]

Morgan was now forty-two yet the sex he had with Kanaya was the first regular sex he had ever had. What is so curious, with all his talk of improving his health, unconquerable lust, desire without affection, is that he had not had all these feelings at the 'normal' age of eighteen or twenty-five or thirty. Sexual passion may not diminish after forty; lust usually does somewhat – but not in Morgan's case. And had there *been* lust in the years of his youth? We know there was some, but the surge of lust he experienced at Dewas was something quite new. He, rather charmingly, put it down to the heat. The real reason was his body's response to Mohammed. He had had perhaps a dozen nights with him. Then Weybridge had subsumed him in 1919–21. Now, at last, his body could have what it wanted, or what Morgan thought it needed (with his equally charming references to his health).

(Does the biographer find all this detail about lust distasteful? Well, less distasteful than uninteresting. What I *do* dislike are the references to slaves, the unabashed using of someone purely for physical sensation. I cannot decide if Morgan doesn't quite mean all he says, whether he is being honest and straightforward and we should not censure him for this, or whether indeed it is not fair to make judgements from a memoir not written for publication. And am I myself being disingenuous if I profess to find sexuality more acceptable if it is prompted by affection and unacceptable if it is extracted under psychological or financial duress? It is the oldest confusion under the sun. But, as Morgan knew, the Kanaya episode does leave an 'unfavourable' impression; and it was one of the rare occasions in his life when he, to whom power and despotism were anathema, confessed to enjoying his own power.)

While at Dewas Morgan did not keep a diary; instead he wrote long and detailed letters. Possibly he had begun to think that even if he never wrote another novel he might one day gain a reputation as a letter-writer; or, indeed, that his letters might help him with his Indian novel when he returned home. (They *were* published in his lifetime, in 1953 in *The Hill of Devi*. And it is interesting, re-reading them again in order to see what else to glean from them for this chapter, that, partisan as I am, I cannot, still, see them as the very greatest of letters. Just as, to me, eccentrically perhaps, Virginia Woolf's diaries are her most lasting memorial, so Morgan's letters will never seem to me among his most memorable writing. I am fascinated by them, because of course they illuminate his character and his life, but they rarely make my heart leap in the way that the novels always, every time I re-read them, make my heart leap and spirits soar. He himself defined one of the reasons why. Second-class writers like Charles Lamb and R. L. Stevenson lack anonymity, they always write with their surface personalities. 'They are letter writers, not creative artists, and it is no coincidence that each of them did write charming letters . . . Literature tries to be unsigned.'[28] Morgan wrote literature: he was perhaps not a wonderful letter-writer because he was a creative artist.*)

He would have been much happier if he had felt inclined to work at his novel: the thought of it was always there at the back of his mind. On the other hand, without the year there would have *been* no novel: back in England it was Morgan's time in India that was the impetus for the second half of the manuscript. Court life at Dewas, the complexities of character of HH, were not the inspiration; it was being in India, observing it as an insider.

He felt especially an insider in August when an elaborate festival took place and he even 'walked barefoot in petticoats through the streets with black and red powders smeared over my forehead, cheek and nose'.

Well, what's it all about? It's called Gokul Ashtami – i.e. the *eight days* feast in honour of Krishna who was born at *Gokul* near Muttra, and I cannot yet discover how much of it is traditional and how much due to HH. What troubles me is that every detail, almost without exception, is fatuous and in bad taste. The altar is a mess of little objects, stifled with rose leaves, the walls are hung with deplorable oleographs, the chandeliers, draperies – everything bad. Only one thing is beautiful – the expression on the faces of the people as they bow to the shrine . . .[29]

---

* Virginia Woolf of course disproved this theory.

The bizarre nature of the festival, the riotous celebration, the 'altar, huddled out of sight amid images of inferior descent, smothered under rose-leaves, overhung by oleographs, outblazed by golden tablets representing the Rajah's ancestors, and entirely obscured, when the wind blew, by the tattered foliage of a banana': it provided Morgan with the catalyst which helped him to finish *A Passage to India*. The festival was to reappear in the final Temple section and would convey the gulf between the Indians and the English in their attitude to matters spiritual. 'By sacrificing good taste', he would write, 'this worship achieved what Christianity has shirked; the inclusion of merriment. All spirit as well as matter must participate in salvation, and if practical jokes are banned the circle is incomplete.'[30] That is why, he now understood, for the English the circle would be – forever – incomplete.

Another aspect of Dewas that was important to Morgan was the palace. Although he once remarked that 'the crude ugliness of this palace presses on me', while he was there and in his memory it mattered as much to him as all the other houses in his life. This was not because he was especially happy there, or because he loved it as a place (he did not); it was because of its imagery of transience. Not only was it in a state of continual flux because 'building, decorations, repairs, drainings and diggings were going on in every direction', but it had always been thus and would always be thus; it was like Melcombe Place in 1896 or Battersea Rise in 1907, and yet pointlessly so – which made Dewas all the more Gilbert and Sullivanish. The inherent restlessness of life in the palace, of the very fabric of the palace itself, became, for Morgan, an image of India and of humanity. When he wrote about *A Passage to India* that 'It's about something wider than politics, about the search of the human race for a more lasting home . . .',[31] he was not only defining the theme that had obsessed him throughout his life – 'no resting place' – he was making the Maharajah and his home a symbol of eternal flux.

27

A Passage to India

Morgan was in Dewas for a little more than six months, from March to October. Since his previous stay in India had been from October to March, he had now experienced a whole year's worth of climate. (Some assiduous critics have declared that this was a deliberate ploy, as if Morgan was determined to 'research' Indian weather, because his novel is constructed around the different seasons; it was, I am sure, a convenient coincidence.) He rarely left Dewas, except for one or two expeditions – notably to the abandoned Moghul city of Mandu – until his final departure for Hyderabad at the end of October. Here he had a happy time staying with Masood and his family:* as with Mohammed, and as was to be the case with his future lovers in England, once the first passion had passed then Morgan wanted and needed to extend his feelings to his lover's entire family. Indeed it is possible that the family, or potential family, since all Morgan's lovers were bisexual, was as important to him as the lover: as if he were trying to re-create and become part of the family that he had missed as a child; or as if he were trying, domestically, to turn the lover into the brother he had always longed for ('I saw that he was my brother'[3] thinks the hero of 'The Other Side of the Hedge' in ecstasy).

At the beginning of January 1922 Morgan saw once more, as Fielding was to see it, Alexandria's 'bright blue sky, constant wind, clean low coastline, as against the intricacies of Bombay'.[4] Here he visited Mohammed. He had told Masood, and Florence, and indeed

---

* However, on one occasion, on an expedition to see a hill fort, Morgan took a short cut up to it and returned 'covered with cactus thorns. He was in agony ... it took three days for Forster to recover completely.'[1] This would be re-worked as Adela's headlong rush down the hillside from the caves after which 'hundreds of cactus spines had to be picked out of her flesh'.[2]

anyone else whom he had told about his Egyptian affair, how much he was looking forward to seeing his lover; and he was, but he longed for sex as well: in India 'I promised myself that on my return I would get you to penetrate me behind, however much it hurt and although it must decrease your respect for me.'[5] It was not to be. As Morgan wrote, confidingly, to Masood, 'I know how sorry you will be for my disappointment here. At Port Said I received a letter from Mohammed saying he was ill';[6] as he would write in his posthumous 'letter' to the dead Mohammed, more curtly, 'your disease had struck'.

He stayed in Egypt for a month, doing what he could, loyal, generous and miserable. But he was not unrealistic and by 1929, when a trip to Egypt with Florence prompted him to finish the 'letter', he wrote with a touching matter-of-factness, with the mixture of realism and sentiment with which his novels are overlaid:

It appears to me, looking back, that you were not deeply attached to me, excited and flattered at first, grateful afterwards – that's all. But if I am wrong, and if lovers can meet after death, and go on with their love, call to me and I'll come . . . I did love you and if love is eternal I may start again. Only it's for you to start me and to beckon. So much has happened to me since that I may not recognise you and am pretty certain not to think of you when I die. I knew how it would be from the first, yet shouldn't have been so happy in Egypt this autumn but for you.[7]

By the end of February Morgan had reached Marseilles. Here occurred an event that, just as much as the year in the East, eased the way to the finishing of his Indian novel: he bought a volume of Proust to read. It was the first, *Du côté de chez Swann*, which had appeared in a heavily revised second edition in 1919, at the same time as the second volume of Proust's novel. The latter had won the Prix Goncourt, making its author instantly famous; three more volumes had appeared during 1920 and 1921 and a fifth would appear in May. It was Virginia Woolf (alerted in her turn by Roger Fry) who had made Morgan resolve to read the great French writer. 'Every one is reading Proust,' she told him in a letter, responding to one of his from Hyderabad, that she had sent to Egypt. 'I sit silent and hear their reports. It seems to be a tremendous experience, but I'm shivering on the brink, and waiting to be submerged with a horrid sort of notion that I shall go down and down and down and perhaps never come up again.'[8] Morgan, too, was responsive to this concept of hidden depths as explored by Proust, and was to say that he 'learned ways of looking at character from him. The modern sub-conscious way. He gave me as much of the modern way as I could take. I couldn't read Freud or Jung myself; it had to be filtered to me.'*9

'The middle age of b[ugger]s is not to be contemplated without horror,' wrote Virginia Woolf in her diary, Morgan having met her by chance in London a week after his return and accompanied her to her and Leonard's house in Richmond. He 'was, we thought, depressed to the verge of inanition . . . But he was charming, transparent' and told them about India, about the sparrows that flew about the palace, about the quarrelling junior and senior branch, about rowing on the lake. Yet, he told the Woolfs, despite the lack of other people to talk to, India 'is much nicer than this. I felt no enthusiasm at seeing my native cliffs again.' Virginia could well understand his response: 'To come back to Weybridge, to come back to an ugly house a mile from the station, an old, fussy, exacting mother . . .'11 Morgan was grateful for her understanding. But his circumstances were, as he knew, of his own making; and he did not complain, nor did he ask for sympathy. By now a complex mixture of inertia, masochism, guilt and anger at his father's death, an exaggerated sense of responsibility for Lily and a deeply introverted streak would keep the forty-three-year-old Morgan for ever in the same cage in which he had been virtually all his life.

And yet there was his novel. There were many and varied reasons why Morgan had left it unfinished; but the fact was it had lain abandoned for ten years, with the result that the gap, the gulf, the lacunae made it far, far harder to re-start. One does not need a vast leap of sympathy to imagine how difficult it must have been for him; so nearly did the Indian novel join the pantheon of the unfinished like *Nottingham Lace* and *Arctic Summer*. Something, nevertheless, some

---

* In 1929 Morgan was to review the English translation of Proust by Scott Moncrieff (the first volume of this had appeared in September 1922). There are two sentences in the review that encapsulate Morgan's writing at its very best: 'All the difficulties of the original are here faithfully reproduced,' he wrote about the translation. 'A sentence begins quite simply, then it undulates and expands, parentheses intervene like quickset hedges, the flowers of comparison bloom, and three fields off, like a wounded partridge, crouches the principal verb, making one wonder as one picks it up, poor little thing, whether after all it was worth such a tramp, so many guns and such expensive dogs, and what, after all, is the relation to the main subject, potted so gaily half a page back, and proving finally to have been in the accusative case.'10

inner strength and inner compulsion, helped him to re-start; it was during the year after his return that this happened.

The key difficulty, it seems, was that he did not know where he was going. In 1951 he would give an explanation for not having finished *Arctic Summer*:

The novelist should, I think, always settle when he starts what is going to happen, what his major event is to be. He may alter this as he approaches it, indeed he probably will, indeed he probably had better, or the novel becomes tied up and tight. But the sense of solid mass ahead, a mountain round or over or through which the story must somehow go, is most valuable, and for the novels I've tried to write, essential.

When Morgan began *A Passage to India* he 'knew that something important happened in the Malabar [*sic*] Caves, and that it would have a central place in the novel – but I didn't know what it would be'. *Arctic Summer*, on the other hand, lacked this focus; what he had 'was thinner, a background and colour only'. Thus, although he had not decided what happened in the caves, he knew, from 1913 to 1923, that they would prove the focus – if he ever managed to finish the book.

As a result of this statement of Morgan's, almost a revelation (because it could be thought that the main impetus for the novel was relations between English and Indian, or the 'Indianness' of India, or a whole host of other themes – and not the incident in the caves), it is possible to understand something of what was going on in his mind during the ten years of writer's block. He had wanted, ever since Masood first suggested the idea in the December of 1910, to write a book about India. But his primary interest was the English *in* India, the antithesis between the one race and the other, not in Indians or India *per se*. All his novels contain antithesis as their central motive. 'Let me think,' he mused in 1952, when asked by an interviewer whether he considered antithesis essential. 'There was one in *Howards End*. Perhaps a rather subtler one in *The Longest Journey*.' It was the freedom of Italy versus the constraint of England in the Italian novels; integrity versus falsehood in *The Longest Journey*; Schlegels versus Wilcoxes in *Howards End*; respectability versus non-respectability in *Maurice*. Each of these antitheses would, in some way or another, be used in the Indian novel. Yet there had to be something more.

By 1914, and the end of Chapter 7, Morgan had set out the basic contrast; but still there lacked 'the sense of solid mass ahead, a mountain'.[12] In the previous novels, marriage had been the mountain: Lilia's, Rickie's, Margaret's, Clive's and Lucy's (proposed) marriage had all been the pivot upon which the novels turned. But Adela Quested, who had admittedly come to India on a quest for a husband as much as for the real India, could not just go blankly home again without having found either. Something had to happen, and that something had to be connected with the cave. But what would it be?

Morgan's own experience in the caves had, he knew, been coloured by his overwrought night and his dawn departure from Masood's house. But he did not want the caves to be the scene of something purely sexual or even purely emotional, he wanted something more than this. Hence his rejection of the early draft in which 'Janet' is, literally, assaulted. On the other hand he did not want to import into his fiction the oddity and fantasy element of the short stories. He knew, by the end of Chapter 7, that there would be an expedition to the caves, as there had been an expedition to the Italian hillside, or a visit to Mrs Failing at Cadover; but he could not decide what should happen or why, even at Dewas where he hoped to be inspired.

Yet he was pleased with the basic plot, for this he did not change: a Mrs Wilcox–ish figure arriving in India to visit her son, a public-school product* who would have seen no joke in Morgan's long-ago letter-ending to Masood, 'from Forster, member of the Ruling Race to Masood, a nigger'.[14] *A Passage to India* was in one sense to be an exploration of this flippant intimacy. The older woman, Mrs Moore, is accompanied by her son's potential fiancée: the young couple had met in the Lake District, an echo perhaps of the heterosexual courtship conventions that might have encircled Merz and Hilda Garnett if

---

* This aspect of the novel, the contrast between the public-school type and the Indian, may have suggested itself to Morgan when he first read Edward Carpenter's 1892 book about India, *From Adam's Peak to Elephanta*: referring to the English concept of Duty he writes, 'The central core of the orthodox Englishman, or at any rate of the public-school boy who ultimately becomes our most accepted type, is perhaps to be found in that word. It is that which makes him the dull, narrow-minded, noble, fearless, reliable man that he is. The moving forces of the Hindu are quite different; they are first, Religion; and second, Affection; and it is these which make him so hopelessly unpractical, so abominably resigned, yet withal so tender and imaginative of heart. Abstract duty to the Hindu has but little meaning. He ... and ... the Englishman ... do not and they cannot understand each other.'[13]

things had been different. Adela Quested,* who lives in Hampstead and who is familiar with 'advanced academic circles, deliberately free', has muddled her life by imagining herself in love with a member of the ruling race whose 'self-complacency, his censoriousness, his lack of subtlety, all grew vivid beneath a tropic sky'. Her passage to India, and her panic reaction to the caves, teach her the truth about herself and about India, although it is Mrs Moore who articulates this truth: 'She felt increasingly (vision or nightmare?) that, though people are important, the relations between them are not, and that in particular too much fuss has been made over marriage; centuries of carnal embracement, yet man is no nearer to understanding man';[15] the words in brackets forming a link with Helen Schlegel's reiterated vision of her own world's 'panic and emptiness'.[16]

What Morgan was not able to define until 1922 was the link, of which the caves would be the symbol, between Adela's wide-eyed, naïve arrival in India and her disillusion both with her relationship with it and with the man she had thought she might marry. This link would be, he began to realise (gradually or in a flash of inspiration?), a court of law: it was the legal system, its machinations, its immovable traditions, its panoply of rules and regulations, that would be the framework for the novel once Adela had been in the caves.† This is why, when Mrs Moore says to Adela, 'you dislike institutions', she is being both perceptive and prophetic: she understands that the younger girl dislikes power and rules, but that also she does not know how to use or avoid them. Adela's tragedy is not so much her neurotic mistake; it is that 'She has started the machinery; it will work to its end'.

Here, in his loathing of the machinations of the law, Morgan is using the vocabulary of his early stories, notably 'The Machine Stops': law, bureaucracy, machinery, order may be contemptible, but modern

---

* Adela is, phonetically, Hilda backwards and Garnett is a two-syllable word with hard syllables like Quested. Adela = Ang. Sax. 'filth', 'mud', a link with the imagery of mud that Morgan had used in Egypt and in the first paragraph of his novel ('the very wood seems made of mud, the inhabitants of mud moving'). But Adela also = Germ. noble. Thus the name has overtones of noble mud, of somebody or something that is superficially impressive but dirty, or morally impure, beneath the surface (the English) and of somebody or something that lives in mud but achieves nobility none the less (the Indian).

† There would also be the not inappropriate resonance of a trial being used, in traditional fictional mode, as a spiritual test for the characters. And the musical imagery of the trial scene (pointed out by Benjamin Britten, cf. p 162) would be evident in its rhythmic construction and in its use of sound, thus linking back to the Beethoven's Fifth scene in *Howards End* ('Panic and emptiness! Panic and emptiness!').

man must know how to sidestep, or how to manipulate, them. In Morgan's eyes a dislike of institutions is perfectly admirable, but it also leads to disaster because a member of the ruling race who does not approve of them, and does not use them to their advantage, will always be an outsider. Thus another impetus for the ending of his Indian novel would be his growing interest in and lifelong distaste for power as the mainspring of human behaviour: Adela shared it and in this Morgan identified with her. What she learnt in India, alas, is that for the Anglo-Indian 'every human act in the East is tainted with officialism':[17] here was the same unwilling pessimism about the possibility of straightforward personal relations that had appeared in the five previous novels.

Here, also, was Morgan's typical way of using small details on a human scale from which to extrapolate larger meanings. In a 1922 article written in the aftermath of Amritsar (where, in 1919, troops had fired on a peaceful crowd of demonstrators, resulting in an upsurge of Indian nationalism) Morgan attributed the flaw in relations between the English and Indian to the former being 'associated with a system that supported rudeness in railway carriages ... We have thrown grammars and neckties at him, and smiled when he put them on wrongly – that is all.'[18] So, in *A Passage to India*, Aziz, friendlily, lends Fielding his collar-stud and Ronny later remarks that 'Aziz was exquisitely dressed, from tie-pin to spats, but he had forgotten his back collar-stud, and there you have the Indian all over: inattention to detail; the fundamental slackness that reveals the race.'[19] Morgan makes a larger point out of this one tiny detail: if people like Ronny are insensitive to friendly personal relations, if he is rude in railway carriages, then he is not sensitive to Indians and is unfit to govern them. Ronny embodies the remark with which Morgan concluded the 1922 article: 'Never in history did ill-breeding contribute so much towards the dissolution of an Empire.'[20]

At the same time Morgan's Indian novel had two important elements* that had not been in any of his others: the parody aspect, and the mystical. The former was a response to what

* Academics have, over the last seventy years, claimed many other 'influences', few of them convincing, for example that Morgan took his theme of 'spiritual quest' from Whitman's poem 'Passage to India' (1871); in fact the novel lacked a title until the last moment when he thought of the poem. It is hard even to make much of a comparison with Kipling's *Kim* (1901), apart from the shared Indian setting and the shared 'contrast between the emotional warmth and the imaginative power of India and the discipline and reserve of the British'.[21]

he had defined in 1915, 'Anglo-Indian ladies, and their theme the disaster of inter-marriage; that disaster obsessed and obsesses them, and the novels that exhibit it read as though written on an elephant's back, high above the actualities of the bazaar.'[22] It is true that many 'pulp' novels set in India did use this theme; but a more frequent one, as in Ethel M. Dell's *The Way of an Eagle*, was that of a naïve English girl who encounters the reality of India but is helped through her trials and tribulations by her love, at first undeclared, for a good man. This is why so much of what Adela and Ronny do is low-key and deflationary. They never fall into each other's arms or have a row, they are merely sensible, sexless and plain: thus they are the opposite of their romantic counterparts. Indeed, romance eludes them always. As she journeys to the caves, and thinks she has seen a black cobra, Adela reflects, 'Nothing was explained, and yet there was no romance':[23] there is only a tedious, uncomprehending middle way eternally blind to the truth. And the truth, Morgan believed, lay in mysticism, something else to which the average Anglo-Indian was impervious.

It is the mystic element that was to be the focus of the three-quarters of the book that Morgan wrote in 1922–3 (thirty more chapters to add to the first seven). When he began writing, the novel was much more in the mode of the first five (set themes, comic dialogue, social observation); after an interval of ten years it became more 'philo-sophical and poetic',[24] in Morgan's own words. (When re-starting, he wondered whether he was over-emphasising the mystic element simply because of the characters being 'not sufficiently interesting for the atmosphere. This tempts me to emphasise the atmosphere, and so to produce a meditation rather than a drama.'[25]) As the critic John Colmer has pointed out, the first version of the 1922–3 manuscript focused far more on the 'rational humanist' Fielding who, when he enters the caves, has normal, human reactions to the oppressive echo and eventually, having recited some Persian poetry that he has learnt from Aziz, shouts '"Go to Hell" . . . and scuttled out like an excitable schoolboy before the avalanche fell.'[26] In his final revision Morgan changed the focus to the intuitive Mrs Moore and the rather sensible, civilised Adela, whose disintegration in the face of the primaeval quality of the caves makes them all the more frightening and unknowable.

Adela encounters Pan, only this time it is a different Pan from the comic, mischievous god of *A Room with a View* ('Pan had been among them – not the great god Pan, who has been buried these two thousand years, but the little god Pan, who presides over social contretemps and unsuccessful picnics.'27); instead he is the malevolent Pan described by Theocritus, creating the panic and emptiness in *Howards End* as well as the panic felt by Adela, whose emotions are identical to the 'terrible foreboding' of 'The Story of a Panic' twenty years before.

The mystic, philosophical aspect of *A Passage to India* is the reason why the novel is seen by many readers as Forster's greatest achievement: they see it as being on a different level from the novels that are 'only' about the English middle class and their personal relations; and they admire the exploration of religious preoccupation, of man's relation to the universe and other such 'large' themes. These are of course important elements in the novel and contribute to its fame and success: religion and philosophy and mystic overtones lift a novel on to a higher plane from the everyday, the domestic and the human. But many competent novelists can philosophise or write imaginatively about mysticism; only the greatest can write well about the ordinary and the everyday without exaggerating. Morgan was one of them. And there are some, myself included, who feel that the last, mystic quarter of *A Passage to India* is unsatisfying simply because it does ignore the reality of dailiness in favour of wider, abstract themes. The comedy, the irony and the surprise of the other novels has, by the end of Morgan's life as a novelist, been abandoned.

The composition of this, his last novel, was slow and uncertain and there is an elegiac quality about it that was not merely discernible with hindsight but even obvious to the percipient: as Middleton Murry was to observe, 'The planning of Mr Forster's next novel should carry him well on to the unfamiliar side of the grave.'28 In fact, had it not been for Leonard Woolf's kindness Morgan might not have finished at all; but Leonard took on the role, one that had never previously been played, of literary confidant and supporter (the kind of role that is often fulfilled by a spouse or lover) and so 'it was only owing to Leonard that I was encouraged to finish it'.29

Completing his novel was also enormously helped by having his letters home by his side. All kinds of details were gleaned from

327

them: knocking someone down on his bicycle, meeting someone in Cairo called Everard Feilding (although there is no way of knowing whether in character he was like the calmly unheroic Fielding of the novel), el Adl having a relation called Aziz (the name makes echoing reference to Gino in *Where Angels Fear to Tread*, who is also tender, sensitive, impetuous and anxious to please). And he drew on every kind of source: the Temple section at the end of the book, for example, was inspired by Cavafy's poetry and vision, by Proust and by the Gokul Ashtami festival, 'the strangest and strongest Indian experience ever granted me'.[30] 'Temple' was Morgan at his most Modernist.

The actual novel-writing was, as usual, only mentioned in Morgan's diary in negative terms. 'India not yet a success, dare not look at my unfinished novel' he wrote during his last weeks there and, back in England: 'At Leonard's advice have read my Indian fragment with a view to continuing it . . . The philosophic scheme of the fragment still suits me.' Three weeks later: 'Sat gloomily before my Indian novel all the morning.'[31] One of the things Leonard did for Morgan was to allow him to be Apostolic again, to detach himself mentally from Weybridge, where he had now lived and worked for over fifteen years. Morgan's novels were all written from the vantage-point of Cambridge values; yet from these he had been distanced for so long that re-creating them in the form of fiction had become vastly more difficult. Is the corollary of this that if Morgan had become a don he might have been an enormously prolific novelist? It is very likely, and the argument that Weybridge provided him with a necessarily detached point of view is not necessarily correct. In a way Morgan was a novelist-in-exile, one who was continually conscious of the opposing pull in his life and had been since *The Longest Journey* days. As if bidding a final farewell to any possibility of returning to the Cambridge idyll, Morgan wrote to Malcolm after finishing his last novel that he had been thinking a good deal about 'whether I had moved at all since King's':

King's stands for personal relationships, and these still seem to me the most real things on the surface of the earth, but I have acquired a feeling that people must go away from each other (spiritually) every now and then, and improve themselves if the relationship is to develop or even endure. A Passage to India describes such a going away – preparatory to the next advance, which I am not capable of describing . . . The 'King's' view over-simplified people: that I think was its defect. We are more complicated, also richer, than it knew, and affection grows more difficult than it used to, and also more glorious.[32]

Since 1913, when he began writing, and 1923 when he finished, Morgan had changed a great deal: the war and Alexandria were the causes. Again it was the intuitive Middleton Murry who realised this. In December 1922 *Alexandria* was published and in May 1923 Morgan's Egyptian essays appeared under the title *Pharos and Pharillon*. An anonymous review appeared in *The Times Literary Supplement* (Morgan believed it to have been by Murry) which made the point that it was in Alexandria that 'Mr Forster first gained the courage of his own vision, and first dared to venture himself wholly into "a field" that is by right his own.' The reviewer did not just mean the field of essay-writing: he meant an angle of vision, a way of looking at things. Quoting Morgan's words about Alexander the Great ('There, in a paragraph, is Mr Forster') he goes on, 'So the story of Alexandria, seen (or it may be refracted) through Mr Forster's mind, becomes a manifestation of himself. Here is a world of events that he can comfortably inhabit; in this garment the very tricks of his mind can be accommodated. He was made for it and it for him . . .'

What is extraordinary about this review, so unusual that I am still not sure that it may not be by Virginia Woolf (we only have Morgan's word for it that it was Murry), is the understanding of the author himself. For, although the remark about the novels being 'not exactly good books, sometimes they were almost childish books' is *im*perceptive, he (or she) is most perceptively aware that:

There is a vortex in Alexandria, and Mr Forster, being sensitive to these disturbances, was drawn into it inevitably. That is how we would explain this book and the shimmering magic that dances in and out of its pages. You may object, if you are interested in these inquiries, that if he were put anywhere else on the earth's surface Mr Forster would be found behaving oddly and looking sideways at creation . . . Therefore we conclude that in Alexandria Mr Forster found a spiritual home; the queer fish found it easier to breathe in those suspiciously crystalline waters.

And the reviewer concluded that in *Pharos and Pharillon* 'Mr Forster has never yet been so convincingly himself or so manifestly different from his fellow-writers.'[33]

But why *was* Morgan set apart, an outsider, someone not unlike his friend Cavafy, 'a Greek gentleman in a straw hat, standing absolutely motionless at a slight angle to the universe',[34] as Morgan put it? Why did Virginia believe in 1921 that he would stay in India because 'he has no roots here'? It was of course because of his homosexuality and was, as well, why he was homosexual: to be sexually set apart suited his inherent set-apartness, and vice versa. In Alexandria the two aspects coalesced: which is why he *allowed* them to coalesce there. By finding his own, personal voice in the city, and in the writing of the guidebook and the essays, he freed something in himself which allowed him to finish his Indian novel and to find his equilibrium. It was why he stopped writing novels; and why the second half of his life was, on the whole, happier. And yet, as many would argue, the creative process undoubtedly feeds on unhappiness; a calm, happy, self-confident understanding of oneself does not allow the fiction to be wrung out.

Morgan spent 1923 working on his novel. By April he offered to let Edward Arnold see 40,000 words of uncorrected typescript: 'It might enable you to see whether the completed work would be of interest to you.'[35] He seemed to foresee that this was the last novel he would ever write. When, in the autumn, he told Virginia that he did not think he was a novelist, she replied, as she wrote in her diary, '"No, I don't think you are" Ah! he exclaimed, eagerly, interested, not dashed. But L. denied this. "I'm not at all downcast about my literary career", he said. I think he has made up his mind that he has much to fall back on.'[36] And he did. It was at this period of his life that Siegfried Sassoon recorded in his diary that Arnold Bennett had 'said the other day that E.M.F. is "the best reviewer in London." And, by the way, F. said that he had definitely decided to do no more reviewing' – a remark that all reviewers make at frequent intervals but it must have seemed genuine enough to Sassoon for him to note it in his diary. On the occasion that he told Sassoon this, at the end of April 1922, Morgan was carrying a volume of Proust – had he only been reading Proust since he bought *Du côté de chez Swann* in Marseilles eight weeks earlier? He talked about the book to Sassoon and after 'a few minutes I felt that I knew more about him than Middleton Murry and all the other critics would tell me in twenty volumes'.[37]

Morgan was soon to become famous, and there was a curious foretaste of the effect of fame not long after this meeting with Sassoon. R. Brimley Johnson had just published a book about male novelists* in which he compared Morgan with Henry James and said of the novels: 'They are distinguished, without blur or hesitancy, really original, and reveal great power in characterisation and the reading of all within a man';[38] he was less sure about the short stories, although he took them seriously. Possibly prompted by a reading of Brimley Johnson's book, in June a reviewer in *The Times* said about some short stories by 'Lucas Malet' that they reminded him of nothing so much as *The Celestial Omnibus* (it had been reprinted in 1920). 'Lucas Malet', really Mary St Leger Harrison, wrote saying she had never heard of it and Mr Sidgwick of Sidgwick & Jackson, who had published *The Celestial Omnibus*, offered to 'send a free copy of that book to any British novelist who, in our judgement, is as distinguished a writer as "Lucas Malet", if that novelist will make a similar public confession in your columns that he or she has never heard of Mr E. M. Forster or read any of his books.'

A week later *The Times* ran a profile claiming for Morgan some of the artistic vision expressed in Beethoven and declaring that his awareness of man's spiritual dimension might account for his having stopped writing.[39] He was, Morgan told Masood,

suddenly famous. A most mysterious transition. Letters every day about me in the Times, ¾ column article upon me, imploring letters from publishers, missives from unknown admirers – all for no reason. I have done nothing. A trivial accident started in the Times. I am pleased and for one of my temperament the experience is good. You can't know – or perhaps you alone do know – the torture my diffidence often caused me, and a boom like this helps me forward.[40]

It certainly helped *A Passage to India*, as did Leonard Woolf's encouragement, the reading of Proust, the 1921 visit to India. Yet none of the contributing factors, nor the vastly greater boom that would come after the book was published, would be enough to draw forth more novels. In the January of 1924, when he noted in his diary that he had finished writing, on the same day telling Leonard in a

---

* Omitting 'established' writers such as Wells, Barrie, Conrad and Bennett, he wrote about up-and-coming 'realists' – Gilbert Cannan, Hugh Walpole, J. D. Beresford, D. H. Lawrence – and 'romantics' – J. C. Smith, E. M. Forster, John Buchan, Neil Lyons, Frank Swinnerton. The latter had, he felt, 'greater promise than any other of his contemporaries'. Women writers were covered in another volume.

letter 'I have this moment written the last words of my novel and who but Virginia and yourself should be told about it first?',[41] he knew that an era of his life was over.

28

Abinger

It was to be the central fact of Morgan's life: that he wrote no more novels after *A Passage to India*. But could it have been possible for him to have done so during the second forty-five years of his Life? Was it really evident to the percipient like Middleton Murry that he would never write fiction again or did he just make a lucky guess?

I think Murry *was* prophetic and that what he realised was that Morgan's moment had come and was now over. As P. N. Furbank was to observe in 1978: Morgan 'received his whole inspiration – a vision, a kind of plot, a message – all at once, in early manhood'.[1] Furbank went on to link this vision specifically to what he called Morgan's experience of salvation, and I have linked it more broadly to everything that happened to Morgan in his early life. Even though his last novel was set in India, somewhere he did not visit until 1912, it is true that the stuff of all his novels was the period up to 1909, the year of Merz's death. Although he finished *Maurice*, he nearly failed to finish *A Passage to India*; he did not consider writing an Alexandrian novel; and he knew that he would never again write fiction. The vision he had first had twenty years before in 'The Story of a Panic' had reached its final apotheosis in the Marabar caves.

So now Morgan's life as a novelist was over. Ever afterwards he would be asked why this was so; and he would give a variety of reasons, depending on his mood and what happened to occur to him. He told Goldie that he was bored by the fictional convention 'that one must view the action through the mind of one of the characters; and say of the others "perhaps they thought", or at all events adopt their view-point for a moment only'. He wished, too, that novelists would recapture medieval writers' interest in death.[2] A year later he told Malcolm that 'The upheavals in society and psychology and physics

333

(all at the same time) are too much for a form of art which assumed a certain amount of stability in all three.'³ And a few weeks after this he said to Sassoon that 'I shall never write another novel after [*A Passage to India*] – my patience with ordinary people has given out. But I shall go on writing.'⁴

Then, when it began to be clear that Morgan was not going to produce another novel, the critics gave their opinions. They saw Morgan as an Edwardian novelist who could no longer write when the Edwardian age had ended and when the Great War had destroyed so many certainties; what they ignored was that although the novels were all written, or begun, before the First World War (the generally accepted ending of the Edwardian age) yet Morgan's novels have remained, to this day, consistently modern. Their setting may be pre-1914 (in *A Passage to India* little details such as an oblique reference to Amritsar make the 1920s the probable, though not definitive, date), their setting may be long ago, but their fictional relevance has never dated. Nor did Morgan regret the past; which is why he would have rejected any claim that he no longer wrote because he was no longer an Edwardian.

But on a personal level he regretted his childhood. He, as much as Proust or May Sinclair or L. P. Hartley, was a writer who drew on his youth for inspiration. It was a time of innocence, but also a time innocent of self-criticism. With each subsequent novel after *Where Angels Fear to Tread* Morgan had to stand back and observe the contents of the bucket that he lowered into his subconscious with an increasing degree of detachment – until, by 1927, he had reneged on fiction altogether and was writing *Aspects of the Novel*, a sensible book, a useful book, a book written in Morgan's inimically light, metaphorical style, but ultimately a book without inspiration. And Morgan never quite forgave the self-consciousness that was the result of his novels being published.

I remember that in one of my earlier novels I was blamed for the number of sudden deaths in it, which were said to amount to forty-four per cent of the fictional population. I took heed, and arranged that characters in subsequent novels should die less frequently and give previous notice where possible by means of illness or some other acceptable device. But I was not inspired to put anything vital in the place of sudden deaths.⁵

Morgan abandoned fiction as his childhood became more distant and as adulthood removed him from its unselfconsciousness. This is partly why he chose not to have *Maurice* published in his lifetime, even in the 1960s when it would have been socially acceptable: he did not want it picked over. More even than *The Longest Journey* it was his personal testament, indeed his swan-song; as long as it stayed in manuscript it could remain so.

But had he 'used up' his childhood? There are other novelists, after all, who have reworked less interesting material more assiduously. Eddie's death, Streatfeild, the man on the downs, Tiddy, none of them was re-created in fiction, and they were only touched on in *Marianne Thornton*. One factor was Lily. A satire on Tonbridge was just acceptable; he could not go further. How she would have laughed if he had 'used' areas of his Life about which she knew and which he might have embroidered for the sake of art. He could not do it: only if Lily had died earlier might Morgan have drawn further on his childhood to use it in fiction. It is no coincidence that Proust's biographer George Painter ended the first volume of his Life (before Proust had begun to write his novel) with the remark that after the death of his father 'Proust realized with vertigo that only his stricken, weakening mother remained to keep him from falling into the past. He stood at last on the edge of the abyss of Time Lost.'[6] When his mother died, Proust could fall into the abyss; Morgan was to have no such dispensation.

Morgan was, as well, nearly impervious to the growing twentieth-century interest in psychoanalysis. When reviewing May Sinclair's *Mary Olivier* in 1919 he described it as being built out of an immense number of details that 'seldom produce a magic glow: indeed, when one looks back at one's own mosaic, it scarcely seems magic enough.'[7] It was as if Lily's no-nonsense streak had produced in Morgan a refusal to fuss, a determination to deprecate, that ultimately inhibited his writing. Of course his mosaic *was* magic; it was just that he would not think of it as such. Thus, when he came to make use of Goldie's words written in his autobiography – 'a happy life, as I look back on it, and the happier because it was followed by such misery. For the time came when I was sent to school'[8] – when Morgan accompanied this quotation by a photograph of Goldie looking most charming and endearing, it did not occur to him to explore the nature of the happiness more closely or why the wide-eyed little boy turned into a slightly crusty young man. Children were not interesting for Morgan, as for so many other people; so he did not want to delve into his own childhood.

Many other reasons have, over the years, been put forward for Morgan's ceasing to write novels, most frequently that the world after the 1914–18 war was a new one that he felt unable to understand with the depth necessary for the novelist's vision. But the overriding reason was well understood by Morgan himself: 'weariness of the only subject that I both can and may treat'. He was bored of writing about heterosexuality, bored of being unhappily homosexual and not being able to write about it; and, as he wrote in a private memoir, 'I have never tried to turn a man into a girl, as Proust did with Albertine, for this seemed derogatory to me as a writer.'[9] Although great art notoriously springs from unhappiness, the source of Morgan's misery was not something that he could – publicly – express. Then, when he was happier, he lacked the impetus to write. His friend Noel Annan was to remark: the reason why he lacked it was 'that people write very often out of unhappiness and that in the 1920s he found a new kind of personal happiness'.[10] This was true, but it was a happiness that was a long time in coming.

Six months after the publication of *A Passage to India* Morgan described himself in his diary as 'famous, wealthy, miserable, physically ugly'. It was how he genuinely viewed himself, for he had no illusions. He *was* famous and wealthy, but neither attribute gave him happiness. Even so he knew he exaggerated. 'I only open this book when my heart aches,' he had written in the September of 1923. Since, in the following year, there were no entries at all between 21 January and 19 August, are we right to conclude that these seven months were happy ones? Certainly they were filled with correcting proofs, anticipating reviews, confronting success.* Yet, at the end of August, Morgan noted, 'too much good luck, and too late. I cannot live up to it.'[11] Something stopped him from enjoying what was by now his. Sassoon, perceptively, had anticipated this. He had remarked two years before:

F. always makes me feel youthful and impetuous, and intellectually clumsy. Why, I don't quite know, for he is a disappointing (and disappointed)

---

* By August 11,000 copies of *A Passage to India* had been sold, 17,000 by the end of the year; 6000 more were sold in the years up to 1936 and the first Penguin edition: of which 300,000 copies were sold by 1943, 600,000 by 1962 and a million copies overall just before Morgan's death in 1970.

creature, in spite of his extraordinarily interesting and brilliant qualities, and the delicate and sympathetic contact of his mind with my own partially polished blunderbuss ... *Something* deters him from writing the good stuff of which he is surely capable. I judge him to be over-sensitive and sexually thwarted. (He once told me that he believed in sexual austerity. But he gives an impression of being sexually starved.) Some driving force is lacking. Yet he stands out as a man of exceptional distinction. I wish he would get really angry with the world. Or fall passionately in love with an Idea.[12]

The anger never would be expressed: at most Morgan one day 'took some pennies out of my pocket and chucked them on the floor ... This is the 8th or 9th time I have lost control in the last three months';[13] nor would the driving force ever be unleashed; but the love for an ideal would be the theme of the second half of his life: the liberal ideal inherited from Clapham, refined by Cambridge and defined throughout the novels, would now become the nub of Morgan's existence. As he remarked in *A Passage to India*, 'life never gives us what we want at the moment that we consider appropriate. Adventures do occur, but not punctually.'[14] His unpunctual adventure was now beginning, just as the other adventure of his novels was ending.

Something that did occur extremely punctually was his and Lily's departure from Weybridge. By a quite extraordinary chance it happened that no sooner had Morgan completed his novelist's life, the one that had been entirely conducted at Harnham from 1904 to 1924, than Aunt Laura's death precipitated their move away from Weybridge to West Hackhurst. The little study overlooking the green which, over twenty years, had lost its water pump and acquired motor cars, the room in which all six novels were written, was now abandoned. It was not an anticipated move; indeed, in the September of 1923 the Forsters had bought the house – although 'the noise of dogs & children has never ceased since we settled to buy, and it is £1075' [£30,000]. But only a year later they were having to decide whether to move, whether to sell one house or the other, or whether to live in both: for West Hackhurst, surrounded by the woods and hills of Surrey, was (and is) remote enough to be deemed a country house; even though once it had been built 'Other houses were built on the brow of that steep southern slope, and others, again, among the pine trees behind, and northward on the chalk barrier of the downs.'[15] Because single landowners owned this part of Surrey and refused to sell it off piecemeal, and because of stringent planning restrictions, the countryside is today as green as it was in the 1920s when the Forsters moved from the more urban Weybridge ten miles to the north.

Eventually they sold Harnham for £1125; yet until the last minute Lily was querulous because now she was not the owner of the house she lived in (Laura had left the lease, of which thirteen years remained, to Morgan). He told Florence, 'she turned round and said she should not feel independent in the house – had been too used to a house of her own to live in some one else's, also said I was "difficult".' Morgan had to assure her that the new house would be hers in every sense except the legal one 'and that I shall live there in the same relationship as I did at Weybridge'.[16] The seventy-year-old Lily thus managed to keep control of both her home and son, in exactly the way that Aziz and his relations believed was every woman's right:

better polygamy almost, than that a woman should die without the joys God has intended her to receive. Wedlock, motherhood, power in the house – for what else is she born, and how can the man who has denied them to her stand up to face her creator and his own on the last day?[17]

Morgan would not deny Lily power in the house; it was, however, agreed that he would now have a room 'in town' to which he would periodically escape or, as it would have been broached to Lily, in which he would sleep over whenever a late engagement precluded the last train to Gomshall, the station for Abinger Hammer, and the walk home from the station. But despite this glimpse of freedom, Morgan still found that 'my daily life has never been so trying'. The main reason was, as he knew, that 'there is no one to fill it emotionally'.[18]

Mohammed had died in the May of 1922 and Morgan went into heartfelt mourning. When he wrote in his diary that 'I want him to tell me that he is dead, and so set me free to make an image of him' he was confessing to a quite recognisable need – to make an image, almost an icon of Mohammed. This he proceeded to do, obsessively brooding on his lover, even though 'I don't want you alive but to know exactly what you were like.' Month after month the remembering and the mourning continued, with Morgan almost detachedly watching his grief. Only after a year could he declare, angrily and realistically, 'half an hour in the bed of the chauffeur who reminds me of Mohammed would cure it. I don't want love'; and by the end of that calendar year, 1923, the one in which Mohammed had not been alive for a single one of its days, he could write in his diary that 'the end of our daily lives together has come'.[19] Sentimentally Morgan was to attribute a far greater influence to his love for Mohammed within the pages of *A Passage to India* than is actually discernible; yet clearly the image of his lover was always at the front of his mind as he wrote, and when he finished writing he laid down his own pen and used Mohammed's pencil to record the fact in his diary.

Later the next year, the young man who looked like el Adl did begin to take some notice of Morgan, who responded as much as he could because 'I had better have such adventures while I can, for there will be no place for them in the pseudo-feudalism of West Hackhurst.'[20] But the chauffeur's wife was jealous and Morgan had to admit that 'She was right (in instinct) to oppose me, and I should be wrong to cause them trouble.'[21] Nevertheless, by the beginning of January 1925, with half the furniture from Harnham taken to West Hackhurst, the chauffeur visited (Lily thought he was going to move furniture). 'The visit was sticky, but friendly & physically superb,' wrote Morgan to his new friend Joe Ackerley, adding that after an hour there was a ring at the bell and the chauffeur's wife and baby appeared. 'A queer ending to my twenty years' sojourn in this suburb'[22] it may have been; at the same time it was a presentiment of the next twenty years at West Hackhurst: they were to be resonant with the kind of sexual activity for which Morgan had longed all the years he had lived at Weybridge. Whereas Harnham was the place to which he unhappily returned when denied the embraces he dreamed of, West Hackhurst was the house to which he returned fulfilled. It was to be almost the refuge where he recovered from the hedonism that had at last become part of his life.

One of the friends Morgan made at this time was Jack Sprott, a university psychologist. In a radio discussion broadcast after Morgan's death Sprott referred to

the change in his general style of life which came about 1925 when he went to live at West Hackhurst. He had by that time met Joe Ackerley, who was a very great friend of his, and I may say, met myself, though that's not particularly important, but we both had a rather unconventional range of friendship, to which we introduced Forster and he enjoyed this very much. And then he broke away from his home to take a flat in Brunswick Square where he could be more independent in the sort of people he saw. He didn't of course desert West Hackhurst by any manner of means.[23]

This was indeed the general tenor of Morgan's life in the years until the Second World War. In the same month as the move from Weybridge he found a small flat near the British Museum in Bloomsbury at 27 Brunswick Square; it belonged to Mrs Marshall, the mother of Ray and Frances who were, like Morgan, close to the Woolfs and the Bells.

At last it had come about: at the age of forty-five Morgan had reached out for independence. He had finally taken the step dreamed of by Lucy Honeychurch twenty years before when she declared, 'I have seen so little of life: one ought to come up to London more – not a cheap ticket like today, but to stop. I might even share a flat for a little with some other girl.' Morgan might, in all the discussions with Lily about whether they should leave West Hackhurst, have made exactly the same kind of remarks; although the latter was unlikely to have echoed the words of Mrs Honeychurch, the character based on her mother, and to have fulminated against typewriters, latchkeys and suffragettes:*

'. . . And call it Duty – when it means that you can't stand your own home! And call it Work – when thousands of men are starving with the competition as it is . . . !'

'I want more independence,' said Lucy lamely; she knew that she wanted something, and independence is a useful cry; we can always say that we have not got it.[24]

It had taken a long time but, finally, Morgan had some freedom, both sexual and domestic: as he wrote in his diary in July 1926, 'Tom [the chauffeur] and my Brunswick Square rooms between them have made me independent of mother.'[25] He had a new circle of friends and acquaintances; he had 'a room of one's own'.

* The peak years of the suffragette movement were 1905–9.

29

Hammersmith

Their life at West Hackhurst was a comfortable one, the elderly matriarch, the middle-aged writer and the ageing maid, attending to each other's needs in a Victorian house, in Edwardian fashion, in a twentieth-century world. Little had changed since Aunt Laura's heyday: the gardener still pottered around the shrubs laid out so carefully in the year of Eddie's death, the drawing-room mirror still reflected the line of the Downs away to the north. In a way the Forsters had come home. Yet they came to a home they should have occupied fifty years before; so that one of the reasons Morgan did not fret about the isolation of life at West Hackhurst was because in some respects he felt he was re-living, re-activating his childhood. This is why he felt so strongly when the Farrers declined to agree to an extension of the lease to cover his lifetime: he felt as if he was being uprooted from Rooksnest all over again. But until he *was* uprooted, by Lily's death, he would continue to extend what roots he could.

When Morgan told Joe Ackerley, ten years after the move, that his mother had given him something Ackerley's mother, and sister, had clearly failed to do, the word 'subsoil' was the key word in his remark:

Though my mother has been intermittently tiresome for the last thirty years, cramped and warped my genius, hindered my career, blocked & buggered up my house, & boycotted my beloved, I have to admit that she has provided a sort of rich subsoil where I have been able to rest and glow.[1]

It was the soil, the earth of West Hackhurst that now made Morgan fulfilled: and thus, as if all the other factors were not enough, even more disinclined to be a novelist. William Plomer wrote

341

that the house's 'Edwardian rhythm, partly sustained by an elderly parlourmaid in uniform, and its atmosphere of leisurely isolation from the workaday world, seemed attuned to [Morgan's] disinclination to grind out book after book in the manner of habitual, professional novelists.'² He could have gone further. Although Morgan wrote about 'eternal West Hackhurst which I connect with no other joy', nevertheless it now partly became the 'childhood and safety'³ that had been symbolised by Rooksnest. His father's house was, he assumed, his final destination.

When, in September 1937, the Farrers agreed to extend the original sixty-year lease for Lily's lifetime, Morgan could not imagine, despite his understanding of the law, that he too would not be able to stay for his lifetime: he could neither imagine nor contemplate leaving. So when he and Lily refused to install running water at the house they refused partly because they did not see the need, but partly because they wanted to annoy their landlord, the landlord who would not agree to give their life the perpetuity they wanted. Visitors to the house remember that if Lily or Morgan felt angry with the Farrers, perhaps because they had suggested a change to a footpath or failed to present a box of plums in the autumn, then Morgan or Agnes would be told to leave the tap running in the kitchen in order to disrupt the supply at the 'big house'. The antiquated water system became a symbol, for both of them, of the reasons why they refused to modernise. They liked being Edwardian, they liked living in Eddie's house just in the way he planned it to be lived in, they liked doing things in the way Aunt Laura had always done them. They wanted, if they chose and not if the Farrers chose, to be able to go on doing so as long as they liked.

Then there was an additional, symbolic, reason why Morgan was quite happy with the one cold tap. In *A Passage to India* he had used the triad of the sky, water and earth as a central image. As Wilfred Stone, one of the most influential Forster critics, a Jungian, remarked in the 1960s about the novel's symbolism:

Water, the source and sustainer of all life, rises to the heavens, falls upon the earth, and ... also symbolizes blood and milk, the basic sustaining and nourishing fluids of life ... Water can drown as well as nourish, but without it there can be no love ... Just as earth, sky and water cooperate briefly for peace and plenty, only to become again antagonists in the hard-baked summer, so the people know only brief seasons of love and understanding. The book is a comment, from a great ironic height, on the stupidity of these divisions . . . it is equally stupid for men to consider themselves above nature . . .[4]

The water symbolism in the novels may have been subconscious,* yet was ever-present; so was the Forsters' obsession with the antiquated nature of the West Hackhurst water supply. When we read, of Mrs Moore, that 'A sudden sense of unity, of kinship with the heavenly bodies, passed into the old woman and out, like water through a tank, leaving a strange freshness behind',[5] we sense that the West Hackhurst water became, for Morgan, a symbol of the disunity with the Farrers. The unforgiving side of his nature, the side of him that had inherited from Marianne the feeling that you did not forgive until, possibly, you asked for the sacrament of the milk at the penultimate moment, that side never forgave the Farrers.

Morgan and Lily repeated the pattern, set at Rooksnest in the 1890s, of stand-offishness: they did not become much involved in village life. Two of the exceptions to this were the occasions in 1934 and 1938 when Morgan wrote the words for local pageants, both of which had music by Ralph Vaughan Williams. After several tableaux re-creating local life over the centuries, the Woodman in the 1934 Abinger Pageant spoke a Forsterian epilogue:

Houses, houses, houses! You came from them and you must go back to them. Houses and bungalows, hotels, restaurants and flats, arterial roads, by-passes, petrol pumps, and pylons – are these going to be England? Are these man's final triumph? Or is there another England, green and eternal, which will outlast them? I cannot tell you, I am only the Woodman, but this land is yours, and you can make it what you will. If you want to ruin our Surrey fields and woodlands it is easy to do, very easy, and if you want to save them they can be saved.[6]

This was one of the major themes of the second half of Morgan's life, as it had been of the first, still obliquely expressed in essays rather than actively in conservationist campaigning. In fact the countryside around Abinger Hammer has, so far, been preserved; it is the countryside around Stevenage, fifty miles to the north-east, that is today under threat – and has been named 'Forster Country'

---

* That Morgan was to some extent aware of the importance of water as a symbol in his life was evidenced by his image of inspiration deriving from the bucket lowered into the subconscious.

in an effort to spread the aura of his ideals over the area. In some ways Morgan was a pioneer conservationist, having foreseen all his life, since 'The Machine Stops'* and since *Howards End*, what would happen during the twentieth century. And on one occasion he made a financial contribution to conservationist efforts. In 1926 he bought a small wood next to West Hackhurst.† It cost £450 [£12,000] and was, he told Masood, 'an awful price to pay for worthless land, but we feared bungalows might be built there, and mother got worried . . . they are building all over the fields behind "Harnham", and the knowledge she has escaped this reconciles her to her residence here.' 'I am quite a good son', Morgan had remarked some months earlier; but, he added sadly, 'this is only recognised intermittently.'[7]

The 1920s thus passed pleasantly by: the occasional book review or article, lunch with Ackerley's artistic and literary friends in London – a comfortable little set of men such as Leo Charlton, Gerald Heard, Raymond Mortimer, Duncan Grant. But it was an exclusive group, that made the outsider feel both embarrassed and excluded. Virginia Woolf used her diary, in the April of 1930, to describe 'the atmosphere of buggery' at Raymond Mortimer's where someone was described as looking 'very pretty in a white suit':

At this the other buggers pricked their ears & became somehow silly. I mean rather giggly & coy. An atmosphere entirely secluded, intimate, & set on one object; all agreed upon the things they liked . . . Morgan became unfamiliar, discussing the beauties of Hilton Young's stepson. 'His skating is magnificent' (then in an undertone deploring some woman's behaviour). This all made on me a tinkling, private, giggling, impression. As if I had gone in to a men's urinal.

What Ackerley had done for Morgan was to make him feel happy about his sexuality; he made him feel normal and unrepentant. And it could only have been *after* getting to know him that Morgan, when asked by Leonard Woolf whether he would like to be 'converted',

---

* In 1928 Morgan's second collection of short stories was published. It consisted of 'The Machine Stops', 'The Point of It', 'Mr Andrews', 'Co-ordination', 'The Story of the Siren' and 'The Eternal Moment'. The volume was to have been called *The Machine Stops* but was at the last moment called *The Eternal Moment*. The change from the polemical, prophesying title to the more philosophical, more sentimental was an indicator of Morgan's frame of mind.
† 'Piney Copse' was left to the National Trust in his will.

responded: '"No" said Morgan, quite definitely. He said he thought Sapphism disgusting: partly from convention, partly because he disliked that women should be independent of men.' (We only have Virginia's not always accurate word that Morgan put forward the latter reason. Far more likely that he found lesbianism disgusting simply because he found women's bodies disgusting, terrifying, the other. He was after all approaching fifty and knew absolutely nothing at all about female sexuality.)

Virginia was fond of Morgan and felt much closer to him than he did to her. Once she noted the names of the six people without whom her life would become meaningless and Morgan was the last, after Leonard, Vanessa, Duncan, Lytton and Clive.[8] She respected him as a writer; she liked his quiet, unaggressive manner, his self-contained quality, his lack of egoism. Three times, in her diary, she compared him, perfectly, to a blue butterfly,[9] and on another occasion described him as 'moth like and evanescent, abjuring fiction';[10] again it was the elusive, flitting, ethereal quality that drew forth this comparison. Only at West Hackhurst did Morgan sit still, rooted; in every other situation he was (again) 'evanescent, piping, elusive, settling exactly *there*'[11] (as does a butterfly but then, as does a butterfly, flying off). Virginia attributed his nature to Lily and told Vanessa that 'his mother is slowly dispatching him, I think – He is limp and damp and milder than the breath of a cow.'[12]

But sexually, away from Lily, Morgan felt far from limp. By 1926, he informed Ackerley, the total number of his lovers (most of them fleeting encounters) had reached eighteen. Although there may seem something rather joyless about the way he carefully counted the fondlings pressed up against the wall, the mutual masturbation in the corner of a park, yet Morgan did not find them so; and some of his lovers were longer-lasting. There was the chauffeur (who seems to have had various names, but was Tom in Morgan's diary) to whom Morgan made love frequently in the spring of 1925: 'Coarseness and tenderness have kissed one another, but imaginative passion, love, doesn't exist in the lower classes. Lust & goodwill – is anything more wanted?'[13] Morgan asked himself rhetorically, knowing that there indeed was more, much more, that he wanted; there was a ship's steward named Frank Vicary whom Morgan had first met in Alexandria; there was Charlie Day, a ship's stoker. With all these young men Morgan chose, unless they were fleeting pick-ups, to become involved in their lives, helping them with money, visiting their families: he wanted the domestic, the caring aspect of sexuality. And yet, by choosing lovers who were intellectually so different from himself, and who were usually bisexual, he denied himself even the possibility of a lasting relationship.

But each time he hoped for continuity. For example, in mid-1926 he began an affair with a policeman named Harry Daley. Daley was twenty-five when they met (all Morgan's lovers were of about the same age) and had led a sexually fulfilled life ever since an Ansell-figure had revealed to him the pleasures of masturbation and had ensured that his future sexual life would be guilt-free: 'Thus began one of the happiest periods of my life; the real beginning of my happy life; the first awakening to knowledge of the pleasure and warmth in other people's bodies and affection.' This was the philosophy that Daley taught Morgan: and there was to be the added coincidence that Daley's Ansell-figure was called Bob Bolton and that through Daley Morgan would meet the lasting love of his life, Bob Buckingham: the similarity in names would, I am sure, prompt Morgan to imbue his own Bob with some of the qualities of Daley's Bob – and, once more, to re-create his childhood, to re-wind his childhood, so to speak, on to a different spool of film.*

Away from West Hackhurst, however, Morgan still felt the outsider, fitting in only partially with Bloomsbury, with Cambridge and with the Hammersmith set for whom, as Daley was to write in the book which gives such a clear portrait of that particular homosexual coterie, 'Hammersmith Broadway was the pleasure centre of this end of London in the same way that Piccadilly Circus was supposed to be for London as a whole.'14 But Morgan did not really enjoy the atmosphere of the 'men's urinal' and wrote in his diary at the end of 1927: 'Now this Cambridge business – Cambridge v. Hammersmith. I really don't like either.' He did not wish, as Ackerley urged, to move his London flat to Hammersmith and when King's, after the success of

---

* Daley's happy, and sexually active, childhood was spent at Lowestoft. His autobiography starts with the sentence: 'In the first decade of the century deep-sea fishermen on the East Coast made a practice of taking their schoolboy sons to sea with them in the summertime.' Descriptions of this happy scene would have been recalled by Morgan when he got to know Benjamin Britten and his lover Peter Pears and stayed with them on the East Coast.

Daley was on close terms with Ackerley and his friends but later felt bitter at being 'taken up' and dropped. *This Small Cloud* (1986), published fifteen years after his death, does not mention them; but is revealing about the Metropolitan Police and homosexual mores of the period.

the Clark Lectures,* offered him a three-year fellowship with the sole stipulation that he live in for six weeks a year, he was very pleased, at once writing to tell Masood in a brief, emotional letter that this success was due partly to him: 'I think of you whenever I am happy because you have done so much to make me happy.'[15] At Cambridge Morgan was, however, made uncomfortable by the 'absence of appropriate work and still more by the knowledge that I couldn't e.g. have Frank to stay, was indeed utterly isolated from the lower classes.'[16]

Cambridge attracts my heart more but depresses me more because as soon as the train slackens at that eel-like platform it's settled who I can know, who not. The two universities disintegrate and degrade their towns. Servile, extortionate manual workers and dons and undergraduates jiggling in their midst.[17]

It was in the first spring of the 1930s that Morgan met the young man who was to be the last and enduring love of his life. Ackerley gave his usual party for the Oxford and Cambridge Boat Race and all the Hammersmith set was there; ever afterwards Morgan was to mark the date, 12 April 1930, as a key anniversary: sometimes favoured friends would be asked to celebrate over dinner.

Bob Buckingham was twenty-eight, slightly older than Morgan's *amours* had been in the past and good-looking in the Antinous/Masood/Mohammed mode (thick, sensual lips, a direct gaze, a stocky, muscular body). He had the additional advantage – and it was the one that ensured the lasting nature of his relationship with Morgan – that he too wanted affection, continuity and loyalty: there is no doubt that if he and Morgan could have married they would have done so. Living together was, however, unthinkable. There was Lily, Bob's job, Morgan's entrenched dislike of making himself noticeable and, too, Bob's bisexuality which made him loath to commit himself entirely to a man. Yet Bob was to be the third great love of Morgan's life, *the* great love of his life he would always consider it, which would last, despite Bob's marriage, until Morgan's death forty years on.

Luckily for the success of the relationship, Morgan, who had given up 27 Brunswick Square at the end of 1928, had just taken new rooms at 26 Brunswick Square. (During 1929 he had had no London base

---

* He gave the eight lectures upon which *Aspects of the Novel* was based between January and March 1927. His fee nearly covered the cost of Piney Copse.

although for three months in the early summer he had rented a couple of rooms from Vanessa Bell at 37 Gordon Square.) Because of his new flat he was able to invite Bob to see him. And so the relationship began, with Morgan hoping that this time it would involve sex *and* love and Buckingham hoping that, through friendship with Morgan, his life might take a new direction, away from the slums of King's Cross where he had been brought up into the new, more literary, more thoughtful world to which he had always aspired.

Just as the relationship with Mohammed had been described as it progressed to Florence, so this with Bob was described both to Ackerley and to Sprott. Sometimes Morgan recognised this need to confide with some dismay: he wrote in his diary about his affair with Tom (the chauffeur), 'Joe Ackerley has been my confidant. It may cause him to despise me.'[18] (Why it should is a mystery: Ackerley himself had many similar affairs, and over his lifetime was far more promiscuous than Morgan. Nor did the latter despise him when his fondness for his dog Queenie superseded all other emotions: although he *was* irritated.)

One of the attractions that Bob held for Morgan was his working-class background and the way he had managed, intelligently and resolutely, to find work for himself as a policeman at a time of high unemployment. Another attraction, apart from his friendliness, good looks and sexual openness, was his sportiness for, as Bob himself put it, 'Morgan, you see, was so unathletic himself that he had a great admiration for athletes . . . He was *scathing* about football and golf – "fools chasing a ball around". But he admired people of intellect who could do athletic things.'[19] Bob rowed, boxed and played football, and yet he was kindly and had a social conscience. We can imagine that he was not unlike Maurice, who 'gave up Saturday golf in order to play football with the youths of the College Settlement in South London, and his Wednesday evenings in order to teach arithmetic and boxing to them.'[20] Morgan would have loved to have the hearty unselfconscious sportiness that Bob, and Maurice, displayed. He would, too, have loved to have the self-esteem that Bob had acquired from having worked hard and earned every penny of what he lived on.

As with Mohammed, the relationship between Bob and Morgan was slow to blossom. From the start Morgan hoped that it would be lasting and was discreet even to Ackerley. Instead of, for example, writing in the tone he had used about one of his pick-ups, 'his carrying on was perfectly extraordinary. It seemed a new sort of intercourse – more like those sea lions we saw diving round their tanks than anything describable in human terms', he told Ackerley, most uncharacteristically, 'I must re-emphasise the need of silence about Bob: the results of his kindness rather disconcerted him I think, and I am most anxious that nothing should get about to vex him.'[21] In other words Morgan, who was by now well over fifty, too well understood his own need for affection and an enduring love, his longing for an affair that would build up a tradition and shared memories, to risk Bob being infuriated and he would not ask for too much too soon; even though, as Morgan admitted to Sprott, 'He is affectionate, hefty, intelligent, enlightened, and *says* he is fond of me, which I do like people to do, and this Bob does often.'

At the beginning of the affair Morgan had two lovers at once (one with the extraordinary name of Surtees Newton whom he had met 'by a certain corner' and who proved 'permanently more than willing'). Then he acquired a third, an ex-policeman named Les; perhaps over-burdened, he soon passed him on to Sprott. But in March 1931, a year after their first meeting, 'Bob fell very violently in liking with me' and for a while seemed to be the fonder for, by June, he was 'in a condition of stability, and as soon as I realise that miracle I should settle down too. We meet every week and are very happy.' That month there was 'a plighting of troths'.

Yet, the same summer, Morgan realised that it was inevitable that a twenty-three-year-old nurse named May Hockey would one day marry Bob. Part of him minded a great deal; part of him was genuinely convinced that 'he is devoted to me and won't give up . . . whatever happens we shall never part.'[22] And so it turned out. For the next year Bob was as devoted and as possessive towards Morgan as he could ever have wished for; so that 1931–2 was the happiest year that he had ever known, filled with loving companionship and the guiltless sex that Morgan had learnt from Harry Daley and continued with Bob. For sex there certainly was.

When Nick Furbank wrote his biography of Morgan in the late 1970s he was loath to elaborate upon Bob and Morgan's sexual relationship and even quoted Bob telling May, as Furbank admitted 'somewhat implausibly, that he had never even known that Forster was homosexual' and May never having 'thought of the friendship with Bob as a sexual one'.[23] It is, however, *just* possible that May either did not know, or successfully deluded herself, about the sexual nature of her husband's affair with Morgan; while for Bob it was clearly easier to deny any such thing than to endure what he might in old age have thought of as an embarrassing revelation. That Morgan and Bob were definitely lovers is clear from the intimacy of their letters, from their loving pose in photographs, and from other details such as Morgan reassuring Bob that he did not have venereal disease. Usually, however, his letters to Bob were relatively circumspect in case May were to read them. It was to Ackerley that he wrote in December 1933, when he and Bob had been 'violently in liking' for well over two years, that a doctor he had consulted 'seemed quite genuine in his disgust, and added that this sort of thing isn't natural and that nature takes it out of you somehow if you go against her'.[24]

The year before, in August, the calm of Morgan's life had been very much shaken. Goldie had died after an operation; at the memorial service Bob compounded Morgan's sadness by telling him that May was pregnant. The fact that Brunswick Square was almost certainly where the conception happened aggravated Morgan's anger; and he was deeply jealous that the spilled seed, the misplaced seed, would bind May ever more closely to Bob and not himself. For a few months Morgan, who had enjoyed the love and security of which he had always dreamed for hardly more than a year, was furious and bitter, not bothering to disguise his feelings in front of Bob's (now) wife and telling all his friends how hurtful 'Nurse Maisey' was; later he wrote that during this winter '[I] pretended I should kill myself'.[25]

The situation was eased by the birth of a boy named Robert Morgan in the spring of 1933;* and to May's enormous and enduring credit she and Morgan started to become friends. As he began to reach towards sixty and she began slowly to fulfil some of the mothering function of the by now nearly eighty-year-old Lily, the two began the friendship that was to last until the end of Morgan's life. Subtly, and charmingly, May managed to avoid destroying the relationship between the two men: and to introduce herself into the magic circle. As the years passed Morgan played the part of lover, best friend, brother and grandfather rolled into one. The Buckinghams decided to have no more children; and by the time their son had his own children, Morgan, and they,

---

* Mohammed's baby son, who only lived for a short while, had also been given Morgan as a second name; Masood's sons were not, although Morgan's closeness to them was made explicit by his being their guardian. Frank Vicary's baby, too, was called Edward Morgan.

had all but convinced themselves that he was their grandfather; the relationship between the elderly bachelor and the family was so close that an outsider would not have known that they were not related; the domestic intimacy for which Morgan had longed all his life had become his.

It was not, of course, the intimacy of a marriage, whether homosexual or heterosexual. But it was as close as Morgan would ever get to one, and was even closer than the symbiosis that had for so long existed between him and Lily since it involved intimacies, both physical and intellectual, that would never exist between a mother and son. Morgan had long known that the true intimacy of marriage would not be his: he was therefore perfectly content with the portion of it that he enjoyed with Bob, and in this respect he was at one with Fielding in *A Passage to India*:

'I shall not really be intimate with this fellow,' Fielding thought, and then 'nor with anyone.' That was the corollary. And he had to confess that he really didn't mind, that he was content to help people, and like them as long as they didn't object, and if they objected pass on serenely. Experience can do much, and all that he had learned in England and Europe was an assistance to him, and helped him towards clarity, but clarity prevented him from experiencing something else.[26]

The description reminds one of Virginia Woolf's remark about Morgan having 'a razor edge to his mind':[27] it was his clarity that kept him from true intimacy. If he, like Fielding, had been shown photographs of Aziz's dead wife he would have 'wished that he too could be carried away on waves of emotion'; he, too, in some curious way felt that he 'had no roots among his own people'. When Fielding finally does marry he turns out to be 'not quite happy about his marriage'. Morgan, in the quasi-marriage he had achieved with Bob, found exactly what he wanted. He avoided what he saw as the claustrophobic side of marriage; he avoided ownership, power struggle, the death of passion, everything that Adela had subconsciously worried about before the episode of the caves; above all, by binding himself to someone working-class, which he would not have done in a conventional marriage, he avoided the fate of Fielding who 'had thrown in his lot with Anglo-India [and by corollary suburban England] by marrying a countrywoman, and he was acquiring some of its limitations, and already felt surprise at his own past heroism'.[28]

'I am happier now than ever in my life,' wrote Morgan in his locked diary in 1934, hoping 'that if anyone reads this book he will get to this'.[29] Earlier he had written much the same thing in his commonplace book: 'From 51 to 53 I have been happy, and would like to remind others that their turn can come too. It is the only message worth giving.' In 1936, when illness made him miserable, he comforted himself with the thought that it was 'nothing compared to the emotional misery from which I am now free'. (He added, 'but for the fear of war I should be cheerful.'[30]) Morgan may have been a successful novelist; he may have been a friend to some of the most interesting people of his day; he may have been acquiring a growing reputation as a commentator and critic. To him none of this was significant. What mattered was that he had found enduring love. Now he was certain both of his own and of Bob's feelings.

Soon, as the months passed, this certainty created something else he had always wanted: a shared past. After Morgan's life had been closely involved with every aspect of Bob's for two or three years there was no going back: they were like Henry and Margaret who, at the end of *Howards End*, realise that 'they never could be parted because their love was rooted in common things . . . their salvation was lying round them – the past sanctifying the present . . . The inner life had paid.' This, to Morgan, was deep, inexpressible happiness; and his inner life had indeed paid. He was achieving continuity, the kind of continuity provided by the Howards End wych-elm. It was, as Morgan himself wanted so much to be, 'neither warrior, nor lover, nor god; in none of these roles do the English excel. It was a comrade, bending over the house, strength and adventure in its roots, but in its utmost fingers tenderness.'[31]

30

Shepherd's Bush

In the June of 1935 Morgan dined with the Woolfs. Virginia remarked, 'he cant get on with "Bloomsbury" & feels, I guess, unattached, & thus takes on public work, which depresses him.'[1] Depression about his public life may have been Morgan's dominant emotion that evening; overall he enjoyed what he had taken on (and never wanted, in any case, to be more attached to Bloomsbury than he was). For it was now, in the middle years of the 1930s, when Morgan was in his mid-fifties, that his life took a new direction unacknowledged by Virginia. Hers would take as it were a posthumous new direction when, with the publication of her letters and diaries, she began to speak for women in a way she could not have anticipated. But it was at this time that Morgan began to speak for humanity. His clear insights, his compassion, his accessibility and his direct, unaffected tone of voice – they all coalesced with his beautiful prose style and began to create a new Morgan, the Morgan of the final third of his life, whom I privately (because it is rather an unappealing word) think of as Morgan the sage.

A Passage to India had been a rare example of a novel that reached all types of readers, neither too lowbrow nor too highbrow. At the same time, as Rebecca West observed, it had 'universal interest' as a result of Morgan's 'insatiable will to understand'.[2] It was for this reason that it became a best-seller, and has remained one; so that when Morgan wrote anything else people read it with the quickening of interest that always does occur if one reads something by a writer one has previously admired. The simple, direct style, the sensible insights began to reach an increasingly large audience: the move from Harnham may have coincided (or was it not mere coincidence?) with the end of Morgan's fiction; the move to West Hackhurst marked the beginning of his new career as a highly respected journalist and broadcaster – and symbol of liberal values.

Liberalism was recognised by most readers as the central theme of *A Passage to India*: liberalism versus imperialism, that old contrast that had been part of Morgan's life since Tonbridge days and that had permeated it ever after. Since 'The Story of a Panic', since *A Room with a View*, since *Howards End* ('"Imperialism always had been one of her difficulties"'[3] reflects Margaret Schlegel), Morgan had been writing about the individual imagination set against the realities of nature and of society: and in his last novel, which is the nearest he ever came to writing political fiction, he evoked the former as the liberal conscience on the broader, social spectrum of India. He asked the question, who shall inherit the earth? – just as in *Howards End* he had asked, who shall inherit England? The answer he gave was a gloomy one, that a solution would never be possible within a political, illiberal structure. '"This picnic is nothing to do with English or Indians"' says Aziz; '"it is an expedition of friends."'[4]

Imperialists did not go on picnics, nor, we can be sure, did Lily; nevertheless, Morgan had voluntarily confined himself to a world which did not go on them. Yet, in some curious way, as he was now beginning to realise, this dualism in his life would be exactly what would propel him towards ever-increasing fame. He himself embodied the liberal dilemma. The reason why people were to listen to Morgan was that he did not now eat bread and cheese beside streams, did not himself move in Adela's thoughtful circles. He was a liberal, but one who continued to eat beef and turnips off family silver with the curtains partly drawn to save the carpet from the sun. The British public were to listen to him in a way they would not listen to the 'Radical out and out'.[5] Morgan had brought liberal values to suburbia and it is this for which he would be famous. He did not choose or want the role of sage: it crept up on him. As Stephen Spender was to observe:

His presence at Congresses of the Intellectuals during the anti-fascist period, and that of young English poets, was an exceptional action produced by exceptional times – like lions walking the streets of Rome on the night preceding the Ides of March. The artist had become de-natured by apocalyptic events.[6]

Reluctant as Morgan had been, initially, to be de-natured, his strong sense of loyalty and commitment to liberal values thrust him into political engagement in a way that he once would have thought quite impossible. He broadcast on the BBC, attracting vast audiences. He wrote articles, sat on committees, attended congresses and signed letters on a whole range of subjects of concern to the liberal conscience – individual liberty, censorship, penal reform and, above all, the rise of fascism. He became someone who could be relied upon to support a liberal cause, and spoke out against the banning of books which offended sexual proprieties such as Radclyffe Hall's *The Well of Loneliness* (1928) or James Hanley's *Boy* (1931). In 1934 he was asked to be the first President of the National Council for Civil Liberties, and in 1942 held that post once more.

The reason why Morgan's writing at this period had so much influence on the British public was that it was not political, it was not rhetorical, it merely expressed the views of someone with whom average readers could identify, yet did so in a manner more intelligent and more humane than was usual. One of the reasons for Morgan's uniqueness as a commentator is and always has been that he speaks to all of us – and even his contemporary readers recognised this.

At the same time he understood the other, the outsider. One or two of his essays of this period are, in some respects, *Maurice* rewritten. 'Jew-Consciousness', for example, begins by describing the two preparatory schools he had attended (the truth, that he had attended the second for only two weeks, would not have allowed him to make his point). In one school it was held to be a disgrace to have a sister, in the other to have a mother.

These preparatory schools prepared me for life better than I realized, for having passed through two imbecile societies, a sister-conscious and a mother-conscious, I am now invited to enter a third. I am asked to consider whether the people I meet and talk about are or are not Jews, and to form no opinion on them until this fundamental point has been settled. What revolting tosh![7]

Having been a Gentile at his first school and a Jew at his second, Morgan went on to say, he knew what he was talking about. In truth it went deeper than this. For various reasons and in various ways he had been a Jew all his life.

Of course, just as there were many readers who could never understand that depth and insight can be cloaked with lightness of touch and irony (how *can* a great novel start with the sentence 'One may as well begin with Helen's letter to her sister'?[8]), so there were readers who could not think of the 'tea-tabling' Morgan as a great liberal thinker; Christopher Isherwood, whose phrase this was, was aware of many people's ignorance when he evoked Morgan as 'the anti-heroic hero' whose 'books and what they stand for are all that is truly worth saving from Hitler; and the vast majority of people on this island aren't even aware that he exists.'9 In another book one of Isherwood's characters discovers the reason:

The whole of Forster's technique is based on the tea-table: instead of trying to screw all his scenes up to the highest possible pitch, he tones them down until they sound like mothers'-meeting gossip . . . In fact, there's actually *less* emphasis laid on the big scenes than on the unimportant ones: that's what's so utterly terrific. It's the completely new kind of accentuation – like a person talking a different language . . .10

Morgan was aware of this technical hindrance to extending his audience. He noted in his commonplace book one day in 1940, having been reading Lord Acton's *The Study of History*, 'ignoring social variety, neglectful of psychology, he appears to this generation as an old man lecturing in a cap and gown;' and he concluded that his own duty was plain enough: 'to talk this late nineteen century stuff with a twenty century voice, and not be shoved out of believing in intellectual honesty and in the individual'.11 He was not afraid of tearing off the cap and gown in the face of accepted certainties, but at the same time he did not seek to replace one set of certainties with another.

When, in June 1939, writing about life 'Post-Munich', Morgan asked the question 'The decade being tragic, should not our way of living correspond?' and concluded 'On the Thursday I returned to the country, and found satisfaction there in a chicken run which I had helped build earlier in the week'; or when, three months later, he implied in 'They hold their Tongues' that Britain's plight was partly due to those 'who have gagged their countrymen for their country's sake' but was also due to 'us, the tongue-holders'12 who did not speak out; in instances like these he was neither being 'unpatriotic' nor reneging on liberal values, he was putting the all-round point of view – in a way that Lord Acton did not. He wrote to Hilton Young, who had criticised the essays: 'The closing down of criticism, and the division of criticism into "responsible" and "illegitimate" are two of the things I am out against, and whose victory would in my judgement hasten the coming of darkness.'13

What Young, and other critics, overlooked was Morgan's Cambridge,

Apostolic, Moorean, liberal insistence on seeing both sides of the question. This was linked to his self-deprecating quality – why do people want to know what *I* think? – and with not being an extrovert. In an essay called 'The Raison d'Être of Criticism in the Arts', first given as a lecture at Harvard in 1947, Morgan mentioned his alleged over-use of the qualifying word 'but' as an exemplar of this:

I have had a university education, you see, and it disposes one to overwork that particular conjunction. It is the strength of the academic mind to be fair and see both sides of a question. It is its weakness to be timid and to suffer from that fear-of-giving-oneself-away disease of which Samuel Butler speaks. The writer of the opposed type, the extrovert, the man who knows what he knows, and likes what he likes, and doesn't care who knows it – he should doubtless be subject to the opposite discipline; he should be criticized because he never uses 'but'; he should be tempted to employ the qualifying clause.[14]

This was the same Morgan who wrote in a war-pamphlet in 1940, in typically low-key tone, 'Much as I long for peace, I cannot see how we are to come to terms with Hitler. For one thing, he never keeps his word, for another he tolerates no way of looking at things except his own.'[15] A fascist dictator was, in his eyes, the person who could not see both sides of the question and who did not use 'but'. As Morgan remarked, famously, in 'What I Believe' in 1939: 'No, I distrust Great Men. They produce a desert of uniformity around them and often a pool of blood too, and I always feel a little man's pleasure when they come a cropper.' (He went on to define the qualities necessary to be a Great Man as 'iron will, personal magnetism, dash, flair, sexlessness';[16] could he have given a fleeting thought to his Tonbridge companion Edmund Ironside who, that year, had become an undisputed Great Man when he was made Chief of the Imperial General Staff?)

When *Abinger Harvest* was published in 1936 David Garnett compared Morgan with three other great writers, all recently deceased, Goldie, Roger Fry and Lytton Strachey.[17] Comparison with the first had especially delighted Morgan. His gloom during the winter of 1932–3 had been partly because of Bob's marriage, but was just as much to do with Goldie's death: he genuinely felt that something irreplaceable had gone for ever. When he later on attributed the lifting of the gloom to Bob's house and baby, he was ignoring the event that had in fact made him happiest during 1933 – the writing of Goldie's biography. It was not for nothing that Virginia wrote to Vanessa in the February of 1933 that 'Morgan also was in high feather, because he's never enjoyed anything so much as writing Goldie's life.'[18] He not only enjoyed it, he discovered a form of exorcism: there is a strong element in it both of identification with his subject and of self-analysis, of his own autobiography.

When, in recent years, after the publication of Goldie's autobiographical notes which formed the basis of the book, Morgan was criticised for leaving out aspects he considered too intimate – Goldie's passionate but unrequited loves for young men, his shoe fetishism – Morgan's strong sense of identification with his subject has been overlooked. How could someone who did not want *Maurice* to be published in his lifetime choose to make public equally intimate aspects of Goldie's life? It was unthinkable. And if the resulting portrait did evoke something of an observer of life rather than a participator, this did not worry Morgan who was, after all, considered this very thing by those who were denied access to *his* hidden depths.

For, even as he grew older, Morgan retained his reluctance to expose himself. *Maurice* was lent to any new friend, almost as a test of friendship, but apart from this one initiation test his homosexuality continued to be concealed from the world. Occasionally this obsession for concealment, which continued even after Lily's death, was the cause of a rather discreditable episode, in particular what Noel Annan has called 'one of his few false steps'[19] when he wrote an article in the *New Statesman* suggesting that a clean-up of homosexuals was not the answer ('where are these people to be cleaned to?') and, since it was unlikely that the death penalty would be re-introduced for homosexuality, the best thing would be if the law were changed but he thought this unlikely to happen. He ended by quoting a judge who had declared that he would be pleased when 'some humane method for dealing with homosexual cases is devised' and concluded that 'in such indications as these there is certainly ground for hope'.[20] His tone was meant to be ironic; but it was far too muted to be apparent as such.

Morgan's critics (Annan labelled them 'Oxford' but they were just as likely to be Leavisites, modernists or people of different political persuasions) at once, but privately, accused him of hypocrisy. Twenty

years later the future author of a biography of the homosexual
scientist Alan Turing attacked Morgan for cowardice and awarded
him the title of Closet Queen of the Century: he felt that Morgan's
refusal to 'come out' was selfish and did nothing to help his fellow
men in the same predicament. 'The publication of *Maurice* could
have been of real practical help to countless gay people . . . Had
he been prepared to come out, it is possible that so prestigious a
figure would have had influence in bringing forward homosexual
law reform.'[21] Hodges labelled him a traitor who had identified
with the oppressor not the oppressed in his refusal to reveal
the truth.

But Morgan had never professed to be courageous, either about
his homosexuality or politically. His 1930s essays, to be collected
in 1951 in *Two Cheers for Democracy*, were through and through
imbued with his own form of detachment. In the first essay, 'The
Menace to Freedom' written in 1935, he began, in typical fashion,
by saying that the menace was not communism or censorship or
conscription but the way our century had forgotten about the
individual and about love. In 'Racial Exercise' in 1939 he pointed
out the absurdity of expecting people to know the names of their
eight great-grandparents. In everything he wrote or said he preached
no received wisdom and rarely became a member of a group.
When, on occasion, he did, he laughed at himself and could never
forget his loathing of authority. Thus in 'Our Deputation' (1939),
a short piece about going to see the Minister, we are not told what
he is going to see the Minister about. It starts in characteristic
deflationary mode: 'Our deputation straggled across Whitehall in
the sleet, harried by taxis upon either flank. It jumped a bank
of slush, slid upon the pavement, caught hands, upsa! and finally
entered the Government Office of its choice.' They ascend a 'huge
and enormous stairway (both adjectives are needed to describe the
architecture)' and sit in a huge and enormous room. When the
Minister arrived,

all rose to their feet. The Minister recoiled as if horror-struck by the
commotion he had created. 'Sit sit down, do please sit sit sit,' he said.
We obeyed. The Minister sat too, supported on either side by important
permanencies belonging to his department.

Having heard them out the Minister asks the Deputation if it 'could
check certain undesirable tendencies . . . The deputation bowed

its head like a flower in a frost, and gazing at my particular bit of the table, I reflected upon the technique which is employed by those in high authority when they desire to administer a snub.'[22]

And so on to the end of the piece which, in so many respects, exemplified Morgan's approach: the domestic detail impinging on a political occasion, the humour, the gentle stabs at pomposity and ostentation, the refusal (even though the article first appeared in the highly politicised *New Statesman & Nation*) to get down to the detail of ideology, creed, stance, approach or opinion.

Isherwood's phrase 'tea-tabling' had become a much-quoted way of referring to Morgan's technique, firmly refuting Katherine Mansfield's famous remark in 1917, 'E. M. Forster never gets any further than warming the teapot. He's a rare fine hand at that. Feel this teapot. Is it not beautifully warm? Yes, but there ain't going to be no tea.'[23] In another way, also, the image perfectly summed up Morgan's life and work. There was the novelist's struggle, protracted over twenty years at Harnham, of expressing true feeling in a manner that would not disturb the teatime ritual: which is why the silver teapot, now wrapped in baize in the flat in Hampstead, is in its way as symbolic as Freud's couch half a mile away in Maresfield Gardens. But also there was the relentless grip of Lily. 'Although it was war-time' recalled Florence Barger's son in his short memoir of Morgan, 'tea was punctiliously served with cucumber sandwiches and cakes on a three-tiered stand by a housemaid called Agnes with a cracked voice but a neat white cap and apron, while the cook, Ruth, hovered in the background.'[24] He was only seven at the time: it was the tea he remembered.

Lily had not changed one bit, in fact she became 'more so'. Morgan asked Sassoon whether he ever had his mother to stay in his flat:

Mine loves being in mine, and fidgets from start to finish, with the result that towards finish she got rheumatism in her leg – would wash up, make beds, although I had arranged for a char. It is very curious, and curiously tiring. Every moment some defect is noted, or improvement suggested, in realms of brushable or breakable objects; dressers are seen to squeak, linoleum to cockle, the scullery blind cord drips into the sink, the looking glass in the bath room hangs too high, don't open that tongue, the bread'll do but not the milk . . .[25]

Did Lily ever know that there were two reasons for the Brunswick Square flat, one to escape her and the other to make love to Bob? If she did, she suppressed the thought into the deepest regions of her subconscious just as she had with Streatfeild; and continued to treat Morgie as the cherished only child attending to his mother's every whim. There is a photograph taken at this time: little more need be said.

Even during the war life was peaceful at West Hackhurst: the only thing that directly disturbed the calm was aeroplanes overhead. 'My plans', Morgan told Isherwood five days after war broke out, 'are i) to live by journalism rather than by government subsidy for propaganda work ii) to give up the Brunswick Square flat and take a cheaper and safer one near Bob iii) to play and make notes on Beethoven Sonatas.'[26] He carried out all three of these plans including, by October 1939, being installed in a flat in Chiswick 'with a lovely view over Turnham Green which reminds me of Harrogate'.[27] Indeed the Beech Lodge, where he had begun *Maurice* while Lily took the waters, did look out on the lawns and trees of the Esplanade in much the same way as the flat at 9 Arlington Park Mansions looked out on the green. But Morgan was never very happy there and used to spend his time, when in London, with Bob and May nearby in Shepherd's Bush.*

The difficulties of wartime travel, and the impossibility of travel abroad, were, for Morgan as for everyone else, acutely painful: 'I have violent longings for fragments of my past – mostly small pieces of scenery abroad, with blurred edges – and I reconstruct partings which I hadn't at the time known would be for so long.'[28] Yet the greatest deprivation was the loss of the freedom to say what one thought. The laws of Defamatory Libel, of Obscene Libel and so on had always hit the writer and the artist; but 'since last September', wrote Morgan in 1940, 'conditions have become much worse, owing to regulations judged necessary for the defence of the realm.' He imagined what the situation would be if Germany won the war, with the press and the universities rigidly controlled. 'The fate of individual writers would be hard. Those of any eminence would be interned or

---

* From 1932 to 1948 they lived at 137 Hartswood Road and from 1948 to 1952 at 129 Wendell Road. When they moved to Coventry in 1952 Morgan was, however, forced to make use of his own flat more often.

shot. This, however painful to themselves, would not, it is true, be a blow to English literature, for by the time writers have become eminent they have usually done their best work.'²⁹

Fear did not, however, stop him from speaking out, even though, again, the manner of the speaking sometimes incurred criticism. In the same 1939 essay that had offended Hilton Young, 'Post-Munich', he asserted that sensitive people see 'with a clearness denied to politicians, that if fascism wins we are done for, and that we must become Fascists to win'. *In the context of the essay* he meant that if the individual Englishman had to defer to state rule in order to defeat Germany, if he could not criticise the government or rail against the Sedition Bill, if he could not be free, then Fascism would have won the day. He did not mean that we should emulate Fascism; indeed, he ended this particular essay by suggesting that the best thing one could do was buy a book or go to a concert or theatre; nor did he mean that everyone should opt out. He was just speaking openly and fearlessly for the liberal intellectual caught up in a time of national emergency.

Similarly, his statement in 1939 that 'if I had to choose between betraying my country and betraying my friend, I hope I should have the guts to betray my country'³⁰ had nothing to do either with Bob Buckingham or his homosexual friends in general or with what have come to be known (although never known to Morgan) as the 'Cambridge spies'. It formed part of an agreement in which Morgan translated his passionate concern for the importance of personal relations and the values of Sophocles' *Antigone* into the foundation of his famous defence of Democracy. He sustained the theme after the war, at the height of the vogue for Planning, when, in the broadcast 'The Challenge of Our Time', he asked the listener, 'when there is a collision of principles would you favour the individual at the expense of the community as I would? Or would you prefer economic justice for all at the expense of personal freedom?'³¹ We know which Morgan preferred.

What mattered above all else was, as ever, love and friendship. The essential prop in Morgan's life was still the continuing love and support of Bob, and the only real crisis he endured during the war years was in the spring of 1943 when Bob applied to join the RAF as an engineer and was also discovered by May to have been having an affair with a girl named Muriel. 'I console,' wrote Morgan after May told him the news (she had 'found her photo & French letters in Bob's uniform'), 'and next have breakdown of grief myself.' Then he tried not to think about it. 'Better to chronicle Ap. 24 dinner of asparagus soup, cold pork, stewed currants [given] to William [Plomer] and Joe [Ackerley] with sherry, two bottles of vin rosé and nearly a bottle of curacoa [sic] drunk. It was grand. After which Bob and I: — felt a bit sick next morning.'[32] In June Bob failed the RAF interview; Muriel married a family friend and promised never to see him again (it is after all fairly unusual for a mistress to compete with both a wife *and* a full-time lover). Yet nothing shook Morgan's possessiveness. 'Don't forget dear', he wrote typically, 'to ring me up Sat between 9.0 and 9.30 as I am v. anxious to hear how the journey went off.'[33]

As to friendship, although he was as shy as ever (Stephen Spender once observed that Morgan's shyness made him actually uncomfortable*) his circle of friends increased with every year that passed. Often he wrote to praise someone's work and a correspondence ensued and then a friendship, as with Isherwood. Or he worked with them, as with Charles Mauron, the translator of *A Passage to India* into French, or Benjamin Britten. Former lovers were rarely forgotten, although if someone chanced to cause Morgan real displeasure he dropped them almost brutally. The real joy of friendship for him was letter-writing: 'to get letters to which one can reply freely is about the only pleasure left in life, seeing people is usually irritating – they will talk & be wise.'[36]

Nor was his modesty ever eroded, even when, as sometimes happened, he was mistaken for someone else.

A young American dining as a guest in Hall was introduced, and delightedly claimed to have read all his books. Asked up to his rooms afterwards, he listened for some time to unexpected topics of conversation, and finally interposed: 'If you are so keen on music, why did you make Captain Hornblower tone-deaf?' Hearing him hailed by someone as 'Morgan' at a London party, an effusive woman hurried over: 'Are you Charles Morgan?' 'No, I'm Morgan Forster.' 'Oh, I'm so sorry: I thought you were the writer.'[37]

It was typical of Morgan, for only he could have done it, that he uttered these words to an interviewer when he was eighty: 'I have been so conceited about myself as a novelist that I had better add that I am quite sure I am not a great novelist.'[38]

---

* They remained friends. Spender, who considered Morgan 'the best English novelist of this century',[34] said that he 'found the effect of knowing Forster was that he became a kind of supplementary conscience tacked on to my own and bringing what I imagine to be Forsterian scruples to bear on my conduct'.[35]

Epilogue

'There are two very great things in my life up to now – yourself and *A Passage to India*,'[1] Morgan told Bob in the 1940s. But the most important thing in his life was Lily. When, two months before the official end of the war, on 11 March 1945, she finally died aged ninety, he felt only grief: the person who had been by his side for the whole of his sixty-six years was no longer there. He told Isherwood: 'I partly died when my mother did.'[2]

He remained tender and courteous to her until the end, sleeping on the landing outside her room during the last night, speaking about their love for each other, then falling into a state of profound, tearful melancholy. Yet almost immediately he began on the task of clearing up, and destroyed almost all Lily's personal papers; those he kept he stuck into a large bound notebook named 'Record of Destruction'. Although the process was undoubtedly cathartic, he came to regret some of his impetuous destruction when writing Marianne's biography ten years later. The extent to which he relied simply on the bound notebook and on the Thornton papers shows how little else remained.

In October Morgan went to a PEN conference in India, in two days flying the distance that had once taken two weeks to cover. It was an interesting visit, filled with people and talks and autographs. Yet on the journey home he wrote in his diary that 'The only first-class thing about me now is my grief.' He added:

I have [been] crying too, thinking of mother, and too often I think of her body going to bits, and of its huddled position in the churchyard . . . I have not given India much, felt a shell. In the Fort at Agra, though, and enjoying myself, I thought that but for her death I could not have come, that it is thus at least her gift to me, and that my remark to her that morning, 'I shall have your love', is not after all macabre. Thanks to her disappearance, and my own fame, I have had this outing at the age of sixty-six.[3]

Thanks to her disappearance! Can it really be that it did not seem consciously to have occurred to Morgan that the presence of Lily had blighted, constricted, restrained his life in a manner that would have been found intolerable by the great majority? That he still felt a good deal of suppressed anger with Lily, an anger that, unlike his grief, had been in no way exorcised, was, however, evident from his reaction to the Farrers' perfectly courteous request that he now leave West Hackhurst. At first he seemed calm about it; then he fell into an irrational fury about the ending of the lease, irrational because of the strength of his feeling and because he had never particularly liked West Hackhurst *as a house* anyway. But its loss became a symbol of what he felt as his rootlessness and he spent 1946 clearing up in a haze of anger and self-righteousness. He wrote in October: 'Bob has had scares in his life but no sorrows. Nothing irreparable. I shall never get my mother again, and I shall never get a home I have known 67 years, for I cannot live 67 years.'[4] The question of where to live seemed almost insignificant compared with having to leave the only ancestral home he had ever known.

Various suggestions were made about the future. In the January of 1946 King's had offered Morgan an honorary fellowship and, hearing that he now had nowhere to live, also offered him 'a large room facing south & fitted with bookshelves'.[5] The room, Morgan was delighted to realise, had been Wedd's. He spent the spring burning more family papers on bonfires, selling and giving away books, sending a lorry-load of things to Dorking market: they fetched £137 (£2500) 'much more than I expected . . . Florence poor darling burst into tears when it went off.'[6] His main preoccupation, he told Plomer, was 'how the cats* are to be killed, how the sundial is to be transported to the church-yard, how one hundred historical books are to be sent to the Inter-allied Library depot.'[7] However, he still wrote the occasional article, for example 'The Challenge of Our Time', again exploring whether the state or the individual should come first, particularly when the individual concerned is a creative artist.

In November Morgan arrived in Cambridge, the plan being that

---

* Morgan and Lily had had cats all their life together. The rather flippant brutality of his tone was only in part a disguise for his sadness. He never had a cat again: without her he could not contemplate it.

he would lodge in Trumpington Street and spend the day in college. At first doubtful if the plan could work ('there is no privacy there & people are always pestering one to be interesting'[8]), he soon began to feel at home and turned down an offer of the Charles Norton Professorship of Poetry at Harvard ('but I am told I may keep off Poetry'[9]). He did, however, make a three-month visit to the United States, giving one or two lectures, travelling through a good deal of the country and attending parties as the honoured guest. In the autumn he had a holiday with Charles Mauron and his wife in the south of France. Then he returned to King's. The tenor of the next twenty-three years was set: King's, travel, friends, articles, a vast correspondence, all the accoutrements of the successful, elder statesman's literary life.

In some ways it was all he could have hoped for: the Morgan who was 'whimsical & vagulous to an extent that frightens me with my own clumsiness & definiteness'[10] (Virginia Woolf) had, whimsically and elusively, slipped, by the back door as it were, into the spot where he should perhaps have found himself forty years before. Physically clumsy he may have been, indefinite about so much in his life (imposing his own views, making a firm decision), but somehow he had manoeuvred himself into the place that, more than any other, was his spiritual home.

Yet some still considered him intolerably elusive, almost cowardly. A younger Kingsman and novelist, Simon Raven, observed that 'A direct question to him would always receive an indirect answer; "yes" and "no" were the least common words in his vocabulary. He equivocated; he withheld; he switched off; he switched on again to take a point out of context; he prevaricated; he giggled and looked knowing; and quite often he sulked.' Raven also castigated Morgan for his idleness; 'he never, on the face of it, had anything at all to do. He was for ever pottering from nowhere in particular to nowhere else . . .'[11] Raven found this especially odd because Morgan still had a perceptive and curious mind and was interested in everything going on around him.

In a sense this was all true; and in a sense it was untrue. What Raven in fact objected to was the age-old grumble: Morgan was elusive, he did not assert himself, he was not a 'joiner', he did not have the qualities that are conventionally thought of as part of being a Great Man. Raven, and others like him, might have been happier had Morgan accepted the offered knighthood in 1949; yet the very fact that he refused it was an inherent part of Raven's complaint. He did not seem to have the same standards as other people; he did not play by the rules as they are conventionally understood.

There were thousands, however, who did understand Morgan's version of the rules, for he became increasingly well known as the years passed. 'I seem to be a Great Man', Ackerley quoted him as saying wearily when, in the 1950s, 'he got more and more bored by the pressure of culture vultures from all over the world, interviewers, biographers, photographers, autograph hunters, sight-seers, and young writers who wanted the best free advice on their voluminous typescripts.' But he never behaved like a Great Man ('iron will, personal magnetism, dash'); as Ackerley wrote:

Few people, I fancy, who may have noticed in recent times an old man carefully descending the steps of the Reform Club and shuffling on his narrow splayed feet along Pall Mall to Trafalgar Square tube station to take a train to his flat in Chiswick Park, an old cloth cap set flat on his untidy head, his stick in one hand and, dangling from the other, a small ancient rucksack containing (could they but see inside) a book or two, a tin of condensed milk, a little butter and bread and an egg for breakfast would have supposed him a wealthy man – or recognised our greatest living novelist, perhaps the greatest living world novelist.[12]

Yet King's accepted and cherished Morgan's individuality, realising what they were lucky enough to have in their midst: a symbol. To the college Morgan was more than a Great Man and more than a Great Novelist. He was civilisation, the liberal intellectual standing on the sidelines watching everyone else going about their business, the representative of values that were, in the twentieth century, being eroded but not yet entirely. It was enough for Cambridge that Morgan *was* and he understood that. In 1952 he declared, when proposing the health of the college at Founder's Feast,

I do not belong here at all. I do nothing here whatsoever. I hold no college office, I attend no committee, I sit on no body, however solid, not even on the Annual Congregation, I co-opt not, neither am I co-opted, I teach not, neither do I think, and even the glory in which I am now arrayed was borrowed from another college for the occasion.[13]

The words are said in a kind of double-irony, like a double-negative: on the surface they appeared light-hearted and ironic and redolent of deeper meaning; in fact they were true, and unrepentantly so. Morgan knew that it was by now enough for him just to be.

As much as in his novels, as much as in his essays, Morgan continued, during the 1950s and 1960s, to represent liberal humanism. The very name E. M. Forster symbolised the importance of personal relations, art, the inner life, the traditions of rural life, the individual; and hostility to the impersonal, the exploitative, the patriarchal, the capitalist and imperialist. Exactly the same themes that had been encapsulated in the novels were now defined by the fact of Morgan's existence, at King's, in the post-war world. In some senses his longevity was another form of statement that the values he upheld would not yet go under.

Nor were the King's years devoid of literary work. In 1948 *The Celestial Omnibus* and *The Eternal Moment* appeared as *Collected Short Stories* and in 1951 the essays written since *Abinger Harvest* in 1936 appeared as *Two Cheers for Democracy*. In 1953 Morgan used his Indian letters and diaries to write *The Hill of Devi* and in 1956 he published *Marianne Thornton*. But the most interesting, and notorious, project of Morgan's last years was his collaboration with Benjamin Britten over *Billy Budd*. Their friendship had begun when, in the spring of 1941, Morgan had broadcast a talk, then reprinted in *The Listener*, about Crabbe. In their American exile Britten and Peter Pears were so stirred by the article that they felt they must come home; and they started work on an opera based on Crabbe's 'Peter Grimes'.

Britten made no secret of having been inspired by Morgan, and the two met in 1942. In 1945 Morgan went to the opera's first night and although he thought the music 'marvellous' wrote to a friend, 'Well might you warn me that the libretto departed from Crabbe. I thought it did so disastrously, and it was so insistent both as narrative and psychology that it imperilled the opera, especially at the end.'[14] Then, three years later, he gave a talk about the poem, the opera and Aldeburgh and concluded by wondering aloud what he would have done if he had written the libretto. The hint was taken and in the spring and summer of 1949 he went to Aldeburgh to work, together with Eric Crozier, on the libretto of *Billy Budd*: the first draft was written during two weeks in March and the revisions were made during August when 'we went through each scene word by word, line by line, testing, strengthening, compressing.'[15]

There were naturally some difficulties, none of them insuperable, for example Morgan was, as always, interested in salvation and Britten in the darker side of the story. When Britten grew irritated with

Morgan and was not as friendly and hospitable as once he had been, Morgan took offence, but there was no rift, only a cooling off. And the opera had been written; it was first performed in December 1951 and became one of the few classics of twentieth-century opera.

Apart from the books and the libretto, and more articles and reviews and lectures, there were a few attempts at short stories, all on homosexual themes,* so that once again they could not be considered for public consumption; the most notable was 'The Other Boat' which completed a story begun in 1913. The opening of this variation on the shipboard romance had been published in 1948 as 'Entrance to an Unwritten Novel'. It described a pubescent called Lionel, and his brothers and sisters, playing on board ship with a 'dusky' boy whom his mother tolerated because 'it doesn't matter on a voyage home. I would never allow it going to India.'[17] In 1957, with Ackerley's help and encouragement, Morgan completed it by showing Lionel, now a member of the Ruling Race, again being 'good to the little Indian' (as Searight had been on board ship in 1912[18]). The tragic ending, after the most erotic scene Morgan ever wrote and preserved ('a tang of sweat spread as he stripped and a muscle thickened up out of gold'[†][19]), was because he 'wanted a catastrophe of the more romantic type where both crash at the height of their powers'.[21] The seventy-eight-year-old Morgan felt an affinity with Lionel and Cocoa. Having noted in his commonplace book that he thought *Howards End* 'my best novel and approaching a very good novel' he remarked that nevertheless he did not care for it because it had 'not a single character in it for whom I care. In *Where Angels* Gino, in *LJ* Stephen, in *R. with V.* Lucy, in *P to I* Aziz . . . and Maurice and Alec . . . and Lionel and Cocoa.'[22]

Stories that Morgan considered second-rate were destroyed; his correspondence could not, alas, be simply thrown in the waste-paper basket, for Morgan's conscience and reliance on friendship would not allow this. He wrote in 1948, during a brief period of depression:

---

* Morgan wrote the first of his erotic short stories in Switzerland in 1911; destroyed all of them in 1922 in 'the belief that they clogged me artistically'[16] (and later rather regretted it); and wrote about a dozen more during the rest of his life. The extant stories were published in *The Life to Come* (1972), and included the wonderful 'The Obelisk' and 'The Classical Annex' (about a museum curator whose son is seduced – eternally – by a statue of a Roman athlete; his fate is not unlike Harold's in 'Albergo Empedocle').

† But cf. the tower of the palace in *A Room with a View* 'which rose out of the lower darkness like a pillar of roughened gold'.[20]

I never finish anything and untidy every room I enter. Masses of unanswered letters, and even when I do answer the envelopes lie about unstamped. If I could settle on a big piece of work . . . I should be happy . . . The letters are a curse. Having lived till 70, having moved about a great deal without being unpleasant, and having on the top of that become famous, I am naturally inundated.[23]

But normally the letters were a pleasure not a chore and the days passed pleasantly and calmly. He wrote in his commonplace book in 1960, rather summing up the pattern of his own life,

Ackerley, Joe, sentence in letter from:
'The days potter by here much the same; sometimes the sad sound of their ticking feet gets into my ears as they disappear into history, carrying nothing in their delicate hands but a yawn.'
Can the day that produced such a sentence be lost?[24]

It could not of course, nor was it for Morgan. But, as he had written in *A Passage to India* years before, 'Most of life is so dull that there is nothing to be said about it, and the books and talk that would describe it as interesting are obliged to exaggerate, in the hope of justifying their own existence.'[25] When Virginia Woolf had killed herself during the war Morgan had written in a letter, 'I think suicide is the best course at the present moment for a pure artist, such as Virginia was. They will have no chance to exercise their art and they cannot be expected to play at hoping for a better state of things to come some day.'[26] Never, throughout his long life, had Morgan considered himself a pure artist. It was the great paradox, the great imponderable, of his life: the writer considered by many to be the greatest novelist of his time never considered himself as such. He did consider himself 'important', for once he wrote in his commonplace book, 'I think though, to be honest, that I am a more important writer than either Fitzgerald or Gray. I have taken more trouble to connect my inner life with the world's, even though I have not been strong enough to stick.' But pure, in the sense of his writing being the most important thing about him, he did not consider he was.

The advantage, for the elderly artist, was that Morgan did not ever feel that his life was over because he did not write any more. He would have liked to write another book after *Marianne Thornton*, but only because he had enjoyed doing it so much, it was exorcism and insight both at the same time; in addition he felt purposeful when he got up in the morning. When Simon Raven complained of Morgan's indolence during the late 1950s and 1960s he might have been more sympathetic towards an old man who would have liked to be occupied but could find no occupation. He also ignored the vast range of activities that *were* part of Morgan's life: staying with friends, going to the theatre and concerts, entertaining visitors, writing letters, reading, listening to the gramophone (he wished he had discovered Mahler earlier).

Morgan continued to write in his commonplace book fairly regularly until 1965 when he was approaching eighty. He went on with his diary as well, although, since the entries after 1949 are still embargoed, it is impossible to know how often or in what detail he wrote in it. In January 1965 he wrote in the commonplace book, 'Mother's Birthday. Her age would be 110. I suppose bones and some muck still remain from her. I have bought her some flowers.' We can imagine him walking slowly and perhaps a little shufflingly down the staircase from his first-floor room at King's, along to the porter's lodge, through the archway and into King's Parade; then crossing the road and going down Saint Edward's Passage or down past St Mary's Church, either route taking him past the small eighteenth-century house in which he had lodged in 1901; and into Market Square where, at the nearest stall, he would have bought some flowers before wending his way back to King's and placing them in a vase, perhaps on the polished table by the window.

After this entry there were only half a dozen more. In April of the same year that Lily would have been one hundred and ten he wrote, 'It is as if there is something inside me inciting me to dawdle and not to concentrate.' Then he noted that the earth originated 4700 million years ago and fossils 600 million years before; these considerations 'help me to concentrate upon what's small and immediate. They compel me to adopt values.'[27] But selective values: in 1969 he accepted the Order of Merit, yet still rejected other honours, true to the tradition of Cambridge men of his background and generation who 'only accepted honours which came after their name, but not before it'.[28]

He had a small stroke at Bob and May's house in Coventry in May 1965 and described his sensations; they included remembering Bob saying '"*Your dear Bob*" – words ever to be remembered.' The final entry in the commonplace book was 11 November 1968: he perhaps planned to write some thoughts about it being fifty years since the first Armistice Day in 1918, but in fact merely noted, quaveringly:

Doubtful whether I shall write more. Have ordered this book (which goes
to College Library)
to go to College Library.
How it rains![29]

It was at King's, in the May of 1970, that Morgan had the stroke
which although not immediately fatal was, as both he and those
around him realised, the final one. He was well enough to go with
Bob to Coventry and there he lay peacefully in bed, in the little
suburban house that was, for him, the last in the line of all the other
suburban houses in his life. Here, very gently and uncomplainingly,
holding May's hand, he relapsed into unconsciousness and died in
the early hours of Sunday morning the 7th of June. 'I do not take
the hour of death too seriously' he had declared ten years before.
'It may scare, it may hurt, it probably ends the individual, but in
comparison to the hours when a man is alive, the hour of death is
almost negligible.'[30]

Acknowledgements

Many people played a part in the writing of *Morgan* and I would like first of all to thank those not mentioned below who helped me domestically, by bothering to answer queries even if the response was, alas, negative, by their interest (either fleeting or heroically sustained over four years), or by supplying me with the photographs: I am very grateful indeed to all these unnamed individuals.

I would also like to thank all those who are listed here, who lent me books or unpublished material, gave me permission to see documents on restricted access, looked something up for me, found out names or addresses, invited me for the night, talked to me about Morgan, or in any other way assisted me in the completion of this book:

Lord Annan, Margaret Ashby, Anthony Atkinson, Mollie Barger, Erasmus Barlow, Harold Baxter, Malcolm van Biervliet, Sue Boase, Lord Bridges, Mark Bridges, Tony Brown, May Buckingham, Andrew Burns, Lionel Carter, Jean Cook, Shirley Corke, Joyce Darling, Clive Dewey, Elizabeth Dupré, Julian Fane, James Fergusson, Nick Furbank, Robert Giroux, Sheila Grant-Duff, Michael Haag, Christopher Harley, Oliver Hawkins, Veronica Hickman, Philip Hoare, Gilbert Hoole, Peggy Jay, Lord Kennet, Francis King, Richard Knolt, Karen Knox, Philippa Lavell, Patrick Libby, Margaret Low, Richard Merz, Roland Merz, Paul Miller, Christopher Moorsom, Kenneth Munro, the late Barry Orchard, Merryck Owen, Peter Parker, Wendy Pearse, Alison Peppé, James Poston, Garry Pownall, John Pulford, Jessica Quirk, Paula Quirk, John Rodenbeck, Tess, Lady Rothschild, Tony Rottenberg, Doc Rowe, Anne Sebba, Miranda Seymour, Roger Shapland, Ann Sieveking, Gunnvor Stallybrass, John Stape, William Streatfeild, E. P. Thompson, H. K. Trivedi, Christopher Wade, Julian Wathen, Mark Wathen, the late Philip Whichelo, Malcolm Williamson, Margaret Wilson, Dan Yergin.

Nor could I have done the research without the efficient assistance of the librarians of the following libraries or archives: British Library;

British Red Cross; Cecil Sharp House; Centre of South Asian Studies, Cambridge; Durham University Library; Greater London Record Office; Heath Library, Hampstead; Humanities Research Center, Austin, Texas; India Office Library; London Library; London School of Economics; Marylebone Reference Library; Minet Library, Clapham; Surrey Record Office; University of Sussex Library; Tonbridge School Library; Trinity College, Cambridge; Trinity College, Oxford; Tunbridge Wells Library; Working Men's College.

But my greatest debt is to King's College, Cambridge. Without the friendliness, courtesy and perfect mix of detachment and involvement of those with whom I came into contact at King's I could not have started this book, or finished it. King's made it plain from the outset that this biography could not be official, authorised or even approved; yet, within these parameters, was continuously helpful. I must also give the Provost and Scholars of King's College, Cambridge my formal thanks for allowing me copyright permission to quote from unpublished Forster material.

Finally, my warmest thanks to those without whom the book genuinely could not have been written: Donald Parry at King's for explaining the copyright situation to me, making me feel just bold enough to begin work, and then reading the manuscript; Michael Halls, Modern Archivist at King's for the first two years, who explained the archive and shared his enormous knowledge and insight; Jacky Cox, his successor, who speedily mastered the archive and gave me all possible advice and friendly help; Ion Trewin and Richard Cohen, his successor, at Hodder & Stoughton, who were impeccable and kindly editors, as was Chuck Elliott at Knopf; and Gill Coleridge, my agent, who gave every kind of valuable help. I am grateful too to Clare Tauben who typed the final draft of the manuscript so expertly and to Belsize Park Pip who did the photocopying for me. But, in the end, it is my husband Chris Beauman who gave me more help than anyone else: his interest never apparently wavered, he read the manuscript at all stages, and he did not flinch from either praise or criticism – both equally important. My eldest son Josh Lacey also made perceptive comments; my middle son William Lacey had the idea for *Morgan* when he read *Where Angels Fear to Tread* and could not find a book on Forster that seemed appropriate; and my youngest son Ned Beauman and two daughters Olivia Lacey and Francesca Beauman 'gave ideas' and were always supportive. I thank them all.

Notes and References

A great deal has been written about Morgan Forster's work. *E. M. Forster: An Annotated Bibliography of Writings about Him* edited by Frederick McDowell, published in 1976, contains 1913 entries; a similar *Guide to Research* by Claude Summers, published in 1991, contains 500 entries that were not listed in McDowell. Hence I could not possibly provide a bibliography of all the books I have looked at: instead I have tried to include a reference to, or quotation from, all the books that have influenced me most, so that these appear in the notes. The same applies to material that is not pure literary criticism directly related to Morgan: I have mentioned in the notes only those books or articles that have been most useful.

Much relevant material is unpublished and I have given as accurate a reference for this as I could, partly because the first two biographies of Morgan had no notes. My policy has been to use primary material rather than to draw on the work of Nick Furbank and Francis King.

Research on the unpublished material has had an unusual quality. The Provost and Scholars of King's College, Cambridge, to whom I am so much indebted, do not allow any photocopying of his papers. Therefore I spent many peaceful hours in the Modern Archive Center at King's, working on manuscripts that were cold from the air-conditioned 'fridge', resting them on a form of foam-rubber platter with heavy bead belts to hold down the pages, copying and copying and copying. There were few constraints, although Morgan's diary post-1949 is embargoed because of the susceptibilities of those still living and so is the manuscript relating his fury at having to leave West Hackhurst.

The discipline of copying certainly helped in my efforts to write an 'inner' biography – there was something very inward-looking about all the hours of copying, the emerging bleary-eyed into the dark of King's Parade for a cup of coffee at the Copper Kettle, the return to the library for another two hours, before it was time to drive south, with Rooksnest on my left, to Hampstead, 'an artistic and thoughtful little suburb of London'[1] where Adela too lived. (In which case, I often thought, she must have seemed a most unlikely bride for Ronny from the start.)

After all the research, all the copying, all the travel, I returned, always, to the novels. Morgan once declared about Sophocles' *Antigone*, 'of all the great tragic utterances that come closest to my heart, that is my central faith.'[2] Of all the great fictional utterances Morgan's – even after four years' work and a lifetime of devotion – remains closest to my heart.

Notes

In an attempt to make the notes as integral a part of the text as possible, I have not abbreviated any names except Morgan's, which becomes EMF; since, for example, Marianne and Lily are called thus in the text I have chosen not to call them MT or ACF (Alice Clara Forster) in the notes.

The library that is most frequently abbreviated in the notes is KCC, King's College, Cambridge. The reference KCC means that the item is among the Forster Papers there. I have not quoted catalogue numbers but the Forster Papers catalogue is ample and clear and the researcher will have no difficulty in tracing items. The names of other libraries are abbreviated after the initial reference, for example DUL for Durham University Library, and catalogue numbers are usually given. If this is not done it is because there are photocopies of the original material at King's College, Cambridge and it is this version I have seen. Some of Morgan's books are abbreviated by a key word, e.g. *Angels* for *Where Angels Fear to Tread*. Other books that are cited frequently are also abbreviated, for example Mary Lago and P. N. Furbank's two-volume selection of Morgan's letters becomes, after the initial reference, *Letters I* or *Letters II*.

If there is more than one reference to the same book or source, and if it is not muddling to do so, the note indicator beside the last reference refers to those preceding it as well. This is to avoid too many note indicators and too many ibids. In the notes I have abandoned op. cit. when possible – for example, *The Longest Journey* is cited in full the first time it is mentioned and abbreviated thereafter to *Journey*.

I have used the most recent Penguin edition of all Morgan's novels except when the Abinger edition is specifically referred to, for example *Journey* Abinger edition. *Journey* refers to the Penguin edition.

When letters have been published they are referred to in *Letters I* or *Letters II*. Unpublished letters (there are about fifteen thousand of them altogether) are fully referenced and given the number assigned to them in the *Calendar of the Letters of E. M. Forster* compiled by Mary Lago (Mansell Publishing 1985), if they are entered there. In this case the number is preceded by a letter referring to the recipient, for example Morgan's first letter to Lily in 1883 is F (for Forster) 304; this is because there are about three hundred other letters to recipients whose name also begins with 'F' such as Fletcher and Ford. If a letter is not entered in the *Calendar* I have given its date, recipient and present-day location. Spellings follow Forster's usage, e.g. Maharajah.

Frontispiece

1 E. M. Forster 'Anonymity' 1925, reprinted in *Two Cheers for Democracy* (1951) Penguin 1965 p 93

Introduction

1 William Plomer *At Home* Jonathan Cape 1958 p 107

2 P. N. Furbank *E. M. Forster: A Life* Volume I Secker & Warburg 1977 p 21

3 E. M. Forster *The Longest Journey* (1907) Penguin 1989 p 24

4 Cf. Frontispiece.

5 'The Enjoyment of English Literature' unpublished lecture Government College, Lahore, 1913 KCC

6 Lytton Strachey *Eminent*

Victorians (1918) Penguin
1986 p 9
7 *The Diary of Virginia Woolf* Volume 1
Hogarth Press 1977 6 November 1919
p 310

Preface

1 *Marylebone Mercury* January 1895
Marylebone Library
2 E. M. Forster *Howards End* (1910)
Penguin 1989 p 23
3 E. M. Forster *The Manuscripts of
Howards End* ed. Oliver Stallybrass,
Edward Arnold 1973 p 4
4 *Howards End* pp 23, 53, 92, 93
5 Father Ronald Knox quoted in John
Betjeman *London's Historic Railway
Stations* John Murray 1972 p 114
6 *Journey* p 63
7 *Selected Letters of E. M. Forster* Volume
II ed. Mary Lago and P. N. Furbank,
Collins 1985 p 172
8 E. M. Forster *A Room with a View*
(1908) Penguin 1990 p 232

Chapter 1   Melcombe Place

1 E. M. Forster *Marianne Thornton*
Edward Arnold 1956 p 250
2 *Room* p 101
3 Henry James *The Portrait of a Lady*
(1881) Oxford University Press 1962 p 1
4 E. M. Forster *Arctic Summer* and other
fiction Edward Arnold 1980 p 2
5 *Room* p 108
6 *The Manuscripts of Howards End* p 3
7 Marianne Thornton to Lily Forster
August 1877 Thornton Papers,
Cambridge University Library
8 Unpublished memoir by Philip
Whichelo in the possession of the author
9 *Marianne Thornton* pp 251, 253
10 *Journey* p 22
11 E. M. Forster *Where Angels Fear to
Tread* (1905) Penguin 1976 p 44
12 *Marianne Thornton* p 254
13 Marianne to Lily 19 February 1878
KCC
14 E. M. Forster *The Locked Journal*
unpublished manuscript KCC p 11
15 *Howards End* p 308
16 *Marianne Thornton* pp 255, 256
17 *Writers at Work*: The Paris Review
Interviews, Mercury Books 1962 p 31,
interview 20 June 1952 with P. N.
Furbank and F. J. H. Haskell
18 E. M. Forster *The Longest Journey*
Abinger edition Edward Arnold 1984
Appendix B 'Uncle Willie' p 294

19 *Journey* p 22
20 Rupert Croft-Cooke *Feasting with
Panthers* W. H. Allen 1967 p 286
21 *Journey* pp 24, 22, 23, 26
22 E. M. Forster *Maurice* (1971) Penguin
1989 p 186
23 Reginald Blomfield *Memoirs of an
Architect* Macmillan 1932 p 35
24 Unpublished memoir about T. E. C.
Streatfeild kindly lent by W. H. C.
Streatfeild
25 *Marianne Thornton* p 249
26 Claire Harman *Sylvia Townsend Warner*
(1989) Minerva 1991 p 5
27 *Marianne Thornton* p 249

Chapter 2   Clapham

1 On the outside of Holy Trinity,
Clapham Common, on the right side as
you face it. With thanks to the Rector's
secretary for information provided.
2 *Dictionary of National Biography*
(*DNB*) entry for Henry Thornton
3 Standish Meacham *Henry Thornton
of Clapham* Harvard University Press
1964 p 2
4 Philip Gardner ed. *Commonplace Book*
(1978) Wildwood House 1988 p 187
5 Meacham op. cit. p 29
6 *DNB*
7 William Cowper 'In Memory of the
late John Thornton Esq November
1790' *The Works of William Cowper*
Volume X Baldwin & Cradock
1837 p 31
8 *Two Cheers* p 198
9 E. M. Forster *Abinger Harvest*
(1936) Penguin 1974 p 268 and *Two
Cheers* p 199
10 *Angels* p 152
11 *Marianne Thornton* pp 75, 175–7, 192,
264, 287–8
12 *Abinger Harvest* p 272
13 *Marianne Thornton* pp 16, 19, 80, 163,
211, 145, 162–3
14 Unpublished manuscript KCC
'Visit to Stisted' 8 November
1910
15 *Marianne Thornton* pp 250, 251,
249, 250
16 Louisa Whichelo to Lily
undated *Record of Destruction*
book: '*Record* of letters,
books etc. destroyed by
me after my mother's death
1945' KCC
17 *Marianne Thornton* pp 252, 251,
253

Chapter 3   Rooksnest

1 T. H. Farrer to T. C. Farrer, Farrer Papers Surrey Record Office 2 November 1880
2 *Marianne Thornton* p 258
3 Lily to Marianne 1 January 1883 KCC
4 Lily to Maimie 1882 *Record of Destruction* p 20 KCC
5 *Marianne Thornton* p 258
6 Lily to unknown correspondent undated *Record of Destruction* p 12 KCC
7 Marianne to Lily 1880s ibid.
8 *DNB*
9 *Marianne Thornton* pp 287, 289
10 *Howards End* p 263
11 Unpublished paper 'Memory' early 1930s KCC
12 *Marianne Thornton* p 269
13 E. M. Forster *Howards End* Abinger edition Edward Arnold 1973 pp 341–4
14 Unpublished manuscript of A Presidential Address to the Cambridge Humanists Summer 1959 KCC, later reprinted in the *Bulletin of the University Humanist Federation no. 11* Spring 1963
15 Louisa Whichelo to Lily 18 March 1893 *Record of Destruction* p 20
16 *Marianne Thornton* pp 274, 269
17 *Howards End* p 93
18 John Ruskin *The Crown of Wild Olive* (1866) quoted Quentin Bell *Ruskin* Oliver & Boyd 1963 p 45
19 *Howards End* p 62
20 Kenneth Clark *Ruskin Today* Penguin 1967 p 269
21 Quoted Jan Marsh *Back to the Land* Quartet 1982 p 6
22 *Howards End* p 263
23 E. M. Forster *A Passage to India* (1924) Penguin 1989 p 303

Chapter 4   Kent House

1 *Journey* p 24, cf. Introduction note 3
2 *Howards End* Abinger edition p 349
3 *Locked Journal* p 145
4 Quoted in Leonée Ormond *J. M. Barrie* Scottish Academic Press 1987 p 101
5 *Howards End* Abinger edition p 350
6 E. M. Forster *Collected Short Stories* (1947) Penguin 1987 pp 31, 33
7 E. M. Forster *The Life to Come* (1972) Penguin 1989 p 35
8 *Howards End* Abinger edition p 350
9 Neville Braybrooke *Seeds in the Wind* Hutchinson 1989 p 66
10 *Locked Journal* pp 144, 146

11 *Howards End* Abinger edition p 350
12 *Locked Journal* p 145
13 *Selected Letters of E. M. Forster* Volume I ed. Mary Lago and P. N. Furbank Collins 1983 p 6
14 ibid. p 11
15 José Harris *Beveridge* Oxford University Press 1977 p 19
16 *Locked Journal* p 147
17 Undated letter EMF to Lily headed 'The Misadventure' by EMF later on, F315 KCC
18 Undated letter Lily to EMF headed 'Wednesday' KCC
19 Lily to EMF 19 March 1891 KCC
20 *Locked Journal* p 147
21 Margaret Ashby *Forster Country* Flaunden Press 1991 p 89
22 Harris op. cit. p 19
23 William Beveridge to his sister Laetitia 10 July 1892 BP IIa Beveridge Papers London School of Economics
24 EMF to Lily 10 May 1893 F329 KCC
25 EMF to Lily May 1893 F331 KCC
26 *Letters I* p 9
27 Louisa Whichelo to Lily 18 March 1893 *Record of Destruction* p 20 KCC
28 *Howards End* Abinger edition p 351
29 Ashby op. cit. p 98
30 'Memory' KCC
31 *Howards End* Abinger edition p 341
32 Louisa to Lily 18 March 1893 KCC
33 *Two Cheers* p 67
34 *Howards End* Abinger edition p 347
35 *Howards End* p 115
36 *Two Cheers* p 68
37 *Commonplace Book* p 215

Chapter 5   Tonbridge

1 *Howards End* Abinger edition p 350
2 *Journey* pp 42, 43
3 *Arctic Summer* p 15
4 EMF to Lily F333 KCC
5 E. M. Forster *Goldsworthy Lowes Dickinson* (1934) Abinger edition Edward Arnold 1973 p 19
6 *Arctic Summer* pp 8, 19
7 *Journey* p 21
8 Septimus Rivington *The History of Tonbridge School* Rivington's 1898 p 316
9 *Journey* pp 159, 43
10 Rivington op. cit. p 329
11 Patrick Wilkinson 'Forster and King's' in *Aspects of E. M. Forster* ed. Oliver Stallybrass, Edward Arnold 1969 p 16
12 *Commonplace Book* p 198
13 *Letters I* p 25
14 EMF's 1956 introduction to a new

edition of *The Greek Way of Life*, *Dickinson* p 213

15 Francis King *E. M. Forster* Thames & Hudson 1978 p 17

16 *Spectator* 27 July 1934

17 E. M. Forster introduction to *The Longest Journey* 1960, Abinger edition p lxviii

18 E. M. Forster letter to Michael McCrum Tonbridge School Archives 12 August 1965

19 *Spectator* 28 July 1933

20 Rivington op. cit. p 300

21 *Journey* Abinger edition p lxix, EMF's 1960 introduction

22 Interview with Gilbert Hoole 4 May 1990

23 *Marianne Thornton* p 27

24 Unpublished report by Martin Perry 1991 in possession of the author

25 H. Sanderson Furniss *Memories of Sixty Years* Methuen 1931 p 127

26 *The Times* 16 August 1916

27 *Oxford Magazine* quoted in *Tonbridge School and the Great War* Whitefriars Press 1923 p 326

28 Pocket Diary 17 July 1898 KCC

29 *Arctic Summer* p 12

30 Pocket Diary 22 September 1898 KCC

31 *Arctic Summer* pp 7, 26, 6, 26

Chapter 6   To Cambridge

1 Rupert Croft-Cooke *The Altar in the Loft* Putnam 1960 p 42

2 Carolyn Heilbrun ed. *Lady Ottoline's Album* Michael Joseph 1976 p 65 and *The Times Literary Supplement* 18 February 1977 p 178

3 *Room* pp 142, 50

4 Cf. Chapter 5 note 31

5 *Writers at Work* p 30

6 Braybrooke op. cit. p 69

7 *Passage* p 316

8 *Arctic Summer* p 26

9 Virginia Woolf to Margaret Llewelyn Davies 31 August 1915 *The Letters of Virginia Woolf* Volume 2 ed. N. Nicolson Hogarth Press 1976 p 63

10 Address to the Cambridge Humanists

11 *Ruskin Today* p 237

12 EMF unpublished diary of his trip to Normandy 14, 23, 26 April 1895 KCC

13 Richard Ellmann *Oscar Wilde* Hamish Hamilton 1987 p 434

14 *Maurice* p 138

15 *Journey* Abinger edition p lxviii

16 *Letters I* p 13

17 Gwen Raverat *Period Piece* (1952) Faber & Faber 1977 p 207

18 *Journey* p 58

19 *The Listener* 11 October 1956, reprinted *Dickinson* p 205

20 Unpublished manuscript of *Malcolm Darling* by Clive Dewey, Chapter 16 p 7. With grateful thanks to the author.

21 *Journey* p 42

22 John Sheppard unpublished Apostles paper 'King's or Trinity' 5 December 1903 KCC

23 *Journey* pp 63, 112, 5, cf. Preface note 6

24 *Maurice* p 31

25 *Letters I* p 16

26 *Howards End* p 176

27 *Letters I* p 16

28 Julian Fane letter to the author 25 March 1991

29 *Letters I* p 16

30 EMF 'Notes on the English Character' 1926 *Abinger Harvest* p 15 (where it is erroneously dated as 1920)

31 Virginia Woolf 'A Sketch of the Past' 1939 in *Moments of Being* ed. J. Schulkind, Chatto & Windus 1976 p 153

32 Evelyn Waugh *Brideshead Revisited* (1945) Penguin 1962 pp 27–8

33 *Journey* p 58

Chapter 7   King's

1 *Locked Journal* 19 July 1912 p 29

2 Pocket Diary 11 July 1898 KCC

3 Richard Cobb *Still Life* Hogarth Press 1984 p 11

4 *Arctic Summer* p 10

5 Article by Bernard Levin in *The Times* 23 October 1971

6 Pocket Diary 9–15 March 1898 KCC

7 Wilkinson in *Aspects of E. M. Forster* p 16

8 *Two Cheers* p 76

9 Sophocles *The Theban Plays* trans. E. F. Watling, Penguin 1965 Act II p 131

10 Theocritus *The Idylls* trans. Robert Wells, Penguin 1989 introduction p 29

11 *Journey* pp 161, 58

12 E. Wingfield-Stratford *Before the Lamps Went Out* Hodder & Stoughton 1945 p 156

13 *Dickinson* p 25

14 Wingfield-Stratford op. cit. p 179

15 *Dickinson* p 61

16 *The Listener* 1 January 1959 p 11

17 *Journey* Abinger edition p 300

18 Christopher Morris *A Short History of King's* Cambridge 1989 p 66

19 *Dickinson* p 22

20 *Maurice* p 32
21 *Journey* p 5
22 EMF to Lily F348 KCC
23 *Letters I* p 36
24 *Basileon* 1 June 1900 KCC
25 *Letters I* p 38
26 *Dickinson* p 29
27 Address to the Cambridge Humanists
28 Leonard Woolf *Sowing*: an autobiography of the years 1880–1904 Hogarth Press 1961 p 148
29 *Journey* p 3, 5, 6
30 J. H. Stape *An E. M. Forster Chronology* manuscript p 37. With grateful thanks to the author.
31 Paul Levy *Moore*: G. E. Moore and the Cambridge Apostles (1979) Papermac 1989 p 197. The details about the Apostles come from this book.
32 J. M. Keynes 'My Early Beliefs' in *Two Memoirs* Hart-Davis 1949 p 81, first read to the Memoir Club September 1938
33 Plomer op. cit. pp 107–8 and cf. Introduction note 1
34 S. P. Rosenbaum *Victorian Bloomsbury* Macmillan 1987 p 128
35 *Letters I* p 39
36 EMF talk given in the 1920s to the Memoir Club, *Journey* Abinger edition p 301
37 *Arctic Summer* pp 66, 64
38 Keynes op. cit. p 83

Chapter 8   To Italy

1 EMF to William Plomer, Plomer Papers Durham University Library brown envelope XX item 5, memo for 23 August 1960
2 *Maurice* p 93
3 *Aspects of E. M. Forster* p 16
4 *Letters I* p 55
5 *Passage* p 303
6 Address to the Cambridge Humanists
7 *Two Cheers* p 75
8 S. Gorley Putt 'A Packet of Bloomsbury Letters: the Forgotten H. O. Meredith' *Encounter* November 1982 pp 77–8
9 Furbank op. cit. p 98 and letter to author 19 July 1991
10 *Locked Journal* 9 October 1910 p 12
11 Lily to EMF undated but on the back EMF has written 'Tunbridge Wells period' and on front 'interference over HOM' KCC
12 Memo for 23 August 1960 Plomer Papers
13 Willie Forster to his sister Laura Forster August 1900

Record of Destruction p 3 KCC
14 *Angels* pp 70, 31, 43, 70
15 EMF to Wedd 1 December 1901 Wilfred Stone *The Cave and The Mountain* Oxford University Press 1966 p 401
16 *Letters I* p 45
17 EMF to Lily 21 August 1901 F374 KCC
18 *Italian Diary* for 3–28 October, 3 October 1901 KCC
19 *Letters I* p 47
20 *Angels* p 160
21 *Italian Diary* 10 October 1901
22 Anon. (Gladys Huntingdon) *Madame Solario* (1956) Penguin 1986 p 15
23 *Italian Diary* 10 October 1901
24 *Madame Solario* p 15
25 *Angels* p 132
26 *Italian Diary* 8, 11 and 20 October 1901
27 *Room* p 31
28 EMF to Dent 13 May 1902 D262 KCC
29 *Italian Diary* 23 October 1901
30 *Room* pp 25, 27
31 *Italian Diary* 27 & 28 October 1901

Chapter 9   Florence

1 E. M. Forster *The Lucy Novels*: Early Sketches for *A Room with a View* called 'Old Lucy' and 'New Lucy' Abinger edition Edward Arnold 1977 p 18
2 Cf. Chapter 2 note 17
3 Jane Austen *Emma* (1816) Penguin 1985 p 60
4 Marianne to Lily June 1878 CUL
5 Address to the Cambridge Humanists
6 Cf. Chapter 4 note 1
7 Louisa to Lily *Record of Destruction* p 25 KCC
8 *Locked Journal* p 145
9 *Room* p 127
10 *Letters I* p 48
11 *Arctic Summer* p 1
12 *Room* p 35
13 EMF to Wedd 1 December 1901 Stone op. cit. p 401
14 *idem*
15 Lily to Louisa 1 December, 3 November 1901 KCC
16 *Letters I* p 51
17 *Life to Come* pp 32, 35
18 *Room* p 55
19 *Letters I* p 51
20 EMF to Dickinson 25 March 1902 D299 KCC
21 *Lucy Novels* pp 45, 67, 11
22 *Letters I* p 52
23 EMF to Dickinson *c.* February 1902 D297 KCC

24 E. M. Forster *Where Angels Fear to Tread* Abinger edition Edward Arnold 1975 p 158
25 EMF to Dickinson 25 March 1902 D299 KCC

Chapter 10   Ravello
 1 EMF to Dickinson 25 March 1902 D299 KCC
 2 *Angels* p 70
 3 EMF to Dent early April 1902 D259 KCC
 4 EMF to Dent 23 April 1902 D260 KCC
 5 Italian Essays Notebook KCC p 41. This may have been an oblique reference to Ruskin's 'three centres of my life's thought: Rouen, Geneva, and Pisa' (*Praeterita* 1885–9 Volume I Chapter IX paragraph 180).
 6 Timothy d'Arch Smith *Love in Earnest: Some Notes on the Lives and Writings of English 'Uranian' Poets from 1889–1930* Routledge 1970 p 63
 7 'Recollectionism' *New Statesman & Nation* 13 March 1937 pp 405–6
 8 'Albergo Empedocle' in *Life to Come* pp 37, 44
 9 Lily to Louisa 3 November 1901 KCC
10 *Room* p 97
11 Cf. note 1 above
12 *Life to Come* pp 36, 46, 48, 52, 62
13 *Baedeker: Southern Italy* 1900 p 172
14 EMF Introduction to *Collected Short Stories* p 5
15 'Three Countries' 1959, reprinted *The Hill of Devi* ed. E. Heine, Abinger edition Edward Arnold 1983 p 290
16 *Collected Short Stories* pp 9, 22, 20, 33, 16, 17, 18, 19
17 'My Books and I' early 1920s, reprinted *Journey* Abinger edition p 302
18 John Meade Falkner *The Lost Stradivarius* (1895) Alan Sutton 1987 pp 83–5
19 Truman Capote *Music for Chameleons* Hamish Hamilton 1981 p 256
20 EMF to Edward Carpenter 12 April 1916 KCC
21 Capote op. cit. p 256
22 E. M. Forster *Aspects of the Novel* (1927) Abinger edition Edward Arnold 1974 p 35
23 *Room* p 65
24 *Ottoline*: The Early Memoirs of Lady Ottoline Morrell ed. Robert Gathorne-Hardy, Faber 1963 p 123
25 *Collected Short Stories* p 33
26 EMF to Bessie Trevelyan 12 March

1920 Trevelyan Papers Trinity College, Cambridge
27 *Journey* p 6
28 *Notebook Journal* unpublished manuscript KCC
29 *Maurice* p 53
30 *Angels* p 66
31 *Notebook Journal* p 146, 28 May 1905
32 David Halperin *One Hundred Years of Homosexuality* Routledge 1990 p 17 quoting T. C. Worsley and J. R. Ackerley
33 *Maurice* p 50
34 Katharine Furse *Hearts and Pomegranates* Peter Davies 1940 p 101
35 Quoted Jeffrey Weeks *Coming Out: Homosexual Politics in Britain*, Quartet Books 1977 p 14
36 Sigmund Freud *Three Essays on Sexuality*: The Sexual Aberrations 1901–5 but this passage added 1910, trans. James Strachey (1949) Hogarth Press 1953 *Complete Freud* Volume VII p 145
37 *Feasting with Panthers* p 286
38 *Room* p 23
39 *Angels* p 37
40 Quoted Claude Summers 'The Meaningful Ambiguity of Giotto in *A Room with a View*' *English Literature in Transition* Volume 30 no. 2 1987 p 173
41 *Arctic Summer* p 60
42 John Colmer *E. M. Forster*: The Personal Voice (1975) Routledge 1983 p 26

Chapter 11   To Greece
 1 *Life to Come* p 38
 2 EMF to Dent 13 May 1902 D263 KCC
 3 *Room* p 36
 4 G. M. Trevelyan to EMF 9 May 1902 KCC
 5 'Three Countries' in *Hill of Devi* p 291
 6 *Baedeker: Northern Italy* 1900 pp 18, 15
 7 *Angels* pp 104, 30, 97
 8 *Room* pp 40, 41, 46, 107
 9 *Journey* p 182
10 EMF to Dickinson 25 March 1902 D299 KCC
11 *Abinger Harvest* p 189
12 *The Times* 23 October 1971 p 6
13 Nettleship and Sandys *Dictionary of Classical Antiquity* Swan Sonnenschein 1901 edition p 36
14 Richard Jenkins *The Victorians and Ancient Greece* Blackwell 1980 p 284
15 *Lucy Novels* p 82
16 EMF to Dent 17 August 1902 D260 KCC

17 Unpublished memoir by Florence Barger kindly lent by Mollie Barger p 1
18 EMF to Dent 25 January 1902 D257 KCC
19 *Room* p 211
20 EMF to Dent 23 April 1902 D260 KCC
21 EMF to Dent 30 October 1902 D269
22 G. M. Trevelyan to EMF 9 May 1902 KCC
23 Raverat op. cit. p 119
24 EMF to Dent 30 October 1902 D269 KCC
25 Cambridge University Library Board of Extra-Mural Studies Papers 55/13 22 November 1902 W. F. Reddaway to Rev. D. H. S. Cranage
26 EMF to Dent 25 January 1902 D257 KCC
27 1903 Diary of visit to Greece 12 April 1903 KCC
28 EMF to Florence Barger 17 October 1912 *Letters I* p 140
29 *Abinger Harvest* p 191
30 Nettleship and Sandys op. cit. p 177
31 *Abinger Harvest* p 192
32 L. Burn *The British Museum Book of Greek and Roman Art* British Museum 1991 p 72
33 *Abinger Harvest* p 192
34 *Room* p 186
35 Introduction to *Collected Short Stories* p 5
36 ibid. pp 96, 98, 102, 105, 10

Chapter 12   Bloomsbury

1 EMF to John Sheppard July 1903 S256 KCC
2 *Arctic Summer* pp 76, 88, 92, 91
3 *Life to Come* pp 32, 35
4 *Dickinson* p 90
5 *Collected Short Stories* p 216
6 BEMS Papers 12/39 letter 426 14 August 1903 and BEMS 55/13 13 November 1903 Miss Wilson to Rev. Cranage
7 *Dickinson* pp 95–6
8 *Lucy Novels* p 85
9 *Angels* p 160
10 *Life to Come* p 51
11 *Notebook Journal* 8 December 1903, 13 March 1904
12 *Arctic Summer* p 240
13 *Diary of Virginia Woolf* Volume 1 p 206 23 October 1918
14 EMF 'Bloomsbury' unpublished memoir *c.* 1920 KCC
15 *Notebook Journal* 21 March 1904
16 BEMS Papers 12/38 letter 142 12 March 1903

17 Lily to Louisa 1 June 1902 quoted Stape op. cit. p 43
18 *Collected Short Stories* p 187
19 *Lucy Novels* p 106
20 *Room* p 61
21 *Notebook Journal* 21 March 1904

Chapter 13   Weybridge

1 *Notebook Journal* 21 March 1904
2 *Pilot* 14 May 1904 p 445
3 *Letters I* p 60
4 *Notebook Journal* 6 July, 7 August 1904
5 ibid. p 2 and *Lucy Novels* p 91
6 *Marianne Thornton* p 279
7 *Journey* p 94
8 *Marianne Thornton* p 276
9 Philip Gardner ed. *E. M. Forster*: The Critical Heritage, Routledge 1973 p 162
10 *Howards End* p 177
11 *Notebook Journal* 18 July 1904
12 *Lucy Novels* p 105
13 *Journey* Abinger edition p 303
14 National Trust sign at Figsbury Rings
15 *Journey* Abinger edition pp lxvii, 306
16 *Journey* p 125
17 *Howards End* p 178
18 *Notebook Journal* 12 September 1904
19 Cf. Chapter 9 note 20
20 M. E. Blackburn and J. S. L. Pulford *A Short History of Weybridge* Walton & Weybridge Local History Society 1991 p 32
21 *Commonplace Book* p 34
22 Blackburn and Pulford op. cit. p 32
23 *Room* p 119
24 EMF to Dent 1 October 1904 D274 KCC
25 EMF to Masood 9 January 1927 KCC
26 *Howards End* p 251
27 *Notebook Journal* 7 August 1904
28 *Howards End* p 252
29 Henry Beveridge to Annette Beveridge 13 May 1894 Beveridge Papers MSS Eur. *c.* 176/197 India Office Library
30 *Letters I* p 61
31 Cf. Chapter 9 note 5
32 *Room* p 129
33 'A Book that Influenced Me' 1944 *Two Cheers* p 226
34 *Collected Short Stories* p 40
35 *Notebook Journal* 8 December 1903
36 *Journey* p 144
37 *Letters I* p 62
38 *Notebook Journal* 31 December 1904

Chapter 14   *Where Angels Fear to Tread*

1 Virginia Woolf 'Old Bloomsbury' early 1920s in *Moments of Being* p 188
2 Virginia Woolf to EMF 21 January 1922 *The Letters of Virginia Woolf* Volume 2 p 500
3 *Journey* p 33
4 EMF to Robin Mayor 5 June 1908 KCC
5 *Commonplace Book* p 101
6 *Notebook Journal* 31 December 1904
7 *Room* p 50
8 *Aspects of E. M. Forster* p 81
9 *Two Cheers* p 114
10 EMF to Trevelyan 28 October 1905 reprinted *Angels* pp 162–3
11 *Angels* pp 84, 134
12 *Arctic Summer* p 77
13 *Poems of Arthur Hugh Clough* ed. Mulhauser, Oxford University Press 1974 pp 98, 108, 111
14 *Angels* p 70
15 *Notebook Journal* 16 March 1904
16 *Angels* Abinger edition p xii
17 *Notebook Journal* 24 February 1905
18 BEMS Papers 12/43 letter 65 16 February 1905
19 *Life to Come* p 12
20 Virginia Woolf 'Mr Bennett and Mrs Brown' *Collected Essays I* Hogarth Press 1980 May 1924 p 320
21 Virginia Woolf 'The Way of All Flesh' June 1919 *The Essays of Virginia Woolf* Volume 3 Hogarth Press 1988 p 58
22 Angus Wilson 'A Conversation with E. M. Forster' *Encounter* November 1957 p 55
23 *Two Cheers* p 65
24 *Howards End* p 305
25 Samuel Butler *The Way of All Flesh* (1903) Penguin 1980 p 302
26 *Two Cheers* p 225
27 *The Listener* 12 June 1952 p 956
28 *Angels* p 64

Chapter 15   Nassenheide

1 K. Usborne '*Elizabeth*': The Author of *Elizabeth and her German Garden* Bodley Head 1986 p 299
2 *The Listener* 1 January 1959 pp 12–13
3 *Notebook Journal* 23 April 1905
4 *The Listener* 1 January 1959 p 12
5 Rupert Hart-Davis *Hugh Walpole* Macmillan 1952 p 50
6 Elizabeth von Arnim *The Enchanted April* (1922) Virago 1986 Introduction by Terence de Vere White p ix
7 *Angels* p 76

8 *The Enchanted April* p 78
9 Leslie de Charms *Elizabeth of the German Garden* Heinemann 1958, quoting Elizabeth's diary for 22 June 1923 p 257
10 *Letters I* p 81
11 *Notebook Journal* 16 April 1905
12 *Letters I* p 78
13 de Charms op. cit. p 103
14 Hart-Davis op. cit. p 50
15 *Notebook Journal* 25 July 1905
16 de Charms op. cit. p 47
17 *Letters I* p 81
18 *Notebook Journal* 15 September 1907
19 *Independent Review* June 1906
20 Gardner op. cit. pp 43, 44, 46, 58

Chapter 16   *The Longest Journey*

1 EMF to Lily 18 August 1905 F408 KCC
2 *Journey* Abinger edition p xlix
3 'Three Countries' in *Hill of Devi* p 294
4 *Journey* Abinger edition p lxvi, 136
5 *Notebook Journal* 31 December 1904
6 Gorley Putt in *Encounter* p 78
7 Cf. Chapter 10 note 29
8 *Notebook Journal* 24 December 1906
9 *Two Cheers* p 76, and cf. Chapter 7 note 8
10 Gorley Putt op. cit. p 78
11 Edward Carpenter *From Adam's Peak to Elephanta* Swan Sonnenschein 1892 p 277
12 *Two Cheers* p 297
13 *Notebook Journal* 23 March 1906
14 EMF to Lily 29 August 1906 F411 KCC
15 EMF to Lily 31 August 1906 F412 KCC
16 Ashby op. cit. p 105
17 *Howards End* pp 36, 325
18 *Commonplace Book* p 95
19 'Uncle Willie' in *Journey* Abinger edition p 294
20 ibid. p lxx
21 ibid. 'Uncle Willie' p 298
22 EMF to Dent 1 October 1904 D274 KCC
23 *Journey* Abinger edition pp 295, 297
24 *Notebook Journal* 31 December 1907
25 Gardner op. cit. p 68 and *Journey* p 141
26 *Journey* p 96
27 *Journey* Abinger edition p lxx
28 Philip Whichelo: interview with author 25 November 1989
29 'Uncle Willie' in *Journey* Abinger edition p 296
30 Working Men's College *Journal* Volume 10 January and February 1907 pp 9, 10, 26, 30

Chapter 17   Clun
1 *Notebook Journal* 12 June 1907
2 *Letters I* p 83
3 *Writers at Work* pp 30, 29, 32
4 *Journey* Abinger edition 'My Books and I' p 303
5 Cf. Introduction note 6
6 *Two Cheers* pp 92, 91
7 EMF 'Inspiration' *The Author* July 1912 p 281
8 *Letters I* p 87
9 Gardner op. cit. pp 83, 87, 96
10 *Journey* pp 74, 235, 60, 70, 119
11 *Howards End* p 177
12 Shelley *Epipsychidion* (1821)
13 *Journey* pp 81, 126, 127
14 *Notebook Journal* 11 April 1907
15 Cf. Preface note 7
16 *Journey* Abinger edition 'My Books and I' p 306
17 Cf. Richard Perceval Graves *A. E. Housman*: The Scholar-Poet Routledge 1979
18 *Notebook Journal* 11 April 1907
19 EMF 'Ancient and Modern' *The Listener* 11 November 1936 pp 921–2
20 *Forster in Egypt* ed. Hilda Spear and Abdel Moneim Aly, Cecil Woolf 1987 p 45
21 *Notebook Journal* 11 April 1907
22 A. E. Housman *A Shropshire Lad* (1896) *Collected Poems* Jonathan Cape 1986 p 62
23 *Locked Journal* 15 July 1944
24 *Letters II* p 287
25 *Howards End* pp 246, 221, 208, 216
26 Thorstein Veblen *Theory of the Leisure Class* (1899) reprinted 1908 Chapter IV
27 *Howards End* pp 211, 102, 137
28 Bryan Bennett and Anthony Hamilton *Edward Arnold* Hodder & Stoughton 1990 p 36
29 *Notebook Journal* 12 June 1907
30 EMF to Bob Trevelyan 11 June 1907 Trevelyan Papers Trinity College Library, Cambridge
31 *Collected Short Stories* p 41
32 *Dickinson* p 31
33 EMF 'The Legacy of Samuel Butler' *The Listener* 12 June 1952 p 956
34 EMF to Bob Trevelyan 8 September 1907 Trevelyan Papers
35 *Notebook Journal* 17 September 1907
36 *Howards End* p 154
37 *Letters I* p 87
38 *Notebook Journal* 7 October 1907
39 *Commonplace Book* p 29
40 *Notebook Journal* 31 December 1907

Chapter 18   *A Room with a View*
1 EMF to Bob Trevelyan 12 September 1907 T224 Trevelyan Papers
2 *Lucy Novels* p 119
3 *Room* p 225
4 *Howards End* p 118
5 EMF to Dent 30 June 1907 D281 KCC
6 *Room* pp 181, 214, 228, 192, 191, 130
7 *Hill of Devi* p 206
8 *Room* pp 141, 51, 52
9 *Collected Short Stories* p 216
10 *Room* Appendix p 233
11 d'Arch Smith op. cit. p 20
12 *Independent Review* May 1904
13 Quoted T. Rahman 'Edward Carpenter and E. M. Forster' *Durham University Journal* December 1986 p 62. Cf. also T. Brown 'Edward Carpenter, Forster and the Evolution of *A Room with a View*' *English Literature in Transition* Volume 30 no. 3 1987 and the same author's 1982 unpublished thesis 'A Consideration of some Parallels in the Personal and Social Ideals of E. M. Forster and Edward Carpenter'; and R. Martin 'Edward Carpenter and the Double Structure of *Maurice*' *Journal of Homosexuality* Spring 1983
14 *Journey* pp 242, 72
15 *Room* pp 129, 34, 47, 223, 187
16 *Notebook Journal* 31, 22, 31 December 1907
17 Jane Austen's *Mansfield Park* (1814) Penguin 1985 p 446
18 *Howards End* p 58
19 *The Listener* 16 July 1959
20 Lily to EMF *Record of Destruction* p 19
21 *Notebook Journal* 4 January 1908
22 Cf. Chapter 14 note 26
23 William Le Queux *The Invasion of 1910* (1906) pp 19, 20, 26
24 *Collected Short Stories* p 146
25 *Notebook Journal* 27 January 1908
26 *Howards End* pp 264, 59, 115, 67, 256, 122
27 EMF to Edward Arnold 10 September 1908 A1159 Edward Arnold
28 *Notebook Journal* 26 June, 9 August 1908

Chapter 19 *Howards End*

1 EMF to Malcolm Darling 12 December 1908 D24 Darling Papers Humanities Research Center, University of Texas at Austin
2 *Notebook Journal* 8 September, 31 December 1908
3 EMF to Darling 12 December 1908 D24 HRC
4 *Notebook Journal* 31 December 1908
5 *Letters I* p 122
6 ibid. pp 122, 134
7 *Forster–Masood Letters* ed. Jalil Ahmad Kidwai, Karachi 1984 pp 97, 103
8 Gardner op. cit. pp 109, 111–15
9 C. F. G. Masterman 'Towards a Civilization', *Independent Review* May 1904 pp 515–16
10 Virginia Woolf *Collected Essays I* 'The Novels of E. M. Forster' November 1927 p 342
11 *Commonplace Book* p 203
12 *Howards End* pp 246, 38, 176, 187
13 *The Letters of D. H. Lawrence* Volume IV ed. Warren Roberts and Elizabeth Mansfield Cambridge University Press 1987 D. H. Lawrence to EMF 20 September 1922 p 301
14 *Howards End* p 178, 118
15 *Two Cheers* p 81
16 *Locked Journal* 3 August 1910
17 *Commonplace Book* p 49
18 Introduction to *Arctic Summer* pp xii, xiii
19 Gardner op. cit. p 123
20 *Chicago Daily Tribune* 28 January 1911 quoted Francis King op. cit. p 47
21 Marjorie Watts *Mrs Sappho*: The Life of C. A. Dawson Scott 'Mother of International PEN' Duckworth 1987 p 35
22 Graham Greene *The Third Man* (1950) Penguin 1971 p 31
23 *Passage* p 271

Chapter 20 *Maurice*

1 Unpublished typescript of Alice Merz's *Diaries* kindly lent by Gail Sieveking 20 July 1909
2 *Notebook Journal* 13 July 1909
3 Alice Merz op. cit. 16 January 1903
4 Quoted Dewey op. cit. Chapter 16 pp 81, 83
5 Dickinson to Roger Fry 24 January 1889 in unpublished MS of the Dickinson/Fry letters ed. Michael Halls KCC
6 Alice Merz op. cit. 20 July 1909
7 Ernest Merz to Malcolm Darling 5 July 1909 Darling Papers Box 53 Centre for South Asian Studies, Cambridge
8 Unpublished report by Monique Stirling 1992 in possession of the author
9 *Ernest Merz: From His Letters*, 30 copies privately printed Newcastle 1910 1 May 1903, 5 July 1909, 1 April 1907
10 Notebook kindly lent by Peggy Jay
11 *Passage* p 256
12 Alice Merz op. cit. 24 October 1906
13 EMF to Darling D26 16 July 1909 HRC
14 EMF to Darling D27 19 July 1909 HRC
15 Terminal note to *Maurice* p 217
16 EMF to Hsiao Ch'ien 1 May 1943 KCC
17 *Maurice* pp 59, 67, 157, 187
18 Epilogue to 1913–14 version of *Maurice* KCC
19 *Howards End* p 327
20 Epilogue to *Maurice* KCC
21 *Letters I* p 285
22 Plomer Papers DUL
23 EMF's letters to Darling p 455 CSAS
24 Article by Evert Barger in *New York Times Book Review* 16 August 1970
25 *Maurice* p 218
26 Cf. Chapter 19 note 10
27 Letter to the author from Peggy Jay 13 March 1989
28 Merz to Darling 19 January 1906 CSAS
29 Alice Merz op. cit. 2 October 1913

Chapter 21 *The Celestial Omnibus*

1 *Notebook Journal* 30 August 1909
2 *Locked Journal* p 1, 24 October 1911
3 Stape op. cit. pp 70, 91
4 *Cambridge University Reporter* 24 October 1910
5 *Dickinson* p 47
6 *Locked Journal* 19 September 1910
7 Anthony Storr *The School of Genius* André Deutsch 1988 pp 97, 120, 124, 128, 136
8 *Locked Journal* 25 January 1911
9 *Marianne Thornton* p 250
10 *Angels* p 84
11 *Locked Journal* 25 January 1911
12 Unpublished memoir by Philip Whichelo
13 Gardner op. cit. p 156
14 *Locked Journal* 21 July 1910, 19 July 1912, 3 August 1910, 16 June 1911
15 *Notebook Journal* 22 November 1908
16 *Locked Journal* 31 December 1909
17 *Letters I* p 102
18 *Locked Journal* 28 July 1910, 5 September 1910, 28 January 1911, 31 December 1911
19 *Commonplace Book* p 217

20 *Locked Journal* 31 December 1911
21 EMF to Darling 12 October 1937 D139 HRC
22 *Locked Journal* 1 November 1911
23 *Arctic Summer* pp 130, 133, 162, 149
24 *Locked Journal* 31 December 1911
25 EMF to Masood 19 August 1912 KCC
26 *Letters I* p 134

Chapter 22   India 1912
1 'Indian Journal 1912–13' *Hill of Devi* p 119
2 W. J. Weatherby 'A Chat with E. M. Forster' *Guardian* 6 October 1989
3 *Letters I* p 203
4 *Journey* pp 195, 199
5 *Letters I* p 140
6 *Hill of Devi* p 119
7 EMF to Lily 8 October 1912 F440 KCC
8 *Dickinson* p 112
9 EMF to Lily 8 October 1912 F440 KCC
10 *Dickinson* p 113
11 EMF to Lily 8 October 1912 F440 KCC
12 *Hill of Devi* pp 123, 122
13 *Dickinson* p 113
14 Ronald Hyam *Empire and Sexuality* Manchester University Press 1990 p 128 and *The Autobiography of G. Lowes Dickinson* ed. D. Proctor, Duckworth 1973 p 178
15 Toby Hammond '"Paidikion": a Paiderastic Manuscript' *International Journal of Greek Love I* New York 1966 p 36
16 *Hill of Devi* pp 120, 127
17 EMF to Lily 8 October 1912 F440 KCC
18 EMF to Malcolm Darling 5 June 1911 Darling Papers HRC
19 *Hill of Devi* pp 124, 125
20 *Letters I* p 138
21 EMF to Lily 23 October 1912 F441 KCC
22 *Hill of Devi* p 126
23 'Iron Horses in India' *Golden Hynde* December 1913 p 35
24 EMF to Masood 2 August 1912 KCC
25 *From Adam's Peak to Elephanta* p 276
26 *Hill of Devi* pp 128, 129, 130
27 *Letters I* p 141
28 ibid. p 145
29 ibid. p 149
30 *Hill of Devi* pp 146, 136
31 *Letters I* p 145
32 ibid. p 147
33 *Hill of Devi* p 137
34 *Passage* pp 39, 96, 67
35 Macaulay's *Works* ed. J. Clive quoted J. W. Burrow *A Liberal*

Descent Cambridge University Press 1981 p 63
36 *Passage* p 80
37 *Commonplace Book* p 29
38 *Passage* p 80
39 Maud Diver *The Englishwoman in India* William Blackwood 1909 p 9
40 E. M. Forster *The Manuscripts of A Passage to India* ed. Oliver Stallybrass, Edward Arnold 1978 pp 59, 124, 229
41 *Passage* p 48

Chapter 23   India 1913
1 *Letters I* p 153
2 *Dickinson* p 114
3 *Letters I* p 155
4 *Hill of Devi* p 141
5 *Dickinson* p 115
6 *Passage* p 76
7 *Letters I* pp 156, 151, 159
8 *Passage* p 257
9 *Hill of Devi* p 145
10 *Letters I* p 159
11 *Hill of Devi* pp 146, 147
12 *Commonplace Book* p 55
13 *Hill of Devi* p 152
14 *Dickinson* p 115
15 J. R. Ackerley to EMF 23 April 1924 *The Letters of J. R. Ackerley* ed. N. Braybrooke, Duckworth 1975 p 13
16 *Letters I* pp 162, 164
17 *Dickinson* p 223
18 *Passage* pp 281, 302
19 *Hill of Devi* pp 157, 156
20 J. R. Ackerley *Hindoo Holiday* (1932) Penguin 1983 p 12
21 *Dickinson* p 115
22 EMF to Malcolm Darling 12 April 1912 D50 HRC
23 *Hill of Devi* p 155
24 *Letters I* p 168
25 *The Listener* 5 December 1940 p 801. EMF returned to the theme of the 'world-mountain' and the individual in *The Listener* 10 September 1953 p 419 *and* 2 December 1954 p 977 *and* 12 March 1959 p 469.
26 'The Temple' *Athenaeum* 26 September 1919 p 947
27 *Dickinson* pp 116–17
28 *Letters I* p 168
29 *Dickinson* p 116
30 *Hill of Devi* p 159, 162
31 *Letters I* pp 162, 170
32 *Hill of Devi* pp 163, 164
33 EMF to Josie Darling 22 December 1912 D15 HRC
34 *Passage* pp 45, 188

35 Dewey op. cit. Chapter 17 pp 32, 28
36 EMF to Bob Trevelyan 26 December 1912 T260 Trinity College, Cambridge
37 *Hill of Devi* p 27
38 *Letters I* pp 173, 174
39 *Hill of Devi* p 172
40 *Passage* p 31
41 *Hill of Devi* p 175
42 Emily Eden *Up the Country* Richard Bentley 1866 5 November 1837 p 15
43 *Hill of Devi* p 179
44 *Passage* pp 31, 32
45 *Hill of Devi* p 184
46 EMF to Lily 17 December 1912 F450 KCC
47 *Hill of Devi* pp 3, 185
48 Anthony Spaeth 'What was Mystery of Marabar Caves for E. M. Forster?' *The Wall Street Journal* 1 February 1988
49 *Murray's Handbook to India* 1920 p 50
50 Norman Douglas *Old Calabria* (1915) Penguin 1962 p 37
51 *Passage* p 138
52 *The Manuscripts of A Passage to India* pp 580, 243
53 *Passage* p 199
54 *Letters II* p 125
55 *Letters I* p 187
56 *Hill of Devi* pp 196, 200, 193
57 *Dickinson* p 117
58 Dewey op. cit. Chapter 17 p 33
59 *Hill of Devi* pp 209, 213, 210, 213, 211
60 EMF to Lily 19 March 1913 F470 KCC
61 *Hill of Devi* pp 217, 223, 219
62 *Passage* p 81
63 *Hill of Devi* p 225
64 EMF to Masood 30 March 1913
65 *Hill of Devi* pp 227, 228

Chapter 24   Weybridge Again
1 Unpublished transcript of conversation between Bob Buckingham and Eric Crozier 5 July 1971 KCC
2 Quoted in the present author's *A Very Great Profession* pp 51, 43, cf. fn p 265
3 *Letters I* p 229
4 EMF to Lily 27 April 1914 F479 KCC
5 *Record of Destruction* KCC
6 *Letters I* p 229
7 EMF to Ackerley 21 October 1924 A53 HRC
8 *Room* p 185
9 *Locked Journal* 10 August 1913
10 *Sowing* p 171
11 *Letters of Leonard Woolf* ed. Frederic Spotts, Weidenfeld & Nicolson 1989 pp 40, 50, 105
12 *Locked Journal* 26 June 1913

13 Virginia Woolf *Letters* Volume 2 July 1913 p 31
14 EMF to Ackerley A131 HRC
15 *Locked Journal* 17, 31, 12 December 1913
16 EMF to Masood 15 August 1913, 20 November 1913 KCC
17 *Locked Journal* 15 May, 3, 1, 3 August 1914
18 *Commonplace Book* p 49
19 Josie Darling to her mother 26 March 1915 quoted Dewey op. cit. Chapter 16 p 47
20 EMF to Masood 2 May 1920 KCC
21 *Howards End* p 73
22 *Letters* p 213
23 Dickinson to EMF 11 December 1914 KCC
24 Quoted Ashby op. cit. p 109
25 *Letters* p 219
26 *The Letters of D. H. Lawrence* Volume II ed. G. J. Zytaruk and J. T. Boulton Cambridge University Press 1981 pp 282–3
27 *Letters I* p 249
28 *Locked Journal* 31 December 1911, 31 December 1914
29 *Letters I* p 216
30 EMF to Florence Barger 27 April 1915 B54 KCC
31 Interview with Mollie Barger 20 October 1989
32 *Letters I* p 216

Chapter 25   Alexandria
1 EMF to Lily 2 October 1915 F489 KCC
2 *Locked Journal* 27 October 1915
3 'The Lost Guide' unpublished MS of lecture given 17 June 1956 KCC
4 EMF to Bertrand Russell 28 July 1917 R357 McMaster University, Ontario, copy KCC
5 *Letters I* p 251 (EMF copied a variation on these lines into his 'Incidents of War' memoir.)
6 E. M. Forster *Alexandria*: A History and a Guide (1922) ed. and pub. by Michael Haag 1986 p 241. Cf. also *Guide to Egypt* Michael Haag 1987
7 *Letters I* p 239
8 'The Lost Guide' KCC
9 EMF to Lily 21 November 1915 F491 KCC
10 E. M. Forster 'Between the Sun and the Moon' 1918, *Pharos and Pharillon* (1923) Michael Haag 1983 pp 87, 88
11 *Howards End* pp 116, 184
12 *Letters I* p 232

13 Lord Northcliffe *At the War* Hodder & Stoughton 1917 p 148
14 'Incidents of War' unpublished memoir written 1915–16 KCC
15 *Letters I* p 233
16 EMF to Dickinson D305, D306, D308 KCC
17 Working Men's College *Journal* Volume 14 March 1915 pp 58, 61
18 *Alexandria* pp 186, 276
19 *Letters I* p 237
20 EMF to Dickinson D305 KCC
21 *Alexandria* pp 37–8
22 Richard Howard in 1971 quoted Jane Pinchin *Alexandria Still* Princeton University Press 1977 p 101
23 *Two Cheers* p 243
24 C. P. Cavafy *Collected Poems* trans. Edmund Keeley and Philip Sherrard, Hogarth Press 1984 p 69
25 'Cavafy' unpublished memoir 1950s? KCC
26 *Letters I* pp 243, 237, 265, 271, 274
27 ibid. p 237
28 EMF to Edward Carpenter 12 April 1916 C115 KCC
29 ibid. 1 July 1917 C120
30 ibid. 12 April 1916 C115
31 *Letters I* p 287
32 *Locked Journal* 11 May 1922
33 *Letters I* p 291
34 Edward Carpenter 'Self-Analysis for Havelock Ellis' 1901 *Edward Carpenter: Selected Writings I*: Sex, Gay Men's Press 1984 p 290
35 *Locked Journal* p 149, 28 August 1920
36 *Letters I* p 291
37 EMF to Florence Barger 10 November 1917 B79
38 *Locked Journal* 8 April 1922
39 EMF to Lily 27 June 1916, 12 September 1916, 19 August 1918, F510, F519, F576 KCC
40 *Letters I* pp 253, 261, 233
41 *The Letters of D. H. Lawrence* Volume IV D. H. Lawrence to EMF 11 April 1923 p 420
42 *Alexandria* pp xxvi, 5, 115
43 *Room* p 41
44 *Alexandria* pp 134, 10
45 V. S. Naipaul *An Area of Darkness* Penguin 1964 p 10
46 *The Listener* 23 December 1948 p 975. The 'Entrance' was written in 1913 and would one day be the opening part of the short story 'The Other Boat', published posthumously.

Chapter 26   India Again
1 *Alexandria* p xxi
2 *Angels* pp 112, 31
3 *Letters I* p 300
4 Vera Brittain *Testament of Youth* Gollancz 1933 pp 475, 477
5 *Letters I* p 308
6 *Dickinson* pp 146, 136
7 Brittain op. cit. p 474
8 *Letters I* p 289
9 *Collected Letters of Katherine Mansfield* Volume II 1918–19 ed. O'Sullivan, Oxford University Press 1987 p 324
10 *Letters between Katherine Mansfield and John Middleton Murry* ed. C. Hankin, Virago 1988 p 390
11 EMF to J. M. Murry dated 4.1.23 but misdated, perhaps in fact 1.4.23 HRC
12 *Locked Journal* 12 August 1919
13 *Arctic Summer* pp 219, 222, 223, 225
14 *Letters I* p 302
15 EMF to Lily 19 March 1916 F503 KCC
16 EMF to Masood 16 May 1920 KCC
17 *Arctic Summer* p 3
18 James Eastwood *General Edmund Ironside* Pilot Press 1939 p 7
19 *Life to Come* pp 151, 145, 162
20 *Passage* p 256, 70
21 *Letters II* p 2
22 Unpublished manuscript 'Mohammed el-Adl' begun August 1922, finished 1929, written in little cream-coloured bound notebook beginning 'Dear Mohammed, This book is for you and me . . .' KCC
23 *Letters II* p 2
24 *Hill of Devi* pp 30, 31, 6, 297, 32, 298, 38, 40, 311, 312, 315, 319, 323
25 Richard Cronin *Imagining India* Macmillan 1989 p 173
26 *Passage* p 160
27 *Hill of Devi* p 324
28 *Two Cheers* p 92, and cf. Introduction note 6 and Chapter 17 notes 6 and 7
29 *Hill of Devi* pp 65, 64
30 *Passage* pp 282, 286
31 *Hill of Devi* pp 41, 311, 298

Chapter 27   *A Passage to India*
1 1970 article by Syed Ali Akbar quoted Pinchin op. cit. p 103
2 *Passage* p 199
3 *Collected Short Stories* p 40
4 *Passage* p 277
5 'Mohammed el-Adl' KCC
6 EMF to Masood 25 January 1922 KCC
7 'Mohammed el-Adl' KCC
8 Virginia Woolf *Letters* Volume 2 p 499

9 *Writers at Work* pp 26–7
10 *Abinger Harvest* p 109
11 Virginia Woolf *Diary* Volume 2 p 171
12 *Writers at Work* pp 26–7; and cf. Chapter 21 note 23
13 *From Adam's Peak to Elephanta* p 269
14 *Letters I* p 102, and cf. Chapter 21 note 17
15 *Passage* pp 89, 96, 147
16 *Howards End* pp 47, 102
17 *Passage* pp 90, 211, 195
18 'Reflections in India' I *Nation & Athenaeum* 21 January 1922 p 614
19 *Passage* p 97
20 'Reflections in India' p 615
21 Leonée Ormond *Kim by Rudyard Kipling* Macmillan 1988 p 31
22 EMF 'The Indian Boom' *Daily News and Leader* 2 February 1915 p 7
23 *Passage* p 153
24 *Hill of Devi* p 298
25 *Letters II* p 42
26 *The Manuscripts of A Passage to India* p 268 and Colmer op. cit. p 156
27 *Room* p 90
28 Gardner op. cit. p 236
29 *Letters II* p 152
30 *Passage* p 355
31 *Locked Journal* 31 December 1921, 12 April, 1 May 1922
32 *Letters II* p 63
33 *The Times Literary Supplement* 31 May 1923 p 369
34 *Pharos and Pharillon* p 91
35 EMF to Edward Arnold 7 April 1923 Edward Arnold
36 Virginia Woolf *Diary* Volume 2 pp 96, 269
37 Siegfried Sassoon *Diaries 1920–1922* Faber & Faber 1981 p 148
38 R. Brimley Johnson *Some Contemporary Novelists* (Men) Leonard Parsons 1922 pp 19, 15, 181
39 *The Times* 7, 8, 10, 17 June 1922
40 EMF to Masood 26 June 1922 M180 KCC
41 Quoted Virginia Woolf *Diary* Volume 2 23 January 1924 p 289

Chapter 28   Abinger
1 P. N. Furbank *E. M. Forster: A Life* Volume II Secker & Warburg 1978 p 132
2 *Letters II* p 26
3 EMF to Darling 10 May 1923 D98 HRC
4 *Letters II* p 45
5 *Two Cheers* p 128
6 George Painter *Marcel Proust*

Volume 1 (1959) Penguin 1977 p 317
7 *Daily Herald* 30 July 1919 p 8
8 *Dickinson* p 8
9 *Locked Journal* 16 June 1911, and cf. Chapter 21 note 14; p 149
10 *The Listener* 16 July 1970 p 82
11 *Locked Journal* 2 January 1925, 30 September 1923, 31 August 1924
12 Sassoon op. cit. p 126
13 *Locked Journal* 2 January 1925
14 *Passage* p 46
15 *Room* p 129
16 *Letters II* p 66
17 *Passage* p 37
18 *Letters II* p 67
19 *Locked Journal* 7 May 1922, 5 August 1922, 30 September 1923, 31 December 1923
20 *Letters II* p 66
21 *Locked Journal* 17 October 1924
22 EMF to Joe Ackerley 19 January 1925 A69 HRC
23 *The Listener* 16 July 1970 p 82
24 *Room* p 214
25 *Locked Journal* 12 July 1926

Chapter 29   Hammersmith
1 EMF to Ackerley October 1938 A453 HRC
2 Draft of obituary prepared by William Plomer 1965 Plomer Papers brown envelope XX DUL
3 *Locked Journal* 15 July 1944
4 Wilfred Stone op. cit. p 313
5 *Passage* p 51
6 *Abinger Harvest* p 384
7 EMF to Masood 16 February 1926, 15 July 1925 KCC
8 Virginia Woolf *Diary* Volume 3 p 299 4 April 1930, p 193 31 August 1928, p 48 27 November 1925
9 Virginia Woolf *Diary* Volume 1 p 291, Volume 2 p 33, Volume 3 p 177
10 Virginia Woolf *Letters* Volume 4 p 221
11 Virginia Woolf *Diary* Volume 4 p 321 13 June 1935
12 Virginia Woolf *Letters* Volume 3 p 266
13 *Locked Journal* 24 March 1925
14 Harry Daley *This Small Cloud* Weidenfeld & Nicolson 1986 pp 23, 5, caption after p 114
15 EMF to Masood 23 July 1927 KCC
16 *Locked Journal* 31 December 1927
17 *Commonplace Book* p 49
18 *Locked Journal* 17 October 1924
19 Eric Crozier's interview with Bob and May Buckingham

20 *Maurice* p 126
21 EMF to Ackerley 1927 undated A179, 14 January 1931 A285
22 EMF to Sprott 1 December 1930 S746, 2 January 1931 S753, 4 January 1931 S754, 6 May 1931 S776, 24 June 1931 S785, 27 June 1931 S787, 11 July 1931 S789, 14 July 1931 S791
23 Furbank *E. M. Forster* Volume II pp 319–20
24 EMF to Ackerley 1 December 1933 A355 HRC
25 *Locked Journal* 7 October 1934
26 *Passage* p 129
27 Virginia Woolf *Diary* Volume 4 p 321 13 June 1935
28 *Passage* pp 129, 259, 312, 313
29 *Locked Journal* 7 October 1934
30 *Commonplace Book* pp 94, 100
31 *Howards End* pp 291, 206

Chapter 30   Shepherd's Bush

1 Virginia Woolf *Diary* Volume 4 13 June 1935 p 321
2 Rebecca West in *Saturday Review of Literature* 16 August 1924 quoted Gardner op. cit. pp 254–5
3 *Howards End* p 197
4 *Passage* p 170
5 *Room* p 129
6 Stephen Spender *The Thirties and After* Fontana 1978 p 187
7 *Two Cheers* p 24
8 *Howards End* p 19
9 Christopher Isherwood *Down There on a Visit* Methuen 1962 p 177
10 Christopher Isherwood *Lions and Shadows* Hogarth Press 1938 p 173
11 *Commonplace Book* p 118
12 *Two Cheers* pp 32, 33, 39, 40
13 *Letters II* p 169
14 *Two Cheers* p 129
15 EMF *Nordic Twilight* Macmillan 1940 p 31
16 *Two Cheers* p 80
17 David Garnett *New Statesman & Nation* 21 March 1936, Gardner op. cit. p 384
18 Virginia Woolf *Letters* Volume 5 February 1933 p 160
19 Noel Annan in *The Listener* 16 July 1970
20 EMF in *New Statesman & Nation* 31 October 1953 p 508
21 *With Downcast Gays: Aspects of Homosexual Self-Oppression* Pomegranate Press 1974 pp 20, 18, published anonymously but identified by Judith Scherer Herz *The Short Narratives of E. M. Forster* Macmillan 1988 p 121
22 *Two Cheers* pp 26–8
23 Katherine Mansfield *Journal* May 1917 Gardner op. cit. p 162
24 Evert Barger 'Memories of Morgan' *New York Times Book Review* 16 August 1970
25 *Letters II* p 95
26 EMF to Isherwood 8 September 1939 I46 KCC (copy)
27 EMF to Isherwood 31 October 1939 I47 KCC (copy)
28 EMF to Isherwood 1942 I54 KCC (copy)
29 *Nordic Twilight* pp 27, 28
30 *Two Cheers* pp 34, 76; cf. Chapter 16 note 9 and Chapter 7 note 8
31 *Two Cheers* p 67
32 *Locked Journal* 2 May 1943
33 EMF to Bob Buckingham 9 October 1935 B1353 KCC
34 Stephen Spender *World Within World* Hamish Hamilton 1951 p 143
35 Stephen Spender in the *New York Review of Books* 23 July 1970 p 3
36 EMF to Plomer 4 September 1939 P129 DUL
37 *Aspects of E. M. Forster* p 24
38 *The Listener* 1 January 1959 p 11

Epilogue

1 EMF to Bob Buckingham 11 June 1938 KCC
2 EMF to Isherwood 26 May 1945 I69 KCC (copy)
3 *Hill of Devi* pp 280, 281
4 *Locked Diary* 15 October 1946
5 EMF to Bob Buckingham 28 January 1946 KCC
6 EMF to Bob Buckingham April 1946 KCC
7 EMF to Plomer 28 July 1946 P215 DUL
8 EMF to May Buckingham 7 November 1946 KCC
9 EMF to Bob Buckingham 8 December 1947 B2078 KCC
10 Virginia Woold *Diary* Volume 1 p 291
11 *The Listener* 5 September 1970 p 237
12 J. R. Ackerley *E. M. Forster: A Portrait* Ian McKelvie 1970 pp 12, 16
13 EMF Address at Founder's Feast 6 December 1952 KCC

14 EMF to Eddy Sackville-West 10 June 1945 Private Collection
15 Eric Crozier 'Writers Remembered: E. M. Forster' *The Author* Winter 1990 p 124
16 *Locked Journal* 8 April 1922
17 *Life to Come* p 203
18 Cf. Chapter 22 note 12
19 *Life to Come* p 210
20 Cf. Chapter 12 note 20
21 E. M. Forster's *Letters to Donald Windham* Verona 1975 p 41
22 *Commonplace Book* p 204
23 *Locked Journal* 19 June 1948
24 *Commonplace Book* p 230
25 *Passage* p 145
26 EMF to Bob Buckingham 4 April 1941 B1759 KCC
27 *Commonplace Book* pp 180, 254, 255
28 Ralph Vaughan Williams, quoted David Cannadine *G. M. Trevelyan* Harper-Collins 1992 p 19
29 *Commonplace Book* p 256
30 Address to the Cambridge Humanists

Notes and References

1 *Passage* p 274
2 *Two Cheers* p 225

Illustration captions

1 *Journey* p 8
2 *Marianne Thornton* p 188
3 *Howards End* p 191
4 KCC
5 *Howards End* p 88
6 *Letters I* p 16
7 Merz to Darling 19 January 1906 CSAS
8 *Commonplace Book* p 217
9 Carpenter to EMF 13 March 1918 KCC
10 *Angels* p 48
11 *Locked Journal* 20 September 1924
12 *Letters I* p 164
13 *Hill of Devi* p 80
14 *Passage* p 89
15 J. A. Symonds *Sketches and Studies in Italy* Smith Elder 1879 pp 48–9
16 Siegfried Sassoon *Diaries 1922–1925* Faber & Faber 1985 10 July 1923 p 49

Illustration credits

Pictures within text
p ii The Provost and Scholars of King's College, Cambridge
p 25 E. M. Forster *Marianne Thornton* Edward Arnold 1956; Margaret Ashby *Forster Country* Flaunden Press 1991
p 87 Cambridgeshire Libraries
p 224 Bryan Bennett and Anthony Hamilton *Edward Arnold* Hodder & Stoughton 1990; Edward Arnold archive
p 289 Frances Spalding *Roger Fry* Granada 1980; National Portrait Gallery © 1978 Estate of Duncan Grant; KCC; Courtauld Institute of Art © 1961 Estate of Vanessa Bell

Between pages 36 and 37
pl 1 The late Philip Whichelo
pl 2 J. H. M. Burgess *Clapham* A. V. Huckle & Son 1929; RCHME Crown Copyright; Marylebone Library
pl 3 KCC; Dick Lewis of Weybridge
pl 4 The late Philip Whichelo; Wychwoods Local History Society; Tonbridge School Library

Between pages 132 and 133
pl 5 The late Philip Whichelo; Trinity College, Cambridge; KCC

pl 6 Francis King *E. M. Forster* Thames & Hudson 1978; Leslie de Charms *Elizabeth of the German Garden* Heinemann 1958; KCC
pl 7 KCC
pl 8 Francis King op. cit.; author's postcard; Egerton Williams *Hill Towns of Italy* Smith Elder 1904; RCHME

Between pages 260 and 261
pl 9 James Poston; KCC; Frederic Spotts; Courtauld Institute of Art © 1961 Estate of Vanessa Bell
pl 10 KCC
pl 11 Author's postcard of statue at Delphi; KCC
pl 12 Sheffield Archives; James Eastwood *How They Did It: General Edmund Ironside* Pilot Press 1939; Robert Liddell *Cavafy* Duckworth 1974; KCC

Between pages 356 and 357
pl 13 KCC
pl 14 Francis King op. cit.; KCC; Hulton Deutsch, Kurt Hutton for *Picture Post*
pl 15 KCC
pl 16 KCC; the late Philip Whichelo; Norman Routledge

Index

Asterisked entries* indicate that there is a photograph in the separate sections of illustrations or among the illustrations in the text. Page numbers in italics refer to complete chapters.

References to titles of the subject's books and other writings will be found under 'Forster, E. M.', subheadings **'books'** and **'writings'**.

Index

Index

Quirk, Robin 235n

'Raby, Miss' 139–40, 207
'Ralph' *see* Forster, E. M., writings: 'Ralph and Tony'
Ravello *109–22*, 151
Raven, Simon 366–7, 371
Raverat, Gwen 71, 129
Rayner, Louise, painting of EMF 87
Reform Club 60, 367
Reid, Forrest 277, 288
Religion, and India 268–9
Richmond, George, portraits by *25*
'Rickie' *see* 'Elliot, Rickie'
'Ronny' *see* 'Heaslop, Ronny'
Rooksnest,* house 6, *30–43*, 55, 56, 102, 131, 155, 196, 199, 202, 219, 342, 343, 376
turned out of 42–3, 51–3, 118–19, 341
revisited 185–6
Rothenstein, William, portrait of EMF 289
Ruskin, John 41, 69, 121, 124, 125, 176n, 219
Russell, Bertrand 287, 292, 309

Salisbury (Wiltshire) 90, 103n, 149–53, 155, 218
San Gimignano* 124–5, 148, 166
Sanger, Charles P. 86
Sassoon, Siegfried 307, 308, 310, 311, 330, 334, 360
on EMF 336–7
'Sawston school' 59, 60, 160–1, 164, 166, 169, 173, 176–7, 179, 208, 209
'Sawstone' 64, 103
Sayle, Charles 113–14, 151
'Schlegels' 201, 213, 220, 222, 322
'Schlegel, Ernst' 227n
'Schlegel, Helen' 13, 73, 102, 150, 156, 157, 168, 203, 220–1, 224, 233, 240, 263, 324, 355
'Schlegel, Margaret' (later Wilcox) 5, 36, 40, 42, 151, 153, 156, 157, 186, 189, 199, 204, 220–1, 222, 226, 232–3, 263, 294, 323, 352, 354
'Schlegel, Tibby' 156, 157, 220, 222
model for 61–2
Searight, Kenneth 253–5, 257, 259, 262, 264, 265n, 283, 284, 286, 299, 300, 304, 369
Seebohm, Hugh 219n
Shelley, Percy Bysshe 195–6, 197, 200
Shepherd's Bush *353–63*
Sheppard, John 83, 86
Shove, Gerald 86
Shropshire 195–200, 209, 220
Sidgwick & Jackson, publisher 223, 231
Simla 63n, 265–6
Sinclair, May 334, 335
Smyth, Austin 83, 85
Sophocles 77–8, 134, 362, 376

Southborough (Kent) 32, 63
Southey, Reginald 11
Spencer, Herbert 267
Spender, Miss, novelist 105
Spender, Stephen 354, 363
Sprott, Jack 339, 348, 349
Steinweg, Herr* 172
'Stephen' 153, 179, 193, 195, 208–9, 223, 369
Stephen, Sir Leslie 19, 160
Stevenage 38, 50, 53, 141, 202, 209, 219, 343–4
school 50
see also Rooksnest
Stevenson, R. L. 192, 317
Stisted (Essex) 26, 37, 213, 241
Stone, Wilfred 342–3
Storr, Anthony 240
Strachey, James 85
Strachey, Lytton 85, 288, 345, 357
on biography 2, 192
and EMF 83, 160, 246n, 282, 283
Streatfeild, Katharine 31n, 182
Streatfeild, Ted 14, 16–17, 18n, 29, 31, 47, 70, 110, 120, 151, 168n, 182, 183, 231, 335, 361
Sturgis, Howard 211
Surrey 42, 122, 153, 161, 176, 337, 343
Swinburne, Algernon 64
Symonds, J. A. 119n, 122, 127n, 207, 210, 211, 216, 232, 284
Synnot, Henrietta 18n
Synnot, Inglis 12, 27, 31, 238–9
Synnot, 'Maimie' (Mary Ann), later Mrs Aylward 12, 31, 32, 89, 90, 103n, 129, 150, 151, 155, 164, 242, 259
elements of, in EMF's novels 149–50

Thatcher, Margaret 221
Theocritus 77, 78, 81, 290, 297, 327
Thomas, Elsie 288
Thompson, E. V. 228, 230, 237
Thorntons 222, 242
Thornton, Henry (great-grandfather) 17, 19–21, 22, 33, 34
Thornton, Henry Sykes (great-uncle) 23, 24, 34n, 201
Thornton, John 19, 20
Thornton, Lucy (great-great-grandmother) 20
Thornton, Marianne* (Great-aunt Monie) 10–11, 14, 17, 18, 25, 26, 61, 164, 364
influence on EMF 22, 32–3, 34–5
turned out of Battersea Rise 22–4, 40, 201
favourite nephews 27, 29, 238–9
legacy to EMF 34, 56, 96, 110, 156, 160n, 181, 203
and Lily 11, 12–13, 31, 32–3, 35, 101, 201
Thornton, Marianne Sykes (great-grandmother) 16, 24
'Tibby' *see* 'Schlegel, Tibby'

403

A Note About the Author

Nicola Beauman was born in London in 1944 and was educated at Newnham College, Cambridge. The author of *A Very Great Profession: The Woman's Novel 1914–1939* and a biography of Lady Cynthia Asquith, she has also worked as a journalist in New York, as a book reviewer for *The Observer* and *The Financial Times,* and as a freelance book editor. She is married with five children and lives in London.

A Note on the Type

This book was set in Garamond, a typeface originally designed by the famous Parisian type cutter Claude Garamond (1480–1561). This version of Garamond was modeled on a 1592 specimen sheet from the Egenolff-Berner foundry, which was produced from types thought to have been brought to Frankfurt by Jacques Sabon (d. 1580).

Claude Garamond is one of the most famous type designers in printing history. His distinguished romans and italics first appeared in *Opera Ciceronis* in 1543–44. While delightfully unconventional in design, the Garamond types are clear and open, yet maintain an elegance and precision of line that mark them as French.

Composed in Great Britain

Printed and bound by Arcata Graphics, Martinsburg, West Virginia